WORDS COLLIDING

A NATION DIVIDED: STUDIES IN THE CIVIL WAR ERA
Orville Vernon Burton and Elizabeth R. Varon, Editors

WORDS COLLIDING

The Debate over Slavery and Black Exclusion
in Nineteenth-Century America

ANDREW F. HAMMANN

UNIVERSITY OF VIRGINIA PRESS
Charlottesville and London

The University of Virginia Press is situated on the traditional lands of the Monacan Nation, and the Commonwealth of Virginia was and is home to many other Indigenous people. We pay our respect to all of them, past and present. We also honor the enslaved African and African American people who built the University of Virginia, and we recognize their descendants. We commit to fostering voices from these communities through our publications and to deepening our collective understanding of their histories and contributions.

University of Virginia Press
© 2025 by the Rector and Visitors of the University of Virginia
All rights reserved
Printed in the United States of America on acid-free paper

First published 2025

9 8 7 6 5 4 3 2 1

ISBN 978-0-8139-5368-7 (hardback)
ISBN 978-0-8139-5369-4 (paperback)
ISBN 978-0-8139-5370-0 (ebook)

Library of Congress Cataloging-in-Publication Data is available for this title.

Cover art: Frame, https://www.briarpress.org/3379; quills, Christos Georghiou/stock.adobe.com
Cover design: Cecelia Sorochin

For Lisa and Cole
with deep and eternal love
and for Barr, Violet, and Hobbes
with the same

CONTENTS

Acknowledgments | ix

Introduction   1

1 Founding Moment: Decoding the Rhetoric   33

2 Ending Slavery: 1817–1833   49

3 Strengthening the Union: 1833–1853   75

4 Preventing Disunion: 1854–1860   127

5 Ending the Civil War: 1861–1865   155

6 Opposing Black Suffrage: 1866–1900   199

Conclusion   235

Notes | 249
Bibliography | 289
Index | 315

ACKNOWLEDGMENTS

Those who write books can be very solitary people. To some extent, they have to be. Otherwise, the research, the writing, the further research, the rewriting—along with the numerous and necessary iterations that follow—do not happen. It can be common, thus, for first-time authors, like myself, to feel startled, even somewhat terrified, when confronted with the basic fact that we need help, a lot of help. The acknowledgments sections of the hundreds of books on our shelves provide compelling evidence of this reality. Virtually all contain long lists of thanked people and poignant remarks about how the book, in its final polished form, would not exist without the insights, suggestions, challenges, and encouragements of so many generous people. These candid and heartfelt pieces of writing, a genre unto themselves, blast to smithereens any delusion that the finish line can be found, much less crossed, as an entirely solo effort. They also attest to the great benefits of mustering the courage to share rough, semi-coherent, gap-filled drafts with others. Every writer does it, because this act of sharing, humbling and disconcerting as it may be, elevates the quality of the finished product in dramatic, unexpected, and undeniable ways. I am sure that I am not the first person to wish that things were different, that the solitary grind could, in fact, be enough. But I've had enough experience as both a student of the craft and as a teacher of it to recognize that this is simply the way things are and that, ultimately, this is a good thing.

And now on to the specific task of thanking the numerous people who agreed to enter my solitary sphere; to read pieces of the manuscript as it developed over many years; to comment on ideas that for so long remained partially realized or out of focus or floating in the air around the page; to provide confessional advice on how they made it through the minutes, hours, days, weeks, months, and years of their own writing processes; to offer sincere, humane, empathic encouragement; and to contribute, with great generosity, selected fruits of their brilliant minds to a book that, in the end, will bear only my name on the front cover.

Thanks must go first and foremost to my PhD adviser, Jim Campbell, and my dissertation committee, which included Jim, Allyson Hobbs, and Richard White. In the latter years of my doctoral program, Jim Oakes, of the CUNY Graduate Center, was an absolutely invaluable interlocutor. These brilliant scholars, eloquent writers, deeply engaged teachers, and all-around excellent human beings guided me through an incredibly challenging and exhilarating six years and have remained essential mentors in the years since. I owe similar gratitude to the extended list of faculty who also contributed important and generous guidance during my graduate student years, including Jennifer Burns, Al Camarillo, Gordon Chang, Justin duRivage, Estelle Freedman, Jonathan Gienapp, David Kennedy, Kathryn Olivarius, Jack Rakove, Vaughn Rasberry, Richard Roberts, Caroline Winterer, and Bryan Wolf. This book is the product of so much that I learned from all of them.

My time in the History Department at Stanford was also greatly enriched by several fellow doctoral students: Branden Adams, Claire Rydell Arcenas, Valerie Deisinger, Destin Jenkins, Risa Katzen, Nicole Martin, Justine Modica, and Alex Stern. It was an enormous privilege to go through my doctoral years with all of them as fellow travelers.

Prior to becoming a PhD student, I spent an instrumental and invaluable year at San Francisco State University, in a master's program that is one of the great national gems of the history discipline. I am enormously grateful for the teaching, advice, and encouragement of Trevor Getz, Barbara Loomis, the late Dawn Mabalon, Molly Oshatz, Charles Postel, Jarbel Rodriguez, and Eva Sheppard Wolf.

ACKNOWLEDGMENTS   XI

I left Stanford in 2022 after eleven years, six as a doctoral student and five as a lecturer, in order to become a fellow at the Kinder Institute on Constitutional Democracy at the University of Missouri, where I spent a full academic year. By this point, I had put considerable time into writing this book, but the fellowship year at Kinder was a crucial inflection point because of the incredibly collegial community there and because of the very manageable teaching load. Deep gratitude to Billy Coleman, Carli Conklin, Alan Gibson, Ferris Lupino, Jeff Pasley, Jordan Pellerito, Al Zuercher Reichhardt, Jay Sexton, and Annie Twitty (now at Stanford).

During the final year of writing, I lived in Charlottesville, where I had the honor of spending three months as a short-term fellow at the International Center for Jefferson Studies. The staff there treat everyone who comes through with the greatest warmth, attentiveness, and inclusiveness. It feels like being welcomed into a family. Particular thanks go to Anna Berkes, Megan Brett, Frank Cogliano, Andrew Davenport, Caitlin Lawrence, John Ragosta, and Endrina Tay.

I presented portions of the in-process manuscript to audiences at both the Kinder Institute and the International Center for Jefferson Studies. During the several preceding years, I presented earlier versions to groups of scholars assembled at the Stanford U.S. History Workshop, the McNeil Center for Early American Studies, the Society for Historians of the Early American Republic's annual conference, and the Stanford Center for Law and History. In all instances, the feedback that I received was incredibly generous and helpful. Thanks to the many individuals who participated, especially to those who participated multiple times.

In the spring of 2024, with the generous financial assistance of the Kinder Institute, my editor at University of Virginia Press, Nadine Zimmerli, organized an extremely valuable manuscript workshop. The participants were Ed Ayers, Kirt von Daacke, Christa Dierksheide, Justene Hill Edwards, and Liz Varon. The feedback provided by this assembly of extraordinary minds was highly encouraging and thought-provoking, leading to several months of revisions that, in my opinion, dramatically improved the book. Special thanks to Ed and Justene, who in the final weeks before I finished the manuscript offered careful readings of revised versions of the introduction and conclusion, prompting several important final revisions.

Throughout the course of this many-year project, I benefited enormously from conversations with several scholars who have dug through many of the same archives and whose articles and books on colonization have informed and shaped my understanding on this complex historical subject: Eric Burin, Nick Guyatt, Sebastian Page, Ousmane Power-Greene, and Beverly Tomek. We do not agree on everything, but it is undeniable that my arguments would be less clear and less developed if I had not had their penetrating insights as reference points.

I am enormously grateful to all of the staff at UVA Press for taking this book on and for guiding me through the publication process—especially Nadine Zimmerli, who has provided unflagging support and who has been instrumental in getting the book across the finish line, as well as Clayton Butler. I owe a special thanks to Peter Onuf, as so many of us do, who gave me a very warm introduction to Nadine after a couple of wonderful COVID-era Zoom conversations between California and Maine. And I owe another special thanks to Liz Varon, who chose this book to be part of UVA Press's A Nation Divided series. Liz, in addition to being a brilliant historian, is also a brilliant lead guitarist, whom I have the great fortune of playing with in a band comprised entirely of Charlottesville-based academics.

I am very grateful to my parents, Ken and Sue Hammann, and my brothers, Greg Hammann and Alex Eichenberg, for being so supportive throughout my life and over the many years that I have been writing a book that I struggled to explain.

And I am eternally grateful to Lisa and Cole, the center of my universe, and to Barr, Violet, and Hobbes, who are very nearly as central. I could not have done this without the five of them. The latter three are dogs (the first is no longer with us), and anyone who knows me well knows how seriously I take the idea that dogs are full-fledged family members. I love and depend on them, almost as much as on Lisa and Cole. But Lisa and Cole are truly in a category alone. Both are dazzlingly gifted writers and awe-inspiring human beings whom I learn from every day and who are the most constant sources of warmth, humor, intellectual stimulation, and encouragement in my life. Two important memories for me are: telling Lisa, in the months before Cole was born, that I might want to leave my career in finance to become a high school history teacher, and witnessing the grace and wholeheartedness with which she agreed to support a change of course that felt, at the same time, right and crazy; six years later, bringing Cole, a first-grader armed with stuffed animal and movie-stocked iPad, to several of my night classes as a master's student at San Francisco State, and listening to him chuckle in the background during seminar discussions, offering light but meaningful reminders that my latest ambition, to become a university professor, was but a piece of a much fuller life. They have been with me through it all, and my love and gratitude cannot be expressed in words. This book is dedicated, with all my heart, to them.

WORDS COLLIDING

INTRODUCTION

> Nothing is more certainly written in the book of fate, than that these people are to be free; nor is it less certain that the two races, equally free, cannot live in the same government.
> —THOMAS JEFFERSON, "Memoir," 1821

> Slavery . . . is able to exalt nonsense and stupidity into the dignity of learning and philosophy.
> —FREDERICK DOUGLASS, *Douglass' Monthly*, 1860

IN 1787, A FEW MONTHS before the Constitutional Convention in Philadelphia that would dramatically revise the United States' organizing document, Thomas Jefferson published *Notes on the State of Virginia*, the first and only book-length publication of his long life. Jefferson—a politician, farmer, and slaveholder in his mid-forties—had written the book several years earlier during the latter part of the Revolutionary War, when he had served as governor of the new state of Virginia. The impulse to write had come from a French diplomat living in the United States, who had sent an information-gathering questionnaire to every state governor for the purpose of learning more about the United States' social, economic, political, and physical aspects. Jefferson took the request quite seriously and composed an extensive and wide-ranging response that ran to more than three hundred pages, divided into twenty-three chapters. In two of these chapters, Jefferson offered critical comments and specific predictions regarding the institution of slavery. Although Jefferson did not necessarily intend his remarks as prompts to action, that is what they would effectively become. A few decades later, they would inform the launch of a political movement that spanned the entire nineteenth century and that involved many of the United States' most celebrated and influential leaders, including, in various ways and to varying degrees, almost half of the nation's first sixteen presidents, numerous cabinet members, hundreds of congressmen, and innumerable state legislators: the movement to remove Black Americans from the United States.

The institution of African slavery, Jefferson proclaimed in a chapter entitled "Manners," was fundamentally unjust and dangerous. "Can the liberties of a nation be thought secure," he asked, "when we have removed their only firm basis, a conviction in the minds of the people that these liberties are of the gift of God?" To this stern judgment, Jefferson added a warning that would be widely invoked over the next eight decades, until 1865, when the Thirteenth Amendment abolished slavery immediately and comprehensively across the United States: "Indeed I tremble for my country when I reflect that God is just: that his justice cannot sleep forever." To underscore this point, particularly its implication that slavery was unsustainable, Jefferson indicated that he saw in the United States' current revolutionary effort a clear trend away from this oppressive system. "The spirit of the master is abating," he observed, "that of the slave rising from the dust, his condition mollifying, the way I hope preparing, under the auspices of heaven, for a total emancipation."[1]

In an earlier chapter entitled "Laws," Jefferson noted, in passing, that he had helped to draft an abolition proposal for the Virginia legislature a few years earlier, while serving on a committee charged with proposing possible statutes for the new state. Although the legislature had not pursued the proposal, Jefferson briefly described its key elements, effectively making available to the American public his view as to how a total emancipation should be pursued. The plan had two elements, both of which he believed to be essential to the task of abolition. First, emancipation should take place gradually, not all at once. All children born to enslaved mothers—enslavement in the English colonies and, in turn, in the United States was inherited according to the mother's condition—after a specified date would become fully and permanently free when they reached a designated majority age, eighteen for women and twenty-one for men. Pennsylvania, in fact, adopted this exact approach, except with higher majority ages, in 1780, just a few years after the convening of Jefferson's committee. Second, emancipation should be combined with a plan of Black expatriation. Those who became free, Jefferson advised, should be "colonized" outside of the country and given various materials to help them on their way to becoming a "free and independent people." During the colony's early years, as it built "strength" and self-sufficiency, Jefferson added, it should receive the "alliance and protection" of the United States.[2]

The second element of this plan, Jefferson admitted, warranted further explanation. "Why not retain and incorporate the blacks into the state," he asked, thus acknowledging, at least implicitly, the gravity of facilitating the removal of a significant portion of the American population. His answer—which would also be widely invoked over the next eight decades, and indeed for decades following the national abolition of slavery—was this: "Deep rooted prejudices entertained by the whites; ten thousand recollections, by the blacks, of the injuries they have sustained; new provocations; the real distinctions which nature has made; and many other circumstances, will divide us into parties, and produce convulsions which will probably never end but in the extermination of the one or the other race."[3]

In simplified terms, white freedom and Black freedom were, in Jefferson's assessment, *incongruous,* a framing that many white Americans would use, during the nineteenth century, as they argued in favor of Black colonization. The two races, according to the future third president, lived in a dangerous state of tension while the institution of slavery existed in the United States, and they would live in an equally, perhaps worse, state of tension if this population were freed and allowed to continue living within the nation's borders. Jefferson gave this view of the nation's racial dilemma its clearest, and most frequently invoked, articulation forty years later, five years before his death. In 1821, in an unfinished autobiography that his grandson would publish during the late 1820s, along with other memorable letters and papers, Jefferson declared, "Nothing is more certainly written in the book of fate than that these people [enslaved Black Americans] are to be free." "Nor is it less certain," he added, "that the two races, equally free, cannot live in the same government."[4]

The vision of the nation's racial future that Jefferson expressed in *Notes on the State of Virginia* and that he crystallized in a retrospective account of his life became the ideological cornerstone of the nineteenth-century colonization movement, which began in 1816 and continued through, at least, 1900. Taking Jefferson's notion that Black freedom and white freedom were incongruous as their starting point, and frequently citing his name to augment their authority, the leaders of this movement characterized the establishment of a national system of Black expatriation as the first and most important step toward eliminating slavery *and* the existentially threatening racial tensions that slavery had fostered. When slavery ended in 1865, after four years of civil war, various white politicians continued to promote the colonization cause, even though the Thirteenth Amendment had obviated one of the movement's originating goals and even though it had done so without making any provision for, or even mention of, Black expatriation. These individuals—among whom were included a vice-presidential candidate and several United States senators—insisted that the Thirteenth Amendment had done nothing to change the fact that Black freedom and white freedom were irrevocably incongruous. Indeed, what it had done, they contended, was increase the magnitude of the race problem more than tenfold, by expanding the size of the free Black population from roughly five hundred thousand to five million.[5]

Words Colliding tells the story of this eight-decade exclusionary movement, from the perspective of the numerous white Americans involved in its promotion and from the perspective of the numerous Black Americans who vigorously and persistently opposed it. The book's specific focus is the debate that surrounded the movement's long-running effort to secure federal support, effectively an effort to make Black colonization a national priority. In telling this story, *Words Colliding* makes three interrelated arguments. First, it asserts that the colonization movement bore significant responsibility for propagating two particular racialized ideas: that Black freedom was a problem in American society and that the exclusion of Black Americans—either from the United States itself, or, at a minimum, from the rights enjoyed by white Americans within the United States—was necessary, inevitable, morally defensible, and even patriotic. The book further argues that as the movement's leaders—which included Henry Clay, James Monroe, Francis Scott Key, Frank and Montgomery Blair, Abraham Lincoln, and John Tyler Morgan, to name but a few—propagated and elaborated these ideas in national politics over roughly eighty years, they ensured that Black expatriation ideology made a broad and deep impression on the racial attitudes of white Americans. Finally, the book argues that Black Americans recognized, from the outset, that this movement could do enormous damage to the interrelated causes of abolition and Black civil rights and, importantly, that this damage did not depend on the movement's success in obtaining federal support. Accordingly, a central element of Black Americans' vigorous and persistent efforts to oppose the colonization movement was the propagation and elaboration of a counterideology, one that stressed racial inclusion and equity as the principles that were, in actual fact, necessary, inevitable, morally defensible, and patriotic for all Americans to embrace.[6]

The idea that Black freedom was something problematic in American society, something that needed to be controlled and restricted, had deep roots in colonial North America. During the second half of the 1600s, various English colonies passed laws and adopted practices that ensured, as the Virginia colonial legislature confirmed explicitly in 1668 with respect to free "negro women," that free Black residents would "not in all respects" enjoy the same freedoms as free white residents. These laws and practices, although not as comprehensive or as consistent across colonies as they would become across states during the nineteenth century, expanded in number and in geography over the next hundred-plus years. By the time of the American Revolution, the legal and practical distinctions between the liberties afforded free white Americans and free Black Americans were very significant.[7]

From the very beginning, laws and practices aimed at the control and restriction of Black freedom had a strong connection to the existence of enslavement, specifically to its racialized basis. It was no coincidence that this developing system of racial exclusion hit an inflection point during the second half of the 1600s. This was the same period during which the use of white and Black indentured labor in the English colonies began to decline significantly and during which Black individuals who were enslaved for life began to become the dominant, ultimately exclusive, form of bonded labor in the English colonies. Indeed, the Virginia legislature's 1668 declaration asserting the necessary inequality of free "negro women" came just six years after the statute that formally racialized enslavement in the colony. In 1662, the legislature established that enslavement would be matrilineally hereditary. In other words, all children born to enslaved "negro women" would themselves be enslaved.[8]

A main reason for this strong legal connection was the fear of uprisings among the enslaved, a significant and growing concern in English colonial society. The crux of this connection was an emerging belief among white colonists that free Black populations had an inflammatory effect on enslaved Black populations. Effectively, white colonists were becoming convinced that free Black populations, simply through the proximal enjoyment of basic freedoms denied to the enslaved, had a tendency to foster unrest among the enslaved and, moreover, contained within them individuals who were inclined to lead slave uprisings. The deeper origins of this English colonial idea are not entirely clear. Indeed, at least one prominent scholar has argued that, in the long span of world history, this idea was not necessarily inherent in societies where enslaved labor was widespread—or, stated differently, that the idea was uncommonly strong in North America. English colonists, themselves, did not offer much in the way of empirical evidence. Typically, they presumed rather than explained, modeling an approach to this controversial subject taken by many colonization advocates during the nineteenth century, especially those living in the Upper Southern states of Virginia, Maryland, and Kentucky, where the notion that emancipation had to be connected with expatriation had the most fervent support.[9]

In order to impede growth of the colonial Black population, several colonial governments restricted the practice of emancipation. Virginia curbed the practice as early as 1691. Various colonies followed suit over the next several decades, including several Northern ones. One mode of restriction was to require government approval for any prospective manumission. Another mode was to require newly emancipated individuals to leave the colony permanently, a prefiguring, in effect, of Jefferson's assertion regarding the necessity of combining emancipation with expatriation. By the time of the American Revolution, laws restricting the practice of emancipation, in combination with other factors, ensured that the rate of manumissions across the English colonies was quite low.[10]

This general attitude of emancipatory restriction and discouragement changed during the first few decades following the Revolution. In the North, the change was permanent. Between the late 1770s and the early

1800s, all of the states north of Maryland took measures to abolish slavery. The first significant action was the Gradual Abolition Act passed by the Pennsylvania legislature in 1780, during the final years of the Revolutionary War. In 1804, the New Jersey legislature completed the regional process when it adopted, after years of failed attempts, a gradual abolition law of its own. In the South, mainly the Upper South, the change was temporary but nonetheless quite consequential. Instead of enacting gradual abolition laws, the legislatures of Virginia and Maryland, among other Upper Southern states, elected to soften their respective manumission restrictions. A wave of emancipations followed that spanned the final part of the eighteenth century and the opening years of the nineteenth century. By 1810, the aggregate free Black population of the Upper South, which had been minimal in 1780, was approaching one hundred thousand, with Virginia and Maryland composing close to 70 percent of the total.[11]

Concern about the effects that the free Black population had on white American society did not, however, evaporate during this period, despite the widespread change in attitudes toward emancipation. The lawbooks of effectively all of the new states evinced this ongoing worry. In the North, a clear indication was the widespread pursuit of *gradual* abolition instead of *immediate* abolition. Gradual abolition laws significantly delayed increases in the size of the free Black population. At the time of their enactment, they freed no one. All enslaved people born *before* the laws' effective dates were exempted. Those whom the laws did free—all individuals born to enslaved mothers *after* the effective dates—gained full freedom only after reaching a predesignated age, usually between twenty-one and twenty-eight. Prior to that, they lived, in effect, as indentured servants, beholden to the individual who claimed ownership over their enslaved mothers. Southern concern regarding Black freedom manifested most clearly, as it had during the colonial period, in laws that constrained the rights of free Black Americans living in the region. Often, states reinstated colonial-era restrictions in their new statute books. Some states, including Virginia and Maryland, went further, implementing a new kind of constrictive law that prohibited free Black Americans from taking up new residences within their borders. These state-level immigration bans reflected and reinforced the basic Jeffersonian sentiment that white freedom and Black freedom were incongruous.[12]

During the 1790s and early 1800s, two events, one in the Caribbean and one in Virginia, fueled a general increase in white Americans' concern regarding the nation's growing free Black population: a protracted slave rebellion and civil war in the French colony of Saint-Domingue, which began during the early 1790s and continued, in various phases, over the next decade; and the so-called Gabriel Prosser Conspiracy in Virginia, which occurred in 1800. The first event spread a persistent and escalating terror throughout the white South, as wave after wave of Caribbean refugees flooded the coastal cities of the United States, carrying vivid and terrifying accounts of racial violence. Writing to a fellow Virginian in 1797, Jefferson, who was at the time vice president of the United States, characterized the events in Saint-Domingue, later known as the Haitian Revolution, as the front end of a "revolutionary storm" that might soon hit the United States. "The day which begins our combustion must be near at hand," he warned. "If something is not done, and soon done, we shall be the murderers of our own children." Three years later, while violence and unrest persisted in the Caribbean, news of an abortive uprising among the enslaved in Richmond spread throughout the South, escalating fears further. According to trial records, newspaper accounts, and rumors, an enslaved man by the name of Gabriel Prosser had spent months, without detection, organizing a large band of enslaved rebels. Governor James Monroe, future president of the United States, had learned of the conspiracy in time to prevent it only because a few enslaved individuals had given warning. This barely averted uprising underscored for many white Southerners just how dangerous it was to live in the midst of a severely and violently oppressed population.[13]

In the months following the Gabriel Prosser Conspiracy, as the Virginia courts ordered and executed the hanging of Prosser and more than twenty others, the Virginia legislature held closed-door sessions to determine what the state should do in response to this disturbing event. The legislature passed a resolution asking Governor Monroe to correspond with the president of the United States "on the subject of purchasing lands" to which "persons obnoxious to the laws or dangerous to the peace of society may be removed." Over the next four years, Virginia's lawmakers passed three more resolutions, keeping pressure on Monroe and his successor as governor, John Page, to pursue the prospect of federally supported Black colonization. Dutifully, both men corresponded regularly on this subject with Thomas Jefferson, who had assumed the presidency in early 1801, shortly after the Virginia legislature's first resolution. During this time, Jefferson tasked various federal officials with exploring several potential destinations, including islands in the West Indies, the Portuguese colonies of South America, unsettled parts of Western North America, and Africa. Ultimately, none of these federal efforts bore fruit. Escalating tensions with Great Britain effectively ended the correspondence between Virginia and the federal government, as the Jefferson administration faced the very real possibility of foreign war. Nonetheless, these colonization-related actions, which remained largely unknown to the American public at the time and for several years hence, set a precedent that would inform the launch of the colonization movement in Washington slightly more than a decade later.[14]

The Virginia legislature's decision to seek federal support for a prospective effort to colonize Black Virginians had a history to it, both inside the United States and outside of it. Jefferson had suggested, in his remarks in *Notes on the State of Virginia,* that the federal government might have a role to play in Black colonization. Around the same time that *Notes* was published, the British government actually began to do, on a small scale, what Jefferson had suggested the United States government would eventually have to do on a large scale. The British government began transporting multiple groups of Black former Americans to a newly established colony on the west coast of Africa, named Sierra Leone. Most, if not all, of the forced emigrants had self-emancipated during the Revolutionary War and had fought for the British against the United States. A few years later, in 1790, a prominent Virginian by the name of Ferdinando Fairfax explicitly recommended federal support in an article published in *American Museum.* "A colony should be settled, under the auspices and protection of Congress, by the negroes now within the United States," he wrote. The new settlement, Fairfax added, should be established in Africa, a location that was full "of the same kind of people" and that was far enough away from the United States to eliminate the possibility of ongoing tensions with white Americans.[15]

This history also provided context for the publication in 1801 of one of the first major American discourses on Black colonization: *Letter to a Member of the General Assembly of Virginia, on the Subject of the Late Conspiracy of the Slaves; with a Proposal for Their Colonization.* The pamphlet, which was written by a Virginian named George Tucker, began circulating at roughly the same time that the state legislature first asked Jefferson for federal support. Tucker, a young lawyer who had studied at William and Mary, Jefferson's alma mater, and who would later publish an early biography of the former president, insisted that the time had come for the state to pursue a plan of gradual abolition combined with a system of federally supported colonization, thus commencing the process of eliminating the dangers caused by the institution of slavery and by the ineradicable tensions that existed between the white and Black races. If "we return to our wonted repose," Tucker warned, "we may chance to be waked again, by a shock that will barely allow us time to see our folly."[16]

In his commentary on the subject of colonization, Tucker rejected as unrealistic the view, asserted by some in the state, that expatriation might be safely avoided if, instead, the legislature adopted laws "denying the negroes some of the most important privileges of a citizen." The Black population, Tucker insisted, would "never rest satisfied with any thing short of perfect equality." Moreover, to do such a thing would be to risk the integrity of the nation's system of republican governance. Relegating the nation's Black population to a state of unremitting oppression, he declared, would make it vulnerable to manipulation by a "domestic faction" or perhaps an "artful and enterprising leader."[17]

One individual that Tucker almost certainly had in mind when he rejected this alternative to colonization was his older cousin and former professor, St. George Tucker, an instructor of law at William and Mary who occupied the chair formerly held by George Wythe, the teacher of Thomas Jefferson, James Monroe, John Marshall, and many other prominent Virginia politicians. Five years earlier, in 1796, while the events of the Haitian Revolution raged in the Caribbean, St. George had published *A Dissertation on Slavery with a Proposal for the Gradual Abolition of It, in the State of Virginia*. The events in Saint-Domingue, St. George asserted, signaled the necessity of abolishing an institution that "threatens [our] destruction" and, at the same time, affirmed that there could be no postemancipatory equality between the white and Black races. Accordingly, the state legislature should pass a gradual abolition law that had embedded within it a provision that excluded the state's Black population—those who were already free and, importantly, those who would become free—from the enjoyment of key civil liberties. Although such a course, he acknowledged, might have the ring of injustice, it also had firm roots in a core principle of republican governance: "Men when they enter into a state of society, [have] a right to admit, or exclude any description of persons, as they think proper."[18]

St. George's ethical defense, we can see clearly, in retrospect, left a key point implicit. When he referred to *men,* he meant *white men.* In other words, the Black men and women living in the United States at the time of the nation's founding had not been, according to St. George's way of thinking, part of that original *entering* moment. Six decades later, in 1857, Supreme Court Chief Justice Roger Taney would assert the same basic sentiment in the majority opinion of the *Dred Scott* decision, which effectively invalidated the idea of Black citizenship under the US Constitution.

St. George understood that in recommending that the Virginia legislature pursue gradual abolition without colonization, he was disagreeing with Thomas Jefferson. The disagreement, though, was only partial. St. George, the pamphlet made abundantly clear, strongly agreed with Jefferson on the essential incompatibility of Black freedom and white freedom. Indeed, he also agreed that the best interests of both races would be served by permanent geographic separation. What he was uncomfortable with was the prospect of making colonization a condition of abolition. Placing severe legal restrictions on Black freedom was, in effect, as St. George explained, an interim step toward a large-scale act of *voluntary* migration. "By denying them [free Black Americans] the most valuable privileges which civil government affords," he stated, "I wished to render it their inclination and their interest to seek those privileges in some other" land, perhaps, he suggested, the "immense territory of Louisiana," which at the time was claimed by the Spanish Crown. Although it was not certain that free Black Americans would find these privileges living under Spanish rule, St. George admitted, there was, at least, a much greater possibility of such an outcome in that new region than if they "remain [here] with us."[19]

The overall plan proposed in *A Dissertation on Slavery* was not, St. George observed, a perfect one. The prospect of systematically oppressing free Black Americans, while not as troubling as a general expulsion, was troubling in its own right, and, of course, voluntary colonization was uncertain. But the simple fact, St. George insisted, was that it was the best plan available. The only two practical options for Black Americans in a postemancipatory United States were severe civic oppression or voluntary emigration.

In asserting such a narrow view of the nation's racialized future, and in expressing hope that the former course might lead to the latter course, St. George foreshadowed two very significant future dimensions of the colonization movement's promotional efforts, dimensions that the movement's opponents would repeatedly highlight over the course of the nineteenth century. First, white legislators could use exclusionary laws as coercive levers, in essence as a means of pushing Black Americans to leave without necessarily forcing them to do so. Generally speaking, colonization advocates insisted on voluntary actions, although, as will be explained in chapter 1, the term *voluntary*, as they conceived it, often had unspoken qualifications. Second, white legislators could use exclusionary laws as colonization substitutes. In other words, if colonization were not an option, exclusionary laws could be used to approximate the effects of full geographic separation.

Two specific facts about the colonization movement's efforts ensured that these dimensions manifested increasingly during the nineteenth century. First, the colonization movement repeatedly failed, except in a few brief circumstances, to gain the federal support that, according to its leaders, was essential to the movement's success. Second, the overwhelmingly majority of free Black Americans strongly and persistently rejected offers of voluntary colonization.

In early 1816, roughly eleven years after the Jefferson administration ceased its efforts to find land for the removal of Black Virginians, a Virginia state legislator by the name of Charles Fenton Mercer learned, for the first time, about the series of events that had followed the Gabriel Prosser Conspiracy. The next day, he unearthed the relevant documents in the legislature's archive—among them, the state legislature's closed-door resolutions on colonization and the secret, five-year correspondence between Governors Monroe and Page and President Jefferson—shared them with various colleagues, and resolved to revive the subject of colonization at the next legislative session in December. Among the many conversations Mercer had on this subject during the intervening nine months, an especially consequential one occurred in Washington during the spring of 1816. Walking through the gallery of the United States House of Representatives during the closing period of the Fourteenth Congress's first session, Mercer encountered Elias Caldwell, a schoolmate from Princeton (the College of New Jersey, as it was known at the time) who currently served as clerk of the United States Supreme Court, and Francis Scott Key, an influential Washington attorney well acquainted with Caldwell. The trio commenced a lively discussion on the merits of Black colonization that continued, over the next few weeks, in the Washington boardinghouse of Virginia Congressman John Randolph, a close friend of Key's. By the end of their time together, Mercer, Key, and Caldwell had agreed to initiate parallel efforts to find like-minded individuals in their respective home states of Virginia, Maryland, and New Jersey. The first two planned to do so in person, while the third, given his ongoing Supreme Court duties, planned to write letters, one of which went to his brother-in-law Robert Finley.[20]

Finley, a Princeton-educated minister then in his late thirties, led a Presbyterian parish in Basking Ridge, New Jersey, roughly forty miles to the west of New York City. Over the course of roughly twenty years in clerical service, he had built a reputation for himself as a revivalist preacher, an advocate for the poor, and a man of influence in the Presbyterian synod of New Jersey and New York. Finley reacted enthusiastically to Caldwell's letter. The idea of colonization was one that he was familiar with and that he found quite appealing, both in terms of its potential to improve the lives of Black Americans and in its potential to foster the end of slavery. He promptly commenced his own canvassing efforts. One of his most significant actions was to propose, at a meeting of interested individuals in Princeton, a draft of a petition for prospective submission to the New Jersey legislature. The petition asked the legislature to make an appeal to Congress that endorsed the idea of federal support for Black colonization—something it ultimately did eight years later. Shortly after the meeting, Finley headed to Washington intent on learning more about Caldwell's efforts and on seeing what might be done for colonization during the next congressional session, slated to begin in early December.[21]

On December 21, one of Washington's main newspapers, the *National Intelligencer,* reported that the Virginia House of Delegates had passed a resolution on the subject of colonization. Mercer had been the resolution's chief advocate, thus fulfilling his earlier promise. The resolution passed the

House by a stunning majority, 137 to 9. The state senate passed the resolution a few days later, with one dissenting vote. The resolution's preamble asserted that Virginia's interest in Black colonization was long-standing and that efforts pursuant to this interest had been irregular in large part due to external factors, not shaky convictions. This statement referred, implicitly, to the state's earlier collaboration with the Jefferson administration and the subsequent end of this collaboration due to events that, over time, gave rise to the War of 1812, which had just ended. The residents of Virginia "now avail themselves of a period when peace has healed the wounds of humanity" to ask the governor of the state to correspond with the president of the United States on this important subject. The state's explicit desire, the resolution expressed, was for the federal government to acquire foreign land that would "serve as an asylum for such persons of color, as are now free, and may desire the same, and for those who may be hereafter emancipated within this commonwealth."[22]

On the same newspaper page, immediately above the resolution's full text, an editorial note offered broader context for this resolution and connected it, explicitly, to an important public meeting planned for later that day: "The attention of many intelligent men in the United States, has recently been turned, with peculiar force, and a corresponding zeal and spirit of perseverance, to the proposition for establishing a COLONY OF FREE BLACKS." To this end, several individuals in the city, the note announced, intended to hold a meeting, later that night, at a local hotel. The sentiments motivating this meeting, the note observed, were "singularly" accordant with the spirit of the recent resolution in Virginia.[23]

Speaker of the House Henry Clay presided over the evening meeting, as a full account published three days later in the *Intelligencer* indicated. Also in attendance were three of the prime movers behind the meeting: Elias Caldwell, Francis Scott Key, and Robert Finley. The fourth, Charles Fenton Mercer, was still in Richmond for the current legislative session and thus did not attend. The December 21 meeting led to two other meetings over the next eleven days, one of which was held in the Hall of the House of Representatives. The end result was the formation of a new organization, the American Society for Colonizing the Free People of Colour of the United States (the American Colonization Society, as it eventually became known, or ACS) and the submission of a congressional memorial asking for federal support. The new organization's sole stated purpose, as its name indicated, was to colonize *free* Black Americans "with their consent, in Africa, or elsewhere." The driving motivations for this project were "philanthropy" and, of equal importance, "the prosperity and happiness of our country." More specifically, as Clay and Caldwell explained, the new organization would offer free Black Americans opportunities for self-advancement and self-government that they could never enjoy in the United States. At the same time, it would facilitate the removal of an oppressed free class that was both "useless and pernicious" and that stood out as a "monument of reproach to those sacred principles of civil liberty" that were the bedrock of the new nation. Collectively, these actions marked the beginning of the eight-decade political movement that is the core subject of this book.[24]

To give these founding efforts a significant boost, Finley published "Thoughts on the Colonization of Free Blacks," a brief but thorough declaration of the motivations and aims for Black colonization from the perspective of a Northern minister. Much of what Finley wrote about slavery and about the nation's free Black population resonated with the earlier commentaries on colonization published by Jefferson, St. George Tucker, and George Tucker, all of whom were from the South and all of whom were slaveholders. There were, however, two important points of contrast. First, Finley offered an extensive discussion of why Africa, which would become the ACS's sole geographic focus, was the ideal destination for a new colony. Jefferson had mentioned Africa as a potential spot but had not expanded much on his reasoning, and both of the Tuckers had pressed for the Western regions of North America. The case that Finley made for Africa contained a striking religious assertion. Colonization was the second phase of a divine plan to bring republican government and Christianity to Africa, with the first phase being the institution of slavery in North America. "Is it too much to believe it possible," he proclaimed, "that *He* who brings light out of darkness, and good out of evil, has suffered so great an evil to exist as African slavery, that in a land of civil liberty and religious knowledge, thousands and tens of thousands might at the appointed time be prepared to return, and be the great instrument of spreading peace and happiness." Such a view of things, Finley acknowledged, might seem radical, but it should not be easily dismissed: "We know that the ways of the great Ruler of the world and director of events are wonderful and great beyond calculation." Many future advocates of colonization, not just religious leaders but political ones as well, would replicate Finley's interpretation as they insisted on the singular appeal of Africa. Many would also replicate Finley's advice about the inscrutability of God's ways.[25]

To this religion-based argument, Finley added a more pragmatic one: Africa's great geographic distance from the United States. While it was true, Finley admitted, that removing Black Americans to the "territories of the United States," as George Tucker had suggested, would diminish the cost and complexity of colonization, "these advantages would be in part counterbalanced, by having in our vicinity an independent settlement of people who were once our slaves." The associated risks, Finley maintained, deserved serious consideration. A nearby colony might well foster unrest among "those who remain in slavery" and encourage growing numbers of them to run away. Moreover, if the colonists became formal allies with "our Indian neighbors" or with other "European nations," they might become "our enemies" in armed conflict—a warning almost certainly informed by fresh memories of Black Americans fighting for the British in the recently ended War of 1812. Neither of these problems, Finley asserted, would manifest if the colony were placed in Africa, especially the latter one: "Removed far from our sight; our contempt of them, produced by their situation, and by long habit confirmed, would gradually die away, and their jealousy and suspicion proportionably decrease." In this way, peace, rather than strife, would be cultivated.[26]

The second point of contrast was that Finley did not put quite as much stress, as his Virginian counterparts had, on the dangers of slavery to white Americans. Stated differently, white fear was not a dominant theme of his pamphlet. This distinction stemmed from the fact that he had lived for most of his life in New Jersey, where fear of uprisings of the enslaved, though certainly not absent, was not nearly as high as in Virginia—according to the 1810 census, New Jersey's enslaved population constituted less than 5 percent of the total; in Virginia, the enslaved portion was nearly 40 percent. This basic geographic difference, as will be seen, shaped the future history of the colonization movement. In very general terms, white Southerners would cling more tightly than white Northerners to the idea that abolition had to be pursued in conjunction with colonization. The simple fact was that fear proved to be a more powerful impulse than benevolence.

On December 30, 1816, just a few days after the founders of the American Colonization Society reviewed a draft of their prospective congressional memorial, a group of Black Americans submitted a "counter memorial" to the *National Intelligencer*. The newspaper's editors published the piece, but not without appending a brief note of disparagement—generally speaking, the *National Intelligencer* was, from the outset, quite supportive of the ACS's efforts. We have "learned with no less concern than surprise," the countermemorial declared, "that divers[e] white persons . . . are devising ways and means for the transportation of your memorialists beyond seas." No matter what the professed intentions of these "false friends and self-styled benefactors" might be with respect to the future happiness of Black Americans, they had no "right," the memorial insisted, to "pass judgment on their condition" or, worse still, to embark on a project designed to push them "into voluntary exile." We "humbly pray your honorable body to interpose your authority," the memorialists stated, "to save them" from such "officious intermeddlings."[27]

If the founding meetings of the ACS were the beginning of the eight-decade movement to remove Black Americans from the United States, this countermemorial was the beginning of the eight-decade effort to oppose this movement. From 1816 through the end of the nineteenth century, the debate between these two groups would be vigorous, contentious, and constant. As this countermemorial suggested, and as this book overarchingly contends, this debate would operate on two levels. On the surface, it addressed the political question of whether the federal government would support Black expatriation and the practical question of whether Black Americans would or would not agree to leave the country. Deeper down, it also grappled with the ideological question of whether Black freedom *was* or *was not* a problem in American society.

During the late eighteenth century and throughout the nineteenth century, the word *race* did not have a broadly agreed-upon definition in the United States. The essential uncertainty underlying the term hinged on whether apparent differences between designated racial groups were changeable or permanent. In a basic sense, the theory of changeability—which historians have largely ascribed to the influence of Samuel Stanhope Smith, the president of Princeton from 1795 to 1812—held that any apparent physical or mental differences between white and Black Americans stemmed from the fact that the ancestors of these two races had lived, for many centuries, on disparate continents under different societal structures and climatic conditions. The implication of this theory, which white Americans often downplayed or did not mention, was that some level of convergence between the two races was already in process in North America, at least in terms of the climate factor, given two centuries of continental cohabitation. The theory of permanence—which historians have largely associated with individuals like Samuel Morton and Josiah Nott, both physicians—generally posited, in contrast, that all physical and mental differences between white and Black Americans were biological, and, moreover, that these differences, when considered in aggregate, mapped onto a hierarchy in which white Americans were fundamentally and unchangeably superior to Black Americans.[28]

In basic historical terms, the theory of changeability seems to have had its greatest influence in American racial discourse from the late eighteenth century through the mid-nineteenth century, while the theory of permanence seems to have had its greatest influence from the mid-nineteenth century onward. But there are two very important caveats to keep in mind. First, throughout this entire hundred-year-plus period, both of these theories, in various forms and to varied extents, were in wide circulation. Thus, both of these theories were available to any American trying to understand the racial landscape in the United States and to form an opinion on the key issues of slavery and Black civil rights. Second, there was nothing to prevent an American engaged in this thought process from manifesting a mix of the two views. In other words, it should not be inferred from the conflicting nature of these theories that every individual in the United States aligned fully with one or the other.

A highly relevant example of a mixed-theory view can be found in Thomas Jefferson's *Notes on the State of Virginia*. In the section where he offered his list of reasons why the Black population could not be retained and incorporated into the United States, he noted "the real distinctions which nature has made" as a key factor. He then spent the next ten pages, far more time than he devoted to his discussion of why slavery should and would ultimately be abolished, describing a variety of ways in which the white race and the Black race seemed to be essentially different: physically, emotionally, and intellectually. The impression that he gave, and it was a fairly strong impression, was that he believed that these differences were largely fixed and biological, and that, on the whole, the white race was far superior to the Black race. In the closing remarks of this section, however, Jefferson inserted a deliberate qualification: "I advance it . . . as a suspicion only, that the blacks, whether originally a distinct race, or made distinct by time and circumstances, are inferior to the whites in the endowments both of body and mind." With this qualification, Jefferson, who had just effectively represented himself as an adherent of the theory of permanence, acknowledged that the theory of changeability might, in the presence of additional evidence, ultimately invalidate some of his racial views.[29]

There are two main reasons why this historical background is important to the long history of the colonization movement in American politics. First, for roughly the first forty years of the movement, from 1816 through the late 1850s, colonization advocates tended to speak about racial variation in terms that accorded more with the theory of changeability than the theory of permanence. In "Thoughts on the Colonization of Free Blacks," for instance, Robert Finley firmly asserted, "That they [Black Americans] are capable of improvement is not to be contradicted." They were demonstrating this capability every day in the United States, Finley noted, despite all of the impediments placed in their way, and, moreover, if one looked outside the United States, one could see clear evidence of their ultimate "capacity for self-government" in the Black republic of Haiti. All that Black Americans required to elevate themselves, Finley claimed, was removal and opportunity: "Place them by themselves in some climate, congenial with their color and constitutions" and "give them the hope of becoming possessed of power and influence, and the pleasure of their invigorated minds will be similar to ours in like circumstances." Finley's core view strongly leaned toward a belief in racial equality, a sharp contrast to Jefferson's core view, which strongly inclined toward a belief in the fundamental inferiority of the Black race.[30]

The countermemorial published in the *National Intelligencer* in late 1816, shortly after the publication of Finley's pamphlet, showed that Black Americans understood that the leaders of this emergent colonization organization were, generally speaking, aligning with the theory of changeability, and were thus breaking with Jefferson. But this purported alignment, as the document made clear, caused more confusion than comfort. "Your memorialists . . . cannot dissemble their astonishment and indignation, that those who profess to acknowledge them their *equals* in all things should make a difference of color the cause of their transportation and banishment." Would not a more reasonable and practical plan for dealing with color-based "prejudices," the countermemorial continued, be the gradual "amalgamation" of the white and Black races in the United States? "In a few generations the odious distinction of color would pass away, and . . . your memorialists would find themselves blended with the great American family—their equals in color, as your memorialists are now acknowledged to be their equals in everything else."[31]

There was, almost certainly, a bit of sarcasm blended into this logic-based rebuttal. The authors of the countermemorial would have been well aware that effectively all of the published discourses on colonization, from Jefferson's *Notes* through Finley's *Thoughts,* expressed strong aversion to the prospect of racial amalgamation. Jefferson, in explaining why the abolition of slavery during Roman times had not required expatriation and why the abolition of slavery in the United States did, had declared: "Among the Romans emancipation required but one effort. The slave, when made free, might mix . . . without staining the blood of his master. But with us a second is necessary, unknown to history. When freed, he is to be removed beyond the reach of mixture." But the logic-based portion of the countermemorial's remarks on amalgamation was also meant to be taken seriously. Many Black Americans, over the next several decades, claimed that the gradual mixing of the races would ultimately cause color-based prejudice to disappear in the United States, thus obviating the colonization movement's entire premise.[32]

The second reason why this historical background is important to the history of the colonization movement is that during the movement's latter decades there was a notable shift away from the theory of changeability and toward the theory of permanence. This shift became notable during the late 1850s and very pronounced by the 1880s and 1890s. As was the case during the earlier period when the former theory held sway, the influence of the latter theory did not necessarily manifest in all colonization publications and speeches, nor did it necessarily manifest in absolutist terms. The theory of changeability continued to have purchase in American racial discourse and thus, to some extent, in colonization advocacy. But the shift was quite visible and indeed consequential, as it contributed to important differences in how white Americans, especially white Southerners, talked about the *problem* of Black freedom and, in turn, argued the necessity of colonization or, at a minimum, the civic exclusion of Black Americans.

On the surface, it seems odd that the long history of this political movement has not been told, at least not in full or, with regard to many of its key moments, in depth. The nineteenth-century records of Congress and of state legislatures, especially in the Upper South and the North, are filled with resolutions, bills, speeches, and debates related to Black colonization. Newspapers and magazines of the time contain extensive commentary on the subject, as do published reports of local-, state-, and national-level meetings organized in support of and in opposition to this political issue. The documentary record of nineteenth-century Black activism—especially the archives of the American Anti-Slavery Society (AASS), the "colored convention" movement, and the most influential Black newspapers of the period, among them the *Colored American, Frederick Douglass' Paper,* and the *Christian Recorder*—abounds with important sources as well. In a very real sense, much of this story has been hidden in plain sight. As a consequence, our collective understanding of the pivotal nineteenth-century debates over slavery and Black civil rights in the United States has been commensurately incomplete.

I began discovering this large volume of primary source material roughly twelve years ago, when I began researching the American Colonization Society. As I learned more about this organization and the wider political movement that it spawned, I found that scholars, on the whole, had dramatically underestimated the magnitude and historical significance of this story due, in large part, to the widespread and, in many ways, quite rational use of four framing conventions.

The first, and arguably the most impactful, convention is the assumption, often more implicit than explicit, that the history of the colonization movement is largely, if not fully, coextensive with the history of the American Colonization Society. This assumption, although problematic in certain ways, is rooted in an empirical fact. For most of the antebellum period, from roughly 1816 to the mid-1850s, the ACS was indeed at the movement's center. However, at no point during this forty-year period was the ACS, as an institution, dictating the rhetoric, strategies, and actions of all of those actively involved in promoting Black expatriation. Many of the most active promoters, like Congressmen Henry Clay and Charles Fenton Mercer, understood themselves to be working on behalf of a cause and an ideology that transcended the ACS. And this was true even when the promoters—as was the case with Clay, Mercer, and many others—were officers of the ACS. Thus, in order to gain a full sense of the scope and impact of the colonization movement's national political efforts, historians need to spend as much time in the congressional record as they do in the institutional archive of the ACS.[33]

This first convention creates even greater challenges when it comes to understanding the history of the colonization movement during the late 1850s, the Civil War, and the postwar decades. During these highly important periods, the ACS was no longer at the movement's center, even though it continued to exist and to wield a measure of influence. From the late 1850s through the early 1870s, the Blair family, specifically a powerful trio of slaveholding politicians from the Upper South, was the chief promoter of Black expatriation ideology in national politics. Then, during the 1880s and early 1890s, the leadership role shifted, somewhat ironically, into the Lower South, the region that during the prewar period had produced the fiercest white political opposition.[34]

The second framing convention is the understandable, but not infallible, inclination scholars have toward studying political movements that succeeded, not ones that failed. The eighty-year effort to make Black expatriation a national cause fell in the latter category. Despite the great number of influential men and women involved in colonization advocacy during the nineteenth century—including presidents, cabinet members, and countless congressmen—nearly all attempts to secure federal sponsorship failed. The historical significance of this movement, however, lies not in the faint marks it left on federal lawbooks but rather in the deep ideological and systemic imprints it made on American society.[35]

The third convention is the common use of 1865, the year that the Thirteenth Amendment was ratified and that the 250-year-old institution of slavery was abolished, as a narrative endpoint or starting point. This framing device—which has the benefit, among others, of underscoring just how important the abolition of slavery was, both to the history that came before and the history that came after—has made it difficult for scholars to apprehend the full scope and significance of colonization advocacy because such apprehension depends on looking through the 1865 moment, not simply toward it or from it. The larger ongoing project of studying slavery's afterlives, to which this book makes a contribution, hinges on scholars writing more histories that have a trans-1865 framing. It is one thing to acknowledge, as effectively all historians do and as a great many Americans do, that political movements and ideas that originated in the debates over slavery continued to have influence in the postslavery debates over Black civil rights. It is another thing, however, to show, with empirical rigor, how and why certain racialized threads carried through the momentous, but not fully discontinuous Thirteenth Amendment—like the idea that the freedom of Black Americans was a societal problem.[36]

The final convention, one that receives further discussion in the next section, is a binary way of thinking that has structured, and in turn constrained, much of the scholarship produced on the history of Black expatriation advocacy—and indeed, in certain ways, the larger body of work on the intertwined histories of slavery and Black civil rights in the United States. For sixty years, going back to the publication in 1961 of P. J. Staudenraus's germinal *The African Colonization Movement, 1816–1865,* historians have spent much ink debating whether colonization advocates were, on the whole, *antislavery* or *proslavery*. Scholars who have ascribed an antislavery label—a group that includes Staudenraus and most of the authors of recent monographs—have tended to focus on advocates' claims that expatriation would encourage the gradual abolition of slavery by neutralizing, as Henry Clay called it, "the great obstacle to emancipation": White Southerners' aversion to expanding their free Black populations. Scholars who have ascribed a proslavery label have tended to characterize such emancipatory claims as disingenuous, highlighting instead the assertion made by Clay and many others that the removal of free Black Americans would make slavery safer and more stable by diminishing the population primarily responsible, according to Southern conventional wisdom, for uprisings of the enslaved. A close, thorough, and long-span analysis of the colonization movement's documentary record, however, makes clear that ambivalence was, in fact, one of the movement's defining features—a crucial insight that binary terms and binary thinking have made it difficult for historians to grasp. For Clay and a great many advocates from the Upper South, the region that provided the movement's dominant political impulse during the nineteenth century, the make-slavery-more-safe objective was inseparable from the emancipatory one.[37]

During the many years that it has taken to research and write this book, I developed a strong appreciation for the impact, both intended and unintended, of word choices. This appreciation came not just from reading the ways in which colonization advocates constructed their exclusionary arguments and the ways that colonization opponents took these arguments apart, but also from the struggle to discern and to articulate, with clarity and precision, how the attitudes toward slavery and toward Black civil rights evinced by colonization advocates related to other prevailing attitudes of the time.

The political history of the movement to colonize Black Americans outside of the United States strongly resists straightforward classification. In a basic sense, this is unsurprising. One of the things that the movement was most known for during the nineteenth century was its complex, nuanced, variable, and, at times, seemingly contradictory rhetoric. The trouble that historians have had trying to understand and contextualize this rhetoric is very much a reflection of the difficulties many nineteenth-century Americans encountered in their own efforts at understanding and contextualization. To navigate through these difficulties, I made two sets of word-choice decisions: First, I decided to preclude myself from using three descriptive terms: *antislavery*, *proslavery*, and *abolitionist;* second, I decided to supplement my use of the word *colonization*, with several additional terms, including *expatriation, exclusion, removal, resettlement,* and *emigration*.

The decision to disallow use of the terms *antislavery* and *proslavery* is one that I did not come to easily, even though it is, as I have come to believe, among the most important that I made in crafting this book. I did not come to it easily because these terms are so useful as shorthand descriptors of slavery-related ideas and actions. This is why historians have used them so widely, and why we continue to use them. They allow us to divide ideas and actions into those aimed at opposing slavery and those aimed at supporting slavery. Problems arise, however, when we try to depict attitudes toward slavery that have complexity and nuance and, even more so, when we try to depict attitudes that seem, not just on the surface but indeed deeper down, to have contradictory elements but that are, in fact, ambivalent. The reason that problems arise is that these paired terms operate with a kind of binary force. If one label does not fit, the other one must: if not antislavery, then proslavery. A similar binary force flows from a three-termed framework that historians have employed—to many constructive ends, to be sure—as a substitute: *immediatism–gradualism–perpetualism*. Because immediatism and gradualism subdivide the antislavery category only, the three-termed framework tends to reproduce the antislavery–proslavery binary in modified form: if not gradualist, then perpetualist. The second reason is that none of these terms have standard, broadly agreed-upon definitions. In effect, the line separating antislavery from proslavery *or* gradualism from perpetualism can shift from scholarly work to scholarly work, its position dependent upon varied, often vague or unspoken, criteria. As several historians have pointed out over the years and as many more can likely confirm based on their own experiences, the potential for mutual misunderstanding in such a historiographical space is high.[38]

As a substitute for the antislavery–proslavery binary, I employ a framework that I developed as part of my work over the last twelve years and that I have proposed, more broadly, in a 2022 article published in *American Nineteenth Century History*. In effect, I revised the three-point framework into a continuum with four elements: immediatism, gradualism, *eventualism* (a new term), and perpetualism. To address the problems caused by inconsistent definitions, I derived the terms' meanings from a single question: When should slavery end? The answers—immediately, gradually, eventually, or not at all (it should exist perpetually)—provide the elements of the framework.[39]

The new term *eventualism* is interpretively crucial to the history of the colonization movement, as will be seen in chapters 3 and 4. It describes a conflicted attitude toward slavery that historians have long lacked the vocabulary to label: an insistence that slavery should and would end at some point combined with an aversion to taking any action to facilitate this end, due to fears of disunion and/or uprisings of the enslaved. Various historians have labeled this way of thinking as a *conservative* or *moderate* form of antislavery. Others, discounting the possibility that antipathy and passivity could coexist, have labeled it proslavery, either explicitly or implicitly: what is not antislavery is by implication proslavery. The problem with the former approach is that *conservative* and *moderate* mean different things to different people. The problem with the latter approach is that, due to the coexistence and interoperation of the two prevailing frameworks, *proslavery* and *perpetualism* have tended to conflate, implying that all those who were not antislavery favored slavery's perpetual existence—an implication contradicted by the documentary record left by many nineteenth-century politicians, among them Henry Clay and numerous other colonization advocates who, during the mid- to late 1830s, switched from gradualist rhetoric to eventualist rhetoric, while at the same time denouncing the perpetualist position increasingly promoted by John Calhoun and many others in the Lower South.[40]

As a side note, I should mention that, in general, I confine the use of this framework to describing the rhetoric and actions of historical figures at specific moments in time. This approach presumes that individuals' attitudes toward slavery could—and often did—change. I also confine the use of this framework to describing the intent behind individuals' rhetoric and actions, not the actual outcomes. The goal is to historicize descriptions of rhetoric and actions and to keep separate any retrospective judgments of efficacy or appropriateness, not to suggest that such retrospective judgments have no place. For instance, although Henry Clay may have spoken and acted, at various points in his life, with an intent of shortening slavery's lifespan, few—if any—of his actions could be said to have actually produced this outcome.

I also decided not to use the word *abolitionist* as a term of analysis. Throughout the book, I use it only in direct quotations or in instances where I make reference to these direct quotations. Generally speaking, *abolitionist,* like *antislavery* and *proslavery,* does not have a stable, widely agreed-upon definition among historians, despite the fact that in recent years, scholars have used it, with a bit more consistency, to refer to the small but quite vocal group of white and Black Americans who pushed for immediate actions against slavery and who insisted that Black Americans deserved full civic equality in the United States. More important, however, is the fact that the term did not have a stable meaning during the nineteenth century. For example, it was not uncommon for Lower Southerners to denounce Henry Clay as an abolitionist for his decision to promote gradual abolition and colonization. Clay, for his part, vehemently rejected the label. The term, as he used it, and indeed as most white politicians used it, applied only to Northern immediatists like Frederick Douglass and William Lloyd Garrison.[41]

There is one more important issue to discuss, and that is usage of the word *colonization* and its variants. Generally speaking, historians have used this term as a standard reference for the movement to geographically separate Black Americans, because it was conventionally used as such a reference during the nineteenth century, by both white promoters and Black opponents. White promoters of racial separation defaulted to this term because, among other things, it helped them emphasize that in advocating for the removal of Black Americans from the United States they were also advocating for the establishment of a foreign colony where Black Americans could go to gain full civic freedom. The term thus had a euphemistic effect. It tended to counterbalance, with notes of humanity and benevolence, the various stark exclusionary claims made by colonization advocates under the Black-freedom-as-a-problem rubric. Black opponents of racial separation commonly used the term *colonization* as well. Because the word was so broadly and persistently used in American public discourse, it served as a convenient shorthand as they argued vehemently against the movement's political efforts and insidious ideology. At the same time, Black activists well understood the term's euphemistic tendencies. And they made sure, depending on the moment and on their specific rhetorical aims, to use substitutes. When they wanted to emphasize the fact that the colonization movement, irrespective of its claims of humanity and benevolence, was fostering the spread of anti-Black prejudice and, in turn, encouraging the proliferation of laws that restricted Black freedom, they used words such as *expatriation, exclusion,* and *removal.* In contrast, when they spoke about the interest that a minority of Black Americans expressed, from time to time, in seeking better lives in foreign locales, they used words such as *resettlement* and *emigration,* especially the latter.[42]

In *Words Colliding,* I decided to follow both of these historical precedents. I use *colonization* as a default reference, as was common on both sides of the debate, and I use the various substitutes in specific moments, as Black activists did, for emphasis. Generally speaking, I use *emigration* when making reference to Black Americans who expressed a self-guided, not externally imposed, desire to leave the country. And I use *expatriation, exclusion,* or *removal* when I want to place particular emphasis on the fact that white colonization advocates, throughout the eight-decade period covered in this book, were dominantly motivated by a desire to expunge the Black population from the United States. In these moments, I am not suggesting, in blanket fashion, that the professions of humane and benevolent intent by colonization advocates were all disingenuous, though in some cases they likely were. Instead, I am seeking to stress that an interest in helping to elevate the free Black population was not the core motivation of this political movement. The striking number of very prominent Americans who founded and sustained the Black expatriation cause were seeking, above all, to make the United States a white nation.

The overall organization of the book is chronological, beginning in 1816 with the founding of the American Colonization Society and then proceeding through the main decades of the national debate over slavery and Black civil rights, the Civil War years, and the early decades of Jim Crow. Each chapter covers a distinct phase of the colonization movement's development. During each phase, as colonization proponents adjusted their rhetoric to suit the current political environment, they associated it with a wide range of potent national political issues, thus elaborating their exclusionary ideology and, in many cases, strengthening its influence. The book's narrative also, quite crucially, tracks the vigorous and persistent movement, led by Black activists, against the cause of Black expatriation and against the exclusionary laws and practices that, they asserted, flowed directly from the issue's promotion. It is important to highlight that undergirding the story of historical change told in *Words Colliding* there is a meaningful element of historical continuity. Throughout the eight decades that this public debate raged in the United States, the same fundamental questions were at its center: Was Black freedom a problem in American society, or was this problem assertion, as Frederick Douglass assessed it in 1889, simply a "delusion and a sham, a crafty substitution of a false issue for the true one"?[43]

Chapter 1 covers the founding, in late 1816 and early 1817, of the American Colonization Society, the effective starting point of the Black expatriation political movement in Washington. It begins by highlighting the complex and seemingly contradictory set of messages conveyed by the organization's largely Upper Southern founding group, notable among them Congressmen Henry Clay of Kentucky and John Randolph of Virginia. It then proceeds to explain, in careful and nuanced detail, how this assortment of remarks was in fact not an indication of self-contradiction but rather a representation of the movement's dual aims, at least from the perspective of Upper Southerners, and of the political sleight of hand that the ACS's leaders felt was required in seeking federal support for a project that was conceived, at least in part, for the purpose of facilitating the eradication of slavery in the nation. As a counterpoint, this chapter recounts the early years of the opposition movement that free Black Americans, led by James Forten, launched during the weeks following the ACS's establishment. It emphasizes that Black activists recognized, from the outset, that colonization promotion had the potential not only to muddy and impede efforts to end slavery but also to strengthen the false notion that Black freedom was a societal problem, and, moreover, to foster a sociopolitical environment in which Black exclusion, through laws and practices, seemed appealing and defensible.

Chapter 2 deals with the first decade and a half of colonization promotion in Washington, the period from 1817 to 1833, when the ACS's Upper Southern leaders came to understand two countervailing political realities. First, in order to generate significant levels of Northern political support they had to clarify and stress the emancipatory effects they hoped that establishing a scalable system of Black expatriation would catalyze in the Southern states. Second, by modifying their promotional message and by succeeding in their effort to increase Northern support, ACS leaders provoked the rise of a significant and sustained opposition movement in the Lower South, the region where slave-based agriculture was growing at a much higher rate than in the Upper South and, thus, where politicians had no interest in facilitating gradual abolition and where they saw any effort to involve the federal government in a slavery-related project, no matter how indirect the proponents claimed the relation to be, as a severe threat to the right of each Southern state to determine its own course regarding this institution.

Chapter 3 covers the tumultuous years between 1833 and 1853, when, in response to a dramatic increase in sectional tensions in Congress, Southern colonization proponents effectively reversed course on their tactic of stressing expatriation's emancipatory effects. Instead of promoting federally supported colonization as a means of propelling the nation toward *gradual* abolition, they tended to characterize it, rather, as a preparatory step toward *eventual* abolition. The revised promotional message that they put forth during this twenty-year period was, in essence, that the free Black population was a root cause of sectionalism and that, accordingly, colonization had great potential to heal and to strengthen the Union. During this twenty-year period, Black activists like Samuel Cornish and Frederick Douglass, among many others, intensified their oppositional actions via legislative petitions, pamphlets, newly launched newspapers, and national and state "colored" conventions. Through these outlets, they vigorously denounced efforts on the part of colonization advocates to make Black expatriation a Unionist project. Furthermore, they explicitly accused the colonization movement of doing as much as any other force in American society to increase exclusionary sentiment among white Americans and to encourage the passage, by state legislatures and Congress, of a growing body of exclusionary statutes, the most hated and worrisome being the Fugitive Slave Act of 1850.

Chapter 4 addresses the brief but pivotal period between 1854 and 1860, when the powerful Upper Southern Blair family displaced the ACS as the main driver of the Black expatriation political movement and when, due to the Blairs' strenuous efforts, colonization nearly became a formal plank of the emergent Republican Party. The Blairs—Francis Preston Blair Sr., Francis Preston Blair Jr., and Montgomery Blair—and their many supporters claimed that Black expatriation was the key to increasing the party's traction in the Upper South and, in turn, establishing a North–Upper South coalition capable of putting down the secessionist movement led by Lower Southern Democrats. They claimed, in essence, that Black expatriation, as a political issue, had the potential to prevent civil war. Black activists saw the Blairs' colonization campaign and the tremendous amount of political support it generated as highly troubling signs, motivating them to work, with even greater urgency, to fill the public sphere with the counter-rhetoric of inclusion and equal rights.

Chapter 5 deals with the Civil War years. In basic terms, it shows the period from late 1861 to early 1863 as the effective high point of the colonization movement's political efforts in Washington and the period from early 1863 to early 1865 as a major turning point. During the early period, as the federal government took escalating actions against slavery, President Lincoln and the Blairs, three of Lincoln's closest advisers at the time, pushed hard to make Black expatriation a concomitant of emancipatory moves taken, or at least considered, by various state governments and Congress. In this rare and, as it turned out, temporary environment, the Republican-dominant Congress debated federal support for colonization with greater frequency than ever before and passed the first and only federal appropriations for voluntary Black expatriation in American history. During the later period, Congress, as part of a very significant political shift, rescinded both appropriations and committed the federal government and the nation to a policy of immediate abolition and inclusion.

Chapter 6 covers the postwar decades, from roughly 1866 to 1900, a period that has received very limited attention from historians who have published on the ACS or on the broader Black expatriation movement. During these years, Southern politicians, like the Blairs and Senator John Tyler Morgan of Alabama, continued to promote Black colonization as a national cause because they saw in the movement's pre-1865 ideology a powerful political instrument that they could use in the post-1865 fight against Black suffrage. In other words, during the postwar decades, those who promoted colonization in national politics did so in significantly revised fashion. Rather than promoting the issue with a dominant aim of obtaining federal support for expatriation, they did so largely in the service of a multidecade campaign to oppose, undermine, discredit, and ultimately neutralize the Fifteenth Amendment, which prohibited race-based voter exclusion, to the great and persistent dismay of many white Southerners. Black activists publicly outed this political strategy and denounced it, over the course of several decades, in various public fora. Moreover, they repeated their longstanding assertion that the promotion of colonization ideology, whether the movement achieved its specific political goals or not, fostered an environment in the United States that made Black exclusion, rather than inclusion, seem rational and normative to large numbers of white Americans.

Words Colliding is ultimately a story about how prominent white politicians in the United States, for nearly a century, pushed the federal government to support a project that would facilitate the expatriation of Black Americans. It is a story as well of how this political movement—building on attitudes expressed in common practices, laws, and influential publications of the colonial and early-national periods—embedded in nineteenth-century America a racial ideology that characterized Black freedom as a societal problem and that, in turn, made the exclusion of Black Americans from the nation's borders, or at a minimum from important civil liberties, seem, from the perspective of many white Americans, necessary, inevitable, morally defensible, and even patriotic. And finally, it is a story about how prominent Black activists, at every step, vigorously opposed this movement's political efforts, repudiated its ideology, in thorough and adaptive terms, and fought, more broadly, against a system of racial oppression constructed on the basis of this ideology's false premises.

Both sides of this very public and heated debate used words as weapons, as instruments in a battle with multiple dimensions. In the most basic sense, white colonization advocates and Black activists battled *each other*, with the former insisting that Black Americans had to leave the United States, for the sake of all involved, and the latter insisting that Black Americans had just as much right to live and rise in the United States as white Americans. In a broader sense, both engaged in political battles with *different opponents*. White colonization advocates struggled against a mixture of Northern and Southern opposition in their efforts to obtain federal support. Black activists—in addition to engaging in a countereffort to sustain Northern opposition—fought doggedly against congressmen and state legislators who used the colonization movement's ideology, with or without attribution, to justify laws that increasingly restricted the scope of Black freedom.

From the broadest vantage point, these two parties locked horns in a great battle to determine whose vision of the nation's racialized future would win out. Black activists insisted that it was their progressive vision, not the antiquated one so stubbornly asserted by the colonization movement, that promised to deliver true national stability and prosperity. In other words, it was the path of inclusion and equality, not the path of exclusion and inequality, that was necessary, inevitable, morally defensible, and patriotic for Americans to pursue.

1

FOUNDING MOMENT

Decoding the Rhetoric

THE AMERICAN COLONIZATION SOCIETY (ACS) was founded in late December 1816 and early January 1817 in a series of meetings in Washington, the second of which was held in the chamber of the House of Representatives. These gatherings were all, technically speaking, private, not private in the sense that they were secret or exclusive but in the sense that they were not occasions for official government business. However, the line between private business and government business was a blurry one. Henry Clay, the current Speaker of the House, presided over all three sessions. Many of those who spoke during these meetings or who helped build the ACS during its early years held significant positions in the federal government's legislative branch or judicial branch. From the former, the roster included Clay and Virginia Congressmen John Randolph and Charles Fenton Mercer. From the latter, there was Clerk of the Supreme Court Elias Caldwell, Chief Justice John Marshall, and Associate Justice Bushrod Washington, the organization's first president. The blurriness between private and public would, in fact, be a defining feature of the ACS over its many decades of operation. One of the organization's core objectives was to obtain federal sponsorship and funds for a system that would expatriate "the free people of color of the United States."[1]

If one considers the various statements made during the ACS's founding meetings, in aggregate, it is hard not to detect elements of internal disagreement, perhaps even confusion. Congressman John Randolph, for instance, made two claims that seemed, on the surface, to pull in opposite directions. He declared that the ACS's separatist plan would encourage "thousands" of slaveholders to emancipate "their slaves" *and* would "tend to secure the property of every master in the United States over his slaves." What kind of organization looked to reduce the size of the enslaved population and, at the same time, make it easier and safer to hold Black Americans in bondage? Furthermore, how did the ACS plan to produce this dual effect? Of further complication, Speaker of the House Henry Clay declared that "it constituted no part of the object of this meeting to touch or agitate, in the slightest degree, a delicate question connected with... [the enslaved] population of our country." The ACS would deal only with *free* Black Americans, he insisted. Debates regarding "emancipation" or the broader subject of "abolition" were out of bounds. "It was upon that condition alone... that many gentlemen from the south and the west" had chosen to attend. And, it was on the same basis, he declared, that he had agreed to participate. How does one reconcile all of this rhetoric?[2]

This crucial first chapter seeks to do just that. Through close contextualized readings of Randolph, Clay, and other key founders, it decodes each of these statements and shows how they fit together into an integrated whole. The chapter makes two main claims: First, the ACS's founding moment expressed a particularly Upper Southern way of looking at the nation's racialized future, one that was grounded in Jefferson's remarks in *Notes on the State of Virginia*—as well as subsequent publications, such as St. George Tucker's *A Dissertation on Slavery* (1796) and George Tucker's *Letter to a Member of the General Assembly* (1801)—and that was further shaped by the growing Upper Southern belief that free Black Americans were the main cause of unrest among the enslaved. Second, the ACS's complex and, in a sense, murky relationship with slavery was a product of the founding moment decision to seek, and to continue seeking, federal sponsorship. This decision brought with it significant political risk. Slavery was the single-most controversial issue in national politics. This fact pushed ACS proponents to make difficult, complicated choices about how they described their new project. What became clear, early on, was that in making these choices they were often walking a fine line between clarification and obfuscation.³

In a broader sense, this chapter asserts that in the seeming mess of statements made during the ACS's founding sessions can be found the keys to understanding the eight-decade political movement that followed. Complexities, tensions, and, indeed, elements of deception were ever-present, because they were, as this chapter shows, inherent to the movement.

ENCOURAGING MANUMISSIONS, MAKING SLAVERY MORE SECURE

John Randolph was forty-three years old in late 1816 and early 1817 when he helped found the ACS. At the time, he had served in the House of Representatives for nearly twenty years. Like many of the ACS's founders, Randolph was a slaveholder from the Upper South, a region that included Virginia, Kentucky, Maryland, Tennessee, North Carolina, Delaware, and, in a few short years, Missouri. He shared these characteristics with several early ACS advocates including Clay, Mercer, Washington, Marshall, and District lawyer Francis Scott Key. He also shared these characteristics with Thomas Jefferson, Randolph's second cousin.⁴

All of these individuals—along with most, if not all, of the society's founders, Clay included—generally agreed with Jefferson's declaration in *Notes on the State of Virginia* that the institution of slavery would and should come to an end. They also agreed with Jefferson's insistence that this end could only be achieved through the establishment of a system for expatriating the emancipated. Thus, although Randolph was the only one who chose to be explicit about his emancipatory hopes during the ACS's founding sessions, he was not alone in harboring them. Washington, the organization's founding president, was one of the first to join Randolph in making his hopes explicit. In January 1818, when the ACS held its first annual meeting in the nation's capital, a tradition it would continue for the next seventy-plus years, Washington celebrated that the new organization would, in effect, provide every slaveholder in the nation "the opportunity . . . of emancipating his slaves without injury to his country." Moreover, he rejoiced in the prospect that the ultimate result of the ACS's efforts would be the "gradual abolition of slavery" throughout the United States. Upon reaching this final point, the American people, he added, could then claim to have erased "the only blot" on their great nation-building experiment.[5]

To understand why the ACS's founders generally viewed the establishment of a system of Black expatriation as an emancipatory catalyst—and thus to clarify Randolph's first claim—we need to look closely at Washington's phrase "without injury to his country." Under what circumstances did Washington and other slaveholding founders view emancipation as injurious? The presumed injury, from their perspective, was the incremental increase in the free Black population caused by each manumission. White Southerners widely believed that free Black Southerners were a major cause of unrest among the enslaved and, of even greater concern, violent uprisings. With this belief as a basis, ACS leaders claimed that aversion to incorporating the emancipated was one of the greatest impediments to manumission and thus one of the most significant obstacles to ultimate abolition.[6]

Robert Goodloe Harper, a former United States senator from Maryland and a son-in-law of the wealthy and powerful slaveholder Charles Carroll, gave this line of thought full explication in a long and uncommonly candid essay about the ACS's emancipatory potential, published in 1818. Harper declared that the "free people of color," by example and through direct influence, "contribute[d] greatly to the corruption of the slaves... by rendering them idle, discontented, and disobedient." Slaveholders, accordingly, considered any act of "emancipation" that allowed "the person emancipated to remain in this country" as a source of incremental "evil." The great promise of the ACS's plan, Harper asserted, was that by establishing a foreign outlet for those who might be emancipated, it paved "the way to... more frequent and easier manumission."[7]

Randolph's second claim, colonization's tendency "to secure the property of every master," was effectively a rearrangement of the first claim—the same basic sentiment expressed with different emphasis. Once again, Harper's essay provided clarification. The institution of slavery, he asserted, was a "terrible mischief lurking in our vitals," one that all white Americans should view with "deep and awful apprehension." The great danger inherent in this institution, he added, increased every year as the enslaved population grew and, importantly, as the existing free Black population grew alongside it. By establishing a system through which the latter population could be decreased over time, the ACS would effectively reduce this accreting danger. Although the instabilities and threats that white Southerners faced would not be fully eliminated until slavery itself was destroyed, the incremental removal of free Black Americans would make the institution less troublesome and more "secure" in the interim.[8]

In essence, Randolph's seemingly countervailing claims about the ACS were simply an expression of the white South's two-dimensional view of the region's free Black population. More precisely, they were an expression of the two-dimensional view that the ACS's Upper Southern founders ascribed to the white South. As will be seen, plenty of white Southerners, especially Lower Southerners, disagreed with the basic premise that slavery in the United States would and should come to an end. Nonetheless, as Randolph, Washington, Harper, Clay, and others saw it, the function of the ACS, indeed part of the beauty of its design, was that it would serve both purposes: encourage manumissions and make the institution of slavery more stable and safe. These two aims, from their perspective, were not at all contradictory. They were, rather, quite rational and consistent. Collectively, they expressed an intention of facilitating the gradual abolition of slavery in a way that, at the same time, reduced the ongoing dangers of living in its midst.[9]

"FREE BLACKS" ONLY

Henry Clay was thirty-nine years old when he chaired the ACS's founding meetings. Although younger than Randolph and Washington and less experienced than both in terms of years served in the nation's capital, Clay was already a significant political force. He had served as Speaker of the House of Representatives with near continuity since 1811, and he had been part of the diplomatic team that negotiated the 1814 treaty with Great Britain that ended the War of 1812. When he returned to the Speaker role after the war, at a time when the United States was brimming with nationalist fervor, he pushed hard to increase the federal government's role in efforts to build out the physical infrastructure (for example, roads, canals, bridges), banking system, and economy of the still-young nation. His decision to lend his name, pen, and voice to the budding colonization movement was very much entwined with this nation-building push.[10]

During the late 1790s, when Clay was barely past twenty, he published two editorials in the *Kentucky Gazette* that called on the state's residents to take action against slavery. Clay had recently moved to Kentucky from Virginia, where he had worked for George Wythe, the William and Mary professor who had taught and mentored Thomas Jefferson and many other influential Virginians, including fellow colonization advocates John Marshall and James Monroe. Kentuckians were, at the time, debating the possibility of revising the state's founding constitution, which had made Kentucky a slave state. Clay argued that the state's youth combined with its relatively small enslaved population created a circumstance in which Kentucky might, without too much difficulty, reverse course on this problematic institution. Employing a tone that, over the next few decades, he would largely avoid when speaking about slavery, he urged Kentuckians to commence the process of abolishing this "enormous evil." How could "any humane man" claim satisfaction with the present situation, he wondered, with "near thirty thousand of his fellow beings around him, deprived of all the rights which make life desirable, transferred like cattle from the possession of one to another"?[11]

Given what Clay said and did not say during the ACS's founding sessions, one might reasonably wonder whether he had fundamentally changed his views on enslavement during the intervening twenty years. When he insisted that "it constituted no part of the object" of these sessions to engage with this "delicate" issue and when he claimed further that his involvement hinged on this exclusion, was he signaling to the nation that he now opposed action against slavery altogether? Moreover, was he indicating that he had come to view slavery as an element of the nation's social, economic, and political fabric that should be perpetual? The answer to both questions, as Clay adamantly declared in statements made in support of Black colonization during the late 1820s, was *no*. So why did he offer these insistent public qualifications during the late 1810s? And why, in making them, did he place so much stress on the idea that the ACS was formed for the sole purpose of facilitating the emigration of free Black Americans?[12]

The answers to these questions become clear if one notes that the ACS was, from the moment of its founding, a political organization that sought money and sponsorship from the federal government. Unlike the various national benevolent societies established around the same time—such as the American Bible Society, the American Sunday School Union, and the American Temperance Society—the ACS was founded on the belief that its success depended on accessing federal resources and influence. Indeed, the first major act taken by the new organization was to draft and submit, in January 1817, a formal petition to Congress, thus commencing a practice that the ACS would sustain for decades to come. The organization also established its headquarters in Washington and, in early 1818, began the process of staging its annual meetings there. A main goal of these meetings, typically held in January during the early weeks of each annual congressional session, was to maximize the number of congressmen and other federal officials in attendance.

In essence, Clay's remarks were the first moves in a long-term struggle to manage a risk inherent in the new organization's political strategy. ACS leaders recognized that their attempts to obtain federal sponsorship could be viewed as a potential threat to a crucial constitutional consensus: The federal government, most Northern and Southern politicians agreed, had no power to interfere with slavery in the states where it currently existed. No matter how much ACS spokespeople expressed respect for this consensus or how much they insisted that federal sponsorship, if legislated, would not undermine it, they understood that some portion of the South would likely assert states'-rights-based objections. After all, Clay's disclaimers notwithstanding, ACS leaders were, in fact, trying to get the federal government involved in a project that, at a minimum, had indirect connections to slavery. The fundamental challenge, therefore, was to explain the ACS's motivations and aims in ways that minimized states'-rights anxiety. And, of course, the organization's leaders had to balance this imperative, at the same time, against the objective of maximizing political appeal.

The two main tactics that the ACS founders developed to thread this political needle were exemplified by Clay in his founding moment remarks. The first was to stress that the organization's sole, official function was to deal with free Black Americans, not with the "delicate" issue of slavery. This calculated circumscription appeared explicitly in the society's founding constitution and guided the text of its first petition to Congress. Over the coming decades, it would become a kind of political mantra. The free-Blacks-only claim served to create rhetorical distance between colonization and enslavement as political issues. It signaled to Southerners and to any individual with potential states'-rights objections that the ACS, by original design, sought to keep its hoped-for involvement with the federal government within the limits prescribed by the Constitution.[13]

There was, however, subtext to this exclusiveness claim, which Clay and other ACS leaders understood from the outset. The term *free Black,* as already noted, referred to two groups of Black Americans: those who had freedom in the present, and those who might gain freedom in the future, by means of slaveholder manumissions or state-based gradual abolition laws. It was far safer to speak about the first group, the *already free,* in congressional debate. This was the group that Clay called to mind in his founding moment remarks. To talk about the second group, the *prospectively free,* was to raise the delicate subject of slavery in the halls of Congress. Prospectively free Black Americans were, after all, currently enslaved—at least until they were manumitted with the intention of subsequent colonization.[14]

Randolph's two claims had made reference to both groups. Clay, out of deference to states'-rights-anxieties, referred only to the first group. This was a calculated deception, but it was a deception that, from the perspective of ACS leaders, had an element of truth. The ACS's plan was to facilitate the expatriation of both groups, and both groups fell, in a manner of speaking, under the rubric "free Black." Over the coming decades, colonization advocates, Clay among them, would shift back and forth between generic and specific invocations of "free Black," depending on whether they wanted to downplay or emphasize the movement's emancipatory potential. When they were petitioning the federal government for support, the generic was, for the most part, the preferred form.

The second tactic was to characterize Black expatriation as a national solution to a national problem. The organization's core message was that Black freedom created problems for *all* white Americans, whether they lived in the North or the South. Seeking federal support for colonization was thus, they claimed, both logical and appropriate. Moreover, it was pragmatic. The resources required for such a large-scale endeavor were national in scale, beyond that which any state could muster on its own.[15]

The ACS's first congressional petition expounded on this nationalist framing by connecting colonization to a basic "maxim" of human history:

the "existence of distinct and separate cast[e]s" was "an inherent vice in the composition of society." The influences of this vice, the petition continued, were so disruptive and "baneful" that they required "the utmost exertion of human energy . . . to remedy or remove it." By this point in the nation's development, it was well understood, the petition continued, that free Black Americans constituted just such a caste. The colonization project that the ACS had conceived and that it now asked the federal government to support, therefore, warranted the "earnest attention" of "every patriot" and of "every enlightened, philanthropic, and practical statesman" in the United States. The "great and beneficial" work of this new organization, the petition added, was in the direct service of the "public good."[16]

It is important to note that this second tactic also served a more subtle purpose, one that would become more obvious during the 1820s as the ACS's Upper Southern leaders struggled to recruit Northern support. By characterizing the free Black population as a national problem and Black expatriation as a national solution, the ACS's Upper Southern founders were seeking to downplay, at least for the time being, the fact that white Southerners generally viewed the nation's free Black population with greater concern than white Northerners did—given, among other things, the former's rising fears of uprisings among the enslaved. In other words, part of their motivation for pushing a national, racialized sense of solidarity was to dissuade Northerners from seeing the ACS's federal petition as an attempt to apply national resources to an issue that was, at root, more Southern than Northern.

"WITH THEIR OWN CONSENT"

The ACS's founding charter contained a phrase that the society's proponents would reiterate, often with great emphasis, over the next several decades: *with their own consent*. They used this phrase to signal that the ACS had no intention of forcing Black Americans to leave the country. Their migration would, in all circumstances, be voluntary. In reality, however, the phrase, which became a kind of ritualistic refrain for Black expatriation advocates, was more complex in meaning than its simple language suggested.

There were, in fact, two forms of consent envisioned by the ACS's founders: one for the already free and another for the prospectively free.

During the society's 1818 annual meeting in Washington, Clay addressed both. In choosing to comment on the prospectively free, Clay broke somewhat with his ban on slavery-related talk, thus hinting that his own hopes for the ACS were broader than he had declared a year earlier. Emancipated individuals, Clay insisted, should have their manumissions conditioned on formal agreements to "leave the country." While this might seem, he added, like an arrangement that would give enslaved individuals pause—since it would require them not just to leave their native land but also their homes, sources of income, friends, and almost certainly family members—the prospect of freedom would, Clay asserted, override any sources of hesitance: "He has placed a false estimate upon liberty who believes that there are many who would refuse the boon [emancipation], when coupled even with such a condition."[17]

To characterize consent given in such a context as voluntary was to stretch the meaning of the word. In practice, this was a kind of coerced consent. Prospectively free individuals (enslaved), based on what Clay said, would have a fundamentally different consent-giving calculus than already-free individuals. Although both groups could choose to reject the offer of colonization, those in the former class who rejected the offer would, in doing so, remain enslaved.

The circumstances of consent were more straightforward for already-free Black Americans. Colonization movement leaders and supporters rarely entertained the notion of forced expatriation, claiming that it would be both unethical and legally unsound. Nonetheless, elements of coercion could and did manifest as colonization advocates spoke about this portion of the Black population as well. These elements typically manifested in statements made by advocates from the Upper South, where anxieties regarding growth in the free Black population were highest. In Virginia, where some of the most outspoken and committed colonization advocates resided, the enslaved population had risen to nearly 400,000, according to the 1810 census—a twenty-year increase of about 35 percent. During this same period, the free Black population had grown from roughly 14,000 to 31,000, an increase of approximately 120 percent. In Maryland, another early seedbed of colonization advocacy, the enslaved population had grown by roughly 10 percent between 1790 and 1810 to around 110,000, and the free Black population had increased at a rate of 325 percent to 34,000, making it the largest of any state in the nation. In both states, slavery was, according to the Upper Southern way of thinking, becoming more and more unstable and dangerous. Faced with such trends and convinced that Southern acts of gradual abolition would not commence until after the ACS had established a scalable, proven system of expatriation, Clay and other Southern advocates professed a commitment to *voluntary* action while at the same time expressing a *strong, often sharply worded,* preference that Black Americans consent to emigration. These expressions easily blurred the line between persuasion and coercion.[18]

Such was the case with statements Clay made at the 1818 annual meeting, during which one of the speakers noted a growing sense of opposition among free Black Americans. Clay wondered aloud why free Black Americans, when given the option to leave the country, would choose to remain. Would they not recognize in colonization, he asked, the opportunity to gain access to the various forms of "happiness" forever denied to them in the United States, as a result of a race prejudice that was effectively ineradicable? Sharpening his tone further, he declared, why would any rational people choose to remain in a country where their lives were "cheerless," "debased," and "humiliating" and where they were, and would always be, considered "aliens to the society of which they are members?"[19]

These were not the remarks of someone who was truly open to the prospect of free Black Americans choosing a course different than the one he recommended. Clay wanted them to leave the United States and believed that it was urgent and necessary that large numbers of them consent to do so *voluntarily*. The alternate scenario, in which large numbers of free Black Americans chose to remain, was simply unthinkable, incongruous with his firm beliefs regarding Black–white relations in the United States. This underlying frame of mind motivated Clay, and many other Black expatriation advocates after him, to address free Black Americans in a way that was presumptive, prescriptive, and, indeed, coercive. To choose against emigration, Clay strongly implied in his remarks, would be to act illogically, self-destructively, and shamefully. Hopefully, he pointedly suggested, white Americans could count on Black Americans to see things in the same obvious light.

BLACK OPPOSITION

In January 1817, the same month that the ACS submitted its memorial to Congress, thousands of free Black Americans gathered in Philadelphia to protest the new organization and to voice strong disagreement with the vision laid out by its founders. James Forten, a wealthy sailmaker and a veteran of the Revolutionary War, chaired the meeting and helped ensure that its formal resolutions were printed and publicized. The fifty-year-old Black businessman was a very prominent figure in the young nation. He had extensive connections with white and Black Northerners, by virtue of his high economic and social status, and over the last twenty years he had emerged as one of the most influential Black activists in the North. He devoted significant time and money to growing Northern efforts to promote the abolition of slavery and to protect, and if possible expand, the legal freedoms of Black Americans. Over the next twenty-five years, until his death in 1842, he also contributed significant time and money to the growing Northern effort to oppose colonization advocacy. For much of this time and beyond, Forten and other leading Black activists identified the colonization movement as the second-greatest enemy of Black Americans, the first being slavery.[20]

During this 1817 meeting, during other such gatherings over the next several years, and in various publications, Forten and his fellow protesters vigorously disputed the messages put forth by the ACS's founding group. They utterly rejected the notion that establishing a system of Black expatriation would foster a wave of manumissions. Why would a system that tended to secure the property of every slaveholder also tend to encourage the same class of people to give up this property? Indeed, it was far more likely, they observed, that the ACS's operations would tend to "stay the cause of ... abolition," or, even worse, "defeat it altogether." In essence, Randolph's first claim was, according to Black activists, either the product of deluded thinking or a calculated deception. His second claim, which stressed the ACS's capacity to secure enslaved property, was, from their perspective, the only truthful thing he had said.[21]

Clay, Black activists noted, had spread his fair share of misleading and harmful propaganda as well. First, what sense did it make for ACS leaders to claim that the natural home of Black Americans lay elsewhere when

Black Americans had lived in North America for as long as white Americans and had contributed just as much, if not more, to the many successes that were, in the present, such a source of national pride? Second, wasn't it preposterous to assume that Black Americans would be better off trading their known lives in the United States for an unknown future in "the savage wilds of Africa," where they would have to build every bit of civilization and governance from scratch? Third, why did ACS leaders believe that free Black Americans were willing to "separate ourselves voluntarily" from their enslaved "brethren," with whom they had deep "ties of consanguinity, of suffering, and of wrong?" And fourth, why did these leaders expect free Black Americans to accept, as self-evident and indisputable, the notion that anti-Black prejudice in the United States was ineradicable?[22]

If, in fact, ACS leaders had truly conceived this colonization plan, "for our benefit," Black protesters summarily noted, we "respectfully" but also firmly insist "that it is not asked for by us." Moreover, we "renounce and disclaim every connexion" with the new organization and "declare our determination not to participate in any part" of its operation. Consent, in other words, despite Clay's expression of confidence, would not be forthcoming.[23]

Black activists expressed particular disappointment that this ill-conceived plan was being promoted by men who were "among the wisest... in this great nation" and "whose names give value to all they recommend." Informing this sentiment was a deep anxiety, one that would intensify in the coming years as the ACS grew and as its traction in Congress increased. Black activists recognized that the colonization movement had the potential to become a kind of prejudice propaganda machine. When Speaker of the House Henry Clay stood in a chamber of Congress and proclaimed that white antipathy toward free Black Americans was effectively ineradicable, when he described free Black Americans as "aliens" despite being native-born, and when he characterized the free Black population as a fundamental impediment to national progress, he broadcasted, from a national stage, a message that racial inclusion was illogical and that racial separation was necessary and unavoidable. Furthermore, when he and a growing number of influential white Americans—politicians, clergy, newspaper editors, etc.—made the same points emphatically and repeatedly, they gave this attitude greater reach and strength. "Who can read colonization sermons, orations, or the *African Repository* ... without forming the most degraded opinion of our colored population, and having his prejudices, rather than his sympathy, increased against them," a Black newspaper declared during the late 1820s. (The *African Repository* was the ACS's official monthly publication.) "To concede so much to prejudice," another newspaper noted with a sense of both frustration and anxiety, "is to deify it."[24]

In practical terms, Black activists understood that the threat posed by the colonization movement's capacity to negatively impact the lives of Black Americans was great and, moreover, that this capacity did not hinge on whether its efforts to obtain federal support succeeded or failed. The more that the movement's high-profile leaders pushed white Americans to view the free Black population through its particular exclusionary lens, the more likely white Americans would be to support and indeed demand incremental constraints on Black civil rights. Colonization advocates were, in other words, from the perspective of Black activists, promoting not just a particular cause but also a particular vision of the nation's racial future. If these advocates failed in their efforts to facilitate large-scale, federally sponsored, voluntary emigration but succeeded in their efforts to convince white Americans that Black freedom was a national problem that demanded urgent action, the oppressive conditions faced by Black Americans would almost certainly worsen. Elected state and federal lawmakers would, quite rationally, react to this attitudinal shift among their constituents by passing laws that pushed Black Americans further and further toward the margins of civil society. Making this prediction all the more certain was the fact that many of these lawmakers were now and would likely continue to be colonization advocates themselves.

In summary, the American Colonization Society's founding moment during the late 1810s was a microcosm of the eight-decade political movement that followed. John Randolph's seemingly countervailing claims reflected, in essence, a modified view of the white South's racial predicament. Generally speaking, the ACS's Upper Southern founders agreed with Jefferson that the enslaved population was a source of great instability and danger in Southern society. However, over the last thirty years, they had come to view the region's free Black population as the greater and more pressing concern. Establishing a national system of colonization, as the new organization proposed to do, would address the white South's complex predicament in two ways. First, it would enable slaveholders to pursue emancipation and expatriation in concert. By making the latter a condition of the former, the gradual eradication of slavery could proceed without any associated increase in the free Black population, and thus without any increase in instability or danger. Second, this national system would help the Southern states decrease the size of their existing free Black populations. This ongoing reduction would further diminish the destabilizing and endangering effects of slavery as white Southerners weathered the long period required for the institution's complete eradication.

Henry Clay's remarks during the founding sessions, in effect, conveyed the new organization's political strategy. Specifically, they showed an acute awareness that the decision to seek federal support carried significant risk. States'-rights-based objections would likely arise no matter how careful the ACS's leaders were in crafting their promotional rhetoric. Nonetheless, it was essential that they do as much as possible to communicate their federal appeals in terms that were politically circumspect. The approach that they devised was to declare that the ACS would deal only with "free Blacks," a "caste" population that, they asserted, caused problems in every state and that fundamentally impaired the nation's experiment in republican governance. In short, the ACS's core mission was to provide a national solution to a national problem, not to undermine the legal foundations of enslavement. Indeed, why would slaveholders choose to be involved, Clay suggested in his remarks, if things were otherwise?

The key to reconciling Randolph's claims and Clay's circumscription is to recognize that the ACS, like all institutions seeking a particular legislative outcome, had two basic objectives: maximizing the reasons for supporting its cause while minimizing the reasons for opposing it. Randolph articulated his claims pursuant to the first objective. Clay made his remarks pursuant to the second one. Because slavery was such an incredibly divisive issue and because colonization had potential associations, at the very least, with the institution, there was tension between these two objectives. If ACS promoters tried too hard to maximize the organization's appeal, by, for instance, hammering on its emancipatory potential, they risked handing potent ammunition to their prospective states'-rights opponents. At the same time, if they were too circumspect, by strenuously denying all connections to slavery, they ran the risk of being uncompelling. Would a significant portion of white Americans in the North, for instance, really buy into the notion that the free Black population was a national problem that demanded a national, federally funded solution? White Southerners would derive considerable satisfaction from diminishing the size of their free Black populations whether slavery was affected or not. But would white Northerners? They did not live with the daily fears produced by the assumption that free Black Americans fomented instability and violence among the enslaved. Why would they support the use of federal resources for a problem that seemed more regional than national—unless, of course, these resources might help foster the eradication of slavery, an institution that, by the late 1810s, the Northern states had all rejected.

A close examination of the ACS's founding moment thus reveals that complexities, tensions, and elements of deception were not only hard to avoid but also that they were, in many ways, there by design. In trying to describe the cause of Black colonization in a manner that was, at the same time, politically compelling and cautious, ACS leaders walked a fine line between clarification and obfuscation. Over the next eighty years, they would continue to walk this line. Political circumstances changed, but these changes, generally speaking, did not simplify the task of balancing these two objectives. Colonization rhetoric was always, to some degree, a challenge to decode and comprehend.

By the same token, a close examination of the Black opposition movement that arose in direct response to the ACS's founding, this chapter shows as well, sheds additional clarifying light. From the late 1810s through the 1890s, Black activists paid very careful attention to what colonization advocates said and did. In newspapers, magazines, speeches, pamphlets, and public protests, James Forten and the many who followed his example contested the movement's political actions, refused the movement's offers of funded emigration, and, most importantly, picked apart and disputed the movement's exclusionary ideology. They recognized, more than any white opponents of colonization did, that this movement had a tremendous capacity to justify and amplify Black oppression, irrespective of whether it succeeded in its efforts to obtain federal support.

2

ENDING SLAVERY

1817–1833

IN FEBRUARY 1824, THE LEADERS of the American Colonization Society (ACS) held their annual meeting in the chamber of the US Supreme Court. Four individuals played significant roles in the proceedings. All of them were Upper Southern slaveholders. Associate Justice Bushrod Washington, a Virginian and the society's president, chaired the convention. Representative Charles Fenton Mercer and George Washington Parke Custis, both Virginians, and former Senator Robert Goodloe Harper, a Marylander, gave speeches.[1]

Over the past seven years, the ACS had presented several memorials to Congress asking for federal support. None had produced any significant action on the part of the national government. Harper and Custis believed that the time had come to draft and submit a new memorial. Mercer disagreed. The ACS should wait, he advised, until it had made more progress on two significant issues. First, there was the fact that although the society had been in existence for seven years, it had failed, Mercer asserted, to generate significant interest in the North. For the time being, "we have few auxiliary societies [in the region], and the subject is little discussed." Northern interest, they all agreed, was key to winning a majority vote in

Congress. Second, there was the open question, Mercer pointed out, of whether a congressional majority would support the assumption, implicit in the memorial, that the federal government had the "constitutional" authority to fund Black colonization.[2]

Both of these issues were tightly entwined with the complex assortment of statements that society leaders had made over the last seven years regarding slavery. What was the society's position on this highly controversial issue, many white Americans wondered? Was it truly founded with the sole intention of decreasing the size of the purportedly problematic free Black caste, as Henry Clay had indicated during the founding meetings? The answer, generally speaking, was no—as explained in chapter 1. A large number of Upper Southern proponents—including Washington, Mercer, Custis, and Harper, as well as Clay—envisioned colonization as a means of bringing slavery to an end in the United States. Their cautious and, at times, misleading statements regarding this objective reflected an awareness of the political sensitivity of their federal appeals. But the great majority of Northerners, Mercer claimed, did not understand this, a main reason why Northern interest was so low. Many in the North, Mercer explained, viewed the ACS as a Southern-led organization whose main purpose was to "more effectually rivet the chains of the slave." In effect, Mercer's message was that politically minded attempts at spinning and blurring the ACS's emancipatory aims had worked too well.[3]

Custis and Harper shared Mercer's concern about a general Northern misunderstanding of the ACS's intentions, but they took a more optimistic view of the prospects for a new congressional memorial. Custis, a wealthy slaveholder and playwright who was the adopted son of former President George Washington, spoke with the most optimism. It was impossible to believe, he insisted, that the "prejudices which still existed in the northern sections of the Union ... could long continue." On the question of the justifiability of federal support, Custis and Harper predicted, with a kind of presumptive confidence, that Congress would soon accept that it had a crucial, enabling role to play in the process of eradicating slavery. The ACS, Custis asserted, was engaged in a global project of "retributive justice," and thus when it appealed to Congress for aid in "restoring" Black Americans to "the land of their nativity" and removing "the fetters from the slave," it could trust that it had the force of "virtue on its side." Harper characterized the aggregate population of free and enslaved Black Americans in the United States as "a cancer on the body politic," as threatening to the nation as a "hostile army" poised to "invade." Any "evil" that threatened the nation's existence, he insisted, called for a national response. Thus, he concluded, it is "to the national government that we must address ourselves."[4]

ACS leaders continued to entertain the prospect of a new memorial after the 1824 annual meeting but, ultimately, did not submit one during that year. The society's next application for federal aid would not take place until 1827. During this interim period, ACS spokespeople spent considerable energy trying to address the problem that Mercer had highlighted: a profound lack of traction in the Northern states. Generally speaking, society representatives adjusted their promotional messages during the mid- to late 1820s in ways meant to dispel the notion that the ACS was, as Mercer had put it, a Southern-led organization whose main purpose was to "more effectually rivet the chains of the slave." The most potent and, as it turned out, controversial adjustment was the decision to clarify and stress colonization's emancipatory potential, a feature that Clay had carefully sidestepped during the ACS's early meetings. The political tactic worked, quite well in fact, as many white Northerners became colonization supporters during these years. However, as ACS leaders soon discovered, this tactic had an unintentional consequence: a significant rise in opposition from the Lower South, the exact phenomenon that Clay, with his sidestepping rhetoric, had sought to prevent.[5]

SLAVE TRADE POLITICS AND THE FOUNDING OF LIBERIA

The ACS's decades-long effort to obtain federal support for colonization began in January 1817, when Representative John Randolph presented the first of many memorials from the society to Congress. Hewing to the rhetorical precedents set by Henry Clay (not Randolph), the memorial avoided any mention of slavery and insisted, with all the ambiguity that Clay had, that the society's sole purpose was "colonizing the free people of color of the United States" with their consent. As rationale for pursuing this "great and beneficial object," the memorialists made two claims, one self-interested and one purportedly humanitarian. First, the "existence of distinct and separate cast[e]s, or classes," like the free Black population of the United States, was "an inherent vice in the composition of society; pregnant with baleful consequences, both moral and political, and demanding the utmost exertion of human energy and foresight to remedy or remove it." Second, free Black Americans deserved far better treatment than they received, at present, in the nation. Like white Americans, they deserved an opportunity to experience true freedom and self-determination in a country of their own. By helping the ACS establish a free Black colony, the federal government, the memorial asserted, would support both of these objectives. Surely such a project, the memorial continued, with its combined force of political imperative and benevolence, deserved the attention of Congress and indeed of every philanthropist and "every patriot" in the United States.[6]

ACS leaders quickly discovered that these initial promotional arguments—although not particularly objectionable in political terms, not yet at least—did not produce a strong impulse to action. In early February, a House committee issued a favorable but largely noncommittal response to the ACS's first memorial. The idea of removing Black Americans from the North American continent received explicit endorsement: "Their distinct character and relative condition render an entire separation from our own States and Territories indispensable." But rather than recommend an appropriation, the committee proposed a joint House and Senate resolution that authorized the president of the United States to consult with Great Britain on the possibility of receiving Black American emigrants in Sierra Leone. If these negotiations failed, the resolution asked the president to seek written agreements with Britain and other relevant countries that would enable the United States to establish its own colony on the African coast. As the congressional session proceeded to its closing day, the proposed resolution did not come up for vote in either chamber. The cause of colonization, it seemed, needed to be wrapped in the cloak of another cause and explained in more compelling ways.[7]

During the eight months that intervened between the end of the congressional session in March 1817 and the commencement of the next full session in December, ACS leaders determined that they would seek federal support under the auspices of suppressing the Atlantic slave trade. This approach had four important advantages. First, the federal government had clear jurisdiction over this issue, as indicated in the Constitution and by the 1807 federal law that had prohibited all further American involvement in the international trade (not the domestic trade). Second, the anti-slave-trade cause had significant political cachet, something the report highlighted, citing recent declarations made by Britain and the United States "to use their best endeavors to effect the entire abolition of the traffic in slaves." Third, the idea of Black colonization in Africa had been represented, for several decades at this point, as a way of ending the international traffic in human chattel at the source, in Africa. The British politicians and philanthropists who had combined efforts to establish Sierra Leone in 1787 had made this association quite explicit, as had early American promoters of colonization. Fourth, condemning the slave trade had become, over the last thirty years in both the United States and in Britain, a way of denouncing slavery by proxy. In both countries, explicitly attacking the immorality of the former was a means of implicitly criticizing the immorality of the latter, but with far less political provocation, since the act of trading in human beings was generally seen, in both countries, as more offensive than the act of owning them.[8]

Over the next two years, the ACS, with Mercer as its lead congressional advocate, tried to push the federal government closer to the point of granting a formal role for the ACS in suppressing the slave trade. The society's key move was to try to make the federal government solely responsible for the enslaved Africans taken into custody by the US Navy. Up to this point in the nation's history, this responsibility had fallen to state governments. Up to this point as well, state governments had typically sold these individuals to American slaveholders. Mercer and other ACS leaders saw a political opportunity amid these facts. They wanted the federal government to partner with the ACS in order to replace the inhumane practice of enslaving these liberated people with the more humane practice of returning them to Africa. And they hoped that this relationship might serve as a starting point for a broader partnership focused on the colonization of free Black Americans.[9]

In March 1819, Congress passed a new law that accomplished some, but definitely not all, of what Mercer and the ACS had envisioned. Congress assigned full responsibility for determining the fate of these recaptured Africans, as they were called, to the executive branch of the federal government and appropriated $100,000 to fund whatever expenses might arise. The president gained the specific power to place supervisory federal agents on the west coast of Africa and to allocate funds to help smooth the recaptured individuals' transition back into African society.

Mercer saw all of this as a great boon to the ACS, at least initially. The federal government would now, once the federal agents were appointed and installed, have a formal presence in the region where the society was trying to establish a colony of Black Americans. Moreover, decision-making authority would reside with James Monroe, who Mercer knew to have past and present interests in colonization. Mercer and other ACS leaders hoped the president would take a liberal view of the law and use it as justification for providing substantive federal support to the society's effort.

During the week following the bill signing, a committee of ACS leaders that included Bushrod Washington secured an audience with Monroe in Washington in order to offer advice on the law's implementation. Shortly thereafter, Mercer met with Monroe privately at the president's Virginia home. He and Monroe were longtime neighbors in Loudon County. Favorable reports of both conversations suggested that Monroe might do exactly what the society had suggested. But in December 1819, Monroe's message to Congress offered an interpretation that hewed tightly to the law's explicit purpose of dealing with recaptured slaves. Although he suggested that the appointed federal agents could identify land in Africa where these individuals might be resettled, he did not authorize the agents to purchase territory, and he explicitly prohibited them from "exercis[ing] . . . power founded on the principle of colonization." Of further disappointment to ACS leaders, Monroe did not, based in large part on advice from the United States attorney general, suggest or endorse ways in which the ACS might join the government's effort or ways in which the government's effort might be conducted such that the society enjoyed indirect benefits. If the ACS wanted a formal and substantive relationship with the federal government, it was evident that more politicking would be needed.[10]

In February 1820, the ACS continued its lobbying efforts by submitting a second memorial to Congress that argued strongly for a federally sponsored African colony as an adjunct to the federal government's present efforts at slave trade suppression. John Randolph once again served as congressional messenger, despite his increasingly strained relationship with Henry Clay. The two men had personal differences, but they were also at odds politically.

The tension between them reflected a larger, emergent conflict within the Democratic-Republican Party, effectively the only party of consequence during the so-called Era of Good Feelings that followed the War of 1812. Clay was an ardent advocate of nation-building, and he believed that the federal government had an expansive role to play in this effort. For instance, Clay supported a federal tariff, a national bank, and federal support for internal improvements (roads, canals, etc.) and education—a political program pushed forward during the 1820s under the auspices of the National Republican Party and then, during the 1830s, the Whig Party. Randolph was a dyed-in-the-wool states'-rights politician who helped to lead an emergent coalition in Congress that strongly opposed most, though certainly not all, attempts to expand the scope of federal power. One of the chief concerns of this political coalition—which gained coherence during the 1820s as the party of Andrew Jackson and then, during the 1830s, coalesced as the Democratic Party—was how any expansion of federal power might be used as a precedent for undermining the right of each state to determine its own course regarding slavery. The document that Randolph, who would distance himself from the society over the next few years, placed before the House of Representatives announced the ACS's imminent plan to purchase land on the west coast of Africa and to begin the long-term project of settling it with Black Americans. The resultant colony, which the society hoped Congress would authorize the executive department to support with funds and other appropriate means, would prove invaluable, the memorial asserted, in combatting the international trade in human chattel. Indeed, without some kind of additional measure, one that looked beyond existing reliance on naval patrols, current suppression efforts, the memorial added, would most likely continue to produce unsatisfying results. What was needed were Black settlements, like Sierra Leone and like that presently contemplated by the ACS, that could help proliferate civilized institutions and Christian morality, and help "dispel the darkness which has so long enshrouded that continent" and allowed barbaric practices like the slave trade to persist. The benefits to be derived from enlisting the ACS in slave trade suppression were, the memorial concluded, "obvious and extreme."[11]

Based on these political premises, what Monroe said in his congressional message, and what ACS leaders articulated in their 1820 memorial, an ambiguous long-term collaboration between the federal government and the ACS commenced during the Monroe administration. The centerpiece of this collaboration was a piece of land on the west coast of Africa acquired by the ACS, with the assistance of the US Navy, in late 1821. ACS leaders and early Black American emigrants named this land Liberia, a moniker intended to signal the new colony's animating spirit of freedom. The colony's capital, established shortly thereafter, bore the name Monrovia, after the president under whose auspices the colony had come into existence. From the outset, Liberia had two purposes. The first, the only official purpose supported by the federal government, was to serve as an entry point for the return of individuals seized by the US Navy as part of its slave trade suppression efforts. To this end, the federal government installed agents in Liberia who served as liaisons between the executive branch, the US Navy, the ACS, and Liberian officials. The first of these coordinated return efforts occurred in 1822, and such efforts continued, on a periodic basis, through the 1850s. The second was to provide a home for all Black Americans transported by the ACS from the United States to Africa. Between 1820 and 1825, the year that Monroe left office, more than three hundred Black Americans voluntarily emigrated to Liberia. Many of them did so as part of sea voyages operated jointly by the ACS and the federal government.[12]

In effect, the Monroe administration subsidized, without explicitly indicating any intent to do so, the founding and early settlement of the colony that ACS leaders envisioned as the future home of most Black Americans. Although the amount of government subsidy and the extent of government involvement during Monroe's presidency fell short of what ACS leaders had asked for after the passage of the 1819 Slave Trade Act, it is undeniable that the federal government played a meaningful role in launching the ACS's colonization effort. Over the next several decades, as ACS promoters continued to seek direct federal support for their exclusionary project, they often highlighted, and at times exaggerated, the federal government's role in Liberia's founding. They also continued to stress the benefits to the United States of having Liberia as a partner in international slave trade suppression and, in later years, as a lever for the expansion of American commerce on the African continent and as an ally in bolstering American naval power in the Atlantic Ocean.

From the beginning, Liberia was a very difficult place to live for Black American emigrants. Disease killed many of the early settlers, as well as several white ACS officials and federal agents. The colony's residents fended off recurrent attacks by indigenous Africans. Food production was a challenge, as was the rudimentary condition of the colony's early shelters and physical infrastructure. Beyond these difficulties, there was significant disagreement, especially during the early years, as to how much the emigrants would govern themselves. All of these aspects improved over time, but for many decades after the founding, these factors compounded the aversion that most Black Americans had for the ACS's colonial project in Africa.[13]

There was, however, from the early 1820s onward, a minority interest among Black Americans in Liberian emigration—as will be discussed, this minority interest became significant enough, at times, to cause serious debate and conflict among Black Americans. By the end of the decade, more than one thousand individuals had voluntarily moved to the colony. Emigration during the second half of the decade was roughly double what it had been during the first half. By 1860, thirteen years after Liberian leaders declared independence from the American Colonization Society, the aggregate number of voluntary migrants exceeded ten thousand, a significant portion of whom were former slaves manumitted on the condition that they *consent* to emigrate. Racial oppression, in its varied and numerous forms, played a very significant role in motivating emigration, although it is important to stress that in choosing a new life in Africa, emigrants, for the most part, had no intention of signaling to the American public that they endorsed the various exclusionary arguments asserted by colonization promoters. Those who chose to emigrate, both free and enslaved Black Americans, looked forward to greater social, economic, and political freedom in Liberia. And they looked forward to the opportunity to contribute to building a new polity in which these freedoms would be guaranteed.[14]

On this last point, it is important to note that even the earliest emigrants had an expectation that they would enjoy a large measure of self-governance. Several ACS leaders, including Henry Clay, had indicated during the society's founding years that the envisioned African colony would ultimately become independent or, if it remained under American rule, would be governed as a protectorate with significant autonomy. Jefferson had laid out similar expectations in *Notes on the State of Virginia* several decades earlier. Two of Liberia's earliest emigrant leaders, Lott Cary and Colin Teague, both of whom were self-emancipated Virginians, fought hard to ensure that ACS leaders, and most importantly ACS officials in Africa, did not backtrack on this expectation. Due to their efforts and those of other early emigrants, the ACS Board of Managers shared increasing amounts of governing authority with Liberians from the mid-1820s until 1847, when the colony became a sovereign nation.[15]

NORTHERN RECRUITMENT

During the ACS's first seven years, roughly 1816 through 1823, white Northerners showed relatively little enthusiasm for the idea of federally sponsored colonization. The society's published officer rolls and annual-meeting speaker rosters were dominated by Upper Southerners, with a few Northerners sprinkled in. The directories that the ACS published showing its growing number of auxiliary societies—branches of the ACS established at the town, county, and state level—reflected a similar imbalance. In 1823, there were roughly twenty-seven auxiliary societies in existence in the United States. Only four of these were in the North. The remaining twenty-three were in the Upper South, mainly in Virginia, Maryland, and North Carolina.[16]

The majority of Northern interest, during the society's early years, came from within the network of benevolent organizations that began spreading throughout the region and, to some extent, into the South during the 1810s. These organizations, which included the American Board of Commissioners for Foreign Missions (founded in 1810) and the American Bible Society (founded in 1816), were typically headquartered in Northern cities and run by an interconnected group of Christian ministers, wealthy philanthropists, and pious politicians. Notable members of this Northern network who gave early support to the ACS were Reverend Jeremiah Day, president of Yale College; Theodore Frelinghuysen, attorney general of New Jersey; and Leonard Bacon, minister of Center Church in New Haven, Connecticut, one of the oldest congregations in New England—in addition to Elias Caldwell and Reverend Robert Finley, who were both from New Jersey and who, as noted earlier, were two of the four prime movers behind the society's founding.[17]

During the ACS's 1824 annual meeting, amid the debate over the propriety of submitting another petition to Congress seeking federal aid,

Mercer had suggested that there were two main reasons for the society's relative failure, thus far, to generate Northern interest. The first was a general assumption throughout the region that the ACS, despite its claims of national relevance, was really a Southern-led project designed mainly for the benefit of Southerners. The second was a strong suspicion, layered atop this assumption, that the main benefit sought by the ACS's Southern leaders was to strengthen the institution of slavery, not, as Randolph, Mercer, and others had lightly indicated during the society's early meetings, to help facilitate manumissions.[18]

Generally speaking, Mercer was not saying anything that other ACS leaders, like Harper and Custis, had not already heard or realized for themselves. However, he was pushing ACS leaders to take this Northern-interest problem more seriously than they had thus far. Until the society figured out how to overcome the combination of indifference and distrust that presently blanketed the North, he advised, its leaders had little reason to believe that a petition for federal support would succeed.

One of the most significant moves made by the society in pursuit of expanded Northern interest was the launch, in March 1825, of a monthly publication, the *African Repository*, which remained in continuous circulation for the next seven decades (in its final years, it was published quarterly). The periodical's first editor was Elias Caldwell. Following his unexpected death, shortly after the journal's launch, Reverend Ralph Gurley, a Connecticut-born Yale graduate, took the helm—over the next fifty years, few wrote more on behalf of the ACS and the cause of colonization than Gurley. Gurley's background as a Northerner, as an ordained minister, and as a graduate of Yale, which had broad and deep connections into the benevolent society movement, put him in an excellent position to help lead the effort to increase Northern interest.[19]

During the mid- to late 1820s, the *African Repository*, under Gurley's guidance (and, for a few initial issues, the guidance of Caldwell), worked several promotional angles in support of the society's larger effort to recruit white Northerners into the fold. Two of these were most consequential. The first was an effort to propagate a Northern-centric account of the ACS's origins. In this version of the society's founding, Finley, who received almost no mention in the official account published by the ACS in 1817, was identified as the chief driving force. The wider colonization movement was characterized as an outgrowth of the burgeoning benevolent effort to reform American society, North and South. And great emphasis was given to the cause's moral and spiritual dimensions, which received the most thorough treatment not in the society's official founding account but rather in the pamphlet Finley published in late 1816.[20]

An example of this promotional tack can be found in the very first article of the *African Repository,* published in March 1825, which claimed that the ACS's founding was "principally" due to the "thoughts and exertions of" Finley. The article also underscored Finley's role in the benevolence movement, his belief that the society's efforts deserved the support of the national government, and his firm conviction that the colonization "scheme is from God." The article, on the whole, carried a notably assertive tone, as if a point were trying to be proved rather than simply stated. The clear implication, at least in retrospect, was that the author was making a deliberate effort to revise an origin story that, viewed in light of the ACS's new Northern recruitment imperative, had given Finley's role insufficient emphasis.[21]

Generally speaking, the propagation of this Northern-centric origin story did what it was intended to do. It helped to draw white Northerners into the fold. But this move produced countervailing effects as well. Mainly, it helped to thicken the cloud of ambiguity and seeming contradiction surrounding the colonization movement. From this point forward, the ACS had two coexistent origin stories: an earlier Southern-focused one highlighting Clay, Randolph, Washington, Mercer, and Key and, now, a Northern-focused one highlighting Finley. If the Southern-focused story fostered a mixture of confusion, suspicion, and *apathy* in the North during the society's early years (and later as well), the Northern-focused one tended, over time, to foster a mixture of confusion, suspicion, and *anxiety* in the South. Unsurprisingly, the production of such confounding effects in the past has created confusion and disagreement among historians in the present, with some leaning more toward the North and some leaning more toward the South in their studies of the movement. Although, generally speaking, this book argues that the dominant impulse for colonization advocacy, throughout the movement's eighty years, came from the South, this argument should not be received as absolutist. Just as it is important to recognize that Finley and Caldwell, both Northerners, played important roles in the ACS's founding, it is essential as well to recognize that white

Northerners, from roughly the mid-1820s through the early 1860s, played an important role in promoting colonization in national politics.

The key interpretive point is this: These origin stories were largely used in the service of political strategy, not for the purpose of establishing an objective historical truth. As such, it was rational, and indeed common, for a colonization advocate to traffic in both, choosing one over the other depending on circumstances. A clear illustration can be found in the example of Leonard Bacon, who became involved with the colonization movement while a student at Andover Theological Seminary during the early 1820s, shortly after his graduation from Yale (two years after Gurley) and shortly before he became the minister of Center Church in New Haven, a position he would hold for nearly sixty years. In an 1823 article published in the Connecticut-based *Christian Spectator,* Bacon noted Finley as "the original projector of the [ACS's] plan." Seven years later, in an article published in the same journal, he asserted that the society had its origins in "the south, with citizens of slaveholding States—themselves, in not a few instances, slaveholders." Bacon's main purpose in the earlier article was to make a regional affinity claim, on the ACS's behalf, for the benefit of the *Christian Spectator*'s largely Northern audience: The ACS was rooted in the same reform impulse that was driving so many Northern Christians to support organizations like the Massachusetts-based American Board of Commissioners for Foreign Missions and the New York–based American Bible Society. In the latter article, his main objective was to reassure Northern readers of the credibility and depth of the ACS's commitment to facilitating the end of slavery. Accordingly, he chose to emphasize the society's roots in the slaveholding states and to suggest that many of the society's Southern founders strongly opposed the rising notion that slavery, with "all the evils . . . [it] has entailed on both portions of the mingled population of this country," should continue to exist in "perpetuity."[22]

The second promotional angle worked by ACS leaders was to clarify and emphasize, much more than they had in earlier years, the society's emancipatory intentions. The decision to effect this rhetorical shift was based in large part on an understanding that white Northern interest hinged on the visibility and credibility of these intentions. It was not enough, they had learned, to deny that the ACS was a Southern institution with Southern aims or to deny that its chief aim was to "more effectually rivet the chains of the slave." Nor, they had learned, was it enough to stress the humanitarian dimensions of colonization: supporting the international cause of slave trade suppression or giving free Black Americans an opportunity to engage in a nation-building project of their own. As a public meeting in Boston, held in 1822, involving congressman Daniel Webster and several prominent others, quite clearly advised, support from "the people of New-England" depended on a clear commitment to the "gradual and prudent, but complete emancipation of those now held in slavery."[23]

An article published in August 1825 in the *African Repository,* which included a transcript of a speech given by an auxiliary-society leader in Virginia, explained that while it was generally known that the ACS's main function was to facilitate the colonization of the nation's free Black population, "we anticipate the day when our fellow-citizens, in every part of the United States" will work toward the "emancipation and colonization of every individual slave." In this dual effort, the author added, we expect the "General Government," not just individuals, to play a crucial role, given the issues' "national" scope and significance and the fact that private philanthropy would never be adequate to the great task of "removing the diseases of the body politic." A reprint of a report from another Virginia auxiliary society, published in January 1826, put similar stress on the ACS's emancipatory aims and expectations, forecasting a moment when, due to the society's perseverant efforts, the American people and their legislative representatives would become convinced that the "best and truest interests" of the nation were served by eradicating "this black and menacing evil."[24]

As ACS leaders and other Black colonization advocates worked these two promotional angles, from the mid-1820s through the early 1830s, Northern interest in colonization expanded dramatically. New auxiliary societies proliferated throughout most of the Northern states. Northern politicians, especially congressmen, began to attend the ACS's annual meetings in Washington in far greater numbers than before. The most striking indication of this regional inflection was the fact that during this period eight Northern state legislatures, two-thirds of the regional total, passed formal resolutions endorsing the idea of federal support for colonization: Connecticut, Indiana, Massachusetts, New Jersey, New York, Ohio, Pennsylvania, and Vermont. The specific language of these resolutions, in several cases, explicitly confirmed the importance of the second angle: clarifying and emphasizing the ACS's emancipatory intent. The resolution from New Jersey endorsed the prospect of "a system of foreign colonization" that would, in addition to providing an "asylum" for the free Black population, ultimately "effect the entire emancipation of slaves in our country." The resolution added: because "the evil of slavery is a national one," the "States of this Union ought mutually to participate in the duties and burdens of removing it."[25]

LOWER SOUTHERN OPPOSITION

During the mid- to late 1820s, ACS leaders noted, with a mix of concern and frustration, that opposition to their cause was building in the South, especially the Lower South. They had expected this, to some degree, given that they were trying to involve the federal government in a project that sought, even if only indirectly, as they insisted, to facilitate the gradual abolition of slavery. Such an endeavor was bound to attract states'-rights criticisms. And indeed it had. As an 1825 article in the *African Repository* observed, the ACS, since its founding, had been denounced not just by Northerners for being too "cold and inefficient" on the issue of slavery but also by Southerners for being "too rash and daring." To counter this emergent Southern opposition, society leaders had, for years, used the strategy of proclaiming, as Clay had during the ACS's founding sessions, their absolute respect for constitutional limits and states'-rights—a formal resolution passed at the society's 1826 annual meeting declared, "The Society disclaims, in the most unqualified terms, the designs attributed to it, of interfering... with the legal rights and obligations of slavery." What ACS leaders discovered, however, was that the second of the two tactical adjustments that they had made in order to recruit Northerners into the fold, clarifying and emphasizing the colonization movement's emancipatory aims, was causing growing numbers of Southerners to view such disclaimers with distrust and to accuse the society of foul play.[26]

High-profile meetings held by the ACS in 1827 and 1828 in Washington caused a significant inflection in this building Southern opposition. These two sessions, both held in January just after Congress reconvened, were significant affairs in national politics. Both were held, with congressional permission, in the Hall of the House of Representatives. And both were presided over by Secretary of State Henry Clay—he had assumed this office in 1825, when John Quincy Adams, also a National Republican, had become the new president. Nearly all of the official delegates announced at the two meetings were current members of Congress, including many from the North. At the 1828 meeting, Clay shared the chairperson role with Secretary of the Treasury Richard Rush, a Pennsylvanian who was, like Clay, a vice president of the ACS. The latter session, in particular, was so well attended, according to the report given in the *African Repository*, that attendees occupied every seat in the chamber, stood in the aisles, and spilled over into the gallery above. The purpose of both sessions was to publicize the society's decision to push hard, once again, for federal support.[27]

In his keynote address at the 1827 meeting, Clay spoke with a force and candor on the subject of slavery that he had studiously avoided in his founding-era remarks, making his earlier aim of political manipulation easier, in retrospect, to see. Clay expressed hope that the society, in all that it had accomplished over the last ten years, had persuaded those living in the South that the "scheme of colonization" was a viable means of eliminating the "curse" of slavery; that it was necessary and appropriate for the federal government to become the ACS's official partner, albeit within constitutional bounds; and, that it was time for the Southern states, capitalizing on the increased scale afforded by federal support, to begin taking actions to facilitate the emancipation and colonization of their slaves. To those from the South who might criticize the boldness of such declarations, Clay emphasized the voluntary nature of this opportunity—involving the federal government deprived no state of its right to choose whether or not to act—while at the same time declaring that to decide *not* to act would be to rage against the inevitability of moral progress. Echoing what Jefferson had said forty years ago in *Notes on the State of Virginia*, Clay declared, "What would they, who thus reproach us, have done? If they would repress all tendencies towards liberty and ultimate emancipation, they must do more than put down the benevolent efforts of this Society.... They must blow out the moral lights around us, and extinguish that greatest torch of all which America presents to a benighted world."[28]

During the weeks following Clay's speech at the annual meeting, Charles Fenton Mercer submitted the ACS's 1827 memorial, the first federal petition in five years, to the House of Representatives. In the Senate, Ezekiel Chambers, from Maryland, presented the document. The memorial, while not as forcefully worded as Henry Clay's speech endorsing it, was nonetheless quite bold. Not only did it clarify and stress colonization's emancipatory potential, but it also ventured onto new legal ground. Rather than leaning heavily, as past memorials had, on the federal government's constitutional jurisdiction over slave trade suppression, the 1827 memorial portrayed colonization as an issue that fell under the federal government's constitutional power "to provide for the common defense, and to promote the general welfare" of the American people—given in Article I, Section 8. For any interest group looking to justify applying federal power to a new object, common-defense- and general-welfare-based arguments were, at once, tempting and risky. States'-rights defenders saw this open-ended section of the Constitution as one of the most, if not the most, worrisome platforms for extending federal reach.[29]

Several senators from the Lower South rushed to oppose the memorial's reception and to express alarm regarding its implications. Robert Hayne of South Carolina, who had in recent years voiced concern about the society's growing political momentum, exclaimed, "Of all the extravagant schemes that have yet been devised in this country, I know of none more wild, impracticable, or mischievous, than this of Colonization." The ACS was, in effect, seeking federal funding for a system that would encourage emancipation, he declared, and the federal government had no "constitutional power" to support such a system. Even if the case could be made that it did, which he rejected, the federal government should still, in deference to "the fundamental principles and settled policy of this country," deny the ACS's request. "Can any man be so blind as not to see and feel," Hayne warned, "the dangerous tendency of the measures recommended to us by this Society?"[30]

Lower Southern anxiety regarding the ACS's 1827 memorial gathered strength over the next several months, especially after a committee chaired by Mercer presented a very favorable, ninety-five-page report to the House of Representatives. "It is not easy to discern any object," the report asserted, "to which the pecuniary resources of the Union can be applied, of greater importance to the national security and welfare, than to provide for the removal . . . of the free coloured population." The committee used only seven of the ninety-five pages to make its case for endorsement. The bulk of the document was colonization-related propaganda: excerpts from ACS annual reports, promotional pamphlets, legislative endorsements, among other things. Some of the most hard-hitting and influential articulations of this Lower Southern anxiety were written by a South Carolinian lawyer named Robert Turnbull and published as part of a pamphlet entitled *The Crisis: Or, Essays on the Usurpations of the Federal Government*, a states'-rights manifesto that, as the title indicated, attacked recent attempts to expand the power of the federal government, notably the federal tariff and the ACS's federal appeals. In two of the pamphlet's later essays, Turnbull articulated why he found the latter issue especially threatening. In order to make their project more "palatable," ACS leaders, he explained, were now "openly" admitting that although "colonization of the free negroes was the first object ... the *great object* was emancipation." It was quite clear, therefore, Turnbull warned, that Southerners had to band together and drive "the Colonization Society ... out of the Halls of Congress." If they failed to do so, the ACS's political efforts might become the "ENTERING WEDGE, with which at some future day, our VITAL interests are to be SPLIT asunder."[31]

In December 1827, in the months following the publication of *The Crisis*, the legislatures of South Carolina and Georgia joined the opposition effort, passing resolutions that asserted their firm protest against the ACS's memorial. Both did so in formal reports submitted directly to Congress, which the United States Senate published soon after. Claiming to speak for the South in general, but in reality articulating a view that was more Lower Southern than Upper Southern, the Georgia legislature expressed dismay that the ACS, an organization that many Southerners had previously favored based on a "general impression" that it dealt only with free Black Americans, was now revealing that its true intention was "to remove the *whole* colored population" of the country. Even more troubling, the report continued, was the fact that the society, in seeking federal support for such a "wild, fanatical, and destructive" purpose, was showing itself willing to distort a crucial clause of the federal Constitution.[32]

This late-1820s political moment in Washington lasted until late April 1828, when the Senate Committee on Foreign Relations issued a profoundly negative report on the ACS's 1828 memorial, a lightly revised version of what the society had submitted a year earlier. Senator Littleton Tazewell of Virginia delivered this report on the committee's behalf at a time when congressional debate over a highly contentious new tariff bill—referred to by Southern opponents, after its passage later in 1828, as the Tariff of Abominations—was coming to a head. Echoing criticisms made by Hayne, Turnbull, and the legislatures of Georgia and South Carolina, the Tazewell Report sharply criticized the memorial for proposing an interpretation of the general welfare principle that threatened the "annihilation of the State Sovereignties themselves." More broadly, it delivered a stern message to the ACS: "Should the objects and plans of that society be in any way connected with the action of this Government, either to invite, to stimulate, to restrain, or to prevent, the exercise of any of its acknowledged or supposed powers, such an institution ... must be looked at with suspicion and distrust."[33]

In the time that had passed between Mercer's favorable committee report in the House and Tazewell's unfavorable report in the Senate, the political composition of Congress had changed considerably. The membership of Mercer's committee had been determined when the so-called National Republicans, who generally favored a more assertive and powerful national government, had control of the House of Representatives. The membership of Tazewell's committee had been chosen when the so-called Jacksonian Democrats, who generally favored state power over federal power, had control of both the House and the Senate. As these two partisan groups had coalesced in recent years, National Republicans had, in general, shown far more support for the ACS's federal efforts than Jacksonian Democrats. The about-face that took place in Congress with respect to the handling of the 1827 memorial and the 1828 memorial can be seen as a direct result of the shift in partisan power from one Congress to the next.

From a broader perspective, the Tazewell Report—along with the strong protests of Hayne, Turnbull, the South Carolina legislature, and the Georgia legislature—marked the beginning of a formidable opposition movement, based in the Lower South, that would impede every major federal effort by the colonization movement over the next thirty-three years, until the Civil War, when the Lower South seceded, in its entirety, from the nation and thus radically reconfigured Congress. In the wake of the Tazewell Report rebuke, Mercer, Gurley, Clay, and other colonization proponents continued to hope that they could, at some point, overwhelm this emergent Southern opposition through an alliance of Northern and Upper Southern congressmen, but they also understood that this opposition was likely to grow, not diminish. Not only had they raised the hackles of Lower Southern politicians, who were largely Jacksonian Democrats, and, to a significant degree, their Jacksonian allies in the Upper South and the North, but they had done so at a time when the most powerful Lower Southern state, South Carolina, was preparing to nullify the 1828 federal tariff—a *usurpation* of state power that Turnbull, one of the leading voices of nullification, had lumped together in *The Crisis* with federal support for Black expatriation.

CLAY'S LAND BILL

After the 1827–28 moment in Congress, the next major political moment for the colonization movement occurred in 1832 and 1833, following an uprising of the enslaved in Virginia that caused a dramatic spike in Upper Southern interest in colonization. The Nat Turner Revolt, as the event became known, occurred over the course of a few days in late August 1831. Approximately fifteen enslaved men, led by an educated and devout man named Nat Turner, killed scores of white Virginians. In the immediate aftermath, white Virginians, in vigilante fashion, killed an even greater number of Black Virginians. Throughout the South, whites of all stations reacted with horror and fear to reports of the uprising—skin color, not slave ownership, operating as the main determinant of emotional response. Many could not help but see this event as confirmation of ideas and predictions expressed by Thomas Jefferson several decades earlier.[34]

The first meeting of Congress following the Nat Turner Revolt commenced in December 1831. Within weeks, several Upper Southerners in the House of Representatives raised the issue of federally supported colonization. One of them was, unsurprisingly, Charles Fenton Mercer. Two fellow Virginians joined him, as did a Maryland congressman by the name of Daniel Jenifer. According to Jenifer, several Upper Southern legislatures were gearing up to consider state-level funding for Black expatriation, making the question of what the federal government planned to do on the issue, if anything, a matter of great relevance and urgency. Around the same time that Jenifer addressed the House, the legislatures of Maryland and Virginia began to discuss actions related to state-funded colonization and, to the astonishment of many in the country, even gradual abolition. Intersecting fears of living with slavery and of living with free Black Americans had instilled in many of the states' white residents a sense that the time had finally come to take some kind of action. If Congress should determine that the Constitution did not allow the federal government to support Black colonization, Jenifer indicated, the states "ought to know this as early as practicable."[35]

The impulse for congressional action on colonization, it turned out, was strongest in the Senate, where Henry Clay, whose position as secretary of state had ended in 1829 with Andrew Jackson's inauguration as president, was its driving force. Beginning in early 1832, Clay proposed a bill that would give, for a limited number of years, all annual federal land revenues to the states. The Land Bill, as it became known, went through various iterations over the next several months, but in rough outline it envisioned a large transfer of $2.6 million per year for five years, $13 million in aggregate. The transfer came with an important restriction, one that suited Clay's political interests without, he hoped, overly narrowing its appeal. Each state government could only use these federal funds for three purposes: internal improvements, education, and colonization.[36]

This was a striking proposal, relative to past efforts to garner federal funding for colonization, but it was not a new idea. Thomas Jefferson had mentioned it on occasion during his retirement years. Congressman Rufus King, of New York, had asked the United States Senate in 1825 to endorse, in the form of a resolution, the prospective use of public land revenue to fund Black colonization and, even more controversially, compensated emancipation. (King, it is worth noting, had served as minister to the United Kingdom during the early 1800s and had consulted, during that time, at the request of President Thomas Jefferson, with the British government on the possibility of expatriating Black Virginians to Sierra Leone.) And more recently, in late 1831, former President James Madison and current Chief Justice of the Supreme Court John Marshall had endorsed the concept in public letters featured by the ACS in the February 1832 issue of the *African Repository*. Both men acknowledged that any move to legislate the use of federal land revenue for colonization would encounter criticism. Critics from the North would likely point out that such an allocation would provide disproportionate benefit to the states where enslavement was legal. As Marshall observed, while Black expatriation was a "common object" of all states in the Union, the slave states were "more immediately interested in it." Critics from the South would likely insist that the federal government had no constitutional power to fund colonization. The former objection, Madison explained, would likely be counterbalanced by a general Northern desire to contribute to slavery's eradication and perhaps also by a general awareness that the South had supplied the majority of the federal public lands. The latter objection, both men indicated, was one that required care and caution but that was not insuperable. All in all, both men assessed the idea with optimism. Madison, who was soon to become the ACS's president, asserted his belief that the "present moment" was quite an auspicious one, both for the "prospects of the Society" and for those who looked, with "hope," toward a future period when "the dreadful calamity [enslavement] which has so long afflicted our country and filled so many with despair, will be gradually removed."[37]

Clay had anticipated both objections and had designed the bill to address each. First, by allocating federal money directly to the states, federal funds became state funds, thereby neutralizing, at least in theory, the question of whether the federal government could, on a constitutional basis, spend money on colonization. On the potential utility of this tactic, Clay derived some comfort from President Andrew Jackson's 1830 message to Congress, in which he recommended that the federal government distribute its "surplus funds," much of which came from public land sales, to the states as a means of ensuring that state power, not federal power, was ultimately enhanced by this funding source. Second, Clay established three authorized uses for the allocated funds, rather than just colonization, in an attempt to diminish the bill's controversiality in the South. In explaining the rationale behind these categories, Clay stressed the "national" benefits that would accrue from investments in any of the three, a move that he hoped would stifle suggestions of Southern advantage. He summarized the prospective national benefits as follows: Investments in education would foster the "moral and intellectual improvement of the people." Investments in internal improvements would afford "greater facility in social and commercial intercourse." And investments in "colonization" would contribute to "the purification of the population of our country."[38]

In early July 1832, after roughly three months of debate, the Senate passed Clay's Land Bill, an unprecedented triumph for the colonization movement. After fifteen years of lobbying efforts in Washington, colonization advocates had finally persuaded the upper house of Congress to make millions of dollars available for their cause. Of course, state governments had the right to spend their pro rata portions on education and internal improvements alone. But the many petitions that Congress had received in recent months and years from states that had explicitly asked the federal government to support colonization suggested that significant dollars would be spent in this area. The Upper Southern states of Maryland and Virginia, where interest in colonization had been particularly strong since the ACS's founding, would, under the terms of the Land Bill, receive a five-year total of roughly $435,000 and $1.1 million, respectively.

The final vote in the Senate had been far more partisan than sectional. The overwhelming majority of *yes* votes had come from the party coalescing around Henry Clay, which would soon become known as the Whig Party. All of the *no* votes had come from the party coalescing around Andrew Jackson, which would soon become known as the Democratic Party. Nearly all Southerners who aligned with the National Republican movement voted with Clay for the Land Bill. Within just a few years, such a vote would prove impossible for Southern Whigs, as inflamed sectional tensions would drive Southern congressmen to vote as bloc on most issues that bore, in any way, on the institution of slavery.[39]

The congressional session closed not long after the Senate's final vote on Clay's Land Bill, leaving the House insufficient time, or so opponents claimed, to debate and vote on the measure. When the next session commenced, in December 1832, Clay promptly revived the bill and succeeded in garnering a second affirmative vote in the Senate in late January. The Land Bill then moved to the House floor, where, after a few weeks of debate, the members voted to remove *colonization,* along with *internal improvements* and *education,* thus leaving the determination of how the distributed funds would be used entirely up to the states. This revision did not prohibit states from using these funds for colonization, but it did eliminate the implicit federal endorsement that called out colonization as one of three allowable expense categories. The main speech made against the colonization element of the bill, during the House debate, had come from a Jacksonian representative from Alabama: "If we can appropriate money to colonize those who are free, why not those who are slaves?" The latter action, he warned, might very well proceed from the former: "It cannot be controverted that abolition is the ultimate purpose of colonization."[40]

When the Land Bill came before the Senate for final approval, Henry Clay expressed regret at the revised bill's diluted form. The specific "objects to which these proceeds were to be applied," he noted, had been of great interest to him. Ezekiel Chambers, the Marylander who had championed the ACS's 1827 and 1828 memorials in the Senate, expressed similar regret, indicating that he refused, on principle, to vote for the bill as revised. Clay chose a different path, voting, with the majority, for the measure.[41]

As it turned out, the House revision made little difference in the ultimate outcome. Once the Senate passed the new Land Bill, with colonization and the other named expense categories taken out, the last remaining piece was for Andrew Jackson to sign it, which he refused to do, thus effecting a pocket veto. Clay was furious, as he made clear in December 1833, when Congress reconvened. The president had acted "despotically" and disrespectfully, Clay declared, when he chose neither to sign the bill nor to veto it in formal fashion. The Land Bill had "attracted great public attention" during the year it had spent in and out of congressional debate, and Congress should have been given the opportunity before the adjournment, Clay asserted, to override a formal veto from the president. (Later in the session, Clay claimed that Congress could have mustered the two-thirds majority required for an override.) Clay then declared his intention to reintroduce the Land Bill in the coming weeks, which he did, and which he continued to do, in various forms, for several congressional sessions to follow. But the bill that Clay had envisioned as a means of making federal funds available for colonization never made it again to the desk of Jackson, or any other president.[42]

In December 1833, around the same time that Clay denounced Jackson's pocket veto, Congress received a message from the president explaining his reasons for refusing to sign the Land Bill. Although he did not mention colonization, the controversial subject had almost certainly been on his mind when he decided to pocket veto the bill. For over a year, the prospective statute had been quite publicly associated with colonization and, in turn, with states'-rights objections to federal support. This made the bill dangerous for the leader of the emergent Democratic Party, with its strong states'-rights ethos, to approve. The two final votes in the Senate in 1832 and 1833, which had both showed strong oppositional solidarity among Jacksonian Democrats, had signaled this political danger, as had two interim votes. A Jacksonian senator from Georgia had twice moved to have "colonization" removed from the bill as an allowable expense category. Although he had failed on both occasions, the overwhelming majority of those who had voted with him were Jacksonian Democrats.[43]

Compounding this political danger, from the president's perspective, was the fact that when the Land Bill arrived on his desk, he was awaiting news of how South Carolina would respond to the Tariff of 1833, also known as the Compromise Tariff, and the Force Bill. Several months earlier, the South Carolina legislature had taken the extreme step of passing a measure that nullified, at least from its perspective, the Tariff of 1832. Since then, talk of South Carolina's potential secession and, even more worrisome, of potential war between the state and the federal government had put Congress and the president very much on edge. Of further concern to Jackson was the fact that the nullification controversy had created a rift among Jacksonian Democrats in the South, with some choosing to sympathize with South Carolina rather than the Jackson administration. As a carrot-and-stick peace offering, Jackson and Congress had enacted the Compromise Tariff and, at the same time, a statute that empowered Jackson to use the nation's military might in order to force South Carolina's cooperation. Signing the Land Bill in these circumstances made very little sense from the president's perspective. Even though Jackson had endorsed, as Clay had pointed out, the basic premise of the bill just a few years earlier—distributing federal land revenues to the states—the proposed statute still bore the stain of colonization-related controversy, even after the House succeeded in removing all three named expense categories. Furthermore, the Land Bill, from the very beginning, had been a Henry Clay project, and Clay, despite being a Southerner, was viewed by many states'-rights hard-liners in the South as one of their greatest foes. Jackson's main political priorities in March 1833, when he effected the pocket veto, were to repair the terrible fracture between the federal government and South Carolina and to do so in a way that commenced the process of mending the rift within his party. The Land Bill, given its specific history, strongly conflicted with both aims.[44]

Jackson's pocket veto marked the end of the first major phase in the long history of the colonization movement in national politics. Between 1816 and 1833, the movement had expanded dramatically from its dominantly Upper Southern roots, garnering a tremendous amount of interest and support from Northern white Americans, especially congressmen and state lawmakers. Within a relatively short span of time, ACS leaders had managed to establish numerous auxiliary societies throughout the region and had garnered formal endorsements, mainly in the form of joint resolutions submitted to Congress, from roughly two-thirds of the region's state legislatures. These accomplishments had hinged, to a significant degree, on a decision to promote colonization with greater clarity and emphasis regarding its emancipatory potential. An unfortunate, though not entirely unexpected, consequence of this decision, from the perspective of colonization advocates, was a significant rise in Lower Southern opposition. This new opposition movement, which operated in parallel with the Black-led opposition movement that had coalesced in 1817 immediately after the ACS's founding, played a decisive role in rebuffing the society's 1828 memorial to Congress and a significant role, albeit one that was not quite as clear and direct, in preventing Clay's Land Bill, with its millions of dollars in potential funds for colonization, from becoming law.

As colonization advocates looked to the future, they continued to hope that at some point they would have enough congressional votes and presidential support to gain federal sponsorship for their exclusionary endeavor. As it turned out, however, political conditions were about to depress their prospects further. Several more failures were on the horizon.

3

STRENGTHENING THE UNION

1833–1853

IN DECEMBER 1833, A GROUP of Black and white activists founded the American Anti-Slavery Society (AASS). Although the new organization would ultimately establish its headquarters in New York City, its founding sessions took place in Philadelphia, at a location just a handful of blocks away from two prominent landmarks. One was the Pennsylvania State House, where in 1787 the Constitutional Convention drafted the document that became the legal bedrock of the United States. The other was Mother Bethel African Methodist Episcopal Church, an institution that, since the 1790s, had served as a national center of gravity for Black spirituality, community support and organizing, and civil rights activism. In early 1817, Mother Bethel Church had hosted one of the first major protests against the newly formed American Colonization Society (ACS). Roughly three thousand Black Americans had attended. The founding of the AASS was, in many ways, a direct extension of this catalytic meeting. It was also a powerful testament to the success of Black activists' efforts, over the past sixteen years, to build and sustain a movement that opposed the cause of Black expatriation.[1]

The leaders of the newly established American Anti-Slavery Society included individuals like James Forten and Samuel Cornish, high-profile

Black Americans who, for many years, had led this opposition movement. Forten, the older of the two, had played a leadership role since the 1817 meeting at Mother Bethel Church, which he had chaired. Cornish was part of a younger generation of Black Americans that had joined the cause during the 1820s. At thirty-eight, he was roughly three decades younger than Forten. Cornish's visibility as a public opponent of colonization had risen considerably six years earlier, when he had cofounded, with support from Forten, *Freedom's Journal,* the first major Black newspaper in the United States. Joining Forten, Cornish, and other Black activists in leading the AASS were white evangelical reformers like Arthur Tappan and William Lloyd Garrison. Tappan was a wealthy New York City merchant who, along with his brother Lewis, had provided considerable funding to the national benevolence movement, a movement that commenced during the 1810s with the founding of organizations like the American Bible Society and the American Colonization Society. Indeed, for a period of time, Tappan had supported the ACS. Garrison, who was twenty-eight at the time of the AASS's founding and thus among the youngest of the organization's early leaders, was a printer and a journalist based in Boston. Over the past few years, he had gained increasing public visibility, as well a significant degree of notoriety, as the founding editor of *The Liberator,* a newspaper characterized by fierce and provocative rhetoric. In 1832, Garrison had generated considerable ire among ACS leaders when he published *Thoughts on African Colonization,* a nearly 250-page pamphlet that contained two sections. The first offered a fierce denunciation of the colonization movement's exclusionary rhetoric, which the pamphlet quoted extensively. The second contained a large appendix that documented, again with extensive quotations, the last fifteen years of Black Americans' opposition to the colonization cause. Garrison's incendiary pamphlet produced significant waves in the North and the Upper South due, in significant part, to support from James Forten, who provided the money needed to ensure the document's broad distribution.[2]

The new organization declared, in the published proceedings of its founding sessions, that it had three main objectives: to promote the abolition of slavery throughout the United States; to gain civic equality for Black Americans; and to discredit the unjust and illogical notion that Black expatriation had any role to play in the nation's future. In regard to all three, not just the third, AASS leaders made clear that they viewed the colonization movement as a chief enemy. For the last decade and a half, the movement's proponents had promulgated a separatist vision of America's racial future that had proven quite alluring to white Americans in the Upper South and the North. A chief function of the AASS, the founding group professed, was to roll back this progress: to convince anyone who supported the ACS, or who was considering supporting it, to abandon the older vision, which emphasized *gradual* abolition and Black *exclusion,* in favor of a newer vision grounded in the principles of *immediate* abolition (with certain qualifications) and Black *inclusion.* The AASS's founding "Declaration of Sentiments" sharply declared: "We regard, as delusive, cruel, and dangerous, any scheme of expatriation which pretends to aid, either directly or indirectly, in the emancipation of the slaves, or to be a substitute for the immediate and total abolition of slavery."[3]

One of the AASS's first acts was to coordinate a congressional petition campaign that pushed the federal government to abolish slavery in areas that, in the society's opinion, were under federal authority: the territories and DC. Petitions began flowing into Congress in growing volume during late 1835 and 1836. Southerners in the House of Representatives reacted immediately and forcefully, seeking enactment of a chamber-level rule that would require the immediate tabling of all slavery-related petitions. One leading proponent of a suppressive rule, a congressman from South Carolina, characterized the petitions as part of a larger effort by the "abolitionists of the North" to "subvert the institutions of the South." Another leading figure, also from South Carolina, asserted the necessity of "repress[ing] the spirit of incendiary agitation" animating these petitions, not just for the sake of the Southern states but also for the sake of the Union. In May 1836, these Southern-led efforts succeeded. With near-unanimous Southern support and substantial Northern support, the House of Representatives enacted what became known as the Gag Rule, which its members voted to reenact, in some form, in every subsequent session until 1844. For most of this time, the Senate, although it did not follow the House in its formal adoption and readoption of a chamber-level rule, largely operated, when faced with slavery-related petitions, in accordance with the suppressive spirit of the House.[4]

As ACS leaders witnessed this series of events in Congress, they worried, considerably, about the prospective effects on their efforts to obtain federal support. Two moments in the Senate during the early part of 1837 gave them significant reason for pessimism. The first occurred in early January, when the Senate Committee on Public Lands rebuked Clay's latest attempt to pass a Land Bill that called out colonization, internal improvements, and education as allowable expense categories. In 1837 the Public Lands committee, after a fairly short review, rejected the bill and, moreover, threatened to push for an "indefinite postponement" if the bill were proposed again.[5]

The second moment took place in late January, again in the Senate, when Clay submitted a memorial from the ACS requesting a congressional act of incorporation. ACS leaders believed that the incorporation memorial, because it did not ask for federal funding or for any direct support of Liberia, was far more innocuous than past memorials and thus had a chance of being considered, rather than immediately rejected, even in the highly sensitive political environment that prevailed in Congress at the time. The immediate benefit to the ACS of such an incorporation lay in the legal authority it would confer. In 1831, the society had obtained an article of incorporation from the Maryland state legislature, largely for the purpose of receiving and, in several cases, fighting to maintain donations that had come through wills. A federal incorporation would, ACS leaders indicated, provide stronger legal footing. Two further benefits, not mentioned in the memorial, would be to boost the society's reputation as a national organization and to establish another dimension to its relationship with the federal government, which remained limited to the society's periodic efforts to transport to Liberia, typically at federal expense, various Africans seized by the US Navy in its international slave trade suppression patrols.[6]

Upon presenting the memorial to the Senate, Clay moved that it be referred to the standing Committee on the District of Columbia. It made particular sense for the federal government to grant incorporation to the ACS, the memorial claimed, because the ACS maintained its headquarters in the nation's capital, where the federal government had specific jurisdiction. Senator John Calhoun, of South Carolina, promptly rose and criticized Clay, a fellow Southerner, for deeming this an appropriate time to submit such a request when, as should be obvious, any "discussion or agitation of the subject" would further inflame sectional tensions in Congress. Clay defended the validity of the ACS's memorial, highlighting that it asked relatively little of Congress and rejecting, with indignation, the suggestion that it had any bearing on the tensions to which Calhoun referred.

The political environment in Washington was the fault of Northern "abolitionists," a group of fanatics, Clay noted, with which the ACS had absolutely no connection. Indeed, abolitionists, Clay added, were "just as much opposed to the Colonization Society as to the slaveholders of the South."[7]

Three days later, the Senate voted decisively against referring the ACS's incorporation memorial to committee. Nearly every Southerner, Whig and Democrat alike, voted against referral, along with many Northern Democrats—a notable shift from the 1832–33 Land Bill congressional moment, when several Southern National Republicans had demonstrated a willingness to break sectional solidarity. This failure, in combination with the Public Lands committee's rebuke, sent a clear signal to ACS leaders. Now was not the time to press the cause of colonization in Congress. Indeed, it would be another five years before the ACS would make another federal appeal.[8]

The sectional solidarity evinced by the Senate vote on the ACS's 1837 memorial was indicative of a larger shift in national politics. From the mid-1830s until the beginning of the Civil War in 1861, Southern congressmen largely voted as a unanimous bloc on any issue that they believed might, in some way, serve as a precedent for diminishing state sovereignty regarding slavery or preventing the institution's further expansion. In basic terms, Southern congressmen insisted that the federal government stay completely away from the institution on the premise that it had no constitutional jurisdiction to interfere with it. Even if there were areas where the federal government *might* have jurisdiction, they added, such as in the nation's capital or in the territories, it should refrain from taking any actions as a matter of deference to the Southern states. Over the coming years and decades, Southern politicians would refer to this attitude toward slavery as the principle of *nonaction* or *nonintervention*.[9]

During these years of political upheaval and dampened interest in federal support for colonization, the colonization movement's leaders, Henry Clay still foremost among them, made three highly consequential adjustments, all of which were aimed at keeping alive the possibility of future federal support. First, they put *increased* stress on the notion that colonization offered a means of solving the national problem of Black freedom. They adapted this message to the highly divisive political environment by asserting, in very bold terms, that colonization, as a political issue, had the capacity to mitigate sectional tensions and, ultimately, to make the Union unbreakable. According to this revised view, the cause of colonization was more patriotic than it had ever been. Second, they put *decreased* stress on the idea that colonization would serve as a catalyst of *gradual* abolition in the Southern states, characterizing federal support for colonization, instead, as a preparatory step toward *eventual* abolition, a stance that comported with the principle of nonaction. Although this was not a rhetorical shift that all colonization advocates made, it was one that, in deference to the new political environment, effectively all Southern advocates made. Third, in support of an effort to revise and reargue claims that federal support for colonization was constitutional, ACS leaders reemphasized the value of Liberia as a slave trade suppression partner and made newer assertions regarding Liberia's prospective value as a commercial and diplomatic ally, two avenues where the federal government had clear jurisdiction.[10]

In making these adjustments, especially the first and the second, colonization leaders, in effect, showed more deference to the South than the North, thus reversing, to a significant degree, the course they had charted over the past decade. They recognized that this reversal would likely result in the permanent loss of some of their Northern supporters, which it did, but they felt that they had no choice. The Upper South was, from the beginning, the region that expressed the most interest in colonization. This was the part of the country where white Americans viewed Black freedom with the greatest concern, because it was here that a very large and growing enslaved population coexisted with a large and growing free Black population. Moreover, if one continued to believe, as many colonization proponents did, that the success of the colonization project depended on obtaining federal support, on top of whatever state governments provided, then one had to prioritize crafting a revised political message that accorded with the strictures of the new political environment, which were largely determined by Southern politicians.

THE BLACK OPPOSITION MOVEMENT EXPANDS

The decade following the launch of *Freedom's Journal* was the first of several major inflection points in the decades-long fight that Black Americans waged against the colonization movement. In the paper's first issue, published in March 1827, the editors announced that *Freedom's Journal*'s central purpose was to broadcast the views of Black Americans on all pertinent subjects—foremost among them, slavery, civil rights, and colonization—directly to the American people, without any kind of mediation by white actors. "Too long have others spoken for us," the editors declared. "Too long has the public been deceived by misrepresentations, in things which concern us dearly." This inaugural issue came out roughly two months after Secretary of State Henry Clay's political performance at the ACS's annual meeting and at roughly the same time that Charles Fenton Mercer presented a very favorable committee report to the House of Representatives in response to the ACS's recent memorial.[11]

Freedom's Journal had two founding editors. In addition to Samuel Cornish, who at the time of the paper's launch was the head of a Presbyterian church located in New York City, where *Freedom's Journal* was based, there was John Russwurm, who was younger than Cornish by several years. Russwurm had been born in Jamaica and had lived, during his childhood, for a time in Canada, before settling in Maine. He graduated from Bowdoin College in 1826.[12]

During the first year that *Freedom's Journal* was in circulation, the paper published several articles and letters to the editor that continued the decade-long trend of repudiating, in public fashion, the ideology of the colonization movement. At the most fundamental level, *Freedom's Journal* refuted, in fierce terms, the core assertion that Black freedom and white freedom were incongruous. An 1827 editorial declared: "Any plan which ... carries with it the idea" that "equal rights" were unattainable for Black Americans *within* the United States was "wholly at war with our best interests." Beyond this, the paper denounced all claims made on the basis of this racialized assertion, most notable among them: (1) the nation's free Black population had to be removed, for the benefit of white and Black Americans alike; and (2) the only safe and practical way to end slavery in the United States was through a system that combined emancipation with expatriation. "We cannot view the Advocates of such sentiments, in any other light," the paper declared, "than that of enemies."[13]

Freedom's Journal ceased operations in March 1829, two years after its launch. While money had been tight during the paper's tenure, financial difficulties were not the main reason for the shutdown. At the time Russwurm was the paper's sole editor. Cornish had left *Freedom's Journal,* for reasons that are not entirely clear, in late 1827. In a series of articles published during the early months of 1829, Russwurm announced a major life decision that would prevent him from continuing as editor. He planned to move out of the country permanently. More specifically, he planned to emigrate to Liberia.[14]

Russwurm acknowledged that this decision would surprise and frustrate many Black Americans, not just because *Freedom's Journal* had been a fierce critic of the colonization movement but also because "the majority" of Black Americans continued to oppose colonization, without compromise. The rationale that he offered was simple: "Here, is a land in which we cannot enjoy the privileges of citizen[s]." Liberia, in contrast, was a place "where we may enjoy all the rights of freemen . . . and where we may not only feel as men, but where we may also act as such." Given these options, "can any man of sound judgment hesitate about the choice of the two?" At the same time, Russwurm insisted, his decision did not indicate or even vaguely imply that he sanctioned the "prejudices" that caused Black Americans so much suffering in the United States: "We deplore them as much as any man; but they are not of our creating, and they are not in our power to remove."[15]

Russwurm's decision to emigrate to Liberia, which accorded with a decision that roughly one thousand Black Americans had made over the last decade, did indeed cause a lot of confusion and consternation among Black Americans. It was not so much the individual choice to leave the country that was troubling but more the visibility that his role as newspaper editor gave to the decision and his choice of destination. In August 1829, a briefly lived newspaper by the name of the *Rights of All*, operated by Russwurm's former partner Samuel Cornish, published an article that argued strenuously against Liberian emigration, suggesting that emigration to Canada, a current topic of conversation in the Northern Black community, was far preferrable. To emigrate to Liberia, the article warned, was to give credibility to the operations and ideas of the "Colonization Society," one of the most "formidable" foes of "the colored people of this country." The organization's "ridiculous doctrine of a *separate people, separate interest, extraneous mass, dangerous evil . . .* is fraught with ten thousand evil consequences" for Black Americans.[16]

During the late 1820s and early 1830s, Black activists asserted, with greater force and frequency than they had during the opposition movement's early years, their belief that the actions and rhetoric of the colonization movement were, in effect, worsening anti-Black prejudice and, in turn, encouraging the proliferation and enforcement of exclusionary laws. The 1829 article in the *Rights of All,* most likely written by Cornish, for instance, accused colonization advocates of fostering a particularly troubling oppressive moment that had occurred recently in Ohio. Following a state supreme court decision that upheld the constitutionality of an 1807 law requiring all free Black residents to post strikingly high bonds or face expulsion, municipal officials in Cincinnati had warned the city's two-thousand-plus Black residents that enforcement of the law, which had been loose for decades, would soon become strict. Shortly thereafter, white mobs attacked the city's Black residents for the better part of a week, inflicting wounds and damaging property. In the immediate aftermath, roughly half of Cincinnati's Black population moved to Canada. "I do not for a moment doubt," the article declared, "but you are indebted to colonization efforts, fourth of July sermons, and orations" for these terrible circumstances. Roughly a year later, in early 1831, an anticolonization meeting held in New York publicly declared that as white Americans become more and more interested in "Colonization . . . they become less active and less friendly to our welfare as citizens of the United States."[17]

Between 1831 and 1835, Black Americans expressed similar sentiments through a series of national conventions held in Philadelphia and New York City. During this time, especially after the Nat Turner Revolt in the summer of 1831, Black Americans faced an escalation of state-level legal oppression. In the North, for instance, state legislatures made it increasingly difficult, in many cases impossible, for free Black residents to attend public schools, to serve on juries, and to vote. In the South, where free Black Americans already lived under highly oppressive bodies of legislation, state legislatures continued to pile additional restrictions on their respective free Black residents. The American Colonization Society was "so awful a foe," a convention officer declared at the 1834 meeting in New York, that it was critical for Black Americans to convene regularly to discuss the "best means to frustrate" its efforts. Indeed, the officer added, "as long at least as the Colonization Society exists, will a convention of colored people be highly necessary."[18]

One of the most direct and pointed denunciations of the colonization movement's capacity to foster exclusionary laws appeared in a pamphlet published in 1834 by David Ruggles. The document, which bore the title *The "Extinguisher" Extinguished! Or David M. Reese, M.D. "Used Up"* and which ran to roughly fifty pages, was the second major opposition pamphlet issued by Northern Black activists in recent years. The first was David Walker's highly influential *Appeal to the Colored Citizens of the World*, first published in 1829, which devoted one of its four sections to protesting the colonization movement's efforts. Ruggles, who was only in his mid-twenties at the time, would make a name for himself over the next several decades as a journalist, a bookstore owner, and a leading member of the New York Vigilance Committee, which conducted self-emancipated individuals into and out of the city via the Underground Railroad—in the late 1830s, Ruggles would aid a very young Frederick Douglass on his way from Maryland to Massachusetts. Toward the end of the pamphlet, Ruggles declared, "The tendency of the Colonization Society is, to produce [legislative] enactments detrimental to the vital interests of the people of color in these United States." He made this statement in response to assertions by Reese, one of several colonization advocates whose rhetoric the pamphlet addressed, that Ruggles had been unfair and imprecise in an earlier speech when he had accused the society of "producing" oppressive laws. "If I said that the Colonization Society produced these enactments, the meaning is, that these enactments are the result of influences produced by the Colonization Society." The validity of this asserted causal relationship, Ruggles added, did not depend on "whether Colonizationists" were able to grasp "these things or not, or [to] take them into their calculations."[19]

UNIONISM AND EVENTUALISM

In December 1837, almost a year after the colonization movement's recent failures in the Senate, Senator Henry Clay presided over the ACS's annual meeting in Washington, DC. The gathering, which was not nearly as well attended as annual meetings of the late 1820s and early 1830s, commenced with Clay accepting the office of ACS president, a role that had been held for the past few years by James Madison, the fourth president of the United States. During the early 1830s, Madison had succeeded Charles Carroll, a former congressman from Maryland and one of the signers of the Declaration of Independence. Carroll had held the office for a brief period following the death of Associate Supreme Court Justice Bushrod Washington, the society's founding president. Clay's election to the society's highest office continued a long-standing tradition. He, like all three of his predecessors, was a slaveholding politician from the Upper South.[20]

The published proceedings of the annual meeting indicated that the society and the broader colonization movement were struggling. The proceedings of the last few years of annual meetings, as well as numerous articles published in the *African Repository* during this period, had indicated the same. There were three main dimensions to the colonization movement's struggle, all of which had roots in the American Anti-Slavery Society's founding in late 1833. First, the Gag Rule political environment in Congress, which the AASS's petition campaign had catalyzed, effectively shut down efforts to obtain federal support for colonization. Those who still desired to obtain federal support at some point, a group that included Clay, did not know how long this political shutdown would last, but the two Senate failures in early 1837, along with the high level of sectional friction in Congress, provided ample reason for pessimism. Second, in response to this indefinite shutdown, many colonization advocates began to push hard for state-level approaches to Black expatriation. Seeking state-level appropriations was a means of avoiding the constitutional objections leveled at efforts to obtain federal appropriations. The leaders of this state-level movement were Maryland and Virginia. In the eighteen months following the Nat Turner Revolt, the legislatures of these two states made the first significant appropriations of government funds for colonization purposes, Maryland in early 1832 and Virginia in early 1833. By the late-1837 meeting, ACS leaders had made progress in convincing colonization advocates in several states to reintegrate their efforts with the society's national operations, but ongoing concerns about the prospects for future federal appeals fueled an ongoing political rift within the colonization movement. Third, in direct response to the AASS's declaration of war against the ACS, a significant number of white Northerners abandoned the ACS and the broader cause of Black expatriation. Some left it for good, choosing to join the AASS instead. Notable members of this cohort were James Birney, a former slaveholder from Kentucky who later become the presidential candidate of the Liberty Party in the 1840 and 1844 elections, and Gerrit Smith, a wealthy landowner and philanthropist from western New York who later become a major funder and ally of Frederick Douglass. Other white Northerners left the colonization movement for the time being, until they could clarify, or reclarify, what the movement's actual motives were.[21]

Against this political backdrop, Henry Clay delivered a speech at the late-1837 annual meeting in which he spoke about the society and the wider colonization movement in terms very different from those used ten years ago when, during his tenure as secretary of state, he had endorsed, with great fervor, the ACS's 1827 congressional memorial. Clay did not call on the Southern states, as he had then, to view the society's success to-date as an indication that the time had come to commence the process of emancipation and expatriation. Nor did he reprimand the ACS's Southern critics for their reactionary desire to "repress all tendencies toward liberty and ultimate emancipation." Instead, he retreated to older rhetorical forms, stressing that the ACS, by design, dealt only with the issue of the nation's free Black population: "We seek neither to perpetuate nor to abolish slavery. Our object is totally different from either, and has been proclaimed and clung to from the beginning of the Society to this hour." And yet, Clay noted, it was a fact, a frustrating and in some ways bewildering fact, that the ACS continued to be attacked by both perpetualists and "abolitionists."[22]

Representative James Garland of Virginia also delivered a speech at the meeting. Much of his address was devoted to denouncing, as many Southern congressmen had in recent years, the "fanatical" and "reckless" actions of Northern activists. Garland's goals, in part, were to blame these "crusaders" for the volatile political environment and to bolster the distinction between promoters of colonization and promoters of "abolition." But he had a larger aim as well, and that was to present colonization as an antidote for this volatility. The cause of colonizing free Black Americans, Garland asserted, "presents a theatre on which the North and the South may rally in mutual confidence," thus supplanting sectional "discord" with harmony. Viewed from this Unionist angle, Garland asserted, further pursuit of the colonization cause had the unimpeachable justification of "patriotism."[23]

In April and May 1838, ACS leaders held two special meetings in Washington to discuss how to address the society's ongoing challenges. The product of these discussions was a published circular, signed by more than fifty Northern and Upper Southern congressmen, that was, in effect, a call to action aimed at white Americans. Gurley, along with a congressman from Ohio and another from Kentucky, composed the document. Among the signers were Clay, Garland, Charles Fenton Mercer, and Francis Scott Key, as well as significant, in some cases majority, portions of the current congressional delegations of Virginia, Kentucky, Indiana, New York, New Jersey, Ohio, and Pennsylvania. The document reflected the two political adjustments evinced in the 1837 speeches of Clay and Garland: *decreased* stress on colonization's emancipatory potential and *increased* stress on colonization's capacity to strengthen the Union, with particular emphasis given to the second. In effect, in this moment in mid-1838, roughly one-sixth of the current congressional membership asked white Americans "of every political and religious creed" to make personal donations that would pull the ACS out of its present financial crisis. And they made this ask in the name of ameliorating the "dangerous excitements" disrupting the nation and giving greater "stability to the Union."[24]

Less than a year later, in early 1839, Henry Clay delivered a speech to the Senate that offered a full expression of the Unionist stance that he, and a great many of his fellow colonization advocates, now assumed on the matter of slavery's future in the United States. The speech was very long and was broadly distributed afterward, in pamphlet form, with an eye toward his next potential presidential run in 1840. The reckless actions of Northern "abolitionists," Clay declared, had dramatically worsened the "prospect of any species of emancipation of the African race, gradual or immediate, in any of the States." As direct evidence, he described conditions in his home state of Kentucky, where the people have been so "shocked and alarmed by these abolition movements" that recent calls for a state constitutional convention, one that might have put gradual abolition back on the table after forty years, had failed by a three-to-one majority. Clay expressed regret that he had, in fact, voted with the majority against the call, but he explained that he had felt "constrained" by the new political circumstances. The prudent course and indeed the only realistic course, he advised, was to accept slavery as a long-term national fact for the sake of the Union. The institution would still, at some point, come to an end, he maintained, but not for "some one hundred and fifty or two hundred years."[25]

Six years prior, during a Senate speech in favor of his Land Bill, Clay had predicted that slavery might end "fifty or a hundred years hence." The new prediction of 150 to 200 years did not indicate that he had come to favor Senator John Calhoun's increasingly asserted idea that slavery was of perpetual benefit to the United States and thus, in his words, a "positive good." Calhoun, a South Carolinian of tremendous political influence, had declared in 1837, during the chamber's recurrent debate over the handling of "abolition petitions," "that the existing relation between the two races in the South, against which these blind fanatics are waging war, forms the most solid and durable foundation on which to rear free and stable institutions." In this moment, and at other times during the mid- to late 1830s, Calhoun tried hard to get Southern congressmen to go beyond the principle of nonaction and to unite behind this emergent doctrine. Clay and various other Upper Southern congressmen refused. Clay reiterated this refusal in 1839, when he declared, in the concluding section of his speech, that he was "no friend of slavery" and that the "Searcher of all Hearts knows that every pulsation of mine beats high and strong in the cause of civil liberty."[26]

The hundred-year difference between Clay's two predictions was, however, quite meaningful. The earlier prediction, at least, had some empirical basis: The 1830 census had shown, for instance, that slavery continued to exist in Pennsylvania, on a small but not insubstantial scale, fifty years after the state's gradual abolition act. The latter prediction had no such grounding. It was, in essence, Clay's way of throwing his hands up in the air and tying slavery's fate to human progress. "What is ultimately to become of Slavery? asks the impatient Abolitionist," Clay wrote to an acquaintance in 1842: "I cannot tell him, with any certainty. [Yet] I have no doubt that the merciful Providence, which permitted its introduction into our Country, against the wishes of our Ancestors, will, according to HIS own good pleasure and time, provide for its mitigation or termination."[27]

Clay's 1839 Senate address was, in effect, a significant break point in his political career and in the attitude that he expressed, and insisted that others adopt, regarding the future of slavery in the United States. From the late 1830s until his death in 1852, during which time he continued to serve as the ACS's president and remained quite active in promoting federal support for colonization, nearly all of what he said and did on the subject reflected the ambivalent elements of *eventualism:* professed opposition to slavery in the abstract combined with demands to leave it alone. This was a stark contrast to the general thrust of remarks that he made during the late 1820s and early 1830s, when he repeatedly portrayed colonization as a potential catalyst of state-based gradual abolition. During the new phase of his political career that began in the late 1830s, colonization was something that he talked about, for the most part, as a preparatory step toward an eventual and more passive abolition process that would occur in the very distant future. All those who believed that slavery in the United States ultimately had to end, a cohort that, in Clay's view, counted him as a long-standing member, were obligated to suppress any desire to act on this belief so that the Union could survive. He underscored this obligation when he proclaimed during his 1839 speech, "Wherever... [the cause of civil liberty] is safe and practicable, I desire to see every portion of the human family in the enjoyment of it. But I prefer the liberty of my own country to that of any other people; and the liberty of my own race to that of any other race."[28]

Many colonization advocates followed Clay's lead, or at least came to the same conclusions, during the late 1830s and beyond. To a significant degree, speaking and writing in eventualist terms became the norm among colonization advocates from roughly the late 1830s through the mid-1850s. This was especially true for Southern politicians. In the new political environment, it was far too risky for elected officials in the South, even the Upper South, to use the bold kind of emancipatory rhetoric that Clay and many others had used from the mid-1820s until the early 1830s as part of the ACS's Northern recruitment strategy. Eventualism, however, did not necessarily become the norm for Northern advocates of colonization. During the late 1840s and early 1850s, in particular, when the national debate over slavery reached new sectionalist heights, several prominent Northern proponents spoke about the future of slavery in ways that made many of the movement's Southern proponents quite nervous and uncomfortable.[29]

SAMUEL CORNISH AND THE COLORED AMERICAN

Black activists continued, during the late 1830s and early 1840s, to pressure the colonization movement into abandoning its misguided and destructive cause, using the same vehicles—newspapers, pamphlets, conventions, and the American Anti-Slavery Society—to express their unwavering opposition. One of their most prolific vehicles was the *Colored American,* a weekly newspaper launched in 1837 by Samuel Cornish, a founding editor of *Freedom's Journal* and a founding leader of the AASS. The new periodical, like *Freedom's Journal,* operated out of New York City, where Cornish, beyond his role as a journalist, was also an influential minister and educator. Cornish did not conceive of the *Colored American* as a replacement for like-minded newspapers run by white editors, such as William Lloyd Garrison, who had operated *The Liberator* out of Boston since 1831, but he did believe that it had a very important and distinct purpose. The new publication, the founding issue declared, was "designed to be the organ of Colored Americans—to be looked on as their own, and devoted to their interests." Indeed, the title of the new paper, the first issue explained, was meant as a rebuke to all those in the nation who would "gladly rob us of the endeared name, 'AMERICANS,' a distinction . . . that we will never yield." One of the paper's chief functions would be to sustain and to continue refining the positions held by Black Americans "on the subjects of Abolition and Colonization," specifically "emancipation without expatriation—the extirpation of prejudice—the enactment of equal laws, and a full and free investiture of their rights as men and citizens."[30]

In keeping with these founding declarations, Cornish flooded the pages of the *Colored American,* which remained in circulation until 1842, with assertions, counterarguments, and criticisms aimed at the colonization movement. The aggregate volume of oppositional material published during these years towered over that which had come before from Black activists, between the late 1810s and the mid-1830s. And although much of what activists said during this later period resembled their earlier statements, at least in basic form, they took as much care as they always had to adjust their rhetoric so that it targeted adjustments made by their foes. As Theodore Wright—a regular contributor to the *Colored American* and, like Cornish, a New York–area minister and AASS leader—proclaimed at a large "anti-colonization meeting" in New York in 1839, we must "always [be] on the alert to meet and oppose and counteract the ever-changing movements of our persecutors."[31]

One of the main counterarguments that Black activists had been making for some time was that efforts to expatriate Black Americans would not, despite what many advocates claimed, cause a groundswell of manumissions or catalyze state-based gradual abolition. Those who made such claims were either deluded themselves or were seeking to deceive others. Instead, Black activists insisted, such efforts would have the effect of making slavery more secure, as Congressman John Randolph had explicitly claimed in one of his two statements during the ACS's founding meetings. A significant portion of Black activists spoke about the movement as if its founders and chief proponents had never harbored any emancipatory aims at all, effectively accusing them of deception and writing off the more sympathetic assessment of self-delusion. Several activists had leveled this accusation between the late 1810s and mid-1830s. Even more were doing so during the late 1830s and early 1840s. An article published during the summer of 1837 declared that the ACS was a scheme developed by "Slaveholders, for the purpose of perpetuating slavery, and rendering more valuable their property in Slaves."[32]

During the earlier decades of the Black opposition movement, however, there had been a minority of Black activists who had refrained from making such blanket accusations, acknowledging that there were, within the colonization movement's ranks, numerous individuals who, despite their delusions regarding colonization's emancipatory efficacy, genuinely desired to see the complete abolition of slavery in the United States. Sympathetic attempts to parse the colonization ranks were still evident during the late 1830s. A letter to the editor of the *Colored American* printed in the summer of 1838, for instance, characterized the speakers at a recent "colonization meeting" as a mix of individuals who claimed that slavery was a "necessary evil" and others who "boldly" declared it "to be . . . the crime of FREE America." Such remarks, however, had become less frequent in recent years. Two articles published around the same time offered an unqualified summative message: "The time was, when good men were colonizationists, ignorantly in unbelief, but that time has passed." In recent years, "God has poured so much light on the subject, as to leave no room for any other [justification], than willful ignorance."[33]

The political adjustments that many colonization leaders, Clay foremost among them, made during the mid- to late 1830s contributed to this hardened viewpoint. The shift from stressing colonization's emancipatory potential toward positing colonization as a mere preparatory step toward eventual abolition signaled, from the perspective of Black Americans, a very concerning shift in the national debate over slavery. This new eventualist position, with its strong connection to the principle of nonaction, foreshadowed, at a minimum, ever-increasing levels of political passivity regarding slavery's future. The colonization movement has "succeeded in lulling to sleep the consciences of this nation on the subject of slavery," an 1839 editorial declared.[34]

The increased emphasis that Clay and other advocates put on colonization's capacity to solve the national problem of Black freedom and, moreover, to serve as a political issue through which white Americans could ameliorate sectional tensions was even more alarming to Black activists. A pamphlet published by Cornish and Wright in 1840 sharply criticized two very prominent colonization advocates—former Senator Theodore Frelinghuysen, who was the current president of the University of the City of New-York (later New York University) and who would be Henry Clay's running mate in the presidential election of 1844, and former US Attorney General Benjamin Butler—for asserting that the American people "were more indebted" to the colonization movement than "any other cause" for the "integrity of the Union." An article in the *Colored American* during the following year blasted ACS spokespeople for insisting "that our existence in this land is an evil of so alarming a character, that, if we are not removed by some means, consequences the most disastrous to the peace and prosperity of the nation must necessarily ensue." Noting the appeals to patriotism embedded in such Unionist rhetoric, a resolution offered at an 1839 anticolonization meeting in New York declared that the "whole action and influence of the American Colonization Society" was "highly destructive to all *true* patriotism."[35]

A main reason why this second adjustment was even more alarming than the first, from the perspective of Black activists, was that they deemed it an accelerant of state-level and federal-level exclusionary legislation. Laws restricting the freedoms of Black Americans had been on the rise in the United States since at least the early 1800s. This trend had hit an inflection point during the years following the 1831 Nat Turner Revolt, when various states in the North and the South tightened or seriously considered tightening their bodies of racially oppressive laws and when the state legislatures of Maryland and Virginia made the first significant, multiyear appropriations for colonization in American history. The mid- to late 1830s, from the perspective of many Black activists, felt like yet another point of inflection. And during this time, they made clear in the pages of the *Colored American,* and in other media, that they considered the spokespeople of the colonization movement to bear significant blame.[36]

In several articles published in 1838, Black activists denounced what they saw as one of the most troubling instances of this exclusionary trend: the disfranchisement of Black Pennsylvanians, an action recommended by a state constitutional convention during the early part of the year. "If we look" at the convention's proceedings, a correspondent of the *Colored American* wrote, "we shall discover the demon of colonization busy at work—doing as she always has been since its first organization, exciting oppression and prejudice upon an already injured but useful portion of the community." In this particular instance, as this article and others made sure to stress, the causal relationship between colonization promotion and the enactment of new exclusionary laws—a relationship that Black activists had been asserting for years—was crystal clear. There was no need for inference. Some convention delegates had invoked the colonization movement's rhetoric and efforts as justification for disfranchisement. And the convention, as a whole, had gone so far as to submit a memorial to the legislature recommending a follow-up constitutional amendment that would authorize an annual state appropriation for colonization purposes. "The adoption of an amendment to the Constitution, by your honorable body, which confines elective franchise to the whites," the memorial asserted, "opens the way for another amendment, not less important, and in its nature closely allied to it." Such a troubling turn of events, the paper's correspondent noted, "should inspire every one of us to take a renewed stand" against the expatriation movement and to "swear eternal hatred to the American Colonization Society."[37]

As the 1840 presidential election approached, Black activists became increasingly concerned that these state-level trends would translate to the national level. Articles published in 1838 and 1839, during the several months preceding the Whig national convention, tried to spur Black Americans to publicly oppose Clay's nomination. If "the mighty energies of this Government are wielded by that fallen angel [Clay]," a letter to the editor warned, and "all the resources of the Government are to be brought to bear upon our expatriation ... what evil may we not anticipate?" Another article declared, "We are a Whig, and vote with the Whigs, and we wish to inform the Whigs, that the President of the American Colonization Society never can be President of the United States."[38]

The *Colored American* also devoted space to sharply criticizing Clay's 1839 Senate speech, in which he had declared his firm belief in the eventualist principle of nonaction and reaffirmed his belief that Black freedom was a very large and worrisome national problem: "In the speech before us, which is intended as a Pacifier, we find no general reasoning from universally acknowledged principles, but on the contrary, a series of special pleadings from unwarranted assumptions." Although, the author added, there were moments when he appeared "to catch a glimpse of Truth," he just as quickly lost them, falling back into the deluded confines of his "bleared vision."[39]

When Clay lost the Whig Party nomination to William Henry Harrison, at the end of 1839, the activists who had issued such severe warnings against a Clay presidency had cause to feel a bit of relief. At the same time, however, they recognized that the still very popular politician's potential to impede the cause of abolition and the cause of Black civil rights remained very high. Clay remained at the helm of a movement that had been and that continued to be, as an article published in 1841 put it, a "VAST ENGINE of persecution and oppression." The colonization movement's capacity to do harm, Black activists fully understood, did not hinge on Clay's election to the highest office in the country or on the wider objective of winning federal support for its separatist scheme. As long as white Americans of great influence in Washington—and of great influence in towns, cities, and states across the country—continued to promote the colonization movement's exclusionary ideology, anti-Black prejudice would likely continue to increase and exclusionary legislation would likely continue to proliferate. In the 1840 pamphlet that Cornish and Wright addressed to former Senator Frelinghuysen and former US Attorney General Butler, the authors asked these particular men of influence to consider, with as much openness and honesty as they could muster, whether it was right for them "to persist in a scheme which nourishes an unreasonable and unchristian prejudice" and "which persuades legislators to continue their unjust enactments against us in all their rigor." And they asked these men to engage in such consideration, recognizing fully that their persistence would amount, in effect, to an attempt to force Black Americans to consent to something that they had "unremittingly rejected from the first."[40]

ACS CONVENTION AND KENNEDY REPORT

In the spring of 1842, ACS leaders decided to stage a six-day convention in Washington. The first day's proceedings took place in the Hall of the House of Representatives, where the ACS had held several annual meetings over the past twenty-five years. Other days' sessions occurred in locations scattered around the city. Recent political developments had given the society's leaders reason to believe that the time was right to reengage with the federal government. Petition-rejection policies in Congress appeared to have declining support. In 1841, the House of Representatives nearly rejected a Gag Rule that it had passed, in some form, every year since 1836. Moreover, recent elections had given the Whig Party a significant majority in both houses. While the idea of federally supported Black expatriation had advocates in both political parties, the Whig Party of Henry Clay, which favored an active role for the federal government in nation-building activities, continued to have far more of them.[41]

The convention's most high-profile participants were Francis Scott Key, Senator James T. Morehead and Representative Joseph R. Underwood of Kentucky, Senator William C. Rives and former Representative Charles Fenton Mercer of Virginia, and former Representative Elisha Whittlesey of Ohio. All, with the exception of Key, were Whigs. Key, a Maryland-born lawyer in his early sixties, was the convention's keynote speaker. Since 1816, when he had been part of the four-person cohort that had launched the ACS, Key had acted as one of the organization's chief promoters and administrators. Aside from his long track record as a colonization advocate, one of the things that made Key an attractive choice for the keynote role was his association with the Democratic Party. In recent years, he had worked in the department of the attorney general under two Democratic presidents, Andrew Jackson and Martin Van Buren, giving him a kind of across-the-aisle appeal.[42]

The arguments that Key gave in favor of federally supported Black expatriation focused on the national benefits of becoming more deeply involved with Liberia, the third political adjustment made by colonization advocates, during the 1833–53 period, in response to the highly sectional and volatile political environment. Key anchored his speech in the international cause of slave trade suppression, an issue that had regained salience in Washington in recent years due to a perception that American naval efforts were proving inadequate and due to frustration that British naval efforts were impeding and complicating American efforts. He then spent a considerable amount of time highlighting the benefits to the American economy of increasing the size of the emergent Americo-African trade in raw materials and finished goods. Over the past decade, American merchants had begun establishing footholds in Liberia and showing the profits that could be derived from the African trade, but their success had been limited by competition from British merchants and conflict with the British navy—the latter was the subject of heated treaty negotiations taking place just down the road from the convention between Secretary of State Daniel Webster and British Trade Minister Lord Ashburton. If the United States government were to assert itself with greater force in West Africa, Key asserted, by establishing significant commercial and diplomatic relationships with Liberia, national wealth and power would dramatically increase. In his concluding remarks, Key knitted all of these political issues together, claiming that they were so closely connected as to be "indivisible." "African commerce calls for the destruction of the slave trade, and to destroy the slave trade you must foster African commerce, and African Colonization is the life of African commerce, and the death of the slave trade."[43]

Through this carefully constructed political pitch, which took him hours to deliver, Key was trying to make the prospect of federal support for Liberia, and, by extension, colonization, appear so appealing as to be nearly unobjectionable. He was also, as he made explicit in numerous instances, seeking to expand the constitutional ground upon which such support could be legislated. Slave trade suppression had afforded the first and only successful inroad toward such support: the Slave Trade Act of 1819 and the informal partnership established between the executive branch and the ACS for the purpose of returning illegally enslaved Africans to their home continent. But this political issue had proven incapable of underwriting a more extensive relationship. Strong objections from Lower Southern congressmen had impeded every effort made by colonization proponents, since 1819, to gain federal support. Colonization movement leaders hoped that their revised and expanded pitch—which added the elements of international commerce and diplomacy, two areas where Congress had clear constitutional jurisdiction—would yield better results.[44]

At no point in his wide-ranging speech did Key mention colonization's emancipatory potential. This was in stark contrast to speeches that he gave during the 1820s and early 1830s. Addressing the ACS's annual meeting in 1828—during the moment when Secretary of State Clay, Representative Mercer, and many others were promoting the ACS's latest congressional memorial—Key, a lifelong slaveholder, asserted, "The Society and their friends have always declared their hope, that emancipation would be a result of the success of their scheme," adding that "emancipation" was a "certain consequence" of "colonization." His main task in this earlier moment had been to sustain and expand Northern interest, which hinged, to a large degree, on colonization's emancipatory potential. At the 1842 convention, Key had a different purpose: to regain political traction for the colonization movement at the federal level. Given this objective, and given the volatile political environment, Key chose to keep the sensitive subject of slavery entirely out of view.[45]

Nearly every convention speaker did the same, making sure that they did so in ways that comported with the Unionist and eventualist messages that Clay emphasized in his 1839 Senate speech. Senator James Morehead, a first-time congressman who had previously served as Kentucky's lieutenant governor and governor, articulated the movement's well-worn disclaimer that the ACS's efforts had nothing to do with slavery. They pertained only, he insisted, to the "less numerous but equally degraded" population of "colored freedmen" who could never enjoy full equality in the United States. At one point, however, he broke ranks slightly, making a light and almost undetectable reference to colonization's potential role in facilitating the end of slavery. But his remark was so vague and oblique as to be unprovocative, particularly because he couched it in decidedly eventualist terms. Morehead spoke of a future liberation that might at some point flow from "the wonderful dispensations of that Being whose ways" were inscrutable to human beings.[46]

Ralph Gurley, the Connecticut-born minister who had for much of the last twenty years served as the editor of the *African Repository* and the ACS's secretary, steered clear of the sensitive subject as well, even though, like Key, he had played a significant role in propagating emancipatory rhetoric during the society's Northern recruitment campaign. The main objective of his convention remarks was to reaffirm the idea that the federal government still had a crucial role to play in colonization, despite the recent somewhat conflictive trend of state government actions, a subject on which Gurley had mixed emotions. These actions were welcome, in his mind, but only if they did not undermine efforts to obtain federal support by casting doubt, as the Maryland Colonization Society had done over the last several years, on the constitutionality of such support. On the first day of the convention, which he had the honor of opening, Gurley offered a series of resolutions that highlighted the various national-benefit claims that Key, in his closing speech, would explicate in great detail. One of these asserted a strong connection between federal support for colonization and strengthening the Union: "Resolved, That at this time, when our country is agitated by conflicting opinions on the subject of our colored population; . . . we are urged by the highest and most affecting considerations that ever roused patriotic and Christian men to action, to adopt a national policy, that shall tend to unite our own citizens, benefit our colored population, overthrow the slave trade, and bless, enduringly, two races of men, and two of the largest quarters of the globe."[47]

The only individual who spoke assertively on the subject of slavery during the convention was Henry Leavitt Ellsworth, the commissioner of the US Patent Office and a member of the ACS's Executive Committee. He did so at a fundraising speech that took place, as an adjunct of the convention's formal proceedings, at First Presbyterian Church in Washington. "Slavery has been, it is, and ever will be, considered by all, with few exceptions, a dreadful evil," Ellsworth declared. "What is to be the remedy?" he continued. "None has been offered at all adequate, that does not include colonization, and without it emancipation it is believed by many, would prove a curse alike to the slave States themselves and to those States where entire freedom prevails."[48]

Shortly after these remarks, Ellsworth made an analogy between the trend of native dispossession, which had spiked over the last decade following passage of the 1830 Indian Removal Act, and the cause of colonization: "If the poor Indians, our red brethren, proprietors of the soil, could not remain in the midst of us, how much less encouragement is there to expect a permanent residence with equal privileges for the more degraded [emancipated] slave." With these remarks, Ellsworth foreshadowed a political tactic that various colonization advocates would employ during the coming decades. The large amount of money the federal government spent on *removal* treaties and on *removal* operations—which, during the mid- to late 1830s, forced tens of thousands of individuals from the Cherokee,

Choctaw, Chickasaw, Muscogee, and Seminole nations to resettle in the Western United States—would be asserted as a compelling legal precedent for federally supported Black expatriation. There was significant irony underlying this tactic. During the late 1820s and early to mid-1830s, Clay and other members of the emergent Whig Party—the party that had been and that would remain the political locus of colonization promotion through the early 1850s—had generally opposed the Indian Removal Act and the subsequent acts of native dispossession. Once federal support for this dispossession was a legal fact, however, a portion of these Whigs—including, during the late 1840s, Joseph R. Underwood, one of the convention's high-profile participants—showed themselves willing to cite Indian removal as a precedent for Black removal.[49]

In the weeks following the Washington convention, a committee led by Key drafted and submitted a memorial that asked Congress to determine how the federal government might bring its massive resources to bear in support of Liberia and colonization. This was the first time since 1837 that the ACS had mustered the confidence to appeal for federal support. The memorial, unsurprisingly, conformed to the argumentative framework expounded by Key during the convention. Citing the fact that "African colonization" had already shown itself to be a very "efficient ally" in both slave trade suppression and Americo-African trade and, furthermore, that the federal government clearly enjoyed constitutional authority over both endeavors, the memorial encouraged Congress to consider what it might do, under the auspices of foreign affairs, "to secure the safety" of the current settlements in Liberia.[50]

The House of Representatives referred the memorial to the Committee on Commerce and charged it with recommending next steps. Toward the end of February 1843, John Pendleton Kennedy, a Whig representative from Maryland, presented a one-thousand-page report that strongly endorsed the memorial's requests. Much of the report was comprised of an enormous appendix that was, quite transparently, a promotional history of the ACS's previous twenty-five years—Kennedy was and would continue to be for many years a colonization supporter. The front section on findings and recommendations reiterated much of what ACS leaders had asserted during the convention and in the submitted memorial but with a very significant addition. The report proposed that the United States consider making Liberia "an American colony." The relationship between the two entities, the report indicated, had been vague and arm's-length for far too long. It was high time, it continued, for a plan to be "devised for the permanent and prosperous guidance" of the African colony. If the federal government chose against such action or if it chose, at a minimum, not to clarify and solidify its connection to Liberia in other ways, the report warned, it would give Great Britain, France, and other European nations the opportunity to intervene, thus diminishing the United States' chances of reaping the many benefits that a closer relationship would afford.[51]

The current session of Congress ended just a few weeks after Kennedy's committee presented its report. When ACS affiliates made a second congressional appeal during the next session, they did so under different political circumstances. Recent elections had replaced the significant Whig majority with a significant Democratic majority. The House of Representatives assigned the new memorial to the Committee on Foreign Affairs. Roughly one month later, South Carolinian Democrat Robert Barnwell Rhett delivered a report on behalf of the committee that was, in clear terms, antithetical to the Kennedy Report. In five terse pages, with no appendix, the committee rejected the idea of making Liberia a national colony, claiming that there was absolutely no constitutional basis for such an action. It also rejected, on similar grounds, the lesser idea of establishing formal commercial and diplomatic ties with Liberia, claiming that the federal government could only make such agreements with sovereign nations—Liberia was a collection of settlements established by a private organization.[52]

The 1844 House report's overarching goal, like that presented to the Senate by Littleton Tazewell in 1828, was to discourage, in strong terms, Black expatriation advocates from making further appeals to Congress. One of the ways it sought to do so, as indicated by the final clause, was to turn the language of Unionism against them. Any benefits gained from federal involvement, the Rhett Report concluded, would come at the "expense of the integrity of the constitution," as well as the "peace and continuance of the Union."[53]

LIBERIAN INDEPENDENCE

During the summer of 1847, Liberia declared independence as a sovereign nation, effectively terminating the system of colonial governance, overseen by the ACS, that had been in place for the last twenty-five years. The formal declaration drew heavily, in terms of language and structure, on the American document of 1776, a deliberate signal to the world, and indeed to the American government, that Liberia had historical and ideological connections to the United States. The authors of the declaration reserved a section of the document for the purpose of explaining why they, and so many other Liberian residents, had chosen "to expatriate themselves from the land of their nativity." They pulled no punches on the subject of racial oppression. In many parts of the nation, the declaration stated, "We were debarred by law from all the rights and privileges of men—in other parts, public sentiment, more powerful than law, frowned us down.... We uttered our complaints, but they were unattended to, or only met by alleging the peculiar institutions of the country. All hope of a favorable change in our country was thus wholly extinguished in our bosoms, and we looked with anxiety abroad for some asylum from the deep degradation."[54]

ACS leaders publicly supported Liberia's decision to declare independence. Aside from the basic fact that many expatriation proponents, over the years, had prospectively endorsed such a move, Liberian sovereignty also neutralized, at least in theory, one of the Rhett committee's main objections to the ACS's 1844 memorial: that the federal government could only establish formal relationships with sovereign nations. Colonization advocates could now claim, as they immediately did, that the United States and Liberia had a firm constitutional basis on which to partner in pursuit of the mutually beneficial aims of slave trade suppression, commercial expansion, and Black expatriation. One of the colonization movement's main strategic objectives, thus, became the formal recognition of Liberia by the United States government. When it became clear that the governments of Britain and France would recognize Liberia first (indeed, the United States would not do so until 1862), calls for recognition in the United States carried added urgency and, in some cases, notes of criticism. At the ACS's annual meeting in 1849, for instance, Joseph R. Ingersoll, a congressman from Pennsylvania, declared, "I regret that other governments have gone ahead of our own, in that which was our peculiar work, and ought to have been our distinguished privilege!" Liberia was, after all, he pointed out, a nation comprised of former residents of the United States that was modeled directly on the American form of government.[55]

Liberian leaders played a significant role in promoting formal recognition by the federal government. The first president of the new nation, Joseph Jenkins Roberts—a freeborn Virginian who had emigrated during the late 1820s and who, during his time in Liberia, had built wealth and influence as a merchant—and several other prominent Liberians published regularly in the *African Repository* and, at various moments, traveled to the United States to appeal directly to American audiences. In the summer of 1849, the *Repository* published a letter from Roberts addressed to the ACS's corresponding secretary in which he gave a glowing account of his meetings with diplomats in England and France and expressed frustration at the relative apathy, or at least indifference, of the American government. The United States "ought to have" recognized Liberia's status as a nation by now, Roberts wrote. It was a shame that it had not done so, particularly given Liberia's specific importance "as an asylum for the people of color" still living there. "I do hope," Roberts added, that the United States will soon change its tune, and that it will not stop at simple recognition but go so far as to provide funds that will help bolster Liberia's stability and growth. "The future success of colonization depends upon" Liberia, Roberts declared. "With her colonization must stand or fall."[56]

In conjunction with their effort to secure recognition and aid from the United States government, Liberian leaders also strongly encouraged Black Americans to emigrate. At times, they did so with the same knowing and pushy tone that white colonization advocates had used for decades. At a meeting held in New York in 1848, a religious leader from Liberia—one of five Liberians in attendance, President Roberts among them—asserted that if free Black Americans "knew what he knew, they would go to Liberia." The reasons for choosing against emigration, he insisted, were far outweighed by the justifications for leaving. "Were they [truly] fulfilling their destiny" in the United States? he asked. In Liberia, he added, there were numerous individuals "who would weep tears of bitterest sorrow if they believed they would have to come back to America," because it was in Liberia that they had finally found "true happiness," the religious leader observed, and they were "unwilling to leave it."[57]

As a complement to all of these promotional efforts, colonization advocates made two other strategic moves in Washington. First, in early 1849, Senator Joseph R. Underwood of Kentucky proposed that the Senate Judiciary Committee issue a formal opinion on whether the federal government could support Black expatriation. Underwood, who had been in Congress since the mid-1830s, had been involved with the colonization movement for roughly the same amount of time. He had been one of the principal authors and signatories of the ACS's 1838 published circular, and he had presided over a portion of the six-day convention in Washington held in 1842. In effect, Underwood was asking Congress to make a final, lasting judgment on a thirty-year-old question. Did the federal government have the "constitutional power" to fund the expatriation of Black Americans to the "Republic of Liberia"—a very deliberate phrase meant as an explicit reminder that Liberia was no longer a colony, but a nation. Underwood also asked the committee to determine whether it was "expedient and proper [for Congress] to make such appropriation?"[58]

As a kind of leading instruction, Underwood noted that there were two important legal "precedents" for such federal action: "the removal of Indians from one part of the United States to another" and "the removal of captured Africans from the United States to the shores of Africa." On the latter subject, it is worth adding that Underwood had been trying for several months to get Congress to reimburse the ACS for helping to resettle more than seven hundred illegally enslaved Africans seized by the US Navy at the end of 1845. In citing these legal precedents, Underwood stated his expectation that members of the Judiciary Committee would, in composing their report, "make a distinction, if they could" between past "appropriations" made for Indian and African removal and a future appropriation for colonization.[59]

The immediate context for Underwood's proposal—which had strong support from his Kentucky compatriot Senator Thomas Metcalfe, a former governor who, like Underwood, was a member of the Whig Party—was an upcoming constitutional convention in Kentucky during which, as Metcalfe explained, the subject of slavery, and perhaps the subject of "gradual emancipation," would receive significant attention. A favorable opinion from the Judiciary Committee, both senators asserted, might very well spark emancipatory actions in the state, either by the convention or by slaveholders, or both. "It is perfectly well known," Underwood declared, that a "portion" of Kentuckians were "willing to manumit their slaves, provided they can be sent from the country." The overarching purpose of soliciting a formal opinion from the Senate was thus, Underwood stated, to determine whether "northern men" were willing to use federal funds for "relieving the country of the slaves, whenever slave-owners may be disposed to manumit them." If Kentucky slaveholders were assured that they would have access to federal colonization support, Metcalfe predicted, "thousands would be emancipated" across the state.[60]

This was fairly strong language from both Underwood and Metcalfe. It constituted a notable break from the eventualist attitude that fellow Kentuckian Henry Clay had modeled in his 1839 speech before the Senate and that nearly every speaker at the 1842 ACS convention in Washington had subsequently evinced. Clay, in fact, made a rhetorical break of his own during this 1849 moment. In a public letter that he distributed in advance of the Kentucky constitutional convention, he expressed his desire to see the delegates endorse a course of gradual abolition and colonization. "I lament" that such a course was not pursued during the late 1790s, he observed—as a young man Clay had expressed support for Kentucky gradual abolition in multiple editorials, published under a pseudonym—but "I should be most happy if what was impracticable at that epoch could now be accomplished." To this declaration Clay added the following qualification—one that, despite his suggestion of equivalence, he had not asserted fifty years earlier—Colonization must be "an indispensable" part of the process of ending slavery in the state. "Without it," he stated, "I should be utterly opposed to any scheme of emancipation."[61]

The public assertiveness of these three high-profile politicians was not an indication that sectional tensions on the subject of slavery had lessened—quite the contrary, in fact. Sectional tensions in Congress were as high as they had been in many years, perhaps ever, spurred on by fierce debate over the potential westward expansion of slavery. The United States had declared war against Mexico in mid-1846, which had raised the question of whether slavery would be allowed or disallowed in territory that might be acquired in the case of an American victory. When the United States won the war in 1848 and acquired an enormous swath of land as a result, the question of slavery's expansion became even more contentious. Northern congressmen, for the most part, opposed expansion, as evidenced by repeated majority votes in the House of Representatives for the Wilmot Proviso, a legal article that sought to ban slavery from all acquired lands. Southern congressmen, for the most part, favored such expansion, or at least opposed the passage of any legal restriction. Some congressmen from the South were so enraged by the prospect of a federal ban that they threatened secession.[62]

The willingness of Underwood, Metcalfe, and Clay to speak of colonization's emancipatory potential during this time is explained by the state-level context of their remarks. All of them were speaking about this potential as it applied to Kentucky alone, not any of the other fourteen states that comprised the slaveholding South. And each state had a right to determine its own course with respect to slavery, a political point on which Northern and Southern politicians broadly agreed. Nonetheless, all three politicians well understood the need to tread carefully on the sensitive subject of slavery's future in the United States.

Within a day of Underwood making his proposal, the Senate effectively denied his request. The vote to "indefinitely" table the colonization proposal was close, 27 to 23, but regionally lopsided. Those who voted against tabling were largely from the North. Senator William Dayton of New Jersey was one of them. Dayton—a Judiciary Committee member, a current Whig, and a future Republican vice-presidential candidate (1856)—made sure to clarify that his opposition to tabling was not an indication of optimism. Although he "would go so far as he who goes furthest in reference to an appropriation by this Government which would relieve us from the curse of free blacks," he did not think it likely that the committee, if it in fact was charged with reviewing Underwood's proposal, would give the endorsement the Kentucky senator was looking for. Those who voted in favor of tabling the colonization proposal were almost entirely from the South—the majority were senators from the Lower South, who voted as a unanimous bloc. One of them was the chair of the Judiciary Committee, a senator from South Carolina, and almost certainly someone whom Dayton had in mind when he gave his pessimistic assessment of what might happen to Underwood's proposal, if referred. Another Southerner who voted in favor of tabling was Jefferson Davis of Mississippi, the future president of the Confederate States of America. Davis expressed great frustration that this issue had been brought before the Senate, denouncing it as yet another attempt, like the current Northern effort to prohibit slavery's expansion into the vast Mexican cession, to meddle with Southern rights. "If the people of Kentucky wish to emancipate their slaves—though I should regret such a course," the matter was for them to pursue alone, Davis stated. The Judiciary Committee's view on the issue of federal support for colonization, he continued, should have no bearing on their decision, and thus the claims of urgency and relevancy made by Underwood and Metcalfe were specious.[63]

The second move occurred in the same year, when Secretary of State John Clayton, an affiliate of the ACS from Delaware, used his authority to authorize a formal fact-finding mission to Liberia. To fill the role of the government's chief representative in this mission, Clayton appointed a man who had traveled there before and who had dedicated the last twenty-five years of his professional life to the cause of colonization: Ralph Gurley. Upon returning to the United States, Gurley submitted a one-hundred-plus-page report of his sojourn to the State Department. For all Liberians, Gurley remarked, formal recognition by the United States was "an object of earnest desire." Indeed, they felt such a strong "attachment to the government and people of" the nation that they might be willing, Gurley noted with an element of prodding, to place Liberia's relationship with the United States above those already established with France and England. In August 1850, Secretary of State Daniel Webster, Clayton's replacement and also an ACS affiliate, presented Gurley's report to Congress. Shortly thereafter, the Senate approved a motion by Henry Clay to print the document. This was a minor success, not a huge one. But nonetheless, just as they had seven years earlier with the Kennedy Report, colonization advocates in Washington had managed to publish a significant promotional document with the stamp of the federal government on its face.[64]

From an even broader strategic perspective, colonization advocates tried to use the added visibility afforded by Liberia's Declaration of Independence as a springboard for reestablishing a broad base of support in the North and the Upper South. One of the main ways they did this was to press, with even more force and urgency, the Unionist message that had become a central element of their promotional strategy since the late 1830s. Colonization advocates could easily discern how Unionist rhetoric would serve their cause, even more powerfully, in an environment where

Northerners and Southerners were fighting bitterly over the issue of slavery's westward extension. At the ACS's 1849 annual meeting, amid impassioned calls for the United States to recognize Liberia, three prominent federal politicians stressed colonization's capacity to stabilize and strengthen the Union. One of them was Robert J. Walker, the current secretary of the treasury. The other two were Richard Thompson and Robert McLane, congressmen from Indiana and Maryland, respectively. Thompson, the most emphatic of the three, claimed, as he addressed the audience in Hall of the House of Representatives, that the ACS was a "common ground on which we can meet, and where we can harmoniously stand." In this moment of great national stress, he declared, "patriots and philanthropists" from "all sections" and "all parties" should support the society's work, because it was through such concerted effort that the nation might "get clear of the influences which almost daily agitate *this Hall*" and leave it in an increasingly fragile state. "Let us maintain the integrity . . . *of the Union of States!*" Thompson proclaimed, "and to the latest generation our posterity shall be blessed in the deed."[65]

LIBERIAN STEAMSHIPS AND THE COMPROMISE OF 1850

During the first nine months of 1850, there was a powerful sense in Washington that the nation might split apart. In addition to the fierce ongoing debate regarding slavery's westward expansion—which had intensified dramatically after California, a large portion of the territory acquired from Mexico, had applied for admission as a free state—Upper Southern congressmen had begun pushing, quite hard, for a strengthened fugitive slave law. Henry Clay, now in his early seventies, returned to the Senate during this time, after a seven-year break. His mandate, as he saw it, was to save the Union. The means to this end, he explained in a speech during the early part of the new legislative session, was to forge a permanent and comprehensive settlement of all slavery-related issues. If legislators from the North and the South operated in the spirit of compromise, he advised, the forging of such a settlement was possible. If, however, they continued to dig their heels in and to divide sharply along sectional lines, there was a real chance that the Union would be "dissolved."[66]

Toward the end of this nine-month period, as sectional fires still raged in Congress, Tennessee Representative Frederick Perry Stanton launched a new effort to obtain federal support for Black expatriation. In his capacity as chair of the House Committee on Naval Affairs, the thirty-five-year-old Democrat, who had recently begun an affiliation with the ACS, presented a report to the House recommending that the federal government sponsor a line of steamships running between ports in the United States and Liberia. In this endeavor, the government would partner with a private company, established by two Southerners, that would provide one-third of the necessary upfront capital and would borrow the remaining two-thirds, at interest, from Congress. The private company would also assume responsibility for constructing the three steamships—state-of-the-art 4,000-ton vessels, estimated at $900,000 apiece—and for conducting their ongoing operations: carrying mail, trade goods, and passengers between the United States and West Africa. The federal government, in addition to providing the construction loan, would supply each ship with a captain from the US Navy and four additional naval officers. And it would reserve the right to convert these ships, as necessary, into armed vessels for wartime purposes or other national objectives.[67]

Stanton's committee report endorsing the Liberian steamer project, in the full scope of its argumentation, brought together all of the major political levers that colonization advocates had pulled over the last decade. The document emphasized that Black expatriation would enhance slave trade suppression efforts, expand American trade with Africa, and gain for the United States, in the nation of Liberia, an important ally on the African continent. The report also connected the issue of Black expatriation with the goal of stabilizing the Union, and it avoided the delicate subject of colonization's purported emancipatory potential.[68]

As Stanton promoted the Liberian steamer appropriation during August and September 1850, Congress passed a set of bills, collectively known as the Compromise of 1850, that many hoped would serve as the kind of permanent and comprehensive resolution that Clay had called for several months before. Congress resolved the nation's two most divisive issues by rejecting the Wilmot Proviso's ban on slavery in the new territories (except in California, which was admitted as a free state) and by enacting a strengthened fugitive slave law. At the end of the year, when the next congressional session opened, President Millard Fillmore declared the Compromise to be a "final settlement of the dangerous and exciting subjects" facing the nation. He advised all congressmen, irrespective of their partisan or sectional affiliations, to commit themselves during the coming months and years to preserving this hard-won peace. "Men of extreme opinions," men for whom "mutual concession" was "unwelcome," might, he suggested, seek to overturn one or more of the Compromise's elements. All in the United States should stand "ready to rebuke" such efforts, Fillmore declared, and should commit to doing whatever possible to preserve the sectional "healing" that the Compromise of 1850 had achieved.[69]

One month after Fillmore effectively declared the principle of nonaction as official federal policy, he attended the ACS's annual meeting in the Hall of the House of Representatives, the first time a sitting president had done so since the society was founded. The roster of other attendees was large and distinguished. In addition to Fillmore, various cabinet members, religious leaders, and numerous congressmen filed into the chamber to hear speeches from Clay, whose health was failing, and from Stanton. Over the course of several hours, the two men portrayed Black expatriation—and, by extension, the Liberian steamer project—as a vital political tool in the post-Compromise environment.[70]

"Colonization," Clay declared, in one of the last oratories he delivered in the nation's capital, "is a common object for the common benefit of the whole country." It offered a solution to a problem faced by every state in the Union, the degrading effects of the free Black population on the white population, and it also offered the only safe, practical means of preparing for slavery's eventual eradication, or, as he put it, using the indirect language that he often employed on the subject, "the final separation of the two classes of persons that now inhabit this country." Northern efforts to bring slavery's endpoint closer to the present, he asserted, had failed. In actual fact, they had pushed this threshold farther into the future. Worse still, he added, they had nearly rent the Union. It was time for Northern agitators to accept these painful realities, he advised, and to look to the future with pragmatism, not idealism. "It took two centuries and more to bring from the shores of Africa her sons now existing in a state of slavery in the United States . . . [and] it may take some two centuries to carry them back," Clay observed. "What . . . is this in the great workings of national existence and the administration of the affairs of this world?" The audience, according to the ACS's report of the meeting, clapped vigorously in approval.[71]

As had been the case twelve years ago in his watershed speech before the Senate in 1839, Clay did not celebrate his eventualist prescriptions. At the same time, however, he did not expound on the empirical reality that he, and all those who spoke about slavery in eventualist terms, well understood, even if they chose not to acknowledge it. Time was no guarantee of slavery's eventual decline or eradication. Indeed, decennial census reports published by the federal government showed that the institution had grown tremendously. Between 1790 and 1850, the population of enslaved Americans had increased from 700,000 to 3.2 million. Moreover, the two most recent census reports showed that between 1840 and 1850, the period during which Clay and many others had insisted on a federal policy of nonaction, the number had grown by 700,000 souls. The amount of Southern wealth that enslaved Americans comprised and the amount of national economic production enslaved Americans contributed had grown commensurately during this period, thus strengthening the institution's economic hold. Clearly, eventualist prescriptions, despite their status quo connotations, had consequences, a point that Black activists had been making, in various ways, for decades. The institution of slavery was becoming harder and harder to uproot—just as a young Clay, writing during the 1790s, had warned that it would: "The sooner we attempt its destruction the better."[72]

Clay's own theory on slavery's eventual path to eradication, as he described briefly in his 1851 speech and in scattered addresses over recent decades, rested on the vague assumption that, as the nation's population multiplied, the unit cost of free labor would eventually fall below the unit cost of slave labor, causing the former to supplant the latter. What this meant, in effect, was that slavery would continue its decades-long record of growth until population expansion and shifting labor costs caused a reversal. But how and when would this reversal come to pass, and how long would it take free labor to supplant slave labor completely? Moreover, how and when would the federal government, or perhaps an aggregation of state governments, establish a scalable system of Black expatriation capable of removing all of the supplanted slave laborers, with their consent, from the United States—something Clay insisted must happen in conjunction with slavery's decline? Clay did not have the answers, and he insisted that the questions were not worth asking. During his 1851 speech, he admonished those who wanted a more precise understanding of how and when slavery would end to "have more dependance upon the wisdom and providence of God than upon their own limited passions and circumscribed reason." The audience loudly applauded this eventualist sentiment as well.[73]

Frederick Perry Stanton addressed the 1851 annual meeting after Clay. As he made his remarks, which repeated some of what he had said in Congress but which also contained new material, the Tennessee congressman made the following striking declaration in support of expatriating free Black Americans: "I maintain that this part of our population is a great element of discord and danger . . . [that] must be removed from our borders, if the peace and harmony of our country are to be maintained." In effect, Stanton took the colonization movement's Unionist rhetoric to a new level. The implication of his declaration, as further remarks made clear, was that Black Americans were to blame for past, present, and future sectionalist tensions. While Stanton did not go so far as to identify them as the root cause of the long-running conflict between Northern states and Southern states, which was slavery, he did claim that their ongoing presence prevented a stable, permanent resolution to this conflict. Although the basic substance of what he said had been, for decades, implicit in the well-worn assertion that white freedom and Black freedom were existentially incongruous, the explicit blame element represented a rhetorical escalation. Black freedom was not just a problem, but it was a problem that Black Americans, by choosing to remain, were responsible for—a fact made all the more blameworthy given the Union's current incredibly fragile state.[74]

In his speech at the ACS's annual meeting, and in other remarks made before the House of Representatives in favor of the Liberian steamer project, Stanton explained this blame construct in greater detail. Specifically, he blamed free Black Americans for two of the nation's most divisive political issues: fugitive slaves and Northern agitation against slavery. On the first issue, he claimed that free Black Americans were significantly responsible for encouraging enslaved people to "escape." Moreover, the simple fact that there was a free Black population in the United States, he claimed, made it easier for fugitive slaves to hide. "If there were none [free Black Americans] at all," Stanton explained, "the fugitive would be easily distinguished and readily traced." The Fugitive Slave Act of 1850, with its enhanced system of enforcement and stricter penalties for noncompliance, would, he predicted, serve as an incremental deterrent and thus have ameliorative effects, but it would not, he advised, solve the fugitive slave problem, since the free Black population remained. "I must confess," he added, "I see no possible escape" from this "evil" predicament aside from "promoting the great and benevolent objects of this Society."[75]

On the second issue, Stanton claimed that free Black Americans were largely responsible for driving the "spirit of abolition" in the North—the core impulse that had produced, among other factors of sectional tension, the congressional petition campaign of the 1830s and the dramatic inflection in anti-extension sentiment during the 1840s. With this population greatly diminished, perhaps even eliminated, Stanton explained, the "symbols and exemplars of a degraded race would be no longer before the eyes of misguided philanthropists," and "fanaticism, becoming merely theoretical, would be shorn of its danger." The ultimate effect of Black expatriation on white Northerners, he predicted with confidence, would be the displacement of divisive radicalism by reasoned pragmatism. The natural consequence of this, he asserted, would be the restoration of "harmony" among the Northern and Southern "States of the Union."[76]

In the months following this high-powered affair in Washington, petitions endorsing the Liberian steamer project—or federal support for colonization, more generally—flooded into Congress from several states: Maryland, Delaware, Virginia, Vermont, Ohio, New Jersey, New York, Pennsylvania, and Rhode Island. Nearly all came with long lists of state legislators affixed to them, and nearly half carried the imprint of the state's governor. Many of the petitions asserted Unionist motivations similar to those stressed by Stanton. One petition from Virginia, signed by scores of legislators and the current governor, expressed strong support for the steamer proposal, "especially in a *national point of view*." Some also endorsed the logic of Stanton's blame-free-Black-Americans formula. Two petitions from Indiana, which were presented to the Senate by Henry Clay and then paraphrased in a brief speech, characterized the free Black population as "the greatest cause of discord" in the country and the Liberian steamer project as an excellent opportunity "to secure the future welfare, harmony, and permanency of the Union."[77]

Newspapers from the North and the Upper South offered public endorsements as well, dubbing this political cause the "Ebony Line." One particularly attentive paper, *The Sun* of Baltimore, published a piece in February 1851 predicting that Stanton's proposal could not fail to pass during the present session. Even when this prediction proved untrue, the congressional session ended in March without a successful appropriation, a letter to the editor published in the same paper a few months later expressed confidence that a federal appropriation would come in the next meeting of Congress. "It is known," the correspondent declared, "that many members, of different parties and sections, are now strongly in favor of it."[78]

ACS leaders and affiliates evinced similar optimism in the several months following the end of the congressional session in March 1851, not sensing in this moment of legislative failure the same kind of foreclosure detected in the Rhett committee's rebuke of 1844. At the ACS's annual meeting in January 1852, Stanton, now a vice president of the society, again spoke in favor of the prospective federal venture. President Millard Fillmore was once again in the audience. Presiding over the meeting was Secretary of State Daniel Webster. ACS president Henry Clay was very ill and would die a few months later. During another lengthy address, Stanton reiterated earlier claims about the constitutional and political viability of a federal appropriation and continued to put heavy emphasis on the "national" appeal of such an action by Congress and the spirit of "patriotism" evinced by all those who offered up support.[79]

After Stanton's speech, Webster addressed the audience. He began by recalling his participation in the society's founding meetings thirty-five years ago and by affirming that although during the intervening years he had not been an especially "active" promoter, he had always believed in the ACS's potential to deliver outcomes of the "highest importance." (Despite his relative quiet over the years, Webster had made similar remarks in a well-publicized speech given in March 1850, the purpose of which was to urge sectional compromise and reconciliation.) Webster then made clear that he warmly endorsed the envisioned steamer project and that he believed in the constitutionality of an enabling federal appropriation. When he closed, he made some remarks that sound quite pointed in retrospect but that he attempted to frame as reasonable and humane. Addressing the nation's free Black population, Webster stated, "Trust to God that in your destiny, in the land of your fathers, you will be happier than you are here, and trust to God also, that when you shall have left us, you will leave us, not less happy than if you were to remain." To present-day ears, these remarks, despite the euphemistic double negative, sound presumptive, patronizing, and callous: in effect, do not worry, the United States will get along just fine without you. To a great many white Americans during the early 1850s, however, they sounded as reasonable and humane as Webster had intended.[80]

FREDERICK DOUGLASS AND THE NEXT GENERATION OF BLACK ACTIVISTS

Black Americans vigorously protested the proposed Liberian steamer project, just as they had all major instances of colonization promotion in Washington over the last thirty-five years. "The whole affair is an ill-concealed attempt to give the support of the government to the scheme of the American Colonization Society," the Pennsylvania Anti-Slavery Society (PASS) annual report declared in late 1850, a few months after Stanton gave his first major speech on the subject in Congress, and just a handful of weeks before the ACS's annual meeting in Washington, where he and Henry Clay addressed an audience that included President Millard Fillmore. A relatively new Black newspaper by the name of the *North Star,* founded in 1847, reprinted the report to broaden its reach and oppositional impact. "Viewed in any light," the PASS's leaders declared, the proposal "deserves nothing but execration and opposition from every true friend of the colored man."[81]

The tremendous amount of white support that the Liberian steamer idea generated, which crescendoed during the latter months of 1850 and the early months of 1851, worried Black opposition leaders. The ACS's high-profile 1851 annual meeting was particularly concerning, with Clay and Stanton speaking in presumptive terms to the president of the United States, numerous congressmen, and various cabinet members about the high probability of a major federal appropriation, the central and heretofore unattainable aim of the colonization movement. Despite their worries, Black activists remained steadfast in their opposition. A "convention of colored citizens" in New York State during the spring of 1851 exhorted Black Americans to hold the line against the Liberian steamer proposal and to reiterate, with great conviction, that "we are not to be forced or enticed from our native land." The convention also counseled Black Americans not to worry too much about the colonization movement's latest attempt to obtain federal support for expatriation. This too will "fail," the convention's report on colonization declared. "Aye," the report added, "even the magic influence of Henry Clay cannot effect it."[82]

What Black activists in the Northern states were most concerned about during this time was not the colonization movement's specific actions in Congress but rather the tendency of these actions to sustain and even accelerate the national trend of de jure and de facto Black exclusion. The conditions faced by Black Americans during the late 1840s and early 1850s were demonstrably worse than they had been a decade earlier, when the *Colored American* had led the Black community's fight against escalating oppression. More and more states had taken actions to disfranchise Black Americans, or to severely limit their access to the polls. Several Northern states had enacted, or had come close to enacting, laws that prohibited Black Americans from becoming new residents. Three of the states that succeeded in enacting such laws were Illinois, Indiana, and Iowa. These new statutes effectively prohibited the migration of free Black Americans across a large swath of the country, since most Southern states already had such laws in place. Indeed, Illinois, Indiana, and Iowa, all of which bordered states in which slavery was legal, passed their anti-immigration laws largely in response to an Upper Southern statutory regime that not only prevented free Black immigration but that also prohibited newly emancipated individuals from continuing to live in their respective home states. At the federal level, the Fugitive Slave Act of 1850 struck terror into the hearts of most Black Americans, not just the self-emancipated who faced greater risk of forcible recapture but also those who were free by law but who faced heightened risk of being kidnapped into slavery by unscrupulous "slavecatchers" who used the law's draconian terms as cover. Collectively, these legislative actions indicated that Black exclusion was a highly potent political issue during this period. Many state and federal lawmakers clearly felt that they could and should, whether in deference to their own beliefs or those of their constituents, or both, sponsor and vote for bills that restricted Black freedom.[83]

This highly tumultuous and trying period was also a moment of generational transition for the Black activist community in the North. James

Forten, the Pennsylvania sailmaker who had been at the center of the fight against slavery and the fight for Black civil rights since the late eighteenth century, died in 1842. Reverend Theodore Wright died in 1847, David Ruggles in 1849, and Reverend Samuel Cornish in 1858. Collectively, these individuals had contributed mightily to the American Anti-Slavery Society, the staging of public protest meetings, the organizing of state and national "colored conventions," the writing and publishing of pamphlets, and the operating, in all aspects, of two major Black newspapers, *Freedom's Journal* and the *Colored American*. They were the generation that had launched, expanded, and sustained the effort—ongoing for three decades at this point—to oppose the actions and ideology of the colonization movement. The new generation of activists that came onto the national scene during this period included Martin Delany, Frederick Douglass, George Downing, Henry Highland Garnet, Frances Ellen Watkins Harper, Robert Purvis, and Charles Bennet Ray—as well as several children and grandchildren of James Forten, among them Harriet Forten Purvis, Sarah Forten Purvis, and William Forten. Most of these individuals had been born during the 1810s, putting them in their thirties during this time of transition. Over the next several decades, they would fight the colonization movement with just as much conviction and vigor as the prior generation had.[84]

Frederick Douglass emerged, during the mid- to late 1840s, as the most dominant voice of this new Black activist generation. Born into enslavement in Maryland around 1818, Douglass self-emancipated in the late 1830s, using Ruggles's Lower Manhattan home as one of his northward waypoints. He eventually settled in Massachusetts, where, within a few years, he gained visibility and influence as a traveling orator working under the auspices of the American Anti-Slavery Society. In 1845, he published *Narrative of the Life of Frederick Douglass, an American Slave*, one of the earliest and most influential firsthand accounts of American slavery. Two years later, after moving to western New York, he cofounded and edited the *North Star*, which he published on a weekly basis through 1851. In that year, he reorganized his journalistic endeavors under the heading of an eponymous weekly, *Frederick Douglass' Paper*, which was in circulation through 1855. These papers were, without doubt, two of the most prominent vehicles of Black activism, and more specifically of Black opposition to colonization, during this period.[85]

In the spring of 1849, at an "Anti-Colonization Meeting" held in New York City, reported in the pages of the *North Star,* Charles Bennet Ray, a veteran leader of the AASS, assailed the colonization movement's tendency to sustain and accelerate the national trend of Black exclusion. Ray, who was forty-one at the time, was a New York City minister, an agent of the New York Committee of Vigilance (which, among other things, coordinated the escape of self-emancipated individuals traveling through Manhattan), and had been a prior owner and editor of the *Colored American,* which ceased publication during the early 1840s. "The American Colonization Society," Ray declared, not only "fosters American caste," but it actually "creates" it, "and then like all other affectionate parents, it nurses dearly, and takes the best possible care of its child that it die not, but live to do its work." Indeed, Ray continued, in surveying the oppressive conditions facing Black Americans in the United States, "there is more of the fruit of the Colonization scheme [in them] than of any existing institution in this land, more than even Slavery itself."[86]

An article published in *Frederick Douglass' Paper* in 1853 reinforced Ray's point with great specificity, blaming colonization promotion for several oppressive measures passed during the intervening four years. "The Fugitive Slave Law of 1850," the author declared, "was a Colonization measure. So also are the laws of Illinois and Indiana . . . and others of other free States, which plead the most infamous penalties and disabilities upon the free colored emigrant." As an expression of concern about the extent to which interest in legalized exclusion and in colonization had grown in tandem in recent years, the author added, "Unless we are greatly deceived in this regard, the Colonization question is hereafter to be a party question, and the election of Congressmen and Presidents are to depend upon it."[87]

During this national inflection point in the long history of Black oppression in the United States, Black activists also highlighted the way in which this inflection served the interests of the colonization movement. It was quite common, as Black activists noted, for colonization proponents to cite existing and new exclusionary laws as evidence that white Americans broadly and increasingly saw Black freedom as a major societal problem. An editorial published in *Frederick Douglass' Paper* in January 1852 denounced Horace Greeley, editor of the *New York Tribune* and a major political force in the North, for this exact behavior: "He points us to the inhuman, barbarous, and unconstitutional legislation of Indiana" and "calls upon the free people of color to take the hint ... and clear out to Africa." The legislation referred to by the author was Article XIII of Indiana's new state constitution, which stated that, henceforth, "No negro or mulatto shall come into or settle in the State." It also specified that fines collected pursuant to this law would be used to fund the voluntary colonization of Indiana's existing Black residents. Article XIII had become part of the new constitution after a landslide referendum, in which more than 80 percent of those casting ballots had voted *yes*.[88]

Black activists were particularly upset with Greeley because of the wider context of his endorsement of colonization. The governor of New York had just instructed the state legislature to consider appropriating funds for the voluntary colonization of the state's Black residents, and Greeley was, in effect, putting his considerable political weight behind this instruction. Moreover, Black activists saw Greeley's endorsement of colonization as a striking betrayal. According to the editorial's author, Greeley had, for many years, manifested a "generous and manly spirit towards the Free People of color," making his recent behavior all the more concerning. In practical terms, the author advised, Black Americans must set aside past feelings and look upon Greeley, going forward, as "among the most effective and dangerous of our foes."[89]

In recent years, Frederick Douglass had made analogous declarations regarding Henry Clay. Although he did not speak of Clay with the same retrospective admiration, Douglass did note, with some appreciation, that the Kentucky politician continued to denounce the Calhounian rhetoric of perpetualism. But in Clay's unflagging promotion of colonization and, furthermore, in his staunch adherence to a belief system that deemed Black freedom a societal problem, the only viable solution for which was removal, Clay worked, quite directly and effectively, Douglass asserted, against the cause of Black civil rights in the United States. And he did so, as Greeley was now doing, under the disarming guise of benevolence and partnership. Commenting on one of Clay's last and most thorough statements on the subject of slavery, the letter that he published in 1849 in favor of gradual abolition and colonization in Kentucky, Douglass characterized its contents as an insidious "blending of good and evil ... of piety and blasphemy, of wisdom and folly." It was exactly because Clay evinced countervailing ideas, as well as countervailing tendencies, Douglass warned, that he should be viewed with particular vigilance. The very fact, Douglass continued, that he distinguished himself, in multiple ways, as being "far above the average class of slaveholders in this country" made him, from the perspective of Black Americans, "all the more dangerous and powerful for evil."[90]

As Black activists highlighted the fact that the colonization movement was fostering oppressive legislation *and* the fact that this fostering effect was, quite directly, serving the movement's political interests, they called the attention of the American public, in a wider sense, to a cycle of self-reinforcement that was inherent to the colonization movement. In effect, the movement's proponents were causing a rise in statutory oppression that they could then, in turn, cite as mounting evidence for the credibility of their assertion that Black freedom and white freedom were incongruous and their deductive claim that Black expatriation was rational, necessary, and even humane. Stated differently, colonization proponents were manufacturing evidence that they could then use to make their arguments in favor of Black expatriation more compelling. And the more compelling their arguments seemed, the more credible calls for further statutory oppression seemed to white Americans—thus completing the cycle and beginning it again with greater force.[91]

On top of all of this, there was the plain fact, Black activists pointed out, that the significant inflection in oppressive legislation and the increased popularity of colonization were causing free Black Americans to worry more and more about the tenability of their lives in the United States. How could it be otherwise, Ray indicated in his speech at the 1849 Anti-Colonization Meeting, when in every attempt free Black Americans made to "seek equal political privileges," "claim civil rights," or, in any fashion, "attempt to rise," they were confronted with the oppressive "spirit of Colonization." The author of the 1853 editorial in *Frederick Douglass' Paper* took the point further, declaring that a significant part of "the object and aim" of "Colonization measure[s]" like the Fugitive Slave Law and the exclusionary laws in Illinois and Indiana was, in fact, "to coerce the 'consent'" of free Black Americans. With this last statement, Black activists highlighted another way in which statutory oppression served the colonization movement's interests. The more concerned Black Americans became regarding their current and future living conditions in the United States, the more interest they might develop regarding the prospect of voluntary emigration. Indeed, during the years following the much-loathed and much-feared Fugitive Slave Act of 1850, the number of free Black Americans who chose to emigrate to Liberia increased substantially. Also during this time, Black Americans debated the subject of voluntary emigration more frequently and more substantively than they had in years, a trend that several leaders of the opposition movement found quite troubling.[92]

During the late 1840s and early 1850s, the new generation of Black activists also decried and sought to discredit the intertwined appeals to Unionism and patriotism being made by Clay, Webster, Stanton, and so many other colonization advocates at the time. In a formal address to the 1853 Colored National Convention, held in New York, Frederick Douglass declared—in carefully chosen words, as was his custom—that the purpose of this important gathering was "not to excite pity for ourselves, but to command respect for our cause, and to obtain justice for our people," and to do all of this "in the spirit of *patriotic* good will." Part of Douglass's intent was to take a word frequently invoked by colonization promoters, place it in a different frame, and then use it against them. Black Americans, Douglass indicated, were the ones acting *patriotically*, as they advocated publicly and peacefully for their civil rights—in stark contrast to colonization movement spokespeople, who were trying to make the specious argument that Black expatriation was an act of patriotism. In another moment of calculated wording, Douglass demanded that white Americans stop characterizing Black Americans as "enemies" of national stability and Union. "We are not malefactors," he declared, nor are we "strangers," "aliens," or "exiles." Those who made such accusations, like Congressman Stanton, who effectively blamed free Black Americans for the current sectional crisis in his speech at the ACS's 1851 annual meeting, were, Douglass contended, being both dishonest and unfair.[93]

In the midst of all of this objecting and counterarguing, Liberia's status as a new sovereign nation created complexity for the Black opposition movement. The rise in emigration interest that followed the Fugitive Slave Act of 1850 was, in fact, partly a continuation of an inflection that commenced in 1848. The ACS's 1848 annual report, published shortly after Liberia's declaration of independence, cited recent public discussions of emigration by Black Americans in Illinois and New York as evidence that Liberian nationhood was producing "a most favorable effect" among the free Black population, especially among "the more intelligent" portion. The report added, with a note of coercion layered on top of this backhanded compliment, that the very unfavorable "circumstances" that Black Americans faced in the United States in recent years would "undoubtedly hasten their decisions" to move to the "free and happy community" in Africa founded by their expatriated brethren. Shortly after the publication of this report, the *North Star* published a razor-sharp countering piece, one that condemned the ACS's use of Liberian independence as a marketing instrument without denying the contemporary rise in Black interest. Colonization advocates invoked "the high sounding title of 'Independent Republic,'" the paper declared, in order to prey "upon the vanity of those possessing more ambition than brain among the colored people of this country." The society was adding the "alluring charms of nationality, independence, wealth, dignity and station" to its baneful remarks about ineradicable prejudice in order to "threaten as well as coax" Black Americans to leave, thus making "an appeal to our 'fears as well as our hopes.'"[94]

Despite such strongly worded rhetoric, Black activists fully recognized that Liberia's declaration of independence was an event of great potential significance to Black Americans, and to the wider African diaspora. When Liberia became a sovereign nation in 1847, it established the second Black republic in the Atlantic World, along with Haiti. Articles in Douglass's newspapers during the late 1840s and early 1850s showed that growing numbers of Black Americans felt compelled to reconsider, at least partially, their former views and to acknowledge that Liberia, in its new form, might enhance white opinions of the Black race's capacity for socioeconomic elevation and political participation. Among this growing number were several outspoken critics of the ACS and the wider colonization movement, including Frederick Douglass and Henry Highland Garnet. Contrasting remarks made by the former in 1848 and 1853 illustrate the point. In 1848, Douglass mocked the new nation, claiming that it was as "dependant as ever she was" and asserting that "this new form" was mainly a ploy to boost the "spirit of Colonization" in the United States. Five years later, Douglass offered the following revised assessment: "Liberia is a fact; tho' she may not be a *fixed* fact, and while we loathe and detest the malign spirit which prompted and brought about her existence, ... we, nevertheless, rejoice in every sign of prosperity given by the young sable Republic, believing that what *men* may have meant for evil, may, under God, turn out for good."[95]

Garnet went much further than Douglass in voicing qualified appreciation for the new nation, and he did so much sooner. Garnet was only a few years older than Douglass but he had been free for much longer, which meant, among other things, that his career as a public advocate of immediatism and fierce critic of the ACS commenced several years earlier than Douglass's. Garnet's entire family had self-emancipated during the 1820s when he was still a child. After escaping enslavement in Maryland, the group settled in New York State, where Garnet studied at the African Free School, earned a degree from the Oneida Institute, and ultimately received ordination as a Presbyterian minister. In early 1849, less than a year after he sharply criticized Black Americans who expressed interest in Liberian emigration, Garnet declared, in the pages of the *North Star*, that his "mind" had "greatly changed in regard to the American Colonization scheme." He still viewed it with a healthy degree of aversion and concern, recognizing its tendency to reject the "possibility of our elevation here," but "so far as it benefits the land of my fathers, I bid it God-speed." Garnet further explained, "It is my firm and sober belief, that Liberia will become the Empire State of Africa," of great benefit to the entire continent, politically, economically, and culturally, and "for our race throughout the civilized world." Although he did not plan to emigrate himself and he did not, by any means, believe that all Black Americans should emigrate, he did feel that "every colored man who sincerely believes that he can never grow to the stature of a man in this country, ought to go there immediately, if he desires."[96]

Black leaders involved in the larger movement against slavery and for civic equality did not, for the most part, change their public opinion of Liberia or colonization as much as Garnet did. Most held views similar to those expressed by Douglass. A strongly worded letter to the *North Star*, published in early 1849, expressed strong objections to Garnet's modified view. "'The American Colonization scheme' confers very few, if any, 'blessings upon the land of our fathers,'" the author declared. While it was a fact worth appreciating that some Black Americans might become "free and grow rich" through emigration, the author admitted, the "nature and character of that 'scheme' is to be learned less from what is the condition of the Republic of Liberia, than from the abominable sayings of its President, the impenitent slaveholder, Henry Clay ... and from the general, universal, invariable false declaration of colonizationists ... that our elevation is impossible here." In effect, according to the author, Garnet was going much too far in his endorsement of Liberia and of individual acts of colonization. By speaking in such open and favorable terms, he was, the author asserted, lending significant credence to the colonization movement's exclusionary ideology, whether he intended to do so or not.[97]

Douglass had warned of this exact thing a year earlier in a brief note attached to Liberia's Declaration of Independence, which he published in one of the first issues of the *North Star*, "We must feel this land to be our home, and make our white fellow countrymen feel the same. If we fail in this, our case is hopeless; but in this we cannot fail." For Douglass and for many ardent opponents of the colonization movement, any act of Black emigration, to Liberia or elsewhere, carried the great risk of confirming, even if only implicitly, the view that white colonization advocates, for decades, had tried to impress on American legislators and the wider American public: White freedom and Black freedom were irrevocably incongruous, and so Black Americans, at some point, had to leave.[98]

The Liberian steamer project for which Stanton had twice sought congressional approval, first in the summer and early fall of 1850 and second in the early months of 1851, and that he had promised, in January 1852, to continue pursuing, faded gradually from the national political stage during the early to-mid-1850s. For at least twelve months following the second moment of failure, until well into 1852, politicians and newspapers in the North and the Upper South continued to endorse the idea. And although Stanton's early-1852 promise produced no congressional action, and little to no debate, the vision of steamships plying the waters between Liberia and the United States, carrying trade goods and passengers, continued to have political traction for a number of years. Remarks appearing in *Frederick Douglass' Paper* in 1853 and 1854 attested to this traction, as did a moment in Congress in mid-1854 when a senator from Indiana briefly pushed for an appropriation, smaller than those proposed by Stanton, that would fund an ACS-led Liberian steamship operation. At the annual meeting of the American and Foreign Anti-Slavery Society (AFASS) in the spring of 1853—an organization that had splintered from the American Anti-Slavery Society during the early 1840s, in part based on a belief that the AASS was not engaging directly enough in national politics, and that had taken numerous Black activists with it—Douglass lamented the fact that the governments of the states and of the nation were still being "called upon for appropriations to enable the Society to send us out of the country by steam!"[99]

In its gradual fading, the Liberian steamer political effort of the early 1850s most closely resembled the Land Bill campaign of the 1830s. Henry Clay had continued to pursue the Land Bill, with its funding mechanism for colonization, for several years after Jackson's 1833 pocket veto and even, to some extent, after the Senate Committee on Public Lands' rebuke in 1837. Stanton and others had acted similarly, choosing not to give up immediately following the second failure in early 1851. Both instances, however, differed markedly from colonization movement appeals to Congress made between 1827 and 1828 and then again between 1842 and 1844, which ended in formal, bookend rebukes from congressional committees, respectively delivered by Littleton Tazewell and Robert Barnwell Rhett, that sent expatriation advocates back to the strategic drawing board.

Despite this specific historical difference, the dominant reason for the failure of the Liberian steamer effort in Congress was the same that it had been in all three previous cases: states'-rights-based opposition from the South. The chief spokesman for the opposition in 1850 and again in 1851 was Abraham Venable, a Democrat from North Carolina. The Constitution, Venable declared, afforded the federal government "no power" to enact Stanton's proposal. "This whole colonization scheme," he added, "is an assumption on the part of this government to control institutions that they have nothing to do with." Venable was one of several Upper Southern politicians whose interest in colonization had been complicated by the movement's persistent efforts to obtain federal support during the politically volatile 1830s and 1840s. Venable acknowledged his past and present interest in a brief aside during his speech, claiming that he supported the prospect of transporting "the free negro population to Liberia," that he had once been a member of the ACS, and that he remained "now, as ever, its friend." Part of his intention was likely to signal to North Carolina constituents who favored colonization that he was not casting aspersions on the Jeffersonian idea that emancipation had to be connected, if and when pursued, with a plan of expatriation. A broader aim, just as likely, was a desire to signal to his constituents and to his fellow congressmen that he endorsed the national trend of free Black exclusion that had so much recent political appeal. "None of us are unacquainted with the peculiar character of that population," Venable stated. "None of us can hesitate to admit that their removal would be a blessing to the white race here."[100]

From the perspective of Black activists, and Black Americans in general, these two instances of failure did little to mitigate the anxiety they felt regarding the political traction gained by the colonization movement in recent years. As a correspondent of *Frederick Douglass' Paper* wrote in the late spring of 1852, roughly three months after the pro-steamer speeches given by Stanton and Webster at the ACS's annual meeting, it was troubling to see the spirit of "colonization or negro expatriation . . . running riot through the land," and it was equally disturbing to see "the executive and the legislature of the nation, as well as many of the states . . . encouraging the scheme." Faced with such circumstances, the correspondent advised, Black Americans must rely heavily on "faith, patience, endurance and perseverance." These, he declared, were the "weapons by which this hydra-headed monster, colonization, will be decapitated."[101]

A strong implication of such statements was that the three main political adjustments made by the movement's leading promoters during the late 1830s and 1840s—expanded arguments regarding the benefits of an Americo-Liberian alliance; increased emphasis on colonization as a Unionist political issue; and decreased emphasis on colonization's emancipatory potential (shift toward eventualism)—had enabled the movement to regain significant political strength. The key inflection point was the late 1840s, when Liberia declared its independence, thus firming the constitutional ground upon which the federal government might engage with the colonization cause, and when the national debate over enslavement, in its various facets, brought the nation to the brink of disunion. In this political environment, colonization advocates found that their adjusted rhetoric had dramatically increased resonance and potency.

Further evidence of this resonance and potency appeared in the expansion of the ACS's public roll of officers (published annually in the *African Repository*) during the early to mid-1850s. Several prominent national politicians allowed their names to be added to the list, an indication that they saw political value in associating with the colonization cause. Four of the most notable were Senator John J. Crittenden of Kentucky, Senator Stephen Douglas of Illinois, Secretary of State Edward Everett, and President Millard Fillmore. Everett gave one of the main addresses at the ACS's annual meeting in Washington in January 1853. Fillmore accepted a position as a life director of the society in the same year, an appointment that required a large donation, which was made on his behalf by a group of individuals in Washington that included current and former congressmen, Crittenden among them. Fillmore's acceptance letter, which the *African Repository* printed, affirmed the outgoing president's "decided approval of the objects of this Society" and his belief that the pursuit of such objects warranted the support of state governments and the federal government. Only with this kind of significant backing, Fillmore noted, would the society have "power adequate to the evil which it is intended to remedy."[102]

When looking backward over the preceding thirty-five years to the ACS's founding moment, the early to mid-1850s was perhaps the peak of the ACS's traction in national politics, up to this point. At a minimum, this moment closely rivaled the society's earlier moment of great traction between the late 1820s and the early 1830s. Ironically, however, this moment was also a kind of endpoint for the ACS, or, perhaps more accurately stated, a major turning point. Over the next six years, as chapter 4 shows, the colonization movement would undergo a dramatic reconfiguration. Although the reconfiguration impulse would come from the Upper South, just as it had decades earlier when the ACS was founded, and would be grounded in the same basic Jeffersonian ideology, it would also push the American Colonization Society to the political margins, where it would remain, through the Civil War, and beyond.

4

PREVENTING DISUNION

1854–1860

BETWEEN 1854 AND 1860, a major shift occurred in the political movement to make colonization a federal project. The impetus for this shift came, as usual, from the Upper South, the region that had, since Thomas Jefferson published *Notes on the State of Virginia* in 1787, shown the deepest and most consistent interest in the idea of Black expatriation. The impetus did not come, however, from within the American Colonization Society (ACS). Instead, it came from a powerful slaveholding family, one that had, over the years, said surprisingly little about colonization and that had aligned, for decades, with the Democratic Party, not the Whig Party (or its National Republican predecessor), where political interest had, since the ACS's founding, been most concentrated.

The family's patriarch and chief strategist was Francis Preston Blair Sr., former editor of the Democratic Party's Washington *Globe* and adviser to President Andrew Jackson. In partnership with his two sons—Montgomery, a prominent Washington attorney, and Francis Preston Jr., or Frank, a rising Missouri legislator—Blair orchestrated a massive effort to promote federally sponsored Black expatriation. This effort sprung from his leadership role, fairly surprising given his long history with the

Democratic Party, in the new Republican Party that formed in the aftermath of the Kansas-Nebraska Act of 1854, with opposition to slavery's further extension as its cornerstone issue. The Blairs' promotional campaign formally commenced in early 1858, when a newly elected Frank gave a speech in the House of Representatives. Over the next three years, from this moment until the presidential election of 1860, their efforts generated a level of interest in Washington for colonization that rivaled those generated by ACS-affiliated advocates during the late 1820s and early 1830s, as well as the early 1850s. Indeed, during this time several prominent Republican congressmen pushed to make the issue of colonization a formal plank of the new party's platform—the first time that a major party had considered such a move.[1]

In spearheading this late-1850s political campaign, the Blairs made a very conscious decision to work *around* the ACS instead of working *with* it. Indeed, it is fair to say that in significant ways the Blairs worked *against* the ACS. The most significant countermove was this: The Blairs rejected the eventualist rhetoric that had become increasingly prevalent among ACS-affiliated advocates since the late 1830s. In Frank's speech before the House in 1858, he advised action with respect to the institution of slavery, not inaction. "The time has ripened," he declared, "for the execution of Mr. Jefferson's plan" of "emancipation and deportation." In making such an assertion, the Blairs were, in essence, characterizing colonization as a catalyst of slavery's eradication. Effectively, they were reviving the gradualist claims made by Clay, Key, Mercer, and many other colonization proponents during the 1820s and early 1830s and supplanting the eventualist position that had become the norm, over the past twenty years, for many colonization advocates, especially those from the Upper South. Given the Blairs' desire to distance themselves from the ACS, they made no acknowledgment of these historical precedents. One of the only references they made to the colonization movement's past was to Thomas Jefferson, the ACS's ideological fountainhead. And, as will be seen, the Blairs referred to Jefferson repeatedly as they sought to gain traction for their revised colonization initiative, invoking his name, ideas, and frequently his exact words as they promoted Black expatriation under the auspices of the emergent Republican Party.[2]

Although the Blairs chose to work around and, in a sense, against the ACS, they showed, during this period of political reconfiguration in the colonization movement, that they operated on the same basic premise that had animated the movement since the ACS's founding: that white freedom and Black freedom were incongruous. The Blairs showed as well, without any doubt, that they adhered to the corollary idea, which expatriation proponents had broadcasted and elaborated for decades, that Black freedom was a serious, existential problem in American society, one that white Americans and their lawmaking representatives had a duty to address.

Black activists noted these facts with great frustration and anxiety, as well as with some disagreement as to how they should respond. In basic terms, they had to grapple with the complicated and unfortunate reality that the Blairs were pushing, with great force and perseverance, under Republican Party auspices, a political issue that they had considered, for the last forty years, to be just as much the enemy of Black Americans as the institution of slavery itself. Moreover, they had to deal with the fact that the Blairs were doing all of this at the same time that they were playing a significant role in building the first major national political party to put a firm stake in the ground against slavery's extension.

THE BLAIR FAMILY

Francis Preston Blair was born in Virginia in 1791, four years after the Constitutional Convention in Philadelphia and four years after Jefferson made public, in *Notes on the State of Virginia,* his views regarding future abolition and racial separation. Blair spent many of his formative years west of Virginia, in the newly established state of Kentucky, admitted in 1792. He graduated in 1811 from Transylvania University, which Jefferson had helped to found in 1780 and which, by the time of Blair's matriculation, counted Henry Clay as a trustee. Two years later, he married Eliza Gist, the stepdaughter of the most recent governor. Over the next decade, the couple had several children, including Montgomery in 1813 and Francis Preston Jr. (Frank) in 1821. By 1830, ambition and opportunity had carried Blair from Kentucky to Washington, from state politics into national politics. Rather than operate as an elected or appointed official, Blair wielded influence as coeditor of the Washington *Globe,* the main paper of the emerging Democratic Party. In this capacity, he had great access to and influence with President Andrew Jackson, who became a lifelong friend.[3]

Signs of Blair's future conversion from Democratic Party stalwart to Republican Party founder started to become apparent during the 1840s. Tensions with the presidential administration of James Polk prompted Blair to resign his *Globe* editorship, and associations with the rising anti-extension (free soil) movement further strained his Democratic affiliation. In 1852, he supported Democratic presidential candidate Franklin Pierce, believing that the New Hampshire man's election would counterbalance states'-rights radicalism in the party and help to sustain the sectional peace achieved, in theory at least, by the Compromise of 1850. Two years later, when Pierce signed the Kansas-Nebraska Act into law, Blair regretted having given the Democrat his support.[4]

The most provocative element of the new federal statute, in Blair's view, and in the view of most Northern politicians, was its repeal of the Missouri Compromise boundary, an east-west line drawn across the Louisiana Purchase, banning slavery in all areas to the north (except Missouri). Both newly organized territories, Kansas and Nebraska, lay above the former line. Due to the repeal, however, and other terms of the new law, residents of both territories could now legalize slavery by popular majority vote. In effect, the Kansas-Nebraska Act had reopened a huge swath of land for slaveholder settlement, ending a thirty-four-year closure that many had believed permanent.

Over the next two years, Kansas Territory became a battleground between free-state interests and slave-state interests. In Congress, the political fight centered on whether the territory's application for statehood, which various Kansans had begun preparing, would include a constitution that legalized slavery or one that prohibited it. In this tumultuous moment, as the presidential election of 1856 approached, the Whig Party disintegrated, no longer able to sustain a partisan bond between Northern and Southern politicians. Two new political parties formed in the aftermath: the short-lived American Party (Know Nothing), which itself disintegrated in the run-up to the 1860 presidential election, and the long-lived Republican Party, which has persisted to the present day.

In this period of shifting loyalties, Blair renounced his decades-long affiliation with the Democratic Party and became one of the Republican Party's few Southern founders. His collaborators in this effort came, to a large degree, from the ranks of Northern Whigs, along with a minority but nonetheless significant portion of former Democrats. The new party's main unifying issue was the anti-extension principle (free soil), the view that slavery, while constitutionally protected in the states where it currently existed, should be kept from expanding beyond its current state boundaries. Though a Southern slaveholder and a lifelong believer in the cause of states'-rights, Blair believed that the time had come to build a party dedicated to this view. The Kansas-Nebraska Act had not only overthrown a thirty-year-old compact between North and South, but it had also repealed a thirty-year-old boundary against slavery's expansion. Even worse, it implied that such expansion was acceptable and that the federal government had no right or obligation to get in its way. On both points, Blair vehemently disagreed.[5]

In editorials and pamphlets written on the Republican Party's behalf, Blair argued that the founders of the nation—especially Jefferson, whom he invoked frequently, setting an example that his sons often followed—had set an important and forward-looking precedent with the 1787 Northwest Ordinance. By banning slavery from the Old Northwest, the founders had indicated a clear preference for slavery's containment and had demonstrated the federal government's power to prevent slavery from expanding into organized territories. The Kansas-Nebraska Act constituted a willful rejection of both precedents. Blair called on Northerners and Southerners to band together in opposition to the Democratic Party's regressive agenda.[6]

One of Blair's main challenges as a Republican Party founder was to recruit fellow Upper Southerners into a party with predominantly Northern origins. To this end, he appealed directly to white voters and politicians of the Upper South who felt duped by the "treachery" of the Kansas-Nebraska Act and who regretted their complicity in the law's divisive effects but who chose to stay quiet for fear that they might "incur the imputation of deserting their own section." Blair made these appeals with urgency and force, insisting that there were a great many patriots in the Upper South who harbored these sentiments. And he expressed hope that a large portion of these like-minded individuals would band together in the next election in support of a bisectional party committed to opposing the Southern "Nullifiers," who seemed intent on either building an American "slave empire" or driving the nation toward disunion and civil war.[7]

The results of the 1856 presidential election showed that Blair's early attempts to forge a Northern–Upper Southern political coalition had failed.

Republican candidate John Fremont obtained only a handful of votes in the Upper South, zero in most states and a small number in Delaware and Maryland. The majority of voters in the region, roughly 54 percent, had cast ballots for James Buchanan, a Pennsylvanian Democrat known to be quite amicable, even deferential, to the Southern agenda. The remaining 46 percent had voted for Millard Fillmore, the former Whig president from New York who had run, in 1856, on the American Party–Know Nothing ticket. A significant portent of the Upper South's rejection of the Republican Party had appeared on the grounds of Blair's rural residence in Maryland prior to the election: the "skull and horns of an old Buck," along with an American flag, in one of his hickory trees. "The occasion of raising this trophy to Mr. Buchanan," Blair remarked, "was taken to denounce me to my neighbors as '*an arch traitor!*'"[8]

The disturbing trends that Blair had seen in the Kansas-Nebraska Act worsened during the first several months of James Buchanan's presidency, which commenced in March 1857. Not only did the new president endorse the movement to make slavery legal in Kansas, but the United States Supreme Court issued a decision in the *Dred Scott v. Sandford* case—Blair's son Montgomery was one of Scott's lawyers—that effectively ratified the Missouri Compromise's repeal. The majority opinion, written by Chief Justice Roger Taney—who was the brother-in-law of the now deceased Francis Scott Key and who had been, many years earlier, a member of an auxiliary colonization society in Maryland—asserted that slave-owning in federal territories was a constitutional right that Congress could not abridge. In effect, this opinion, in all that it said and all that it implied, swept the legal ground out from under the anti-extension principle. If Congress could not pass laws regarding the status of slavery in federal territories, then it could do nothing, or very little, to prevent slavery's extension.[9]

Taney's majority opinion had another element with which the Blairs took issue, though, to be clear, not to the same extent. The court declared that Black Americans were not, at least under the terms of the Constitution, citizens of the nation. Taney's basic argument was that nothing in the national government's originating documents indicated that the founders considered free Black Americans to be federal citizens—though he did not deny the possibility that they could become citizens of particular states. The existence of a free Black population in the country at the time of the founding was, Taney stated, entirely a consequence of enslavement, or, more specifically, the decision to import enslaved labor. In this context, it was commonplace for white Americans to consider free Black Americans to be "part of the slave population rather than the free." And it was normative for the former to feel that the latter "had no rights which the white man was bound to respect."[10]

In one of the many speeches that Frank gave as part of the Blairs' campaign in favor of Black expatriation, he called this part of the court's decision a "monstrous doctrine" that the chief justice had "interpolated into our Constitution" as part of a last-ditch attempt to "render Slavery compatible with the principles of our free government." It is worth noting, however, that the doctrine characterized as monstrous by Frank resembled, at least in basic terms, something that colonization advocates had been saying or at least implying for decades: Black freedom was a serious problem in American society, and thus it made sense that white lawmakers, for many decades, had taken actions to restrict it. While the specifics of the thought processes might differ somewhat, the message was similar: Black exclusion in the United States was a practice that was historically grounded and, from the perspective of white Americans, eminently rational. Furthermore, in a very real sense, it did not matter all that much whether colonization advocates like the Blairs criticized the *Dred Scott* decision, celebrated it, or refused to judge it. In all circumstances, they could point to it as yet another powerful indication that Black freedom and white freedom were irrevocably incongruous and that colonization was thus the best course forward for the nation.[11]

THE COLONIZATION MOVEMENT SPLINTERS

In the months following the *Dred Scott* decision, Francis Preston Blair Sr. conferred with his sons and decided that it was crucial for the three of them to spearhead a new colonization initiative on behalf of the Republican Party. The formal launch, they concluded, would take place during the early weeks of the new congressional session, with Frank, a freshman congressman, taking the promotional lead. Blair had come to believe that colonization was the key political issue that would enable the Republican

Party to draw a significant number of Upper Southerners into the fold. This belief hinged on a basic assumption about the slaveholding South, one that Jefferson had asserted in *Notes on the State of Virginia* and that ACS advocates had promulgated for decades: The process of ending slavery, however pursued, had to include a plan of Black expatriation. As Frank declared in Boston in 1859, in an address to a high-powered audience that included the current governor as well as the literary luminary Ralph Waldo Emerson, "The removal of the manumitted slaves is a *sine qua non* in every State that looks to deliverance from Slavery." As Southern slaveholders themselves—Frank and his father were current slaveholders; Montgomery had been a slaveholder until fairly recently—the Blairs insisted that they understood, as well as anyone, the depth of this Southern conviction.[12]

Given their long histories in the South, specifically the Upper South, however, the Blairs also understood something that they did not make explicit, although recent history made it fairly easy to discern. White Upper Southern legislators and voters, the main target of their Republican Party recruitment effort, tended to side with their Lower Southern counterparts in opposing, or at least indicating an unwillingness to support, any restriction on slavery's expansion. This had been the case, to a significant degree, since the Missouri debates nearly four decades earlier and, to an even greater degree, since the South's mid-1830s defensive reaction to rising "abolitionist" agitation in the North. During the congressional debates that culminated in the Compromise of 1850, for instance, Upper Southern and Lower Southern congressmen had repeatedly voted against the Wilmot Proviso with unanimity, or near-unanimity. During the 1853–54 debates over the Kansas-Nebraska Act, they voted with similar solidarity for the repeal of the Missouri Compromise, claiming, or at least indicating with their votes, that this thirty-year-old geographic restriction violated the Constitution. Then, in the 1856 presidential election, when the emergent Republican Party asserted anti-extension as one of its core issues, voters throughout the Southern states almost unanimously rejected the party's candidate. Of the roughly 1.3 million votes cast for Republican John C. Fremont, Southern voters provided fewer than 600 of them, much to the Blairs' chagrin.[13]

The Blairs were betting, in essence, that the promotion of colonization under Republican Party auspices would help white politicians and voters in the Upper South get over their opposition to slavery's restriction. But this recent history gave them significant reason for doubt. Although they knew that plenty of Upper Southern whites continued to prefer an eventualist view of slavery's future over a perpetualist one, they also knew that this eventualist view continued to be informed by a widespread belief that geographic *expansion,* not geographic *restriction,* had a key role to play in slavery's future eradication. The diffusion theory, as this belief was called, held, among other things, that geographic expansion tended to diminish the density of slaveholding and thus to diminish, over time, the extent to which slaveholding interests drove the politics of a state (or territory). Thomas Jefferson and other Upper Southern politicians had espoused this theory during the debates over Missouri's admission, decades earlier. Various Upper Southern legislators had done the same during the debates that produced the Compromise of 1850 and the Kansas-Nebraska Act. Among them was Senator Joseph Underwood of Kentucky, one of the colonization movement's most stalwart advocates in Congress, who declared, "If you permit slavery to become diffused, it will enable States that have a disposition . . . ultimately to become free States, to do so much sooner than they possibly can if you confine slaves within their present limits."[14]

But the simple fact was that the Blairs had little choice in the matter. Anti-extension was an immoveable cornerstone of the Republican Party, because it was an attitude toward slavery's future that the majority of Northern politicians and voters had gathered behind, including many who publicly supported colonization. Thus, if the Blairs were going to draw a significant number of Upper Southern politicians and voters into the Republican fold, they had to find ways to make anti-extension more palatable to Upper Southerners. One of their main tactics was to bring the political issues of anti-extension and colonization together through the vehicle of Thomas Jefferson. On the former issue, they repeatedly stressed that Jefferson had been instrumental, during the 1780s, in establishing the ordinance that banned slavery from the vast Northwest Territory and that he was thus one of the originating proponents of the anti-extension principle. On the latter issue, the Blairs made a habit of quoting, in their writings and speeches, certain remarks that Jefferson had made on the subject, especially a passage from his unfinished autobiography, which was now in broad circulation due to the publication of several edited editions of his papers. Frank invoked the autobiography passage—"Nothing is more certainly written in the book of fate, than that these people (the negroes) are to be free; nor is it less certain that the two races, equally free, cannot live in the same government"—in the opening of his germinal speech in Congress in early 1858, and on several other occasions over the next few years, as he served as the main face of the Blairs' efforts to promote Black expatriation.[15]

Such invocations had multiple purposes. There was the obvious: the fact that Jefferson's name conveyed a sense of founder-era mythos and thus burnished any cause with which it was associated. But in the Blairs' particular situation, Jefferson's name also provided a sense of Southern history and continuity for both anti-extension and colonization. This history and continuity were of particular importance to their efforts to promote the latter issue, given their decision to work around, and in certain ways against, the ACS, the organization that had been at the center of colonization politics for several decades and that had attracted considerable support, over many decades, from the Upper South. Frank announced this highly consequential decision with a pointed remark in his 1858 speech. The "efforts of the benevolent society that has labored so long in vain to form a community in Liberia, which would draw hence its kindred emancipated population, and establish a nation there to spread civilization and religion over Africa" had "failed."[16]

The Blairs differentiated their Black expatriation project from that of the ACS in three key ways, all of which dovetailed with current political trends. The first difference was geographic. The Blairs' project focused on Central and South America as a destination for free Black Americans, instead of Africa. The Blairs knew that over the last several years, following the Fugitive Slave Act of 1850 and then the *Dred Scott* decision of 1857, a small but growing minority of free Black Americans had expressed interest in the possibility of emigrating to places within the Western Hemisphere: Central America, South America, and the Caribbean. They also knew that the overwhelming majority of free Black Americans had long viewed the ACS's African-focused project with disdain and distrust. Suggestive indications of the wisdom of the Blairs' geographic differentiation came almost immediately. Two weeks after Frank's congressional address, James Theodore Holly—a rising leader in the Northern Black activist community who had, in recent years, expressed interest in Black emigration to Haiti—sent Frank a letter characterizing his speech as the commencement of "a new era." Many Black Americans, Holly predicted, "can and will easily reconcile themselves to the irresistible fate of local separation from the whites of this country, when they can locate on the same continent, within a few days sail of the scenes of their nativity," to which he added, "This can never be the case in African colonization, since by this scheme they are not only expatriated from their country, but also exiled from our Western World."[17]

The Blairs also understood that American imperialism in Latin America and in the Caribbean had become a major rallying cry for many Southern politicians, especially those interested in expanding the United States' slave-based economy and in bolstering Southern power in Congress through the addition of new slave states. Recent high-profile events such as the State Department's failed effort to acquire Cuba from Spain and William Walker's temporary conquest of Nicaragua underscored the strength of this political trend. The Blairs strongly opposed this kind of imperialism, believing it to be one among many Slave Power efforts to dictate federal policy. They hoped that by shifting the geographic focus of colonization from Africa to Latin America and the Caribbean, they might turn this imperialistic impulse away from the propagation and perpetuation of slavery and toward its ultimate eradication. As Frank explained in his 1859 speech in Boston, instead of allowing "buccaneering" types to expand this "poisonous" institution further, the national government should sponsor an effort through which Black Americans could carry the values of American government and free labor southward, into the tropical regions of the Western Hemisphere, making significant money in the process. "Are the young merchants of Boston and of America," Frank declared, "indifferent to an enterprise which would give to our commerce ... such an empire?" Furthermore, were they not intrigued by this singular opportunity to pursue economic gain in a way that granted "the inestimable blessing of liberty" to Black American while, at the same time, "removing from our midst the only cause which threatens the prosperity and stability of our Union?"[18]

The second difference was that the Blairs incorporated a relatively recent piece of race "science" into their separatist arguments, one that ACS advocates had not adopted with the same vigor. In a promotional address given in Cincinnati in late 1859, Frank warned the audience that the ongoing cohabitation of white and Black Americans would ultimately cause the two distinct races to "merge into a mongrel race, inferior to either of the original types." In making this assertion, he referred, without specific attribution, to a theory of racial hybridity that had gained traction in the United States, in recent years, due in significant part to the publications of physicians Samuel Morton and Josiah Nott. This theory, as Frank applied it, propelled the sense of urgency associated with colonization beyond that supplied by the well-worn claim regarding the inevitability of a future race war. Every moment that white Americans hesitated to support the Black race's removal, Frank indicated, was a moment in which they allowed this process of degradation to continue. Indeed, he added quite deliberately, every moment that the "system of Slavery" continued to exist in the United States was a moment in which this process gained more and more traction, given the system's "inevitable tendency" to corrupt "the blood of both races."[19]

The third main point of difference, relative to the ACS, was the fact that the Blairs characterized the establishment of a national system of Black expatriation as a catalyst of slavery's eradication, not simply a preparatory step toward that eventual outcome. In effect, they reverted to the gradualist position on slavery that colonization advocates had broadly taken during the late 1820s and early 1830s. This was quite significant and quite deliberate on the Blairs' part. It constituted a repudiation of the eventualist position that had become increasingly normative for ACS spokespeople, especially those from the South, over the last two decades. Indeed, in recent years, the leadership of the ACS had gone so far as to adopt an internal rule intended to keep society rhetoric on the subject of slavery within tight boundaries. During the ACS's 1852 annual meeting, when Stanton and Webster had stressed the Liberian steamer project's Unionist benefits, a Virginian officer of the society successfully enacted the following policy: "That the publication of schemes of emancipation, and arguments in their favor, in the *African Repository,* and other official documents of this Society, is a departure from our fundamental law, and should be excluded from such documents." This action was, in significant part, a reaction to the fact that, during the late 1840s and early 1850s, it was not uncommon for Northern colonization advocates to express support for the principle of anti-extension. Two of the most high-profile examples of this trend were

Senator William Dayton of New Jersey and Senator Thomas Corwin of Ohio, but there were many others.[20]

The Blairs viewed the Kansas-Nebraska Act as a betrayal of the spirit of Unionism and as a very worrisome indication of the Slave Power's dominance in federal politics. In this new political environment, they believed that it was counterproductive to promote colonization in this narrowed, eventualist fashion. Addressing a large audience of Republicans at a rally at the Cooper Institute in New York in early 1860, ahead of the autumn presidential election, Frank chided white Southerners for showing too much deference, in recent years, to the "latter-day" Democratic Party, which was demanding greater and greater guarantees of slavery's national sanctity, which was demanding further expansion of slavery's geography westward and southward, and which was threatening disunion if their demands went unmet. Coming from a family with ties to Virginia, Kentucky, Missouri, and Maryland, he claimed to know for certain that there were many in the Upper South who did not "look upon slavery as a good" but rather as an "evil thrust upon us," and who had no "desire to dissolve the Union" in order "to extend slavery." It was imperative, thus, in this moment of national crisis, Frank proclaimed, that freedom-loving and Union-loving Southerners align with like-minded Northerners, under the banner of the Republican Party and under the auspices of anti-extension and colonization, in pursuit of the presidency in the election of 1860.[21]

REPUBLICAN SUPPORT

From the beginning, the Blairs' efforts to promote colonization generated strikingly positive results among Northern Republicans, an important stepping stone in their effort to recruit Upper Southerners into the party. Frank's speech in the House of Representatives prompted many Northern Republicans to send letters of endorsement, and others to express personal favor in public addresses or congressional speeches. The Blairs worked to give these endorsements visibility by reprinting them in pamphlet versions of Frank's speeches. The public address that Frank gave to the Mercantile Library Association in Boston, published in 1859 under the bold heading

The Destiny of the Races of This Continent, contained a ten-page appendix devoted to just such a purpose.[22]

The roll of luminaries who endorsed the Blairs' colonization project between 1858 and 1860, or who spoke generally in favor of Black expatriation during this time, included governors, congressmen, journalists, and other Northerners of influence. Among the noteworthy were two former congressmen with past connections to the American Colonization Society. The first was Gerrit Smith, a wealthy man from western New York who vigorously supported the ACS until the mid-1830s. In the decades since, he had opposed the society with equivalent vigor, denouncing it publicly in his capacities as an affiliate of the American Anti-Slavery Society and, later, the American and Foreign Anti-Slavery Society, as well as in his role as a funder and correspondent of Frederick Douglass's various newspapers. The Blairs had mailed Smith a copy of Frank's germinal speech in the House of Representatives shortly after Frank delivered it in early 1858. Smith responded by sending two letters to Blair Sr. and one to Frank, all three of which were reprinted in the appendix to Frank's 1859 Boston speech. "Among all feasible things," Smith wrote, "there is nothing that, in my judgment, would so much promote a peaceful abolition of Slavery as your son's plan." The overwhelming majority of the "whites in the Slave states," he agreed, "would be in favor of emancipation, could an outlet for the emancipated be afforded." To these strong words of endorsement, he added two important qualifications. The Blairs should employ "no form of compulsion" in their efforts to promote colonization and they must "be careful" not to "offend the blacks, or invade their self-respect." The Blairs, in the various speeches they gave over the next two years, would only partially comply. While they consistently professed their commitment to voluntary expatriation, they nonetheless often promoted the colonization cause in ways that Black Americans found both coercive and disrespectful.[23]

The second noteworthy individual was Frederick Perry Stanton, the former Democratic representative from Tennessee who had spearheaded the Liberian steamer initiative in Congress between 1850 and 1852. During the mid-1850s, after finishing a ten-year term in Congress, Stanton had migrated northward, first to Kansas Territory and ultimately to Washington, DC. By 1860, he, like the Blairs, had left the Democratic Party for the Republican Party. In the summer of that year, while campaigning in

Missouri in support of Frank's reelection to Congress, Stanton made an affirmational connection between his earlier expatriation effort and the current one being led by the Blairs. Stanton said that he cherished "a fellow feeling" with Frank regarding the nation's racial future, one rooted in a mutual belief "in the policy of sending the free blacks to some part of Central or South America, where they can be separated and left to elevate themselves, and to relieve this country of their presence."[24]

Among currently serving congressmen, several Northern Republicans endorsed the Blairs' colonization project or spoke generally in favor of Black expatriation between 1858 and 1860. Of these, three stood out: Senators Lyman Trumbull of Illinois, Benjamin Wade of Ohio, and James Doolittle of Wisconsin. The latter, over the next ten years, would be the Blairs' chief Northern ally in Congress with respect to colonization promotion. All three men represented states formed out of the Northwest Territory, a region where the spirit of Black exclusion had been strong for many decades and where it had notably risen since the late 1840s. And all three, in the approbatory speeches they gave before Congress during 1859 and 1860, quite clearly indicated that they, like the Blairs, believed that the time had come to save the nation from Slave Power politics and that colonization had an important role to play in this saving effort. Addressing the Senate in the spring of 1860, Doolittle declared that the United States had only one "wise and practical" path forward with respect to the vexing issue of slavery: "the peaceful and gradual separation of the races, for the highest good of both"—the very same path, he emphasized, "proposed by Jefferson, [and] concurred in and sustained by Washington, and Madison, and Monroe, and Clay, and Jackson." Along this path lay the only "truly republican solution of this whole negro question." The two other potential paths, he explained, the first guided by "northern fanaticism" and the other by "southern fanaticism," were both illogical and self-destructive. The former looked to "unconditional emancipation" and racial equality, while the latter looked to slaveholding imperialism and perpetual enslavement. Ultimately, both worked against the best interests of the nation and of the white race to which it belonged.[25]

All three senators recommended that colonization become a central element of the Republican Party's agenda. Wade, in a speech to the Senate on a slavery-related resolution, urged that Black expatriation "be ingrafted into our platform as a fundamental article of our faith." Trumbull asserted that "the idea of the deportation of the free negro" should become "part of the creed of the Republican Party." In support of this assertion, he quoted several past remarks from Henry Clay in favor of colonization. And, he quoted Jefferson's famous "nothing-is-more-certain" statement from 1821, the one that the Blairs so often invoked. Colonization, Trumbull added, was not just an idea that Republicans should gather behind but also one that Northerners and Southerners should join together in supporting. On this issue, he declared, "we may come together as our fathers did of old in their struggle for independence" and, "as brothers," begin the combined work of gradually ending slavery and "relieving the country of the evils of a large free negro population."[26]

All three politicians had another reason for urging that colonization become an official party plank. As Trumbull explained it, he was sick of Democrats calling him a "Black Republican," ignoring the fact, borne out by his statements and actions, that he strongly opposed civic equality for Black Americans. Wade expressed similar sentiments, declaring that he wanted "to hear no more about negro equality." Republicans, he insisted, "shall be as glad to rid ourselves of these people, if we can do it consistently with justice, as anybody else can."[27]

The Washington, DC–based newspaper the *National Era,* which had become a primary organ of the Republican Party, published articles that bolstered these messages. This was surprising in a way and unsurprising in another. It was surprising given the fact that the newspaper had denounced the American Colonization Society in the past. But it was unsurprising given how strong the shift in favor of Black expatriation was that the Blairs had catalyzed within the Republican Party and the fact that Republican proponents were stressing expatriation's capacity to facilitate slavery's eradication. "Nine-tenths" of the Republican Party, a speech reprinted in the *National Era* in the spring of 1859 declared, supported the "colonization of the free people of color and emancipated slaves." In this respect, as in its conviction that the federal government had a right to "exclude Slavery from the Territories," the Republican Party, the article noted, was "treading in the footsteps of Thomas Jefferson" and "endeavoring to realize the dream of his life": a racially homogenous nation based entirely on free labor.[28]

PUBLIC REBUKES

In January 1859, Frederick Douglass launched a new paper: *Douglass' Monthly*. This was the third incarnation of the self-edited periodical that he had been publishing since 1847. The first had been the *North Star*, and the second had been *Frederick Douglass' Paper*, which overlapped briefly with the new paper. Over the past twelve years, both had served as primary mouthpieces in the fight against the colonization movement: the "twin-sister of slavery," as one of Douglass's writers dubbed it in the late 1840s. In the inaugural issue of *Douglass' Monthly,* Douglass made it abundantly clear that his new paper would serve the same crucial purpose: "Upon one point we wish to be especially explicit, and that is, upon no consideration do we intend that our paper shall favor any schemes of Colonization, or any measures the natural tendency of which will be to draw off the attention of the free colored people from the means of improvement and elevation here." He added, "Now, and always, we" will demand that "we are Americans; *that America is our native land; that it is our home; that we are American citizens* . . . and that it is the duty of the American people so to recognize us."[29]

In an editorial published in the third issue, which came out in March, Douglass took direct aim at the new Blair-led effort to promote Black expatriation. Referring to Frank's high-profile speech in Boston in early 1859, the one attended by former Governor Nathaniel Banks and Ralph Waldo Emerson, Douglass dismissed Frank's promotional arguments as the same "specious sophistries" that colonization advocates had put forth for decades. In essence, there was not much new to hear, and thus there was not much new for opponents to say. All of this expatriation rhetoric, he explained, derived from the "ridiculous untruth" that "the black free man and the white free man cannot live in the same territory on terms of political and economical equality." One of the main reasons for giving Frank's rhetoric any substantive attention in the paper, Douglass stated, was to highlight, in stark terms, "the hideous deformity enclosed in his apparently humane views."[30]

It was for this same basic reason that, during the late 1840s and early 1850s, Douglass had often reprinted Henry Clay's remarks on colonization, racial prejudice, and enslavement—which he had characterized as a dangerous "blending of good and evil." Douglass wanted, as mentioned in chapter 3, to prevent Black Americans from softening at all in their efforts to denounce and undermine the colonization movement. He advised eternal vigilance against the effects of exclusionary messages delivered in the guise of benevolence and partnership. One of the effects that continued to worry him was that, given the growing sense of pessimism and distress among free Black Americans, more and more individuals would view emigration as the best option for relief and self-improvement. Another deeply concerning effect was that the colonization movement's rhetoric, with its repeated claims of benevolence and fairness, would appeal to more and more white Americans. By insisting that Black Americans deserved a chance for full and equal citizenship, but only on the condition that they pursue it outside of the United States, colonization advocates offered white Americans a comforting and satisfying self-deception—one that enabled them to view expatriation, and indeed statutory acts of exclusion, as being in the best interest of the nation's Black population.

As the presidential election of 1860 approached, Douglass and other Black activists used the pages of his monthly and various other outlets to denounce the alarming number of Northern Republicans who were endorsing the Blairs' revised colonization plan and, worse still, recommending that the issue become a party plank in the upcoming presidential election. In April 1860, at a meeting in New York City's Zion Church attended by more than one thousand people, George Downing, a prominent merchant and one of the AASS's longest-standing members, criticized these Republicans for embracing, in starkly opportunistic fashion, the cause of "shipping off the negro." Their main purpose, he insisted, was to counter the "charge of being 'negro-worshippers'" or Black Republicans. One month after the meeting at Zion Church, at the American Anti-Slavery Society's annual convention, also held in New York, Robert Purvis, a wealthy Philadelphian who was also a veteran society member, blasted "Republicans leaders" for trying to make colonization part of their fundamental "creed" or, going further, insisting that it become "a plank in their platform." Purvis declared himself absolutely unwilling to support a party, even one "opposed to the extension of slavery," whose leading figures were working "to expel us from the country." This was exactly, he proclaimed, "what your Bateses and Wades, Blairs, Doolittles and Greeleys are now doing," adding, "It is the old spirit of African Colonization revived under a new name; it is the old snake with a new skin—nothing more, nothing less." Purvis spoke with particular authority on the "old spirit of African Colonization" because he, like Downing and Douglass, had fought against the colonization movement for many years at this point. Purvis had the added distinction of being the son-in-law of the now deceased James Forten, a fact he underscored by quoting from the resolutions proclaimed by Forten and others at the first anti-ACS meeting in early 1817.[31]

THE CONSTRAINED THINKING OF THE ACS

The negative impact that the Blairs' colonization project had on the ACS's traction in national politics did not go unnoticed or unmet by the institution's leaders. The impact was most significant in the North as the Whig Party, the locus of colonization politics for several decades, disintegrated. During the late 1850s, in significant part due to the success of the Blairs' rival colonization campaign, fewer Northern congressmen attended the society's annual meetings in Washington, and effectively none allowed their names to be added to the society's published list of vice presidents. Society advocates made speeches, wrote letters, and published articles in an attempt to mitigate this decline. In what they said and did, they behaved predictably. The ACS's efforts at rebuttal and defense showed a remarkable and even surprising consistency, considering the extent to which the Blairs had changed, and benefited from changing, the terms of colonization advocacy. In effect, the society was mired in its own past, constrained by views that limited the range of its response.[32]

Constrained thinking was on full display at the ACS's 1858 annual meeting, held at Trinity Church in Washington, less than a week after Frank Blair's inaugural colonization speech in Congress. ACS leaders, despite their fervent and unshakeable commitment to the larger cause of racial separation, remained unwilling to consider any emigration destination other than Africa. The money and energy invested in Liberia over the years, combined with the pride associated with what had been accomplished, undoubtedly contributed to this unwillingness, as did the fact that the ACS still had an informal partnership with the federal government to return "recaptured slaves" to the continent. But the preference for Africa also had deep religious roots, as Reverend Robert Finley had indicated in his 1816 pamphlet and as ACS advocates had reinforced throughout the intervening years. Reverend Phillip Slaughter of Virginia, an officer of the society, repeated this rationale in a speech that he gave during the 1858 meeting. God intended for Black Americans to return to Africa for the great and noble cause of transmitting civilization and Christianity. The implication of this claim was just as striking as it had been when Finley had made it forty-two years earlier: God had, in effect, conceived the Atlantic slave trade and the institution of slavery in North America as instruments of racial uplift. "This is a great mystery which I cannot expound," Slaughter admitted, echoing a qualification that Finley had made in his pamphlet. "I can only see that what men mean for evil . . . God often means for good." Thus, as Slaughter further explained, the ACS's preference for African colonization should not be understood as indicating opposition to the prospect of geographic and commercial expansion in Latin America. It was, rather, an expression of their firm conviction that Black Americans had no role to play in these expansionary efforts.[33]

Over the course of his speech, Slaughter showed another element of institutional constraint. Many ACS leaders continued to adhere to the eventualist view of slavery's future that had become increasingly dominant within the colonization movement, especially its Southern wing, over the last two decades. "Time is a necessary element in human progress," Slaughter declared. "What is of long growth is of slow decay, and the inveterate evils of many ages cannot be eradicated within the hour-glass of one man's life." The effective message was this: If God created slavery as a vehicle for bringing civilization and Christianity to Africa, then the ACS and its supporters could rest assured that slavery would eventually end, and that free (and freed) Black Americans would eventually leave American shores and resettle on their ancestral soil. Slaughter, it is worth noting, was the prime mover behind the resolution, adopted by ACS leaders in 1852, to ban emancipation-related remarks from the society's publications.[34]

In conjunction with their persistent adherence to eventualism, which remained rooted in concerns about alienating Southern supporters, ACS leaders also continued to avoid the subject of slavery almost entirely, allowing themselves only oblique and highly qualified references to the subject, as exemplified in Slaughter's above remark. Another example can be found in the text of a speech given by the society's president, John Latrobe, in January 1859, a few days before Frank Blair delivered his high-profile colonization speech in Boston. Latrobe, a Maryland lawyer who had been involved with the colonization movement since the 1820s, had served as the president of the Maryland Colonization Society for many years before, during the early 1850s, replacing Henry Clay as president of the ACS. His early 1859 speech, which occurred at the ACS's annual meeting held at the Smithsonian Institute in Washington, was the effective launch of a speaking tour that was meant, at least in part, to rival the Blairs' promotional efforts. By August of that year, he had delivered the same speech or variations of it to audiences in Virginia, New York, New Jersey, Pennsylvania, and Ohio. Although Latrobe tried to give African colonization a fresh political varnish by invoking the zeitgeist of American expansion—"we look forward to the future of Liberia, as we do to the future of California and Oregon"—and by claiming, based on a mix of data and anecdotes, that opportunities in Africa for building national wealth were as attractive as ever, he made no mention at all of slavery, or of the society's original, now quite latent, aim of using colonization to encourage individual manumissions and to facilitate slavery's eventual abolition. Instead, he recapitulated the standard elements of the ACS pitch—Liberia as a beachhead for slave trade suppression, missionary efforts, and commercial investment—and tied them all together with the society's standard disarming refrain: "Colonization concerns itself with the free alone."[35]

Saying the same things that the society's advocates had been saying for years did not prove an effective rebuttal strategy for the ACS. Over the course of 1859 and throughout 1860, as the Blairs drew more and more prominent politicians to their Central American colonization project, political interest in the ACS and African colonization declined further. ACS leaders, especially those formally responsible for raising funds and establishing new auxiliary societies, noted the mounting number of Blair endorsements with concern and frustration. In March 1860, the society's traveling secretary wrote an open letter to the *Ohio State Journal* in response to an endorsement he had seen, printed in the pages of the paper, from Governor William Dennison of Ohio. The agent took umbrage at the fact that the governor had "seen fit . . . to endorse the proposition" for Black colonization "on this side of the Atlantic." Beyond concern and frustration, the letter also carried an undertone of embarrassment. For decades, Ohio, and the states of the Lower North generally, had been sites of significant support for the ACS. Now, prominent state and federal politicians from the region were coming out in force for the Blairs' rival plan.[36]

Despite the poor state of its political appeal, the ACS actually managed to obtain $325,000 in federal money during 1859 and 1860. However, this success, which came in the form of two separate congressional enactments, indicated no positive trend for African colonization in national politics. Instead, it signaled a continuation of a decades-old relationship between the ACS and the federal government for the resettlement of "recaptured slaves." In recent years, the United States Navy had bolstered its slave trade suppression efforts in the Atlantic. Inevitably, such stepped-up efforts brought numerous "recaptured slaves" into the temporary care of American naval officers and, under the terms of the 1819 Slave Trade Act, the president of the United States. During 1859 and 1860, alone, the US Navy seized more than two thousand Africans as part of its Atlantic Ocean patrols. President James Buchanan followed the precedent of past executives, notably Monroe and Fillmore, and looked to the ACS for aid. Congress supported him by appropriating $325,000 for the settlement and temporary support of the seized individuals in Liberia.[37]

The two laws passed to effect this appropriation, however, did not signal any change of attitude in Congress with respect to the ACS, a fact underscored by Senator Henry Wilson in reply to certain objections from Lower Southern Democrats, always on the lookout for ways in which federal support for such actions might threaten slavery. The longtime free soiler from Massachusetts, who was by no means an avid supporter of colonization, declared that the question before the Senate was whether to reimburse the ACS, an organization he was "not disposed to defend," for a "bargain" struck with it by the president of the United States: "For myself, I see in the law of 1819 enough to authorize the President to make this bargain; and my own heart impels me to give it a prompt and decisive vote." Most in Congress viewed the $325,000 appropriation in the same legal light, allowing the 1859 and 1860 bills to pass both houses with considerable majorities and to become law under Buchanan's signature.[38]

One might expect that the ACS and its auxiliaries would have tried to capitalize on this bit of momentum by reviving the practice of memorializing Congress, or the tactic of using congressional allies to put aid bills, like the 1850 Liberian steamship proposal, before the national legislature. One might also expect that, faced with such a mighty challenge from the Blairs for national attention, ACS leaders might have mounted a more vigorous defense and might have tried to revise their political message to more closely match that of the Blairs. Part of the reason for the ACS's limited response was the fact that the society's stable of political allies had shrunk, and not just because of its declining appeal in the North. Many of the society's most prominent federal advocates had died, Henry Clay, Charles Fenton Mercer, and Francis Scott Key foremost among them. Compounding the effect of individual mortality was the Whig Party's demise. But there was another reason as well, more intentional in nature than circumstantial. Many of the ACS's leaders and remaining sympathizers believed that the highly sensitive political moment, one in which Lower Southern cries of disunion were gathering volume, called for caution, moderation, and, in a sense, quiet on all slavery-related issues, in the hope that the purportedly halcyon years following the Compromise of 1850, the years in which both parties and both sections had declared themselves committed to the Union above all, might return. Engaging in loud and conflictive debate with the Blairs and their mounting cadre of Central American colonization supporters would have run counter to this sentiment.

In a very real sense, then, the ACS's political marginalization between 1858 and 1860 was the result not just of what the Blairs did but also of what society leaders felt they could not do.

ELECTION OF 1860

The presidential election of 1860 was the moment that the Blairs had had in their sights since 1856, when the Republican Party's first foray into electoral politics had produced dismal results in the Upper South. Prior to the 1860 Republican national convention, the Blairs and their allies organized state Republican conventions in Missouri and in Maryland. Frank took primary responsibility for the former, while Blair Sr. and Montgomery focused on the latter. The resolutions of both conventions, unsurprisingly given Upper Southern preferences and the Blairs' direct influence, voiced strong support for colonization as a formal Republican Party issue.[39]

At the Maryland convention, Montgomery sought to reinforce the party's connection to Black expatriation by connecting the issue with another major Republican project: the Homestead Act, a bill currently before Congress that sought to encourage and facilitate increased settlement in the nation's vast Western territories. Two of the Republican Party's defining causes, Montgomery declared, were "the homestead law," which would "prevent the Africanization of the Territories, by giving them as homesteads to the free white race," and the "plan of procuring, in some neighboring country, a region where the free people among us of the African race may also, in accordance with the wise and humane counsels of Mr. Jefferson, be given homesteads and a country of their own." The goal of these carefully worded remarks was not just to underscore, for Upper Southern ears, how thoroughly colonization had been incorporated into the party's creed but also to rebut ongoing race-baiting attacks. Strong and clear party support for these two causes, Montgomery proclaimed, "will silence the false clamor against us, that we maintain the equality of the negro, and favor amalgamation." While such clamor had succeeded in fomenting opposition against the Republican Party in the past, it would no longer, Montgomery claimed, have the same effect, since the Republican Party had made clear that it hewed to "the Jeffersonian plan of separating the races."[40]

At the Republican national convention, held in Chicago in May 1860, the Blairs initially pushed for a presidential nominee from the Upper South, believing such geographical affiliation to be essential to the aim of generating Republican votes among Upper Southern whites. Their preferred candidate was Edward Bates of Missouri. In addition to his credentials as a player in national politics—during the 1820s, Bates had served as a United States district attorney and in the House of Representatives, and then, in 1850, President Millard Fillmore had offered him the position of secretary of war, which he declined—Bates was a long-standing ally of the Blairs, and unlike many Upper Southern politicians, he was willing to stand, publicly, for free soil *and* Black expatriation. Bates had made both stances explicit in an open letter written in March 1860 and subsequently published in various Missouri newspapers. In this letter, he made sure to note that, although "for many years" he had supported the ACS's project of removing Black Americans to Africa, he now favored the "tropical regions of America" as a destination. This revised plan of colonization, he stated, was "a far better prospect both for us and for them."[41]

Ultimately, the Republican national convention, after many nominating ballots, chose Illinois politician Abraham Lincoln as its presidential candidate. The Blairs quickly shifted their support to Lincoln and became some of his most fervent proponents over the coming months. They did so not just because they were, at least for the time being, party loyalists but also because he suited their Upper Southern recruitment agenda in at least two ways. First, Lincoln had been born in the Upper South, Kentucky specifically, and had married into a slaveholding family from that state. Second, in addition to being an avowed anti-extensionist, Lincoln had, during the 1850s, stated on several occasions that he preferred that slavery come to an end in combination with some form of Black expatriation. In a public eulogy for Henry Clay, his political idol, given in Illinois's state capital in 1852, Lincoln had praised Clay's perseverant role as a colonization advocate and had declared, "If as the friends of colonization hope, the present and coming generations of our countrymen shall by any means, succeed in freeing our land from the dangerous presence of slavery; and, at the same time, in restoring a captive people to their long-lost fatherland . . . it will indeed be a glorious consummation." More recently, in 1857, in one of many heated engagements with Stephen Douglass, his chief rival in Illinois politics, Lincoln had expressed pride in the fact that "a very large proportion" of the Republican Party's members favor the "separation of the races." He then added the following remark: Although the project of colonization, when ultimately pursued, would be challenging, "'when there is a will there is a way;' and what colonization needs most is a hearty will."[42]

In late February 1860, Lincoln, then still a prospective candidate for nomination, had affirmed these sentiments when he addressed an audience gathered at the Cooper Union for the Advancement of Science and Art. The venue was the same one that Frank Blair had used one month earlier to deliver one of his many speeches in favor of the Republican Party and Black expatriation. It was also the same venue that Robert Purvis used later that spring to denounce the Republican Party's escalating support for this political issue. Lincoln made this affirmation, as the Blairs so often did, using Jefferson as his rhetorical authority: "It is still in our power to direct the process of emancipation, and deportation, peaceably, and in such slow degrees, as that the evil will wear off insensibly; and their places be, *pari passu*, filled up by free white laborers"—a direct quotation from Jefferson's unfinished autobiography, the same source that contained the "nothing is more certain" quotation habitually invoked by the Blairs.[43]

Lincoln received the Republican Party's nomination for president of the United States a few months after his Cooper Union address. By late fall, when the election took place, he had three opponents: two from the Democratic Party, which had splintered along sectional lines, and one from the Constitutional Union Party. The candidate of the Southern Democratic Party was John C. Breckinridge, a Kentuckian who had served, since 1857, as James Buchanan's vice president. Breckinridge's Democratic rival was Stephen Douglas, the Illinois senator who had shepherded the controversial Kansas-Nebraska Act through Congress in 1854, and who, in recent years, had redeemed his reputation in the eyes of many Northerners by opposing the Lecompton movement that sought to legalize enslavement in Kansas. The newly formed Constitutional Union Party ran Tennessean John Bell, a former Whig, as its presidential candidate. Nearly sixty-five at the time, roughly fifteen years older than the next-oldest candidate (Lincoln), Bell had served in Congress for most of the last three decades, commencing his first term in the House in 1827. In 1854, he had gained the distinction of being one of the only senators from the South to vote against the Kansas-Nebraska Act. Generally speaking, Bell's party platform decried sectional conflict and favored a revival, in some form, of the Unionist detente that had prevailed during the years following the Compromise of 1850. Bell's vice-presidential running mate was Edward Everett, who had served briefly during the Fillmore administration as secretary of state. The Constitutional Union Party's position most closely resembled that evinced by ACS leaders during the 1850s, which emphasized nonintervention, eventualism, and Unionism. Indeed, both Bell and Everett were known ACS affiliates. Bell's affiliation was fairly recent, commencing in the mid-1850s. Everett's association with the ACS stretched back roughly thirty years.[44]

Lincoln and the Republican Party won the 1860 election by a large margin. Lincoln garnered nearly 1.9 million votes, compared to roughly 1.4 million for Douglas, 850,000 for Breckinridge, and 590,000 for Bell. The result seemed to be a powerful mandate for the Republicans, and indeed it was, in a sense. In electoral college voting, Lincoln had taken eighteen out of thirty-three states, suggesting wide support for the party's most prominent plank, restricting the spread of slavery. But from the Blairs' perspective, there was great cause for concern. All of Lincoln's electoral college votes had come from the North. None had come from the Upper South. Furthermore, in the Upper South, the target of their multiyear campaign to make colonization a central issue of the Republican Party, three out of seven states—North Carolina, Delaware, and, to their great dismay, Maryland—had gone for Breckinridge, the candidate most closely associated with perpetualist views of slavery's future. Missouri, the Blairs' other home state, went to Stephen Douglas, with the remaining three—Kentucky, Virginia, and Tennessee—going to the Constitutional Union candidate, John Bell. In aggregate, Lincoln and the Republican Party attracted fewer than 30,000 votes across the seven-state region. Clearly, the Blairs' vigorous effort to use colonization as a lever to draw Upper Southern voters into the Republican fold had failed, an ominous portent given their professed belief that a bisectional Republican Party was needed in order to avoid civil war.

Frederick Douglass had mixed feelings about the Republican Party, both as the election of 1860 approached and after Lincoln won the election late that year. He expressed these sentiments in a series of articles in *Douglass' Monthly*, published between June and December. On the one hand, while he understood and appreciated why fellow activists like George Downing and Robert Purvis refused to support the party—indeed, Douglass himself did not vote for Lincoln—he looked with a measured sense of optimism at the fact that a major national party had finally adopted a plank against slavery. After the Chicago national convention in May, Douglass remarked that while he would have much preferred the Republican Party to have "committed to the doctrine of 'All rights to all men,'" he nonetheless wished it success in the coming election. In December, after word came down that Lincoln had triumphed, Douglass celebrated that a man of *"anti-slavery reputation"* was, for the first time in American history, going to hold the nation's highest elected office. Not only did this signal a dramatic shift in the North's attitude toward slavery, but it also showed that Northern voters had the willingness and the strength to overpower the "haughty and imperious slave oligarchy," even when faced with threats of "disunion."[45]

On the other hand, Douglass acknowledged the dispiriting fact that, over the last two years, many Republican leaders had endorsed colonization on the floors of Congress and in other high-profile venues, and that they had done so, in many cases, with rhetorical alacrity. Frank and Montgomery Blair first and foremost, but also Senators Trumbull, Wade, and Doolittle, as well as Horace Greeley, the editor of the Republican *New York Daily Tribune,* and the editors of the Republican *National Era* had all pushed to make colonization one of the party's central causes. Although the Blairs' attempt to make colonization a *formal* plank of the Republican Party had ultimately failed—the national convention in May 1860, with little debate, had chosen against such a course—their three-year promotional effort had clearly succeeded in creating a sense of connection between the Republican Party and this much-loathed issue and in giving renewed vigor to the idea that Black expatriation had a significant role to play in bringing slavery to an end.

In articles that he published before and after the election, Douglass tried to downplay the future significance of this trend to his readers. Generally speaking, he chose not to call out, by name, the Blairs or the many other Republican leaders who had publicly endorsed Black expatriation. He also avoided documenting and rebutting the many speeches given by these individuals in promoting the issue. Instead, he spoke in general terms about the recent tendency of Republican leaders to offer "miserable concessions to popular prejudice" in pursuit of political success, the implication being that their exclusionary rhetoric was motivated more by tactics, chosen for the particular moment, than actual belief. And he expressed confidence, or at least hope, that this trend—fueled, he suggested, by a minority cohort—would not guide the party's future strategy. "I certainly look to that party for a nobler policy than that avowed by some connected with the Republican organization," he declared. "Surely," he added, one could reasonably expect that Republican leaders would "not fall into the mistake or the crime of competing with the old parties in the old worn out business of feeding popular malignity, by acts of discrimination against the free colored people of the United States."[46]

5

ENDING THE CIVIL WAR

1861–1865

IN DECEMBER 1862, ROUGHLY TWENTY months after the Civil War began, President Abraham Lincoln sent his second annual message to Congress. In it, he proposed three constitutional amendments that he hoped would provide a framework for abolishing slavery throughout the nation, in the four Border States that had remained in the United States and in the eleven states that had seceded to form the Confederacy. The first amendment offered federal compensation to any slave-state government that completed a plan of gradual abolition by January 1, 1900. Compensation would be determined by multiplying the number of enslaved people living in each state, as recorded in the 1860 census, by some to-be-determined per capita dollar amount. The second amendment declared that all enslaved Americans who had gained their freedom during the course of the war would be "forever free." And the third amendment authorized Congress to "appropriate money" for "colonizing free colored persons with their own consent" outside the United States.[1]

The justifications for recommending such a course to the nation and, in particular, to the fifteen slave states should, by this point in the war, Lincoln declared, be clear to all. The "rebellion" would not have commenced without the existence of slavery in the United States. It stood to reason, therefore, that "without slavery it could not continue." Beginning the process of abolishing this institution, he indicated, was therefore the key to ending the war and to restoring the Union. Moreover, it was the course of action that would save an enormous number of American lives and that would save the tremendous cost of many more years of large-scale combat. There were many in the slave states, most notably the advocates of perpetual slavery, who would offer a range of objections to what he recommended, Lincoln acknowledged, but to them he posed a simple, preemptive question: "Can we do better?"[2]

As part of his justificatory remarks, Lincoln offered commentary on the proposed colonization amendment, and on the larger issue of the future of Black Americans in the United States. "I can not make it better known than it already is that I strongly favor colonization," Lincoln summarily declared. To this strong endorsement, he added two main qualifications. First, all decisions to emigrate must be voluntary. Second, despite his strong desire to facilitate Black expatriation on a large scale, this position, he insisted, did not stem from a desire to appease white Northerners' anxiety that emancipation would cause "freed" Black Americans to "swarm forth and cover the whole land." "Why should emancipation [in the] South send the freed people North," he queried, since the main reason Black Americans had "fled North" in the past was their enslaved condition. "In any event," Lincoln concluded, even if such a migration did commence, "can not the North decide for itself whether to receive them?"[3]

Earlier in his message, Lincoln had made a few relevant remarks on colonization as well. "Applications have been made to me by many free Americans of African descent to favor their emigration," he stated. Although for the time being, many of those expressing interest, he explained, seemed opposed to emigrating to Liberia or Haiti, the two countries most open to accepting them as "citizens," Black American interest in voluntary colonization, he noted, seemed to be "improving." Indeed, he added, it would not be "long" before "an augmented and considerable migration to both these countries" began in the United States.[4]

Looking back at the long eighty-year history of the colonization movement, the year 1862 was the effective high point of the long effort to obtain federal support. Between March and December of that year, Congress legislated the first of only two major appropriations for Black expatriation in American history; a House select committee that Frank Blair served on recommended $200 million in federal funds for the emancipation and expatriation of the enslaved populations of the Border States; and the federal government formally recognized the nations of Liberia and Haiti, after refusing for many years to do so. And then in December 1862, Lincoln asked Congress and the American people to amend the Constitution such that each slave state could, with the aid of significant federal funds, abolish slavery in a way that was similar—though not identical, as will be shown—to the approach that colonization advocates had pushed for decades, and that Thomas Jefferson had recommended almost eighty years ago.

The Blairs had played a very significant role in making this high-point moment happen. From the time Lincoln took office, they had been three of his closest and most influential advisers, and they had pushed the issue of colonization with great fervor since the start of the Civil War. Montgomery was the closest in proximity, serving as a member of Lincoln's cabinet. Frank was in Congress representing Missouri, one of four slaveholding states that remained in the Union. And Blair Sr., who split his time between homes in Maryland and Washington, DC, was a frequent correspondent and visitor of the president, doling out advice, as had been his custom for years, from behind the scenes.

Ultimately, however, the Blairs' fervent efforts to ensure that the federal government abolished slavery in the way that they insisted was crucial to the nation's future stability and prosperity failed, despite the momentous events of 1862. In early 1865, Congress passed a joint resolution endorsing the Thirteenth Amendment, which, when ratified by the requisite number of states later that year, abolished slavery immediately across the United States, with no provision for or even mention of Black expatriation. The turning point, in fact, was Lincoln's message to Congress in December 1862. During the twelve months that followed, especially after March 1863, the colonization movement precipitously lost traction in national politics. This chapter tells the story of how and why an unprecedented window of political viability opened for the colonization movement during the first part of the Civil War and then closed shut—never to reopen, despite further attempts by the Blairs and others—during the Civil War's final years.

THE BLAIRS AND LINCOLN

Up until the colonization movement's moment of political reversal in 1863, the Blairs were three of President Lincoln's most trusted and influential advisers. The Blairs had initially come to know Lincoln through Frank, whose Upper Southern state of Missouri shared a border with Lincoln's Lower Northern state of Illinois. During the late 1850s, Lincoln and Frank had crossed paths numerous times. As leading figures of the Republican Party in the region, the two moved in political orbits with significant overlap. In 1858, each had supported the other's effort to secure a seat in the Thirty-Sixth Congress (March 1859 to March 1861): Lincoln going for the Senate against incumbent Stephen Douglas, and Frank seeking a second term in the House. Around this time, Lincoln had also helped make the *Missouri Democrat,* a Republican Party paper founded by Frank and his cousin B. Gratz Brown in St. Louis, the official mouthpiece of the party in Illinois. In late 1860, after vigorous effort on the part of all three Blairs to get Lincoln elected as president, the family's relationship with him strengthened. With some friendly prodding from Blair Sr., prodding that Lincoln did not yet mind, Lincoln appointed Montgomery to one of his seven cabinet posts, that of postmaster general. By this time, Frank was back in Washington, having regained the Missouri seat in the House of Representatives that he had lost in the 1858 election. Blair Sr. mainly resided, during the Civil War years, in Silver Spring, Maryland, roughly ten miles north of the nation's capital, more than close enough for him to make frequent trips into Washington to talk political strategy with his sons and with Lincoln.[5]

The Blairs saw in Lincoln, in his background and his political beliefs, a great deal of common ground. Lincoln was born in 1809 in the slave state of Kentucky, in an area of farmland roughly one hundred miles southwest of the Lexington–Frankfort area where Montgomery and Frank were born in 1813 and 1821, respectively. When Lincoln was roughly seven years old, he and his family moved to the free territory (soon-to-be free state) of Indiana, joining with the many others who migrated around this time from the Upper South to the Lower North. Around 1830, the Lincoln family moved westward into Illinois, the state that Abraham Lincoln would call home for the rest of his life. Roughly twelve years later, Lincoln married a woman from Kentucky, Mary Todd, whose family had considerable wealth in land and in enslaved people. As an Illinois lawyer, a state legislator from 1834 to 1842, and a congressman from 1847 to 1849, Lincoln absorbed and evinced the views on enslavement and Black–white relations that many in this border region, especially those with Upper Southern roots, had long held—views commonly associated with Thomas Jefferson.[6]

From the moment the first shots were fired in the Civil War, all four men understood that prolonged military conflict would undermine slavery's institutional strength in the United States—at a minimum due to the trend of self-emancipation that was certain to arise, as it had during the Revolutionary War and the War of 1812—and would open up new legal avenues through which the institution might be diminished or abolished altogether. Furthermore, all four men had indicated, in various statements before the war, that they viewed slavery as an institution that should and would come to an end. The nation's future stability and progress, they claimed, depended on slavery's eradication. The Blairs, Frank especially, had conveyed these sentiments repeatedly as they had pushed to make Black expatriation a central political issue for the Republican Party. Lincoln had conveyed them repeatedly as well, notably when he asserted in high-profile speeches in 1858 and 1860 that the nation "cannot endure, permanently half slave and half free" and when he proclaimed that "slavery is wrong" and that a large portion of the nation shared this conviction.[7]

Lincoln and the Blairs also understood that the secession of eleven slave states had radically changed the composition of Congress, thus, in effect, combining the broadened span of legal options with a significant expansion in the range of what was politically viable to pursue. This compound effect fundamentally altered the political environment in Washington regarding slavery in all its facets, including the subject of Black expatriation. At the end of 1861, nineteen Northern states had representation in Congress at a time when only six Southern states had a congressional presence—the four Border States of Maryland, Kentucky, Missouri, and Delaware, as well as the seceded states of Virginia and Tennessee, which continued to send a handful of Unionists to Washington. In effect, the power of free-state interests over slave-state interests in Congress was overwhelming and without precedent.

A letter from Blair Sr. to President Lincoln in November 1861 illuminated what he hoped, and what he trusted Lincoln hoped as well, might be accomplished in this moment of expanded possibilities. The federal government should take actions to facilitate "the gradual removal of Slavery from the Seceding States of the Union" and, by implication, the four remaining Border States. "There can never be peace or union, within our national confines while the principles of Liberty and Slavery remain here to confront each other." As he closed the letter, he highlighted the necessity of combining colonization with abolition. "The period has come which Mr. Jefferson saw would arrive, rendering the deportation or extermination of the African Race from among us, inevitable."[8]

For the time being, and for at least the next thirteen months, Lincoln largely agreed. Indeed, by this point, Lincoln and the Blairs were already working behind the scenes on at least one potential destination for prospective emigrants, a region of Colombia that an American business, the Chiriqui Improvement Company, had been working to develop for the past few years. Other federal officials involved in this effort were Secretary of the Interior Caleb Blood Smith and Senator Samuel Pomeroy of Kansas.[9]

The new administration's most significant early move against enslavement occurred during the summer of 1861 with the enactment of what became known as the First Confiscation Act. The new law, which Frank had voted for in the House and which Lincoln had promptly signed, dictated a formal policy for dealing with self-emancipated individuals who sought refuge with the Union army, as several hundred individuals had already done during the first months of the Civil War. In basic terms, the statute authorized the Union army to emancipate enslaved Americans forced to labor on behalf of the Confederate army. More broadly and consequentially, it established a direct connection between waging war and emancipating enslaved people. The First Confiscation Act made it clear that Lincoln and Congress believed that wartime emancipations should be irreversible. Although in establishing this particular stance, neither Lincoln nor Congress was yet insisting that slavery throughout the Confederate states and the Border States must, during the course of war, come to an end, both were signaling comfort with the prospect of slavery contracting as a result of the war.[10]

An important issue raised by the First Confiscation Act was the question of what the federal government should do with Black Americans who liberated themselves under the auspices of the law. This question had come up during the debates in Congress over the summer, and, in December

1861, Lincoln gave the question direct attention in his first annual message to Congress. The federal government, Lincoln observed, had a duty to ensure that these freed people, who were under the protection of the Union army, were "provided for in some way." On this point, he suggested the prospect of a federally sponsored project that would offer, to those who desired it, the opportunity to leave the United States. Such a project, Lincoln maintained, was justified by both legal precedents and current circumstances. On the question of whether the federal government had the "constitutional power" to acquire foreign territory, Lincoln claimed that "Mr. Jefferson" had resolved this issue decades earlier with the Louisiana Purchase, when he had "yielded his [legal] scruples on the plea of great expediency." On the question of whether the government had the power to appropriate money for colonization, a more ambiguous legal matter, Lincoln remarked, "Does not the expediency amount to absolute necessity?" To these remarks, Lincoln suggestively added that this political issue might, in the near future, become even more timely and significant due to prospective "enactments" by various states and that "it might be well to consider, too, whether the free colored people already in the United States could not, so far as individuals may desire, be included in such colonization."[11]

With these carefully chosen words, Lincoln signaled three things. First, he wanted Border State legislatures to consider whether they would be willing to pursue gradual abolition if the federal government showed that it was willing to support colonization. Second, he wanted free Black Americans to consider whether they might, in light of such potential support, have greater interest in leaving the country, on a voluntary basis. Third, Lincoln was communicating an expectation to Congress. During the current session, he expected the nation's legislature to consider doing what it had consistently refused to do over the past thirty-five years: mobilize the resources of the federal government in support of a national effort to expatriate Black Americans.

EMANCIPATORY MOVES

The high point of the colonization movement's eight-decade effort to obtain federal support began in the spring of 1862 and persisted for roughly a year. In order to understand how and why this singular political moment occurred, it is helpful to view it through the lens of enslavement's three legal geographies. This was the lens employed by Lincoln, the Blairs, and the overwhelming majority of Republican Party congressmen and cabinet members during the many debates over slavery during the Civil War.[12]

The first legal geography was composed of the Western territories and the District of Columbia. According to Republican Party principles, this collective region fell under the jurisdiction of the federal government and thus was a place where Congress could legislate slavery's future. During the first several months of 1862, the Republican-dominated Congress, with Lincoln's full support, passed two laws that abolished slavery across this entire geography. Relatively speaking, these were the least surprising of the emancipatory moves made by Congress and Lincoln during this inflective year, since both had been attempted with the support of many congressmen (including Lincoln) during the late-1840s debates that had preceded the Compromise of 1850. Nonetheless, they were quite significant because they signaled what Congress and Lincoln could accomplish armed with the huge majority of Republican votes afforded to them by the secession of eleven Southern states.

The law that abolished slavery in the nation's capital, enacted in April 1862, sent another signal as well, one that was quite important to the Blairs and to Lincoln given emancipatory moves that they were contemplating in the two other legal geographies. The DC Abolition Act contained a $100,000 appropriation for voluntary colonization, the first significant federal appropriation for Black expatriation in American history. Republican James Doolittle of Wisconsin, the Blairs' close political ally, had proposed the appropriation as an amendment to the bill during the floor debate in the Senate. In offering his reasons for pressing the amendment, Doolittle delivered a speech replete with Jefferson references: "When we accept the solution of Jefferson, which falls neither into the fanaticism of the one nor the blindness of the other, we shall then see the beginning of the end of that irrepressible conflict, more of race than of condition, which has disturbed us so long." He added: "Until it be solved, there can be no permanent peace."[13]

Nearly 70 percent of Northern Republicans voted in favor of adding Doolittle's appropriation to the final bill, a public indication that the Republican Congress was willing, at least for the time being, to earmark federal funds for voluntary colonization when those funds were part of a legislative move against slavery. Lincoln validated this indication when he returned the signed bill to Congress. In a congratulatory note highlighting the law's historical significance and suggesting its prospective relevance as a legal precedent, Lincoln declared, "I am gratified that the two principles of compensation, and colonization, are both recognized, and practically applied in the Act." In addition to the $100,000 expatriation appropriation, the bill had set aside roughly $1 million to compensate each slaveholder, roughly $300 per emancipated individual.[14]

The second legal geography consisted of the eleven slave states that had seceded to form the Confederacy, thus placing themselves on wartime footing in terms of constitutional law. The most important and consequential move against enslavement in this region had begun during the summer of 1861 with the passage of the First Confiscation Act. In July 1862, Lincoln and Congress bolstered this emancipatory policy by enacting a more expansive Second Confiscation Act, which authorized the Union army to emancipate a larger portion of enslaved people living in the Confederate states. In conjunction with this law, Congress made a second appropriation for colonization, in the amount of $500,000. For the second time in a matter of months, the Republican Congress signaled willingness to fund voluntary colonization in conjunction with emancipation.[15]

The culmination of the federal government's expanding policy of military-based emancipation was the Preliminary Emancipation Proclamation, issued by Lincoln in September 1862. As commander in chief of the Union army, Lincoln declared that, as of January 1, 1863, all enslaved individuals in areas of active "rebellion" against the United States would be "thenceforward, and forever free." As part of the momentous proclamation, Lincoln indicated his intention to recommend to Congress, when it reconvened in December, a federal plan that offered compensation to states not "in rebellion" that "voluntarily" enacted gradual or immediate abolition. He also indicated that the federal government would continue its work in support of voluntary colonization. In effect, he foreshadowed the three-amendment proposal that appeared in his December message to Congress later that year.

The third legal geography was comprised of the four Border States: Maryland, Kentucky, Missouri, and Delaware. From Lincoln's perspective, this region, which according to the 1860 census contained roughly one million enslaved residents, was not on wartime footing with respect to constitutional law because it was still part of the Union. Although this did not mean that wartime considerations had no bearing on Lincoln's attitude toward slavery in this region, it did mean that he felt a much greater duty when dealing with this region, versus the Confederate states, to honor each state's right to determine its own course regarding the institution.

During the early months of 1862, Lincoln recommended to Congress a bold new policy regarding this third region. He asked the nation's legislative body to pass a joint resolution proclaiming the federal government's willingness to use federal funds to encourage gradual abolition in the Border States. Nothing of the sort had ever been proposed by a sitting president, nor even debated, to any significant degree, within the walls of Congress. The Confederacy, Lincoln argued, was still holding out hope that it might persuade the four Border States to secede. If the legislatures or constitutional conventions of these four states could be encouraged to initiate gradual abolition, through an offer of federal funds, the Confederacy would have to relinquish this hope, ending the war much sooner than otherwise. The amount of money required for such emancipatory encouragement Lincoln did not specify, but he did claim that the significant expense of providing such encouragement would pale in comparison to that of protracted war—an argument he would forcefully repeat nine months later in his annual message to Congress.[16]

Later in the spring of 1862, after Congress passed a joint resolution endorsing Lincoln's request, the House of Representatives established a Select Committee on Emancipation and charged it with four purposes. First, the committee should determine "whether any plan can be proposed and recommended for the gradual emancipation of all the African slaves, and the extinction of slavery in the States of Delaware, Maryland, Virginia, Kentucky, Tennessee, and Missouri, by the people or local authorities thereof"—in other words, whether there were laws or constitutional articles in any of these states that might hinder the pursuit of gradual abolition. (Virginia and Tennessee were included as part of the Border State emancipatory aid concept since certain politicians in these states had remained loyal to the Union and had retained their seats in Congress.) Second, it should assess "whether such an object is expedient and desirable." Third, it should judge "whether [the] colonization of such emancipated slaves on this continent or elsewhere is a *necessary concomitant of their freedom,* and how, and in what manner, provision may be made therefore." In effect, the committee was being asked to opine on whether, as had been the case with the majority of Liberian emigrants over the last four decades, expatriation would be a condition of emancipation. Fourth, it should "inquire and report how far, and in what way, the government of the United States can and ought equitably to aid in facilitating . . . the above objects."[17]

All six named states had seats on the committee, with Frank Blair serving as Missouri's delegate. Joining these six Southern representatives were two Northern representatives, one a Democrat from Pennsylvania, and the other a Republican from Indiana.[18]

In July 1862, during the packed closing days of the congressional session, the select committee recommended a bill that was, in scale and concept, utterly without precedent. The bill proposed $200 million in funding for emancipatory encouragement purposes. To compensate states that chose to adopt abolition laws, either gradual or immediate, $180 million would be set aside. The former involved compensation payments stretched over time; the latter resulted in a lump sum distribution. In both cases, the amount of compensation due to a particular state would be determined by multiplying the number of enslaved individuals in the state at the time the abolition law was adopted by $300, the per capita level of slaveholder compensation appropriated by the DC Abolition Act a few months earlier. The remaining $20 million in funds would be "for the purpose of deporting, colonizing, and settling the slaves so emancipated . . . in some state, territory, or dominion beyond the limits of the United States."[19]

With this particular phrasing, the Upper Southern–dominant committee implied that colonization *should* be a concomitant of emancipation. This was, in effect, the committee's response to its controversial third charge. The committee communicated this implication by choosing to omit the word *voluntary* or the phrase *with their own consent* from the text of its $20 million recommendation. These omissions, although not explicitly acknowledged as such, constituted a departure from the recent precedent set by the $100,000 colonization appropriation made by Congress a few months earlier in conjunction with the DC Abolition Act. This law had explicitly required that emigration decisions be voluntary.

The extensive commentary accompanying the report, which dedicated roughly two-thirds of its length to the subject of colonization, strengthened this implication considerably. Drawing extensively on rhetoric used by Frank in his colonization speeches of 1858 to 1860, the report stated, "Much of the objection to emancipation arises from the opposition of a large portion of our people to the intermixture of the races, and from the association of white and black labor. The committee would do nothing to favor such a policy; apart from the antipathy which nature has ordained, the presence of a race among us who cannot, and ought not to, be admitted to our social and political privileges, will be a perpetual source of injury and inquietude to both." On this basis, the report continued, "the committee conclude that the highest interests of the white race, whether Anglo-Saxon, Celt, or Scandinavian, require that the whole country should be held and occupied by those races alone." The forceful tone employed here and elsewhere in the report conveyed the same message that Border State congressmen had repeatedly sent in recent months: Certainty of postemancipation racial separation was imperative.[20]

It was in this third legal geography that the moment of political reversal for the colonization movement manifested during the early part of 1863.

BORDER STATE RESISTANCE

Around the same time that the House Select Committee on Emancipation recommended its momentous $200 million bill, President Lincoln sent a message to Border State congressmen. Before the adjournment, Lincoln wanted to impress on these thirty-or-so individuals how essential he believed Border State abolition was to winning the war and restoring the Union and how committed he was to supporting Border State abolition with federal funds, despite the high prospective cost. He expressed hope that over the upcoming four-plus-month recess, Border State congressmen would endorse the emancipatory aid concept to the people and legislators of their states. At the same time, he offered a warning. War had already significantly diminished the stability and the economic value of enslavement in all of their states. If Border State lawmakers refused to accept the current offer of assistance, they needed to understand that a similar future offer was highly unlikely. The "mere friction and abrasion" of war would almost certainly do the work of abolition for them, and they would receive "nothing valuable" in exchange.[21]

In response, most Border State congressmen expressed a strong aversion to emancipatory action. In a formal reply signed by a majority of their number, they conveyed frustration at being asked, after demonstrating loyalty to the Union by rejecting secession, to give up one of the basic rights guaranteed by the Constitution, "the right to hold slaves." Resistance to the present offer and to the earlier Border State Resolution, they insisted, did not derive from a general feeling that the institution of slavery "ought to be cherished," or even that it should never be abolished, but rather from a sense that the Border States were being treated unfairly: "We [are unable to] ... see why sacrifices should be expected of us, from which others, no more loyal, were exempt."[22]

The sentiments expressed in the Border State congressmen's majority opinion were indicative of behavior that many of them had shown between March and July 1862. During the debates over the territorial abolition law, the DC Abolition Act, the Border State Resolution, and the Second Confiscation Act, most of the representatives and senators from the region, Frank Blair being the main exception, expressed strong opposition. Their numbers were small, relative to the overwhelming numbers of the Northern-dominant Republican Party, and so their protests were mostly symbolic. They had little to no chance of persuading a large enough cohort of Republicans to vote against the party's emergent emancipatory agenda. Nonetheless, they made sure to read extensive condemnatory speeches into the congressional record. Their main lines of criticism were that Lincoln and the Republican Congress were reneging on a prewar promise to leave slavery alone in the states where it existed and, moreover, that the various federal emancipatory efforts were violations of the Constitution.[23]

At various points during these four months, however, some Border State congressmen indicated a tentative willingness to take action against slavery. They did not express this willingness with much enthusiasm, typically, but rather with a sense that, under the right circumstances, they might be open to making such a sacrifice. One of the most forthright among the handful of congressmen leaning in this direction was Senator Garrett Davis of Kentucky. During the floor debate on the Border State Resolution, Davis indicated that the Border States might be willing to consider emancipatory actions if the federal government committed, more formally, to "pay[ing] a reasonable price" for all liberated individuals and to funding a "system of colonization ... by which the emancipated slaves *will* be removed from the country." In effect, he wanted Congress to revise the resolution, which was fairly broad in its language, to include these specific commitments. Greater certainty on these crucial issues, Davis stated, would go a long way in persuading the Border States to "enter upon the work."[24]

Over the next few months, as the Republican Congress pursued its expanding emancipatory agenda, the attitude of Border State congressmen softened, to some extent, on this issue. Most still felt that the Republican Congress and president were changing the rules of the game on them, as conveyed in the majority-opinion response to Lincoln's July message, but in the final paragraphs of this response they qualified their opposition to emancipatory action. "While differing from you as to the necessity of emancipating the Slaves of our States," the twenty-one signatories (including Davis) wrote, "we are not unwilling" to consider such action if "you and our brethren of the loyal States sincerely believe, that the retention of Slavery by us is an obstacle to peace and National harmony." However, the message added, the Border States would only consider such action if they had an explicit commitment from the federal government to fund slaveholder compensation and to finance "the deportation and colonization of the liberated slaves"—in effect, a forceful, collective reiteration of Davis's earlier request.[25]

What was particularly noteworthy about the rhetoric of Border State congressmen during this four-month period was its tone. It was resistant and indignant, expressing more confidence in opposition to the administration's expanding emancipatory agenda than was warranted, given the small minority position that Border State congressmen occupied. In the rare moments when they expressed a tentative willingness to cooperate, they tended to speak as if delivering an ultimatum: we will only *consider* taking action against slavery if Congress commits, in advance, to the large-scale funding of slaveholder compensation and colonization. The confidence that Border State congressmen showed during this period was, to a significant degree, performative. Beneath their repeated complaints about broken promises and constitutional violations, as well as their ultimatums, was a clear understanding that there was little they could do to guide the federal government in a different direction. The tide of emancipation was clearly rising. The unmistakable implication of Lincoln's warning to them was this: Border State congressmen needed to bring a different tone and attitude to the next session of Congress if they wanted to have any chance of abolishing slavery on their own terms.

PUSHY VOLUNTARISM

During this high-point moment in the long history of the colonization movement, a fundamental difference of opinion became clear. Border State congressmen, generally speaking, wanted a level of certainty regarding the expatriation of the emancipated that neither Lincoln nor the Republican majority in Congress was willing to support.

This difference of opinion had begun to crystallize quite early during this four-month period, in late March and early April, when the Senate debated whether to add a colonization appropriation to the DC Abolition Act. An initial proposal had come from Garrett Davis of Kentucky, who recommended a $100,000 appropriation to be used by the president for the "purpose" of colonizing "all persons liberated" by the new law. James Doolittle, the Wisconsin Republican who continued to be one of the Blairs' chief allies in colonization promotion, quickly offered a substitute, one that added the phrase "with their own consent," effectively changing an appropriation for compulsory colonization into one for voluntary colonization. Doolittle's substitute eventually passed the Senate and became, as indicated earlier, part of the final bill presented to Lincoln. When Lincoln signed the DC Abolition Act into law, he and the Republican majority in Congress established a clear precedent for voluntary colonization.[26]

On the path to the bill's final vote, two moments in the Senate signaled that the Republican Congress would almost certainly adhere to this precedent, no matter how loudly Border State congressmen insisted that emancipation had to be connected with expatriation. First, Doolittle's substitute failed the first time it came up for vote because, as Doolittle explained upon presenting it a second time in slightly revised form, many senators had made the erroneous assumption that they were voting to fund "compulsory colonization" rather than voluntary. Doolittle's second attempt, based on a clarified understanding of what was being proposed, succeeded by a margin of seventeen, the bulk of which came from Republicans who had switched their *no* votes to *yes*. Second, two Republican senators fiercely rebuked Davis for his stubborn insistence that colonization had to be a condition of emancipation. One of them was Henry Wilson of Massachusetts, who scolded Davis for claiming, as he recently had, that to emancipate without expatriation was to knowingly facilitate a race war. "No, sir, no!" Wilson vehemently declared. "Emancipation does not inevitably lead to an exterminating war of races." Such an assertion, Wilson stated, had "no basis whatever to rest upon, either in reason or history." Implicit in Wilson's rebuke was frustration not just with the recent race-war remarks of Davis and other Border State congressmen but also with decades and decades of such remarks from Upper Southern colonization advocates, who invoked Jefferson's race-war prediction as if it were an incontrovertible truth rather than an opinion. Simply proclaiming, "'I know it,'" Wilson insisted, was not all that was required to prove an opinion right. In the tense moment that followed Wilson's sharp rebuke, not a single Republican senator chided him for his tone or sought to qualify his remarks.[27]

Over the next few months, Davis and other Border State congressmen nonetheless persisted in their calls for certainty regarding expatriation. At one point during the session, Davis declared: "I have said and believe that slaves will never consent to voluntary colonization." Many enslaved individuals in his home state of Kentucky, he explained, had refused offers of manumission conditioned on Liberian emigration. "The idea of voluntary colonization to any considerable extent is all moonshine."[28]

The difference of opinion became even clearer in July when Congress passed the $500,000 colonization appropriation and when it passed the Second Confiscation Act. Both actions followed and reinforced the DC Abolition Act's voluntary precedent.[29]

The Border State congressmen's insistent calls for certainty regarding the expatriation of the emancipated were, if one looks at certain historical facts regarding the Upper South, not at all surprising. For decades Henry Clay and other Upper Southern colonization advocates had shown themselves to be equally inflexible. Indeed, on numerous occasions, Clay and others had declared, unequivocally, that no matter how much they wanted to see the institution of slavery come to an end, they would, for the sake of the Union and for the sake of its white inhabitants, oppose all actions against slavery that did not mandate the expatriation of the emancipated. In accordance with this view, offers of manumission in the Upper South often included a legal condition that required the prospective freed person to *consent* to emigration. Over the last forty years, the majority of Liberian emigrants had been individuals emancipated in such fashion, something Davis had alluded to in his speech. In other words, each person had been given two options: freedom in Africa or continued enslavement in the United States. More broadly, over the last seven decades, every state of the Upper South had inscribed the essence of this exclusionary attitude into their lawbooks. All had enacted statutes that required newly emancipated individuals to leave the state permanently.[30]

Lincoln made a few notable attempts during this uncertain moment to ameliorate Border State concerns regarding colonization. Mainly, he made statements that publicly affirmed his own commitment to the issue and indicated his belief that Black Americans would eventually leave the United States in significant numbers. In his July message to Border State congressmen, for instance, Lincoln stated, with a sense of confidence likely not as strong as he indicated, that "room in South America for colonization, can be obtained cheaply, and in abundance; and when numbers shall be large enough to be company and encouragement for one another, the freed people will not be so reluctant to go."[31]

Lincoln's most significant attempt took place in August 1862, after Congress had adjourned, when he asked his recently appointed commissioner of emigration, a former ACS official by the name of James Mitchell, to invite a group of prominent and influential Black Washingtonians to the White House for a meeting. The widely published formal account of proceedings showed Lincoln asking these men to lead a vanguard colonization movement from the United States to Central America. Recent appropriations in Congress had made it his "duty" to promote colonization, he explained, and furthermore the "cause" was one that he had supported "for a long time." As justification for making such a bold request, Lincoln used language that, in essence, expressed the colonization movement's well-worn claim that Black freedom and white freedom were incongruous: "Your race suffer very greatly ... by living among us while ours suffer from your presence." To this, Lincoln added a striking elaboration. "But for your race among us, there could not be a war." Repeating the point, with added precision, he intoned, "Without the institution of Slavery and the colored race as a basis, the war could not have an existence." In effect, Lincoln employed the same basic blame-the-oppressed formula Frederick Stanton had used during the early 1850s, when, in support of the Liberian steamer project, he characterized free Black Americans as the root cause of American sectionalism.[32]

These were sharp words, arguably the sharpest uttered by Lincoln before or after on the subject of colonization. To them, he added the following pushy admonishment: Do not consider the request to resettle in Central America only from "an extremely selfish" standpoint. Although as higher-status Black Americans, you might have good reason to doubt the extent to which you would benefit personally, "you should [be willing to] sacrifice something of your present comfort . . . to help those who are not so fortunate as yourselves." More broadly, he added, you should be willing to make such a sacrifice "for the sake of your race."[33]

In making such pushy remarks, Lincoln engaged in a practice that had deep roots in the colonization movement: speaking presumptively and provocatively in an effort to coerce consent. Henry Clay, Lincoln's political idol, had for decades been a chief practitioner. At the ACS's first annual meeting in Washington in 1818, for instance, Clay had explained, with a presumptive air, why he believed Black Americans would, in growing numbers, leave the country willingly. No rational and respectable group of people, Clay had asserted, would choose to remain in a nation where their lives were "cheerless," "debased," and "humiliating," and where they were and would always be considered "aliens to the society of which they are members."[34]

Over the coming weeks, newspapers from various parts of the country published accounts of Lincoln's meeting with Black Washingtonians. Indeed, the day after the White House convening, Horace Greeley's *New York Daily Tribune,* one of the nation's main Republican newspapers, published the official government transcript—presumably communicated to the *Tribune* and other press outlets by Mitchell or someone in Lincoln's administration—in an article placed on the front page, center and top. Because it was a full reprint, the article included all of the above quotations, as well as other separatist affirmations Lincoln made during the meeting.

The article's headline included two declarative subheadings: "He Holds That the White and Black Races Cannot Dwell Together" and "He Urges Intelligent Colored Men to Exert Themselves for Colonization."[35]

Through the published proceedings of this orchestrated meeting, Lincoln sent a message to Border State lawmakers that he understood and appreciated their preference for colonization. He also signaled that although he was unwilling to support compulsory colonization, he was willing, in the interest of making voluntary colonization more certain, to push Black Americans, using forceful language, to cooperate in such a national effort. More broadly, Lincoln delivered a message to the nation as a whole, to white and Black Americans alike, and in specific to all of the state and federal lawmakers involved in the ongoing pivotal debates over slavery, that the president of the United States still favored an approach to abolition that incorporated Black expatriation.[36]

DENUNCIATIONS AND REAFFIRMATIONS

Black Americans had a lot to say about Lincoln's August meeting in the White House. Frederick Douglass characterized the president's remarks as offensive and absurd: "the language and arguments of an itinerant Colonization lecturer, showing all his inconsistencies, his pride of race and blood, his contempt for negroes and his canting hypocrisy." By declaring that the "presence [of Black people] in the country is the real first cause of war," Lincoln was strongly implying, as colonization advocates had for decades, Douglass asserted, that "their removal" was essential to ending sectional strife once and for all. This kind of thinking, which employed the scornworthy device of blaming the victim, Douglass insisted, was as wrongheaded as it had ever been. A letter to the editor published in the *Christian Recorder,* the official journal of the African Methodist Episcopal (AME) Church, a Christian denomination founded by Black Americans several decades earlier, agreed with Douglass's assessment: "The existence of slavery is what brought the war about, and I am sure that the colored people are not the authors of slavery."[37]

Widespread newspaper reports of the August meeting, however, also prompted fear among Black Americans. Lincoln's exclusionary proclamations came on the heels of a congressional session that had appropriated hundreds of thousands of federal dollars for Black expatriation. For the first time in American history, colonization was a viable issue in national politics. As long as Lincoln and the Republican Congress continued to see political value in colonization, further federal actions were a real possibility. A letter to the *Christian Recorder* printed one month after Lincoln's White House meeting remarked, "For more than one generation associations of white men, entitled Colonization Societies, have been engaged in plans and efforts for our expatriation.... Now the American Government has assumed the work and responsibility of colonizing us in some foreign land ... and is now maturing measures to consummate this scheme."[38]

Some Black Americans, during this tense moment, expressed concern that federal support for voluntary colonization might presage more coercive measures down the road. A *Christian Recorder* correspondent warned that "*voluntary* emigration ... [was] simply the stepping stone to *compulsory* expatriation."[39]

Douglass and other Black activists used a combination of tactics to oppose this worrisome political trend and to mitigate this upwelling of fear. First, they insisted in articles, speeches, and convention resolutions that Black Americans were, as they had always been, wholly opposed to leaving the country. An editorial letter addressed directly to Lincoln, reprinted in *Douglass' Monthly* later that fall, declared, "I trust, good Mr. President, you will not rend your garments when I tell you that the question of colonization ... has long been settled by a unanimous determination to remain, and survive or perish, rise or fall with the country of our birth." A statewide religious conference in Indiana, around the same time, issued the following formal declaration: "We are now, as ever, unalterably, inflexibly, and determinedly opposed to all and every plan and scheme of colonization." Voluntary colonization, these declarations forcefully indicated, was no more likely now than it had ever been.[40]

Second, they attempted to placate fellow Black Americans who feared a potential shift from voluntary to compulsory expatriation. Reverend Henry McNeal Turner, a young Washington minister of rising influence within the AME Church, encouraged the readers of the *Christian Recorder* not to take Lincoln's remarks too seriously. His motives were largely political, Turner claimed. Lincoln "knows as well as anyone, that it is a thing morally impracticable, ever to rid this country of colored people unless God does it miraculously." Frances Watkins Harper, a veteran American Anti-Slavery Society leader and women's rights activist, offered a similar message: "I anticipate no fresh trouble from this new [colonization] movement." Lincoln's "dabbling with colonization just now suggests to my mind the idea of a man almost dying with a loathsome cancer, and busying himself about having his hair trimmed according to the latest fashion."[41]

Third, Black leaders publicly accused colonization advocates, as they had done for decades, of dramatically worsening racial oppression in the United States and, unconscionably, giving these worsening effects a cover of respectability. As they did so, they continued to highlight the insidious ways that separatist rhetoric, even if couched in benevolence, operated. In an article published in the fall of 1862 entitled "The Spirit of Colonization," Douglass, noting recent acts of violence against the Black residents of various Northern cities, blamed colonization advocates for creating the very conditions that prompted such "bloodthirsty proceedings." By repeatedly citing racial violence as evidence of a "purpose of Divine Providence to compel the colored race in America to emigrate," Douglass asserted, colonization advocates gave this violence "an air of philosophy, piety and respectability," effectively goading "negro hating mobocrats" on in "their fiendish work." Later in the same issue, Douglass accused Lincoln of personal complicity in such racial violence. "In urging his colonization scheme," Lincoln "furnish[ed] a weapon to all the ignorant and base, who need only the countenance of men in authority to commit all kinds of violence and outrage upon the colored people of the country."[42]

The fourth tactic was to continue to push back against the emigration interest that a minority of Black Americans, a growing minority since the early 1850s, had expressed in the Northern United States. Beginning with the passage of the Fugitive Slave Act in 1850, Black Americans had increasingly looked outside of the country for places of refuge from this threatening law, as well as the ever-growing number of exclusionary statutes passed by state legislatures. Some moved into southeastern Canada, joining preexisting communities composed, to a significant degree, of self-emancipated, former Americans. Others, close to five thousand between 1851 and 1861, decided to emigrate to Liberia under the auspices of the ACS. The most public and significant indication of rising interest occurred during the summer of 1854, when a large number of Black Americans gathered for a three-day "National Emigration Convention" in Cleveland. One of the chief organizers was Martin Delany, who, for a period during the late 1840s, had co-led the *North Star* newspaper with Frederick Douglass. Included in the published proceedings of the convention was a pamphlet penned by Delany entitled *Political Destiny of the Colored Race, on the American Continent*. In it, Delany asserted "emigration" as the "sure, practicable and infallible remedy for the evils we now endure" in the United States. Over the next several years, Delany would be one of the most outspoken leaders, among Northern Black activists, of Black-led emigration.[43]

Delany, at the time of the convention, had built a public reputation that approached but did not quite match that of Douglass, Henry Highland Garnet, or several others who had been active, for many years, in the American Anti-Slavery Society, the American and Foreign Anti-Slavery Society, and various national- and state-level "colored conventions." He was, nonetheless, an individual of growing influence and considerable ambition. Born in the western portion of Virginia in 1812, three years before Garnet and five or six years before Douglass, Delany had made his career in the medical field, ultimately as a community physician in Pennsylvania. Prior to the early 1850s, he had shown little to no interest in emigration, except as an opponent, although he had made a few qualified remarks about the significance of Liberia's nationhood and future success during the late 1840s. Delany's interest level spiked during the early 1850s, as living conditions for free Black Americans in the North significantly worsened and after a painful personal experience in which, due to the actions of a group of white students at Harvard Medical School, where he had recently matriculated, Delany was expelled by the administration. This act of racial prejudice strengthened his growing conviction that little could be done by Black activists, despite their herculean efforts, to eliminate, or even significantly diminish, white-American aversion to the fair and equal treatment of Black Americans.[44]

During the late 1850s, while living for a time in Canada, Delany commenced an effort to spearhead a Black-led emigration movement to Africa. Garnet, who continued to live in the United States and who presided over a church in New York that both Samuel Cornish and Theodore Wright had previously led, also became a vocal proponent of African emigration during this time. Garnet led the establishment of a new organization, the African Civilization Society, the stated purpose of which was to contribute to the elevation of the "African race" by "encouraging" the voluntary migration of a portion of the Black American community to Africa. Delany, for his part, embarked on a several-month trip to the African continent, where, with some assistance from Liberian officials, he sought a new piece of land where Black emigrants could resettle. Neither Delany nor Garnet, both made abundantly clear, had any intention of endorsing, through their new emigration project, the long-running efforts of the American Colonization Society. Nor did they intend to validate, even indirectly, the society's exclusionary ideology. However, both showed at least some willingness during this time, to the great dismay of Douglass and many other Black activists, to engage with ACS leaders as arm's-length allies.[45]

Over the next handful of years, until roughly the end of 1862, a bitter fight ensued among Northern Black activists. The majority strongly criticized Garnet and Delany for their actions. While these critics routinely qualified their remarks by stating that they had no issue with individuals who, based on their own assessments, chose to emigrate to Africa, they vehemently objected to any organized effort by Black Americans to encourage and facilitate emigration to Africa or to any other foreign destination. Their biggest concern, as Douglass stressed in an 1859 article published shortly after the African Civilization Society's founding, was that this new organization did, in fact, have a strong tendency to validate the colonization movement's exclusionary ideology, no matter what Garnet and others said. "No one idea has given rise to more oppression and persecution toward the colored people of this country, than that which makes Africa, not America, their home," Douglass proclaimed, to which he added, "The natural and unfailing tendency of the African Civilization Society ... will be to keep life and power in this narrow, bitter and persecuting idea." At a large public meeting held in the spring of 1860 for the purpose of debating the African Civilization Society's merits, George Downing brought an even more strident tone to bear against the organization, as he accused it of acting, in effect, as an "auxiliary to the negro-hating American Colonization Society." Following these remarks, and other pointed criticisms from Downing, a fistfight nearly erupted in the building, at which point Garnet called for the discussion to be tabled and for everyone to depart.[46]

As this minority interest persisted during the early years of the Civil War, Douglass and others spoke with heightened force against it, claiming that any Black-led efforts to encourage and facilitate emigration had a powerful tendency to divide Black Americans at a time when unity was especially important. Douglass expressed particular alarm during the spring of 1862, when he received word that a group of Black Americans had petitioned Congress for emigration support. "If anybody wants to go out of the country let him," Douglass remarked, "but let him not petition in the name of the colored people." To do so, he worried, was to "give new life to the delusion, that the colored people are ever going to leave this, their native country."[47]

The final tactic that Black leaders employed during this time was to frame, in qualified but nonetheless optimistic terms, the Civil War as a gateway toward a better future for Black Americans. These notes of optimism became stronger during the first half of 1863. On January 1, Lincoln issued, as he had indicated three months prior that he would, a formal Emancipation Proclamation. With this wartime measure, he freed, at least in theory, millions of enslaved Americans living throughout the Confederate states, an act that Douglass called, while addressing an audience at the Cooper Institute in February, "the greatest event of our nation's history if not the greatest event of the century." Of particular note, from the perspective of Black Americans, was the fact that the proclamation made absolutely no mention of colonization, in contrast to the preliminary version issued in September 1862 and in contrast to the trio of constitutional amendments proposed by the president in his annual message to Congress in December. With respect to the latter, Douglass had reprinted, before the Emancipation Proclamation's issuance, a scathing article from *The Liberator* that had denounced the president's "renewed" colonization proposal as an "insult and an outrage" that would likely have the deplorable effect of strengthening "popular prejudice" against Black Americans. In the days following Lincoln's proclamation, a correspondent of Douglass's paper offered a revised assessment of the president's attitude toward Black expatriation. "This war," the author declared, "will educate Mr. Lincoln out of his idea of the deportation of the Negro." This assessment, as it turned out, proved prescient. Lincoln's message to Congress in December 1862 was the last time that he publicly endorsed the removal of Black Americans from the United States.[48]

Over the next several months, Black activists asserted another reason for optimism. During this time, with Lincoln's approval, the Union military began recruiting Black Americans, free and formerly enslaved, into its ranks. Douglass characterized this enlistment trend as a means through which Black Americans could settle, on the basis of "perfect civil and political equality," the long-standing question, "what shall be done with the negro?" "Tonight," he added, "we stand at the portals of a new world, a new life and a new destiny." Douglass gave this speech in New York in May 1863, at a time when he had decided to end publication of *Douglass' Monthly* so that he could help the Union army recruit Black soldiers. Indeed, one of the chief purposes of his May speech was military recruitment. The same was true of a speech he had delivered a few weeks earlier at Henry Highland Garnet's church. The earlier gathering had closed with following resolution: "We believe that as we shall manifest competency and valor in the field," the civic "rewards" due to Black Americans will no longer be withheld. And, we believe, accordingly, "that the bugbear, 'Colonization,' which has so troubled the American people, will not, out of respect for the feelings of loyal Americans, be ever again agitated."[49]

TURNING POINT: MISSOURI EMANCIPATION BILL

In late July 1862, less than a week after Frank Blair and the Select Committee on Emancipation recommended a bill that offered $200 million in emancipatory aid to the Border States, Senator John Henderson of Missouri sent a letter to Abraham Lincoln. Henderson began by apologizing for not replying sooner to the president's recent message to the congressmen of the Border States. A schedule conflict had prevented him from attending the meeting hastily organized by his fellow legislators to compose a reply. Henderson had voted for the Border State Resolution in April, one of only a handful of Border State congressmen to do so, and the content of his late-July letter made it clear that he remained quite open to the concept of using federal money to encourage the adoption of abolition laws in the Border States. Although he did not agree, in full, with Lincoln's justificatory claims, he did agree that the people of the Border States should, for the sake of the Union and their own particular interests, seriously consider the government's offer. Henderson promised Lincoln that during the four-month recess he would carry the offer back to Missouri and give it his strong endorsement, noting, however, that there was no certainty that the state's lawmakers would respond favorably.[50]

Henderson had good reason to doubt the willingness of Missouri lawmakers to cooperate. In early June 1862, he had traveled from Washington to Jefferson City, Missouri's state capital, to participate in a session of the Missouri State Convention, a legal body convened for the purpose of dealing with, among other things, slavery-related matters that were constitutional, and thus beyond the reach of the legislature. A main piece of business debated by the June convention had been a gradual abolition bill proposed, by a member, in response to the congressional Border State Resolution. Within hours, members had voted, by an overwhelming majority of 52 to 19, to lay the bill on the table. Henderson had opposed the tabling. Little, if anything, was to be gained, he declared, by repeatedly invoking the language of nonintervention and "cry[ing] aloud that our institution of slavery is about to be destroyed." The time had come, he insisted, for Missourians to accept the fact that the Civil War had fundamentally changed the attitude of the federal government and much of the Northern public toward slavery.[51]

An observer of Missouri politics during the 1850s would have had considerable difficulty identifying John Henderson as one who would, a handful of years later, criticize Missouri politicians for states'-rights intransigence. For most of his political career, since joining the state legislature in the late 1840s, Henderson had moved in state and federal politics as a loyal slave-state Democrat. Even during the partisan reconfigurations following the incendiary Kansas-Nebraska Act of 1854—when the Blairs had led a small minority of Missourians into the Republican Party and when the American Party and Constitutional Union Party had emerged as powerful rivals of the Democratic Party—Henderson had not wavered. In fact, by the mid- to late 1850s, he had become one of the Democratic Party's prominent operatives in Missouri. It was not until 1861, when he strongly opposed secession, that he traded his Democratic affiliation for a Unionist one. What all of this meant, in practice, was that Henderson had helped to build the very ideological inflexibility in Missouri that so frustrated him at the state convention of 1862.[52]

When Henderson returned again to Missouri after the July congressional adjournment, he spent several weeks giving speeches in favor of the federal government's offer of emancipatory aid. Addressing a large audience in Hannibal toward the end of August, Henderson spoke, once more, with great force about the importance of releasing past expectations and accepting the reality of the present. Roughly one-third of slaves in Missouri, he estimated, had already been "lost . . . and those that are left are almost worthless." There was little doubt, he asserted, that the "death-knell of African slavery in this country" had sounded. Henderson also impressed upon the audience the need to act quickly. The federal offer of emancipatory aid was the product of a unique and temporary circumstance, Henderson warned. Had the June convention passed a gradual abolition bill, Henderson noted with regret, Missouri would be in a far better position to count on funding for compensation and colonization, the latter of which he characterized as a "*sine qua non*," or an essential condition. All was not yet lost though, he advised. At the next session, Congress might "accede to the proposition of one or two States . . . perhaps more, if speedily made." Beyond that, however, "I expect no such thing."[53]

In keeping with this sense of urgency, Henderson brought a bill for the abolition of slavery in Missouri to the next session of Congress, which convened in December 1862. His proposed law had two key elements. First, it required the federal government to pay the Missouri government $25 million if its legislators, or delegates in the case of a constitutional convention, chose to pursue abolition within prescribed time frames. Second, it gave Missouri lawmakers the option of enacting immediate abolition or gradual abolition. If they pursued the first option, enslavement in the state would end fully by July 1866, at which point the federal government would deliver the entire $25 million. If they pursued the second, it would end fully by July 1885, in which case the federal government would disburse funds over time in four installments.[54]

Henderson chose not to include any language about colonization in the proposed Missouri Emancipation Bill. On the surface, this seems odd, since in his Hannibal speech, back in August, he had declared colonization as a *sine qua non* of emancipation. Over the next several weeks, however, as the Senate debated various versions of the Missouri Emancipation Bill, including an alternate version from the House, introduced by a Missouri representative, that did contain a voluntary colonization provision, Henderson made it clear that he still believed colonization to be a crucial issue. In response to various questions about the willingness of Missourians to take action against slavery at the present time, Henderson asserted that the majority supported doing so but only on terms that combined emancipation with colonization. The second senator from Missouri, who, it should be noted, did not support the Missouri Emancipation Bill, agreed with Henderson on this point. In the recent state election, he observed, all of the candidates who favored taking action against slavery indicated, as a qualification, that they were "opposed to any scheme of emancipation unless deportation was connected."[55]

Henderson had two motives for passing a bill that avoided any specific mention of colonization. The first of these he made explicit: He wanted to give Missouri leaders the latitude to decide how the allocated funds would be spent, how much they would use for "colonization" versus "emancipation." The second motive was implicit but nonetheless strongly indicated by remarks that he made during the Missouri Emancipation Bill debate. The general language of his bill preserved the possibility that Missouri could take a more coercive, perhaps even compulsory, approach to colonization—in other words, one that was not bounded by an explicit voluntary colonization provision. Henderson implied this motivation when he asserted that the majority of Missourians would only support emancipation if it were combined with colonization. He did so again, earlier in the debate, when he claimed that the original emancipatory aid bill proposed by the House Select Committee on Emancipation, in July 1862, "*required* [the] deportation" of the emancipated. One final indication can be found in remarks that he made at the very beginning of the Senate debate, when he proposed his bill as a substitute for the alternative from the House. As part of broader commentary offered on the expanded range of federal power in wartime circumstances, Henderson indicated that the "negroes of Missouri [might] be freed or removed from the State" under the government's constitutional authority to "secure the people against the incursions of an existing war."[56]

Henderson did not specify how Missourians might pursue a more coercive or compulsory approach to colonization, but history indicated two paths. First, they could offer financial incentives to freed Black Americans in an attempt to obtain their consent to leave the country. In the past twelve months, at least one congressman had suggested that the *federal* government take such an approach: an Illinois Republican who was a close friend of Lincoln. Second, and more straightforward, Missouri lawmakers could pass an abolition law that made expatriation a condition of emancipation: Those who consented would gain freedom; those who did not would remain enslaved or would be banished from the state. The latter approach, which Senator Garrett Davis of Kentucky had alluded to in a speech given the prior year, had direct precedents in Upper Southern state laws that expelled freed Black Americans after emancipation and in Upper Southern legal practices of allowing manumission, by contract or by will, to be conditioned on expatriation.[57]

In mid-February, after several weeks of debate, the Senate voted to pass a version of the Missouri Emancipation Bill that looked more like the one Henderson had proposed than the one that the House had passed earlier in the session. The bill authorized federal compensation to the state in the case of gradual abolition or immediate abolition, and it made no mention of colonization. Although the bill contained revisions that Henderson found frustrating—the dollar amount of compensation had been reduced from $25 million to $20 million, in the case of immediate abolition, and from $25 million to $10 million, in the case of gradual abolition, and the required completion dates had been significantly shortened in both scenarios—he still supported the prospective law. "This bill is not exactly as I would have it," he admitted, but "I sincerely hope it will be passed just as it stands."[58]

To his great delight, the Missouri Emancipation Bill passed the Senate by a substantial margin, with roughly three-quarters of Republicans voting *yes*. To his frustration, but not his surprise, every Border State senator who cast a vote, aside from himself, voted *no*. Several of them, including his fellow Missourian, had signaled their votes in advance by speaking out against the bill during the weeks-long debate. Most, in some form or other, had explained their opposition in the promise-breaking and Constitution-violating terms that they had used to protest every emancipatory action taken or considered by Congress during the momentous four-month period in 1862. As a senator from Kentucky put it, "Leave this institution where the Constitution has left it" and "leave it to the people of the States, to do with it as they may think proper." In other words, despite all that had happened during two years of civil war, nonintervention was still, in the view of most Border State senators, the only constitutionally defensible and politically respectable attitude for the federal government to take regarding slavery.[59]

When the Senate bill transferred back to the House for further debate, several Border State representatives also spoke out against the prospective law. Much to Henderson's chagrin, three of them were from Missouri. All three spoke on the last day of February 1863, just a few days before the close of the current session, after a House committee had revised the bill such that it now offered compensation for immediate abolition only. The most extensive critique came from James Rollins, a slaveholder who represented "the largest slaveholding district in the State." Although he softened his criticisms by professing his willingness to endorse abolition in Missouri under certain conditions, the conditions he specified were not on the table. "Better [to] pass no bill at all on the subject," he declared, than to enact the "law in its present shape." Rollins asserted that he wanted Missouri to have the option to pursue *gradual* abolition and, even more importantly, that he wanted greater certainty regarding the expatriation of the emancipated. To emphasize the strength of his conviction on these points, especially the latter, he invoked the venerable Henry Clay, by reading into the congressional record, in full, the high-profile letter that Clay published in 1849 endorsing the pursuit of gradual abolition and colonization in Kentucky. In the letter, Clay declared, as he had many times before, his belief that colonization should be "an indispensable condition" of emancipation.[60]

The ultimate fate of the Missouri Emancipation Bill was limbo. The congressional session ended in early March before the House of Representatives voted on the revised bill. Even if this vote had occurred, time would still likely have run out, since the Senate would still need to approve any revisions made by the House. Henderson was intensely frustrated, as he made clear in a private letter. The series of deliberations that had taken place in the House after receipt of the Senate bill, he declared, amounted to a "d—d [damned] farce." Henderson singled out Senator Charles Sumner for blame, claiming that he was absolutely "bent on destruction of the bill" and suggesting that he had worked behind the scenes to impede its progress in the House. In making these accusations, Henderson might well have recalled portentous remarks Sumner had made moments before the February vote in the Senate. "I shall vote for this bill," Sumner declared, only "because I know it is to go back to the House of Representatives," where "I trust [that] a bill will be at last matured that will embody the true principle which ought to govern this great question." Sumner, it was well known, wanted to fund immediate abolition only and had effectively no interest in supplying Missouri with federal funds that might be used for Black expatriation.[61]

As Henderson left Washington for the congressional recess, the last-chance warnings that he had given to Missourians during the summer of 1862 likely echoed in his mind. The Missouri Emancipation Bill had failed during the stub congressional session of late 1862 to early 1863, and there was very little reason to believe that it would be revived during the next session, the start date for which was a long nine months away. And although Henderson blamed Sumner for the bill's failure in the House, he could not deny that the votes and rhetoric of his Border State colleagues had strongly undermined his cause. By continuing to reject the legitimacy of emancipatory moves made by the federal government as part of the Civil War or, at a minimum, by continuing to make emancipatory demands that the Republican Congress refused to meet, Border State congressmen were radically diminishing the probability that slavery would be abolished in their states in the Jeffersonian mode that they so strongly preferred.

In effect, as the next session of Congress showed, the window of political viability for federally supported colonization that had opened less than twelve months earlier was now closed.

IMMEDIATE ABOLITION WITHOUT COLONIZATION

Roughly nine months after the Missouri Emancipation Bill's ambiguous death, John Henderson returned to the Senate committed to a different approach to ending slavery. On January 11, 1864, Henderson proposed that Congress recommend to the states, by means of a joint resolution, a thirteenth constitutional amendment that would abolish slavery nationally and immediately, with no provisions for slaveholder compensation or colonization; several other congressmen, during the session's opening weeks, did the same. The moment was a stunning one. National immediate abolition was the most radical approach to ending slavery, and it was one that had never really been contemplated, in any substantive way, prior to the Civil War, because the three-quarters state majority needed to ratify such an approach had never been achievable. In effect, Henderson was recommending an approach grounded in the principles of Northern "abolitionists" like Frederick Douglass and William Lloyd Garrison, men long denounced by both parties and sections as reckless and fanatical. And he was doing so in his capacity as a senator representing a slave state, knowing full well that, less than a year earlier, he had fought vigorously to obtain federal funds that would enable Missouri to pursue abolition in a way that afforded compensation to slaveholders and that facilitated the colonization of the emancipated, possibly on a compulsory basis.[62]

Henderson's striking political move in early 1864 was part of a larger and somewhat curious political shift in the Border States. The front edge of this shift had become apparent in the fall of 1862, when elections in Missouri and Maryland for the next Congress, the Thirty-Eighth, produced numerous wins for candidates who had made explicit promises to take action against slavery. Over the next twelve months, especially after the Thirty-Seventh Congress adjourned in March 1863, emancipatory interest visibly strengthened in Missouri and Maryland, and indeed across all of the Border States, causing a previously dominant Unionist political affiliation to be undermined by the rise of Unconditional Unionism. The latter moniker had existed before in Border State politics, but without strict and clear definition. During 1863, it came to signify a break with Unionist views considered too conservative and counterproductive. Unconditional Unionists believed, generally speaking, that the time to take action against Border State slavery had come, and that the need for action was so urgent that emancipatory conditions, like slaveholder compensation and colonization, had to be abandoned.[63]

Wartime *abrasions,* over the course of 1863, had contributed significantly to this Border State political shift. Perhaps the most significant abrasion had been the Union army's emancipation and enlistment of enslaved men in the Border States, particularly in Missouri and Maryland. For much of the year, Union army leaders had conducted these emancipatory enlistments irregularly and without full federal sanction—technically, the Emancipation Proclamation had authorized such enlistments in the Confederate states only. By the end of 1863, however, the practice was official federal policy, making the Union army a fully empowered emancipatory force in the Border States. Many who became Unconditional Unionists during this time viewed these military developments as final signals that Border State slavery would not survive the war.[64]

At meetings held in Maryland during the second half of 1863, Unconditional Unionists had publicly denounced the behavior of their delegates in Congress during the recent legislative sessions, expressing particular frustration, even embarrassment, that not a single senator or representative from Maryland had voted for the Border State Resolution during the first half of 1862. Votes cast against the resolution did "not represent the *interest* of the *people* of Maryland," a pamphlet from one of the meetings had declared. As former Maryland Representative John Pendleton Kennedy explained in December 1863, the "demolition of Slavery" had become a "present and irresistible reality." If the people of Maryland "do not adjust this question upon the basis of speedy Emancipation, it will soon adjust itself without their assistance." At no point in this speech had Kennedy—a colonization advocate for roughly two decades, and the congressman who, in 1843, had presented to the House of Representatives a thousand-plus-page committee report that had strongly endorsed federal support—spoken of colonization. Now was not the time, Kennedy indicated, to place conditions on emancipation.[65]

John Henderson had made similar remarks during the summer of 1863 at yet another meeting of the Missouri State Convention, several months after the failure of the Missouri Emancipation Bill. Whether Missourians were willing to concede that the war was about slavery (Henderson for his part remained unwilling to do so), they could not deny, Henderson asserted, that the persistence of slavery in the state made them, from the perspective of Confederate leaders, an appealing prospective ally. Missouri's "present position, . . . struggling to maintain slavery against the current of events, constantly invites . . . aggression." The solution, in Henderson's mind, was obvious. Missouri should abolish slavery and serve notice "to the people of the seceded States that we are not of them, and, under no circumstances, will we be with them." At one point during the convention, a delegate had proposed a resolution asking Congress to "enact such laws as shall be efficient for the removal of all slaves, hereby emancipated, beyond the limits of this State." Henderson had voted with the majority to dismiss the resolution, an indication that he now viewed federal support for colonization as effectively off the table. Declarations that resisted reality tethered the state to the past. A more logical course, Henderson believed, was to accept reality and look to the future.[66]

When Henderson returned to Washington to take his seat in the newly constituted Thirty-Eighth Congress, many Border State senators and representatives joined him in affiliating with the Unconditional

Unionist position, as the elections of the fall of 1862 presaged. In the Senate, four of ten regional delegates identified as Unconditional Unionists. In the House, Unconditional Unionists took half of the region's seats, fifteen out of thirty. This visible reconfiguration of Border State representation indicated a merging of Northern and Upper Southern attitudes on slavery. In a basic sense, this was the merger sought by the Blair family between 1858 and 1860. The crucial difference was that colonization had been the Blairs' merger vehicle. Now, after nearly three years of civil war, the vehicle was immediate and unconditional abolition.

In April 1864, after several months of debate, the Senate passed a joint resolution endorsing the addition of a thirteenth constitutional amendment. The resolution passed easily, 38 to 6. More than half of the senators from the Border States, including Henderson, joined the Northern Republican majority in approving the resolution, the first time since the war had begun that a Border State majority in either chamber had voted in favor of emancipatory action by the federal government.[67]

On the day before the final vote, Henderson offered a lengthy explanation, largely for the benefit of "northern men," of the radical political shift in the Border States. To ensure that he said nothing more and nothing less than he intended, he read word-for-word a speech that he had prepared in advance. "This is a practice of which older Senators do not approve," he acknowledged, but the imperative of precision, in his mind, took precedence over tradition. A chief goal of Henderson's speech was, quite plainly, to diminish the sense of triumph that Northern Republicans might feel in this moment. The Border States' shift in stance on slavery, he indicated, should not be viewed as a Northern victory over Southern minds. Sentiment against slavery in the United States, Henderson asserted, had originated to a significant degree in the minds of Southerners: "It was Washington, Jefferson, Madison, Marshall... and others in their own land who had stamped slavery with the most decided disapprobation." Over the years, this sentiment had become muted by sectional tensions deriving from the clash of "extreme men on both sides": those in the North who demanded immediate abolition on moral grounds and those in the South, particularly those in South Carolina, who defended slavery's indefinite perpetuation by claiming slavery to be "morally right." Although a great many in the South had refused to accept this Southern claim of moral rectitude, they had also rejected the Northern idea that morality had a higher legal claim than the Constitution, leaving the "majority of our people" in a difficult predicament: "They confess that the moral law condemns it, but that the Constitution tolerates it." Faced with no clear or desirable path in either direction, toward abolition or away from it, many in the South had resigned themselves to the passive, and they hoped Union-preserving, stance of nonintervention.[68]

The "friends of slavery," in contrast, chose an alternate course. They broke apart the Union to preserve the institution, driving the country into civil war and, ironically, providing the terrible circumstances that clarified, for the majority of the nation, the need for abolition. If the friends of slavery "made war once," Henderson solemnly observed, "they may make it again . . . Therefore the restoration of slavery is a restoration of political strife." How can a nation, faced with such facts, "leave slavery to fester again in the public vitals?"[69]

Over the course of the protracted debate that ended in the Senate in April 1864, the issue of federal support for colonization had barely come up. Even Border State congressmen who strongly opposed the prospective thirteenth amendment and who smarted at colonization's omission recognized that whatever leverage they had once possessed was gone. The Republican majority in Congress was no longer trying to persuade the region's lawmakers to cooperate. Border State congressmen could denounce, if they chose, the new approach to ending slavery, but Republicans had little reason to listen.

In this new political environment, Black expatriation had become, in a sense, an obsolete political issue in Congress. Border State congressmen were, for the most part, no longer demanding it. Northern Republican congressmen were, for the most part, no longer entertaining it as a possibility. Fittingly, in the early summer of 1864, prior to the close of the current session, the Republican-controlled Congress voted to repeal the two existing federal colonization appropriations, $600,000 in total. Expressing support for the repeal, Senator Henry Wilson of Massachusetts characterized the 1862 appropriations as "folly" and the issue of federal support for colonization as over: "The whole idea has exploded."[70]

Henderson, who was still a slaveholder, had addressed his own decision to give up on colonization, at least as a federal political issue and perhaps for good, when he had delivered his carefully worded speech to the Senate in April. "The evils of amalgamation and consequent deterioration of race are often presented as insuperable objections to the proposed [thirteenth] amendment," he noted. "Such evils may be great, but unless it be certain that the freedom of the slave will increase these evils, no such objection can be well sustained." Before closing, Henderson offered a suggestive, summative declaration of his revised position regarding the postemancipatory freedom of Black Americans. "I will not be intimidated by the fears of negro equality," he declared. Without explicitly acknowledging past statements that he had made asserting the fundamental incongruity of white freedom and Black freedom, Henderson professed a willingness to wait and see whether the "negro" had "mental qualities entitling him to a position beyond our present belief." "If so," he added, "I shall put no obstacle in the way of his elevation." However, Henderson added, the matter of Black civil rights in a postslavery United States was not the issue before the Senate at this time. "Whether he shall be a citizen of any one of the States," Henderson noted, "is a question for that State to determine." To give this point added stress, he declared, "We give him no right [here] except his freedom, and leave the rest to the States."[71]

THE BLAIRS' PERSISTENCE

In the months and years following Lincoln's late-1862 message to Congress, the last time the president publicly endorsed the prospect of large-scale Black expatriation, the Blairs continued to promote colonization with undiminished vigor. Part of the reason that they did so was that they knew that the president had not given up entirely on the issue. In various private discussions, he continued to explore the possibility of facilitating colonization in Central America, South America, the British West Indies, and other destinations. Indeed, as late as the early months of 1865, shortly before his assassination, Lincoln spoke with General Benjamin Butler twice on the subject. These actions—combined with the fact that Lincoln rejected the resignation proffer of James Mitchell, the federal commissioner of emigration, during the second half of 1864—indicated to the Blairs and other members of the president's inner circle that he retained a measure of hope, though almost certainly a much-diminished measure, that a portion of the Black population would ultimately agree to leave the United States. At the same time, however, the Blairs understood that Lincoln's public silence was meaningful. It was a calculated response to congressional Republicans' declining willingness to support colonization, a decline forcefully underscored, during the summer of 1864, by the repeal of the two earlier appropriations. The Blairs' decision to continue promoting colonization vigorously, despite Lincoln's public silence and despite the negative congressional trend, illuminated a fundamental difference between them and the president on this controversial subject. In basic terms, for Lincoln, political considerations outweighed ideological ones; for the Blairs, the reverse was true.[72]

During 1863 and 1864, Lincoln felt compelled to give serious consideration to the effects that his public statements and actions regarding colonization might have on his relationship with congressional Republicans. He had, of course, given serious consideration to his positions on all major political issues since the Civil War had begun, but the approaching presidential election of 1864 heightened his vigilance. It is quite likely, thus, that the conviction that informed Lincoln's decision to avoid mentioning colonization in the early-1863 Emancipation Proclamation, the first indication of his public silence, strengthened considerably over the next twenty-two months, as the election neared. During this period, as the negative trend in Congress became more and more clear, two pieces of bad news surfaced that provided Lincoln added reasons for silence. During the first half of 1863, newspapers reported that an ongoing effort to colonize Black Americans in Colombia, under the auspices of the Chiriqui Improvement Company, had produced dismal results. Similar news came out during the first half of 1864 regarding an ongoing effort to colonize Black Americans on the island of Île-à-Vache, near Haiti. The second instance involved the actual emigration of at least a few hundred Black Americans. A report from the secretary of the interior to the Senate, published in the *New York Times,* characterized the "enterprise" as utterly "disastrous" and indicated that all of the emigrants were in the process of being returned to the United States. In both cases, rumors of corruption, some of which pointed at federal officials, darkened the news further.[73]

The Blairs persisted in the face of this strong political headwind. During the spring of 1863, Montgomery—who, for the time being, was still a member of Lincoln's cabinet—gave two especially forceful speeches in favor of colonization to audiences in Ohio and New Hampshire. Despite Lincoln's several-month silence and the recent failure of the Missouri Emancipation Bill, with its underlying colonization agenda, the postmaster general spoke about the prospect of large-scale Black expatriation with as much passion and presumption as ever. The "President's plan" of racial separation, a reference to the trio of amendments proposed by Lincoln in December, Montgomery asserted, was clearly the wisest and most practical path forward for the nation. The approach of combining "emancipation and colonization" was one that, over the past eighty years, many of the most revered "patriots" in American history had endorsed. "Washington, Jefferson, Madison, Monroe, Jackson, Clay, and [many] others" from the South had been "advocates" of such an approach, as had many "patriots of the North." Indeed, one of the only groups of Americans that had opposed this course of action, Montgomery claimed, was the cohort of "ultra abolitionists" in the North that preached the reckless and historically disproven doctrines of Black inclusion and "equality." Their alternative vision of the nation's future, if pursued, Montgomery declared, would prove to be an utter "failure from the start" and, he added, would ultimately lead to a "war of [racial] extermination."[74]

Senator Henry Wilson of Massachusetts wrote to Lincoln twice in the summer and fall of 1863 to express great frustration with the content and tone of Montgomery's speeches. Wilson was particularly incensed by the address in New Hampshire in which Montgomery denounced Northern *ultra abolitionists*. He recognized that Montgomery was engaging in a kind of criticism by proxy, attacking those in the North who were most well-known for supporting Black inclusion and equality as a means of throwing shade on congressional Republicans, like Wilson, who held similar views. "I never heard a single Republican approve" of what Montgomery said in his New Hampshire address, Wilson declared. "Blair is universally denounced for his speeches and actions and," Wilson warned, "is every hour setting men against you." Wilson closed the second letter to Lincoln with a promise, and a threat: "On the opening of Congress—when the pressure of the elections are over—the war he has made causelessly upon us will be repelled—at any cost."[75]

During the first half of 1864, as the president engaged in a fight with Wilson and the majority of Republican congressmen over the terms on which Confederate states might be readmitted to the Union, the Blairs continued to behave in ways that many Republicans found inflammatory and divisive. Frank, for instance, delivered a fiery address in the House of Representatives in February in which he denounced several congressmen in Missouri and Maryland for suddenly and opportunistically becoming advocates of immediate abolition without colonization. Although the Blairs were generally supportive, at this time, of the political shift toward immediate abolition, they had grown increasingly frustrated with Republican congressmen's declining interest in colonization, and they lay part of the blame for this decline at the feet of Border State congressmen who, Frank claimed, were engaging in political "chicanery" to boost their careers. It was absurd, he declared, to take as true claims made for immediate abolition and against the necessity of colonization by those who had, until recently, opposed any and all emancipatory actions taken by Congress and the president: "I submit it to the candor and good sense of the country which proposition is the most benevolent and humane toward this oppressed and much-abused African race—that of Jefferson and Lincoln or that of the Jacobin leaders of Maryland and Missouri." Although Lincoln had been quiet on the subject of colonization for more than a year, the Blairs continued to speak as if the president remained committed to a policy of emancipation and expatriation.[76]

In September 1864, roughly two months before Lincoln faced a very uncertain contest for reelection, the president sent a short message to Montgomery: "You have generously said to me more than once, that whenever your resignation could be a relief to me, it was at my disposal. The time has come." Montgomery returned a note to Lincoln on the same day with his formal resignation as a member of the president's cabinet. Lincoln had decided that his close association with the Blairs had indeed become a political liability, as Henry Wilson had warned. The Blairs agreed. Lincoln would have the best chance at reelection if Montgomery no longer had a high-ranking position in the administration.[77]

Four days after he resigned, Montgomery gave a speech at the Cooper Institute in which he strongly affirmed his desire, despite his resignation, to see Lincoln reelected. He made no mention of colonization in the address. The omission was not an indication that the Blairs had given up on the cause that they had promoted, with great fervor, for the last seven years but rather a political concession made, in this particular preelection moment, for Lincoln's benefit. Indeed, the Blairs resumed promoting colonization with great fervor in 1865. And, as chapter 6 shows, their fervent advocacy persisted for several years beyond the war, even though the political headwinds that blew against the issue of federally supported colonization became even stronger.[78]

In effect, during the final years of the Civil War, the Blairs and Lincoln made a fundamentally different calculation on the issue of Black expatriation. Lincoln's public silence indicated his decision to prioritize his reelection objective, which depended at least in part on harmonizing his political positions with congressional Republicans and diminishing his exposure to bad news. The Blairs' forceful persistence as colonization advocates reflected their long-standing and unwavering conviction that the abolition of slavery, a prospect rising quickly on the horizon, had to be pursued in conjunction with a national plan of Black expatriation.

There was something else of significance going on as well, two points of attitudinal distinction that were discernible even during the early years of the Civil War, when the Blairs and Lincoln were largely on the same page. First, in general, Lincoln chose not to promote the issue of colonization with the same consistency that the Blairs evinced. A significant illustration of this contrast can be found in events surrounding the Border State Resolution. The resolution's text, as composed and submitted to Congress in March 1862, made no mention of colonization, an omission Garrett Davis of Kentucky had complained about during the Senate's debate. The Blairs had anticipated such objections and had advised a different course. The day before Lincoln delivered his resolution to Congress, Montgomery had urged him to address the subject explicitly. Lincoln rejected the advice, despite Montgomery's indication that his father, whose opinion Lincoln greatly valued as well, also endorsed the inclusion. Two days after Congress received the resolution, the *New York Times* published a letter written by Montgomery that, in addition to endorsing Lincoln's decision to advocate emancipatory action in the Border States, heavily stressed the importance of federally supported colonization as an inducement to such emancipatory action. It was crucial for the federal government, Montgomery explained, to give white Americans in the Border States "assurance" that "the blacks... are to be regarded as sojourners when emancipated, as in point of fact," he added, "they are, and ever will be."[79]

Second, Lincoln never indicated, in any significant or sustained way, that he was open to the kind of compulsory connection between emancipation and expatriation that the Blairs indicated, in various moments, they believed was crucial. In a speech given the day after Congress passed the DC Abolition Act, for instance, Frank remarked that although he did "not believe that compulsory colonization" would be "necessary," he did not "regard it with any abhorrence." Indeed, he added, "I look upon it [expatriation] as the greatest boon we can confer upon this race, greater by far than the gift of personal freedom in the land in which they must forever remain in a condition of social inferiority, among a people who will treat them with every imaginable indignity." A few months later, in July, Frank also signed his name to the House select committee report on Border State slavery that, in addition to devoting many pages to arguing the necessity of colonization, proposed a bill that, as noted earlier, implied support for making expatriation a condition of emancipation.[80]

The key factors of these two distinctions, beyond political considerations, were life experience and geography. All three Blairs were, or had been, slaveholders for many decades, and all three had resided, for their entire lives, in areas where enslavement was legal. Lincoln was not and never had been a slaveholder, and although he had been born in a slave state, Kentucky, he had lived since early childhood in Indiana and Illinois, where enslavement was illegal. These fundamental differences in background translated into different levels of conviction regarding the colonization movement's Black-freedom-as-a-societal-problem ideology. While the Blairs and Lincoln generally agreed that racialized slavery had created circumstances that made it incredibly difficult, if not impossible, for white and Black Americans to coexist on equal terms, the Blairs refused to accept the possibility that large-scale emancipation would not, at some point, be followed by large-scale expatriation. The former without the latter, they insisted, would be cataclysmic. In simple terms, the prospective expatriation of a large portion of the Black population was, for Lincoln, a preference. For the Blairs, it was and always had been an absolute necessity.

In October 1864, Black leaders from across the nation gathered in Syracuse for a very public, four-day meeting. Delegates from seventeen states, including some Confederate states, attended. Frederick Douglass served as the meeting's president. On the first day, he delivered a brief address in which he articulated the convening's overarching purpose: "We are here to promote the freedom, progress, elevation, and perfect enfranchisement, of the entire colored people of the United States." A publication of the meeting's proceedings distributed after the convention elaborated Douglass's statement with a declaration of the rights claimed by Black Americans in this great and pivotal moment in the nation's history: "We declare that all men are born free and equal; [and] that no man or government has a right to annul... this fundamental principle," "as citizens of the Republic, we claim the rights of other citizens," and "as natives of American soil, we claim the right to remain upon it." On this last point, the declaration added, "Any attempt to deport, remove, expatriate, or colonize us to any other land, or to mass us here against our will, is unjust" and hereby rejected.[81]

A mix of hope and concern informed these public statements. The Emancipation Proclamation issued by President Lincoln and the endorsement by the Senate of a proposed thirteenth amendment strongly suggested that the end of slavery was finally on the horizon. However, for national abolition to become a reality, the House of Representatives still needed to endorse the amendment, and the requisite three-quarters of the states still needed to ratify it. Moreover, the abolition of slavery, as these statements made clear, was viewed by Black leaders as but a first step in a larger move toward equal rights—an enormously significant first step, to be sure, but a first step nonetheless. In other words, the leaders and participants of the late-1864 convention wanted Congress and the president to know that they expected more from the federal government than just the end of enslavement. They expected no more talk of expatriation as a prospective federal project, and they expected further actions that would guarantee full civic equality with white Americans.

The repeal by Congress, just a few months earlier, of both federal appropriations for colonization was clearly a reason for hope, as was the fact the president had not mentioned the subject publicly in nearly two years. Other reasons for optimism were serious congressional discussions, earlier in 1864, to establish a federal agency that would help protect and uplift the growing population of newly emancipated Americans. During the early part of 1865, the Senate and House reached final agreement on a bill to move forward with this effort, thus establishing what became known as the Freedmen's Bureau. This agreement came shortly after the House voted to endorse the proposed thirteenth amendment, which twenty of twenty-seven states ratified shortly thereafter, indicating that the end of slavery was most likely near.[82]

There were, at the same time, however, several reasons for concern. It remained plain and incontrovertible that the president of the United States had endorsed the prospect of Black expatriation on several occasions during the first half of the Civil War. In two especially high-profile instances—his meeting with free Black Washingtonians in August 1862 and his message to Congress in December of the same year—he had given his endorsement in strongly worded terms. Even if the Republican Congress remained opposed to giving federal support to the colonization cause, the president's earlier endorsements would continue to resonate in the ears of many white Americans, in part because of his tremendous national stature, but also because the Blairs remained insistent that he had not changed his mind on the issue and because they continued to use their own considerable influence to carry the colonization movement forward. The abolition of slavery, they argued, would make the issue of colonization more urgent and relevant, not less. In early 1865, Henry McNeal Turner, a Black chaplain in the Union army and a future bishop in the African Methodist Episcopal Church, sent a letter to the editor of the *Christian Recorder* warning Black Americans that the issue of colonization would not soon be left behind: the "subject is being, of late, very much spoken of," and "as soon as this rebellion is over, it will be the chief topic in every legislative department, from Congress down to town councils."[83]

Beyond all of this, various congressmen indicated, during the legislative sessions of 1864 and early 1865, that they continued to adhere to the colonization movement's exclusionary ideology, whether or not federal support for colonization was a viable issue. For instance, during the relatively short debate that resulted in the repeal of the two colonization appropriations, a senator from Maryland declared that although he supported the proposed repeal, he remained convinced that Black and white Americans could not "live together in social and political equality." A Republican senator from Kansas went further, asserting that while he agreed with Senator Wilson of Massachusetts that "the idea of deportation is exploded," he did "not agree with him as to the separation of the two races," especially as it pertained to the South. Indeed, earlier in the session, this senator had proposed that the federal government facilitate the migration of Black Americans to an area set aside for them in western Texas. He explained: Although the war had generated a "large measure of public sympathy for the colored race," the end of the war would almost assuredly be followed by a resurgence of racial conflict and oppression in the slave states. To bolster the appeal of his colonization proposal, the Republican senator quoted Jefferson's famous "nothing is more certain" remark regarding the essential incongruity of Black equality and white equality, the same quotation that the Blairs habitually invoked.[84]

Black Americans were acutely aware of all of this. They knew that the abolition of slavery would put questions regarding the freedom of Black Americans at the center of national and state politics, and that the prospective answers were very uncertain. The biggest question, one that the Syracuse convention preemptively answered in the affirmative, was whether the federal government would guarantee the full civic equality of Black Americans. The second question, if the answer to the first question were *no,* was whether the federal government would, at a minimum, guarantee certain key rights. The third question was what state legislatures and constitutional conventions would do in response to either scenario. To what extent would they cooperate, and to what extent would they seek to find ways to continue what in most states were fairly comprehensive regimes of Black exclusion? Senator John Henderson had given a terse and potentially ominous answer to these questions in the spring of 1864, when, after explaining his reasons for supporting the proposed thirteenth amendment, he had declared, "We give him no right except his freedom, and leave the rest to the States."[85]

With such worrisome future prospects in mind, the late-1864 Syracuse convention embedded a crucial message in the document that it published and distributed afterward. Although "prejudice" would likely continue to influence "social and domestic relations" in the United States, "in the matter of government, the object of which is the protection and security of human rights, prejudice should be allowed no voice whatever." Implicit in this declaration was an assertion that claims of ineradicable prejudice and of the essential incongruity of Black equality and white equality, like those made by colonization advocates for decades, should not be used by congressmen or state legislators as justification for laws that restricted the freedoms of Black Americans.[86]

6

OPPOSING BLACK SUFFRAGE

1866–1900

IN THE FALL OF 1865, Black Americans convened the first annual meeting of the National Equal Rights League, an organization launched during the Syracuse convention of the prior year. Over the course of three days in Cleveland, convention speakers expressed serious concerns regarding the future of Black Americans in the United States. Without denying the enormous step forward that was the Thirteenth Amendment of the Constitution, the imminent ratification of which seemed fairly certain, the meeting reiterated declarations from the 1864 convention that characterized the abolition of slavery as a first step in a larger process. The federal government needed to guarantee the same rights of citizenship to Black Americans that white Americans had long enjoyed, the 1865 meeting's leaders stressed, if the former were to have any real chance of preserving and building out the basic freedom afforded by the national abolition of slavery.[1]

William Forten, son of James Forten, and a prominent Pennsylvanian activist in his own right, confessed to the convention that he found himself "enveloped in clouds of sombre threatening." "We have been deserted," he declared, "by those whom we faithfully supported, and *insolently informed that this is a white man's country, though it required the strong arms of over*

200,000 black men to save it." Although white and Black Americans "can fight and *die* together... in defence of the spangled-banner," he stated, the former has told the latter that "we must find homes in some Territory separate to ourselves, as white and black men cannot live together upon terms of equality." That Black Americans found themselves in such a "crisis" after all that had just transpired, he observed, was depressing, concerning, and, indeed, galling.²

As Forten's remarks indicated, the colonization movement, and its exclusionary vision of the nation's racial future, was still very much alive in late 1865. Neither the Civil War nor the Thirteenth Amendment had ended it. In acknowledgment of the movement's persistence and as confirmation of Black Americans' strong and unwavering opposition, the convention passed and published a formal declaration: "That we have no sympathy with any movement having for its object, the Colonizing of Colored Americans on the coast of Africa, or elsewhere... [and that] we regard the subject of emigration... [as] calculated to divert the minds of our people from the all important subject of enfranchisement." One of the targets of this declaration was the still active, but politically diminished American Colonization Society. The other, the more significant one, was the Blair family, which after two years of declining influence with Lincoln and the Republican Party, was trying, with notable success, to use Black expatriation as one of the rallying points for a new, reconceived version of the Democratic Party.³

The Blairs' political strategy had been quite apparent in a speech delivered by Montgomery the day before the Equal Rights League convention began in Cleveland. Addressing a large audience in New York City gathered at the Cooper Institute, where nearly six years earlier Abraham Lincoln had delivered a speech that had become one of the cornerstones of his presidential campaign, Montgomery proclaimed, "If the negroes are ever to be free, equal and independent, they must have a place of refuge set off and secured to them." Congressmen who sought to confine "two nations" of people within the United States were not true "Republicans," he declared. Nor were they, despite their insistent claims, real "friends" of the Black race. Those with the clearest vision of the nation's future, he maintained, were those who understood that the Civil War and the Thirteenth Amendment, by abolishing slavery, had made colonization an urgent national issue, even more urgent than before. "Now that the sword has done its work in cutting the cancer [of slavery] from our constitution," the sword must now be employed to excise "every morbid root, lest the ulcer be renewed, and never may be healed."[4]

The Blairs, still politically astute and well-connected, understood they had little to no chance of persuading the federal government to support colonization. Recent events had made this quite clear. Although many Republican leaders had voted in favor of colonization appropriations during the early 1860s, they had done so largely because they had seen these appropriations as a means of encouraging Southern states to take voluntary action against slavery. When no Southern states took action, and, moreover, when events of the war made it increasingly clear that immediate national abolition via constitutional amendment was a viable, indeed preferred, political path, the Republican majority took colonization off the table, repealing the two appropriations made during 1862 and passing the Thirteenth Amendment, which strongly repudiated the Blairs' ongoing claims that emancipation and expatriation had to be connected. With slavery now a thing of the past, any reasonably savvy politician could see that while the Republican Party reigned in Washington, the issue was dead. So why were the Blairs continuing to push Black expatriation as a national imperative?

There were three reasons. First, the Blairs remained firmly committed to Jefferson's vision of a postslavery United States. The abolition of the institution had not changed their long-held belief that white freedom and Black freedom were incongruous. This way of thinking had rigidly shaped their worldview for the last ten years and indeed, as they had suggested during this time, for their whole lives. The continued promotion of colonization was thus, from their perspective, both logical and absolutely essential. To their way of thinking, abolition had increased the magnitude of the Black-freedom problem roughly tenfold. Second, they believed that many white Americans continued to feel the same way that they did about the free Black population and that, accordingly, the continued promotion of colonization, whether federal support was a viable political objective or not, would draw many white Americans into the Democratic Party fold. Third, and of greatest relevance to this chapter, the Blairs worried greatly that the Republican Party would pursue the cause of Black suffrage in the coming years. Such a course fit with the professed values of many in the party and, at the same time, suited Republican electoral interests, since party leaders could likely count on millions of newly free Black Americans to vote for their candidates.

The ongoing promotion of colonization would be of particular value in opposing a congressional move toward Black suffrage, the Blairs believed, since the right to vote was one of the most valued and impactful freedoms in the United States. In other words, if white freedom and Black freedom were incongruous, then it stood to reason that Black voting rights presented a tremendous threat, arguably the greatest threat, to the nation's future. The fact that colonization had been promoted over the course of so many decades by some of the most revered statesmen in American history would make its continued promotion, the Blairs believed, especially impactful. Jefferson, Key, Clay, Webster, Lincoln, and so many others had vigorously and persistently insisted that Black freedom corrupted the inner workings of each state, undermined the strength of the Union, and prevented the nation from realizing its great and exceptional potential. By tapping into this high-powered body of rhetoric, the Blairs could enhance the credibility and strength of their arguments against Black suffrage.

This chapter argues that the tight connection that the Blairs established, during the years immediately following the Civil War, between promoting Black expatriation and opposing Black suffrage persisted in national politics until the early 1900s. During this four-decade period, as colonization advocates accommodated themselves to the new political environment, they translated Black expatriation from a political *goal* into a political *instrument*—not completely, but to a significant degree. At first, they used this instrument to fight the proposed fifteenth amendment on Black voting rights. When this failed, they applied this instrument in a multidecade-long effort to undermine, discredit, and ultimately neutralize Black suffrage throughout the South.[5]

Before proceeding, it is important to make a few qualifying and clarifying remarks. During the post-1865 decades covered in this chapter, the colonization movement's efforts to obtain federal support were much less centralized and influential than they had been during the pre-1865 decades, when the ACS and the Blairs had provided considerable coherence and strength. In the most basic terms, the movement had far less traction in Congress than in any prior period. These facts were especially true beginning in the early 1870s, when the Blairs faded from the national political scene. And they remained true for the remainder of the nineteenth century despite the fact that the ACS, still in existence, continued to promote the cause of Liberian colonization.[6]

However, this chapter's main argument is less about the persistence of the colonization movement's efforts to obtain federal support and more about the persistence of the movement's ideology in the national debate over Black suffrage. In essence, this chapter's narrative and analysis proceed from a basic insight: The various white Americans who promoted colonization from 1865 until the early 1900s—most of whom were Southerners, at first the Upper Southern Blairs and then later, somewhat ironically, a cohort of prominent Lower Southern figures—did so with a clear understanding that the goal of *geographic* exclusion was largely out of reach. Their more immediate goal was *political* exclusion. And they pursued this goal, in significant part, through the use of a racialized ideology that, over the past several decades, colonization advocates had embedded deeply and broadly in American society.

From a broader perspective, what colonization advocates did during this period was to carry Black-freedom-as-a-problem ideology across the threshold of the Thirteenth Amendment, thus creating an afterlife of slavery. In the early decades of the postslavery era, many prominent white Americans sought to keep the colonization movement's slavery-era ideology alive because they believed that it had particular utility in the fight against Black suffrage. In making this argument, this chapter also illustrates an even larger point, one that pertains to the entire racial history of North America, and one that eminent historian Barbara Fields has made, quite emphatically, in her pathbreaking scholarship on race: "Ideologies do not have lives of their own." They cannot persist in society without human agency. If they do persist, it is because certain members of that society continue to find them useful.[7]

FIGHTING THE FIFTEENTH AMENDMENT

During the summer and fall of 1865, the Blairs formally broke with the Republican Party. Tensions with party leaders like Senators Henry Wilson and Charles Sumner, which had grown dramatically since 1863 and which had prompted Montgomery's resignation from Lincoln's cabinet in 1864, had convinced the Blairs to seek a new political platform. The assassination of Lincoln in April 1865, whom they had continued to support despite these tensions, was one of the final straws. The Blairs decided to return to the Democratic Party, where Blair Sr. had made his journalistic career, and to rebrand it as the party of Jefferson and Jackson, not the party of Calhoun. And they sought to draw into this new coalition Republicans of the "Lincoln-Johnson stamp" who opposed the party's "new" Republican agenda of racial equality, especially the possible incorporation of Black Americans into the national electorate.[8]

As the Blairs stumped for the Democratic Party during the mid- to late 1860s, they repeatedly used colonization ideology to characterize Black suffrage as fundamentally misguided. At a large convention in Maryland in early 1866, during the run-up to the mid-term congressional elections, Montgomery declared firm opposition to the idea "that if we carry out our democratic principles of the equality of men that we land in negro suffrage." This was not the view of the nation's "founders," he insisted, especially not Jefferson, who firmly believed that it was "impossible" for Black Americans to "remain among us and be participators in the Government." In June of the same year, Frank expressed similar sentiments as he addressed a "grand conservative meeting" held in the state capital of Missouri. Rather than choosing to invoke Jefferson, as he had so often over the years, Frank invoked God. God had "never" intended the Black race to "share our Government," Frank admonished. Indeed, until the United States removed "these negroes from our midst" and established a true "white man's Government," the American people, he maintained, would have to live with the knowledge that they were violating divine will.[9]

The peak moment of the Blairs' instrumental politicking occurred during the presidential contest of 1868. Horatio Seymour, the former governor of New York, ran as the Democratic Party's presidential candidate, with Frank as the vice-presidential candidate. In the numerous speeches that he gave in support of the Democratic ticket, Frank leaned heavily on the phrase "white man's Government," with its strong and presumptive message that Black political freedom was wrong and dangerous. By this time, Congress had already passed federal laws ensuring Black suffrage in

Washington, DC, the territories, and all of the Confederate states that rejoined the Union—the latter being a stipulation of the sweeping and controversial Reconstruction Act of March 1867—and it had begun debating a constitutional amendment on Black suffrage. In late September, as Frank addressed an audience in Indiana, he denounced all politicians who refused to accept that racial "separation" was the "remedy for the evils which threaten . . . to destroy our form of government." This time, for authority, he urged his listeners to remember the "prophetic language" of Jefferson: "Nothing is more certainly written in the book of fate than that they (the negroes) are to be free. Nor is it less certain that the two races, equally free, cannot live in the same Government." The quotation—which the Blairs, Lincoln, and others had used many times before—had an unmistakable subtext: The first prediction had come to pass; the second was still to be realized.[10]

Blair and Seymour ultimately lost the election to former Union General Ulysses S. Grant and Congressman Schuyler Colfax, signaling, along with the congressional election results of 1868, that Republican dominance in Washington would continue. The Democratic Party ticket, however, garnered 47 percent of the national popular vote and majorities in several Southern states and a few Northern ones, including New York, the largest state in the Union. While these facts did not translate into the kind of political power that the Blairs sought, they did suggest that the party's exclusionary rhetoric resonated with large numbers of white voters.

When Congress reconvened during the months following the election, the Republican majority continued to push for a voting rights amendment. Senator Doolittle—one of the Blairs' longest-standing political allies and, like them, a former Republican who had turned Democrat—invoked colonization rhetoric as he spoke against the prospective law. Recognizing that there was little he or other Democrats could do to block the Fifteenth Amendment's passage, he made sure, nonetheless, to place his sentiments on the record. After making ritualistic references to Jefferson's strong views against racial inclusion and quoting one of Lincoln's declarations regarding the impossibility of the "two races living together on terms of social and political equality," Doolittle suggested that Congress's time and energy would be better spent finding and acquiring a "home in the tropical regions" for the country's Black population. If, he advised, the Republican majority continued to refuse this long-prescribed course, then it should, at least, accept the folly of the proposed amendment. Any attempt to establish and sustain political equality on a national basis, Doolittle insisted, was doomed to failure. The power to oversee suffrage was one of the most "sacred" and consequential powers in a democracy and as such, he admonished, it should be left to the states.[11]

UNDERMINING THE FIFTEENTH AMENDMENT

The Fifteenth Amendment passed both houses of Congress in 1869 and was ratified by the requisite number of states in 1870. By the end of that year, every former Confederate state had reentered the Union. These states were represented in Congress almost exclusively by the Republican Party, due in significant part to the votes of Black Americans that the 1867 Reconstruction Act had ensured across the former Confederacy and that the Fifteenth Amendment now protected on a national basis. Over the next several years, Black voting in these states contributed significantly to the installment of the first Black politicians in Congress and to the widespread election and appointment of Black Americans to state- and local-level government offices.[12]

Large numbers of white Americans in the former Confederate states fiercely opposed this political transformation. They had done so during the late 1860s prior to the Fifteenth Amendment's ratification, and they continued to do so after. Some tactics involved forms of illegal manipulation; others were extremely violent. Newly founded white supremacist organizations, like the Ku Klux Klan and the Knights of the White Camelia, contributed to both types of actions. In general, efforts to exclude Black voters were most notable in the Lower Southern states that had Black majority or near-majority populations, like Alabama, Louisiana, Mississippi, and South Carolina.[13]

In May 1870, roughly four months after the Fifteenth Amendment's ratification, Congress passed a law aimed at curbing these constitutional violations. The Enforcement Act of 1870 augmented the federal government's power to prosecute Fifteenth Amendment violators and authorized the president to mobilize the United States military and state militias to ensure local compliance. In 1871, Congress established an investigatory committee, the Joint Select Committee to Inquire into the Condition of Affairs in the Late Insurrectionary States, in order to assess the Enforcement Act's effectiveness and to determine whether the federal government should take incremental actions. Frank Blair, who had returned to Congress as a senator from Missouri in early 1871, served on this committee.

In 1872, when the committee reported its findings, Frank signed his name to a minority report issued by seven (including himself) of the committee's Democrats. While the committee's majority saw ample justification for continuing and perhaps escalating the federal government's enforcement role in Southern elections, the minority cast doubt on the logic of intervention. In stating their position, the minority members did not defend the many documented acts of electoral violence, but they did, in a sense, normalize them, and they used colonization ideology to do so. Congress should have known, the report declared, that "a conflict of races must be the inevitable result" of any attempt to effect a "peaceable joint exercise of power, among such discordant bodies" of Americans. "Man's puny statutes cannot repeal or nullify the immutable ordinances of the Almighty. Those whom God has separated let no man join together." If congressional leaders continued on their present course, "absorbed in the idea of this newly discovered political divinity in the negro," the minority report warned, they must accept that they were risking the destruction of the "glorious form of government bequeathed to us by our fathers." Just as the Civil War had proven that "no government could exist 'half slave and half free,'" current events were proving that "no government can long exist 'half black and half white.'"[14]

Frank's term in the United States Senate ended the following year, making these disparaging remarks about the Fifteenth Amendment some of the last words—though not *the* last—that Frank, and the Blair family more broadly, contributed to the long-running, intertwined discourses on enslavement and freedom in the United States. After spending much of the next two years back in Missouri in a state of rapidly declining health, Frank died in St. Louis in 1875 at the age of fifty-four. Blair Sr., the patriarch, died the following year in Maryland at eighty-five. Montgomery, the last member of the Blair triumvirate, lived for seven more years and still had a bit more to say.

The violent attacks on Black voters in the Lower South—efforts to undermine the Fifteenth Amendment that the minority report had characterized as unsurprising and, in a sense, inevitable—continued throughout the 1870s. Horrific instances of election-related violence occurred in Colfax, Louisiana, in 1873; Vicksburg, Mississippi, in 1874; and in various locations in South Carolina in 1876, to name but a few such moments. These events were part of a rising trend of social, economic, and political oppression faced by Black Americans living in this region that was enabled, in significant part, by the Republican Party's declining interest in Southern federal oversight and the Democratic Party's resurgence across the region. In 1878, roughly eighteen months after the election of President Rutherford B. Hayes and the subsequent final withdrawal of federal troops from the South, an editorial in the *Christian Recorder,* still one of the most prominent Black periodicals of the time, offered a very discouraging view of the prospects facing Southern Black Americans. The sectional "reconciliation policy" of the new president, the editorial declared, "encourages our enemies to use every means to trample and bind us down where we were before emancipation."[15]

Faced with such troubling circumstances, many Black Southerners moved, or at least considered moving, out of the South. Some looked to places in the North, Kansas being a popular destination. Others moved from the Lower South to the Upper South, hoping to find less oppression than they had encountered when living in states where Black voting, because of the relative size of the Black population, seemed to be most resented. And some considered leaving the United States altogether. Just as a portion of Black Americans had shown increased interest in emigration to Africa or the Caribbean during the 1850s and early 1860s, when racial oppression had escalated to disturbing levels, a portion of the population showed increased interest during the late 1870s and 1880s in response to similarly troubling circumstances.[16]

Articles and speeches published during the late 1870s and early 1880s in the *African Repository,* the still-active journal of the still-active American Colonization Society, seized on this trend. The fact that racial oppression in the South was pushing more and more Black Americans toward emigration, ACS leaders asserted, offered proof of the organization's long-maintained, central principle: Full freedom for Black Americans was practicable only on foreign soil. Although the ACS had never recovered the political traction that it had enjoyed during its first forty years—prior to the late 1850s, when the Blairs pushed it to the margins of national politics—the organization had not disbanded. During the late 1860s, its leaders had insisted, like the Blairs, that the end of slavery had increased, not decreased, the relevance and urgency of Black expatriation. After the ratification of the Fifteenth Amendment, ACS leaders had continued to broadcast this message. While, generally speaking, they differed from the Blairs in that their primary intent was not necessarily to oppose or undermine Black suffrage, they often expressed sentiments that tended to validate these aims. What good were rights of citizenship and voting for Black Americans, an ACS leader asked at the 1877 annual meeting, when these rights were "reddened in a war of races or trampled with contempt, which no constitutional amendment can amend in the constitution of our nature?" During the 1880 annual meeting, the society's president remarked that Black "oppression" was "as potent to-day" as it had been a century earlier, due in large part to the predictable failure of "amendments" and statutes intended "to overcome the prejudices and the influences of Caste." To these observations, he added the following conclusory remark: "The slave question has been settled, but the Negro question is still an open one."[17]

In the midst of this national conversation on Black migration/emigration from the South and Black civil rights, a conversation Congress ultimately joined in 1880 with the publication of an extensive investigatory report, Montgomery Blair contributed an essay to a star-studded forum on Black voting published in the venerable *North American Review*. His piece contained the Blair family's last major public statement on Black expatriation. The article posed two questions in the title: "Ought the Negro to Be Disfranchised? Ought He to Have Been Enfranchised?" Blair answered the first question with a *yes* and the second with a *no*. In support of these assertions, he repeated the same claims that he, Frank, Doolittle, and many other colonization advocates had made for decades: "The races could not live together as equals," and "deportation" had to follow "emancipation." He also reiterated the claim that neither Jefferson nor any of the emancipation-favoring "fathers" had "contemplated making the negro a voter." Against this rhetorical backdrop, Montgomery declared, "to incorporate" Black Americans into "our system is to subvert it."[18]

This article proved to be one of Montgomery's final acts on the national political stage. He died in 1883. As he made these remarks in the *North American Review*, he understood that he was engaging in his own subversive effort: using the pre-1865 rhetoric of Black expatriation to undermine the post-1865 constitutional amendment that protected Black suffrage. In other words, he was using slavery-era ideas and language to contest a postslavery-era constitutional action. Over the next two decades, such efforts to subvert the Fifteenth Amendment would intensify. Interestingly, the main regional impulse would shift, for the first time in American history, from the Upper South to the Lower South. The state right to self-determine with respect to slavery had been nullified and, with it, the Lower South's main motivation for opposing the Black expatriation political movement. Lower Southern politicians now saw the movement in a new light.

DISCREDITING THE FIFTEENTH AMENDMENT

Lower Southern politicians and journalists began to play major roles in this subversive political effort during the mid- to late 1880s. Among the most notable figures were Carlyle McKinley, a reporter for the *News and Courier* of South Carolina; Henry Grady, editor of the *Atlanta Constitution* of Georgia; and John Tyler Morgan, United States senator from Alabama. Collectively, these men argued for Black expatriation with a level of vigor comparable to that evinced by the Blairs during the late 1850s and 1860s. As they applied colonization rhetoric to the ongoing project of repudiating the Fifteenth Amendment, these Lower Southern propagandists frequently used phrases like "Negro Problem" and "Negro Question" as shorthand references for their messages. These were not phrases, to be clear, that they created or that only they invoked. Such word combinations—and variants of them, such as "Race Problem" and "Race Question"—had circulated for years as Americans with a range of racialized attitudes had publicly debated the institution of enslavement and the prospect of Black civic equality. However, during the mid- to late 1880s, McKinley, Grady, Morgan, and other Lower Southern propagandists sought to turn these terms into exclusionary slogans, phrases that called to mind the colonization movement's

Black-freedom-as-a-problem ideology. A chief purpose of this rhetorical move was to take the fight against Black suffrage to another level by discrediting the perceived legitimacy of the Fifteenth Amendment.[19]

One of the pivotal moments of this "Negro Problem" propaganda campaign was the publication, in 1889, of *An Appeal to Pharaoh: The Negro Problem and Its Radical Solution,* authored by Carlyle McKinley. This popular two-hundred-plus-page book went through three editions, the last of which was released in 1907, by which point many Southern states had enacted laws that effectively disfranchised Black Americans. The "radical solution" recommended by McKinley was federally sponsored colonization, an act of "practical patriotism" that, he insisted, it was the "duty" of all white Americans to support. Central to his arguments in favor of colonization was his claim that the Fifteenth Amendment had proven, without doubt, to be a failed "experiment." The federal government had disregarded the "law which from the beginning has commanded and compelled the separation of the races," and the nation was "now groaning under the consequences of our transgression." He added: "Does any man believe for a moment, that, if the Negro were not here, and if it were proposed by any person or power to bring him here *now* to take his place among us, to share our heritage and citizenship, to be established here on the footing now conceded to him . . . he would be allowed to set foot on American soil on any terms?" While it was clearly impossible to change the past and to prevent the decisions that had brought the Black race to North America, McKinley observed, there was something very real to be "gained . . . if we accept the broad principle that it *would be* our duty, clearly, to deny him a place among us, if he had not already secured a foothold on our territory." Acceptance of this exclusionary principle enabled a clear view of the proper path forward, he insisted. White Americans, irrespective of party and region, must give up on all this legal "experimentation" and commence the process of restoring the United States to "the exclusive control of the white race."[20]

During the same year that McKinley published his "Negro Problem" treatise, celebrity editor Henry Grady delivered a much-publicized speech in Boston on the same subject: the "race problem," as he named it. The problem's fundamental cause, Grady declared, was the fact that for the last few decades the United States had enacted laws that contravened the "universal verdict of racial history." Never before had "two races . . . lived anywhere at any time on the same soil with equal rights in peace." The consequences of this contravention, Grady observed, had been dire, especially for the South, which had borne the brunt of the "race problem," but also for the nation as a whole, which remained, decades after the closing of the Civil War, fraught with sectional tension. The fact that the issue of Black freedom continued to cause strife among white Americans was, Grady solemnly observed, tragic. The United States would take a large and important step forward, he advised, if the Northern states would simply respect each Southern state's "inalienable right" to defend itself "against an ignorant or corrupt suffrage." The "race problem" was really the only significant impediment to a "perfect Union."[21]

In his closing remarks, Grady made direct reference to colonization. Among the various possible futures available to Black Americans, two, he noted, seemed most probable. First, the Black race might continue living in the nation as a "forever dislocated and separated" people. Second, this alienated population might finally, as many had long predicted, seek "homes again in Africa."[22]

Senator John Morgan of Alabama, a former Confederate general who had entered Congress more than a decade earlier as part of the late-1870s Democratic Party resurgence in the South, expressed sentiments similar to those of McKinley and Grady in articles entitled "Shall Negro Majorities Rule?" and "The Race Question in the United States," published, respectively, in 1889 and 1890 in the New York–based *Forum* and the Boston-based *Arena*. Morgan, a well-known critic of Black suffrage, insisted, as Grady had, that the Southern states should be allowed to deal with the issue of voting rights as they saw fit. "Public opinion" in each state polity, he declared, should be trusted to determine the proper course. And, like both Grady and McKinley, Morgan placed the project of addressing and resolving the "race question" in a broader nationalist context, claiming that the key to restoring "peace and harmony" in the country was to eliminate the "friction" produced by the "presence," "political power," and "social aspirations" of the Black race. Full and permanent resolution of the "race question," Morgan explained, depended not just on white Americans dealing directly with Black suffrage but also on them supporting Black expatriation, something he expressed confidence they would do. At some point in the future, Morgan predicted, Black Americans would finally accept the fact that the "peace and prosperity ... [of] both races" depended on their voluntary removal. In that crucial moment, "the financial aid of our people and government," he predicted, would pour "forth freely" in support of this long-awaited, national "deliverance." And what a "great deliverance it will be!"[23]

In essence, the propaganda pieces of McKinley, Grady, and Morgan had three messages, all of which proceeded from the colonization movement's core premise that Black freedom and white freedom were incongruous. First, the Fifteenth Amendment was an unfortunate and misguided political act that had produced enormous issues for the nation. Second, the nation needed to take near-term actions to address these issues while the long-term solution to the "Negro Problem," the expatriation of the nation's Black population, gradually came to fruition. Third, because the Southern states had the most experience dealing with the "Negro Problem," in all its aspects, the federal government should give them the latitude to lead the way.

NEUTRALIZING THE FIFTEENTH AMENDMENT

In December 1889, Senator Morgan and two other senior senators from the Lower South, Matthew Butler and Wade Hampton of South Carolina, launched a highly public and, as it turned out, short-lived effort to appropriate $5 million in federal funds for the voluntary expatriation of Black Americans. This was the first time, since the middle years of the Civil War, that any lawmaker had put the issue before Congress in such substantive fashion and with such vigor. Formally introduced by Senator Butler, the proposed legislation would have made the quartermaster general of the US Army responsible for taking in application letters from emigrants, arranging their transportation out of the country, and managing the pool of appropriated funds. In essence, the Butler Bill, as it became known, sought to establish the federal government as the financial sponsor and chief administrator of a national system of colonization: the roles that Mercer, Key, Clay, Kennedy, Stanton, Lincoln, and the Blairs, among many others, had tried for many decades, largely without success, to get it to assume.[24]

These seasoned congressmen—Butler and Hampton, like Morgan, had served continuously in the Senate since the late 1870s, having been elected as part of the same moment of Democratic Party resurgence that had given Morgan his seat—fully understood how improbable it was that the Butler Bill would pass, or even make notable progress toward such an outcome. Neither national political party had shown any significant interest in federally supported colonization since the late 1860s, when the Blairs had made this issue central to their efforts to oppose a prospective fifteenth amendment, to get Democrats elected to Congress, and to promote the presidential candidacy of Horatio Seymour, with Frank as his vice-presidential running mate, in the election of 1868. Moreover, at this particular moment, the Republican Party held both chambers of Congress as well as the presidency, the first time this had happened in roughly fifteen years. These large and obvious political impediments strongly suggested that the three senators had ulterior aims. The first and most immediate was a desire to oppose, on a preemptive basis, the Republican Party's expected attempt to reinvigorate federal enforcement of the Fifteenth Amendment. The party's official platform in the 1888 presidential election had indicated that congressional Republicans were likely to pursue an election reform bill during the sessions from 1889 to 1891. The second aim, as the text of their speeches made clear, was to broadcast numerous hours of "Negro Problem" propaganda from the congressional stage and have it documented in the congressional record. Two intended effects of this broadcast were to further discredit the Fifteenth Amendment and to bolster the claimed legitimacy, or at least defensibility, of ongoing efforts in the Southern states to work around and, in effect, neutralize Black voting rights. During the late 1870s and 1880s, these efforts had expanded beyond outright violence and fraud to include various quasi-legal methods of restricting Black suffrage, such as poll taxes, property requirements, and redistricting.[25]

In the very long oratories delivered by Butler, Hampton, and Morgan in support of the proposed bill, the three Lower Southern senators, all who were former Confederate army generals, brought together, in quite deliberate fashion, the main arguments made by colonization advocates over the last seventy years. In aggregate, they declared racial separation to be the only logical, lasting solution to the "irrepressible conflict" between white and Black Americans. They identified this conflict, specifically the "presence amongst us" of the Black race, as a major obstacle to the founders' dream of a "more perfect union." On this basis, they insisted that colonization was a patriotic endeavor that transcended the divisions of section and party. They cited past "appropriations" for the removal of the "Indians" and "to exclude the Chinaman"—racialized actions deemed crucial to the "general welfare" of the nation—as legal precedents for the current proposal. They insisted that colonization was, to a significant degree, a humane endeavor, since it offered Black Americans an opportunity to enjoy full civil rights in a nation of their own. And they burnished the validity of all of these assertions by extensively quoting Jefferson, Webster, Lincoln, and other past colonization advocates, as well as more recent ones like McKinley. They also celebrated the fact that "so many publications touching this subject" had come before the American people in recent years, a clear indication, they suggested, that "public opinion" increasingly favored Black expatriation. Nowhere in their speeches, however, did these men acknowledge the tremendous irony underlying their current actions. For the majority of the colonization movement's seventy years, their Lower Southern forebears had fiercely and unflaggingly denounced all efforts to involve the federal government in colonization.[26]

The senators' addresses devoted considerable time to asserting connections between the political issues of colonization and Black suffrage, even though the bill had nothing to do, at least formally, with the latter subject. One of the great benefits of colonization, the senators claimed, was its capacity to facilitate an urgent and essential course correction in American government. The Fifteenth Amendment, based as it was on the false premise that the grant of political equality to Black Americans was adequate to the task of overcoming deep-rooted racial aversion, had proven to be a reckless and destructive political experiment, they asserted. Instead of producing the intended ameliorative effects on racial tensions, it had exacerbated, especially in the South, the high levels of "friction and collision" between the white and Black races. Hampton, one of the two South Carolinians involved in promoting the Butler Bill, noted, with regret, the ill-fated decision of the Senate in 1825 to reject a proposal by Rufus King to fund a federal program of emancipation and expatriation—again without acknowledging that Lower Southern congressmen, most notably South Carolinian Robert Hayne, had led the opposition. Referring to the current funding proposal, Hampton remarked, "better late than never," adding that there was "no time . . . more opportune than the present" to solve the "grave problem confronting us." The "destiny" of the United States, he declared, must be placed fully in "the hands" of the white race.[27]

Several months later—with no indication that the Butler Bill was going anywhere, but nonetheless with the speeches of Morgan, Butler, and Hampton inscribed into the congressional record—Henry Cabot Lodge, a Massachusetts Republican in the House, proposed the kind of increased election oversight that the Butler Bill speeches had preemptively disparaged. In rough outline, the Lodge Bill sought to establish a petition process through which groups of people in any state could seek election oversight from the federal government. The bill passed the House by a slim majority and then transferred to the Senate, where it met an aggressive Democratic Party filibuster. One of the senators who spoke most extensively during the filibuster was James Z. George of Mississippi. Like Morgan, Butler, and Hampton, George chose to strengthen his criticism of Black suffrage by making reference to the large, historical body of colonization rhetoric.[28]

George's filibuster speech, which began in late December and ended in January, actually had two aims, not one. In addition to opposing the Lodge Bill, George sought to defend his home state against accusations that recent electoral revisions made by a state constitutional convention that he had helped to lead were, in actuality, thinly disguised attempts to disfranchise Mississippi's Black population. Over the course of his remarks, George offered an elliptical defense of his state's actions. Rather than admitting what some Mississippians had been more than happy to acknowledge—Black disfranchisement had, indeed, been a chief goal of the constitutional revisions—George accused the state's Northern critics of willfully ignoring their own region's historical records. The North, he asserted, had a long history of excluding Black Americans from the electorate. Some parts of the North, he added, had in fact continued this trend during the Fifteenth Amendment era by applying restrictive mechanisms similar to those adopted by Mississippi during its recent convention, which included a formal literacy test and a heavy poll tax. Indeed, the overarching "judgment of the American people and of the American states" had long been, George observed, that "the negro was an unsafe depositary of political power." To give these declarations further strength, George invoked the memory of Lincoln and made specific reference to the revered politician's long-standing support of colonization. In particular, George pulled a quotation from Lincoln's second annual message to Congress during the Civil War: "I can not make it better known than it already is that I strongly favor colonization." Northern congressmen who criticized Mississippi's recent constitutional reforms, George indicated, were acting as if "all this [national history] is forgotten."[29]

In effect, Morgan, Hampton, Butler, and George tapped into the long history of colonization promotion for ideas, quotations, and celebrity names that they could use to make the case that the federal government should allow the Fifteenth Amendment to become a dead letter. The constitutional ban on race-based voting restrictions not only contravened decade upon decade of state laws and practices in the North and the South, but it also, they stressed, contradicted the dictates of Jefferson, Webster, Lincoln, and so many others who had loudly and consistently proclaimed, throughout the nineteenth century, that Black freedom and white freedom were incongruous. Any attempt to reinvigorate enforcement of the Fifteenth Amendment, the senators indicated, made no sense in light of this history. Rather than doubling down on a fundamentally misguided constitutional action, Congress should recognize as necessary and valid the South's ongoing efforts to neutralize the Fifteenth Amendment and to prevent further damage to the American political system. Considered from this vantage point, Mississippi's new constitution deserved praise, not criticism.

COUNTERARGUMENTS AND INTERNAL DEBATES

From the fall of 1865, when William Forten addressed the National Equal Rights League, through the political events of the late 1860s, 1870s, 1880s, and 1890s, Black activists vigilantly tracked and countered the rhetoric and actions of the Blairs and their allies, the American Colonization Society, and the "Negro Problem" propagandists of the Lower South. In effect, Black activists continued, as they had since the late 1810s, to oppose the colonization movement at every turn. While they took some comfort in the fact that the viability of this political issue in Washington had greatly diminished, they understood that ongoing promotion of colonization had the capacity, as it had since the ACS's founding moment, to motivate and justify acts of exclusion that took place within the borders of the United States. And they were well aware of the instrumental merger of pro-colonization rhetoric into the anti-Black suffrage cause.

The first phase of Black activists' countering effort took place during the late 1860s and early to mid-1870s as they fought for the Fifteenth Amendment's passage and then for its enforcement by the federal government. Through newspapers, public addresses, and national and local civil rights conventions, Black activists continued to disavow all connections to the colonization movement. And they denounced all those who used its historical authority and its ideas to oppose or undermine Black voting rights. At a national convention in January 1869, organized by Forten, Henry Highland Garnet, and Frederick Douglass, among others, Black activists blasted ongoing claims that the United States was a "white man's country" and thus not a place where Black Americans should have the right to vote. The United States, the convention declared, was and had always been a "black man's country" as well. The right to vote in this nation "is ours because it is yours, and for the same reason."[30]

Articles published in the *New National Era,* a newspaper that Frederick Douglass helped to found in 1870, accused colonization advocates of contributing significantly to the election violence that Black Americans continued to encounter after the Fifteenth Amendment's ratification. "Emissaries of the Colonization Society," one article declared, "are giving encouragement to negro-hate by impressing the people with an idea that the black man has no right here as a freeman." Another article characterized the society's "persistent efforts" as "deeply hurtful" and fundamentally opposed to the "interests of our newly enfranchised people."[31]

The second phase of this effort occurred during the late 1870s and early 1880s, when Black Southerners expressed growing interest in emigration, as noted earlier, and when Black leaders once again engaged in a public debate on this highly charged subject. During this time, Black Southerners sent numerous petitions to President Rutherford B. Hayes and to Congress seeking federal aid for resettlement in Liberia. If the federal government would not do more to protect the civil rights of Black Americans, these missives indicated, then its representatives should at least have the decency to support their emigration to a nation where these rights could be enjoyed. Black Southerners also sent numerous requests for aid to the American Colonization Society, their longtime foe. Several leaders of the African

Methodist Episcopal Church, Henry McNeal Turner foremost among them, publicly endorsed this trend of Black emigration to Africa and began advocating for its expansion, following in the footsteps of Henry Highland Garnet and Martin Delany, who had promoted African emigration during the late 1850s and early 1860s.[32]

In an article published in *Frank Leslie's Popular Monthly* in 1880, Frederick Douglass, now in his sixties and still one of the most influential Black activists in the nation, warned Black Americans, as he had so many times before, of the messages implicit in any Black-led emigration movement. Given how sensitive and uncertain the current political environment was, Black Americans who actively promoted voluntary emigration, or who just simply spoke in ways that encouraged it, were, in effect, absolving the federal government of its constitutional duty to enforce the Fifteenth Amendment. Moreover, they were lending credence to a "pernicious" exclusionary discourse that, over many decades, had proven very detrimental to the cause of Black civil rights. If certain individuals were in such desperate straits that they felt they had no better choice than emigration, then, by all means, Douglass conceded, they should leave. The overwhelming majority of Black Southerners, however, should reject this trend and simultaneously demand, with heightened force, that the federal government fulfill its constitutional promise to defend their right to vote. It was crucial, during this tumultuous time, that Black Americans avoid speaking or acting in ways that might backfire. In Black-majority states like Louisiana, Mississippi, and South Carolina, where the Black-led emigration trend was most common, Douglass pointed out, colonization "agents" were currently canvassing the land and blaming Black residents for their own political "persecution," asserting that Black suffrage, even though constitutionally guaranteed, was intolerable to white residents.[33]

Between late 1882 and early 1884, the *Christian Recorder* printed a particularly heated exchange between Henry McNeal Turner and the paper's longtime editor, Benjamin Tanner, on the highly contentious subject of Black-led emigration. The two men were almost identical in age. Both had been born free, not enslaved, and both were very prominent figures in the African Methodist Episcopal Church. Turner became a bishop of the denomination at roughly the same time that this heated exchange began. Tanner became a bishop during the late 1880s. Their geographic origins, however, were quite different. Turner was a native of Georgia who, after sojourns in various parts of the United States during the 1850s and 1860s, had returned to his home state following the Civil War. Tanner was a native of Pittsburgh. At the time of his public argument with Turner, he had lived for many years in Philadelphia, where the *Christian Recorder* was based.[34]

The argument between these two prominent figures was an extension of a debate among AME Church leaders that had been ongoing since the late 1870s. The *Christian Recorder* had covered this debate extensively, giving plenty of space to the remarks of AME leaders like Turner who favored emigration, while at the same time making clear that the paper's formal position was one of opposition. The specific catalyst for the multiyear back-and-forth was an article that recounted a meeting that Tanner, as well as several other Black ministers, had in late 1882 with leaders of the Pennsylvania Colonization Society (PCS), which was based in Philadelphia. The society's leaders had organized the meeting with an intent of persuading Tanner and others to use their influence to increase Black American interest in emigration. Tanner, as the published account indicated, used the meeting as an opportunity to reject this offer, in strong terms, and to repudiate, as Black Americans had done so many times before, the society's delusive and insidious views regarding the nation's racial future. In stubbornly promoting the "false" and misleading "theory that the races must be kept apart," Tanner indicated, the society relentlessly reinforced the idea that the United States was not the "black man's country" and that Black Americans could only experience unfettered freedom in Africa. This was not, no matter how colonization advocates framed it, Tanner asserted, a humanitarian cause.[35]

Turner, in the months following the publication of this article, sent several angry letters to the *Christian Recorder*. As a general matter, he denounced Tanner for claiming to speak for all Black Americans on this incredibly important subject. Tanner lived in Philadelphia, not the reconstructed South, and thus he had the luxury of considering Liberian emigration in terms of "technicalities and theories." Southern Black Americans did not have this luxury, Turner asserted. The white population and the white-controlled institutions of the South consumed their "sweat and blood" like "vampires." The American Colonization Society, whatever its past faults were, was offering Black Americans a "place of refuge" from this "red tide of persecution," and such an offer, Turner declared, deserved serious consideration, not a brusque dismissal. "I know we are Americans to all intents and purposes," Turner declared, but "I see no other shelter" from the "horrors of American prejudice" than "African colonization."[36]

Turner also took strong issue with a specific assertion that Tanner had made, during the PCS meeting, regarding the nation's racial future: "the typical American would not be a white man or a black man; but a harmonious blending of all the races." This was, in essence, the same kind of amalgamationist prediction that Douglass and many other Black activists had been making for decades. "What a solution of the Negro problem," Turner exclaimed. "Every man who advocates the bleaching out of the Negro race, is an absolute fool," completely ignorant of the "scientific operations of nature." One of the greatest problems afflicting Black Americans, Turner declared, was a lack of "race patriotism," a sense of collective strength and pride. "Two-thirds of our race have no faith in themselves, and because they have none in themselves individually, they do not have any in each other." Emigration to Africa, Turner declared, would begin the process of ameliorating this condition, as Black Americans would gain the opportunity to help build a great "civil and Christian Negro nation," a global "seat of power and influence" for the Black race.[37]

Tanner responded to Turner's scathing remarks with frustration and indignation. Only a minority of Black Americans, he asserted, subscribed to the divisive and warped concept of "race patriotism" that Turner expounded. Declarations in favor of racial essences and destinies, Tanner admonished, were dangerously counterproductive. They tended to strengthen the belief that white and Black Americans were "natural born enemies" and the expectation that the latter group's fate lay elsewhere. Black Americans must "stop looking upon themselves as aliens in their own country," Tanner declared, and Turner must stop talking in ways that reinforced this wrong and damaging perspective.[38]

The third phase of this post-1865 opposition effort began during the late 1880s, when Black activists recognized the concerning rise in "Negro Problem" propaganda. In two public addresses delivered in Washington, DC, in 1889 and 1890, Frederick Douglass fiercely attacked the various publications coming out of the Lower South under this rubric, disparaging the intentions of those who authored the propaganda, picking apart their arguments, and reframing what he felt was a national conversation on race and civil rights that had gone terribly awry. Douglass blasted the phrase itself as "an anachronism, a misnomer, a false pretense, a delusion and a sham." There was a "great national problem," to be sure, but the problem, he declared, was not one caused by Black Americans, perpetuated by them, or embodied by them—even though the phrase, in its literal formulation, suggested all three. The "true problem," Douglass insisted, was the "white men ... [of the South], who by fraud, violence, and persecution, are breaking the law, trampling on the Constitution, corrupting the ballot-box, and defeating the ends of justice." By insistently shouting, "problem, problem, race problem, negro problem," Southern propagandists were trying to create a sense that all of these violations of law were inevitable and thus, in turn, justifiable. The real issue at hand, Douglass proclaimed, was that the "United States Government made the negro a citizen" and, for the time being, it remained to be seen whether it would "protect him as a citizen."[39]

In both speeches, sections of which he commonly reprised in addresses given over the next five years, prior to his death in 1895, Douglass noted with concern, though not necessarily surprise, that certain "Negro Problem" propagandists were continuing to push the cause of Black expatriation. He also noted that effectively all of the propagandists were basing their exclusionary arguments on a false premise of the slavery era: "No two people so different in race and color can live together in the same country" on equal terms. For disparaging effect, he associated this premise, at one point, with John Calhoun, the outspoken perpetualist who had defended Black enslavement as the only means through which white and Black Americans could coexist. But Douglass, as much as any Black activist living in the United States at the time, understood that there was an even stronger historical association between this premise and the colonization movement, a cause that Calhoun had vigorously opposed. Indeed, Douglass had previously warned Black Americans to be more wary of the rhetoric of Clay than that of Calhoun, because the former portrayed himself as an ally of the Black civil rights cause, maintaining that Black oppression in the United States, while necessary and rational, was not something to celebrate and insisting that white Americans had a duty to help Black Americans out of this oppression by supporting the colonization movement. Several decades ago, Douglass had warned Black Americans not to be taken in by this odd mixture of messages, but rather to see it plainly for what it was: an insidious "blending of good and evil."⁴⁰

As a fifty-year veteran of the fight against the colonization movement, Douglass understood just how much damage the movement's exclusionary rhetoric had done and still could do to the cause of Black civil rights in the United States. Throughout his activist career, Douglass had often expressed just as much concern, if not more, about the oppressive actions that such rhetoric might encourage and that such rhetoric might be used to justify, as he did about the possibility that such rhetoric might actually lead to large-scale expatriation. Indeed, in his 1889 and 1890 speeches, Douglass explicitly rejected the idea that Southern "problem orators" were promoting colonization out of any real desire to see significant numbers of Black Americans leave. These propagandists, he insisted, would almost certainly impede large-scale emigration if Black Americans ever attempted it. "Negro Problem" propagandists, Douglass declared, were far too interested in retaining and exploiting Black labor to allow such a thing to happen. Their real aim, he asserted, was to create a political environment in which white Southerners could, without significant opposition, "defy the constitution and the laws of the United States, especially those laws which respect the enfranchisement of colored citizens."⁴¹

NATURALIZING PREJUDICE AND DIMINISHING THE MEMORY OF SLAVERY

During the several decades following the abolition of slavery, as prominent white Southerners used colonization ideology as a political instrument in the fight against Black suffrage, they contributed significantly to yet another controversial trend. Although this trend did not have nearly the same level of direct negative impact on the lives of Black Americans, it nonetheless served, indirectly but consequentially, to further impede the cause of racial equality in the United States. The trend, in basic terms, was to diminish, on a national level, the perceived significance of slavery's impact on the American past and, by extension, the American present. Colonization advocates contributed to this diminishment trend—which, to be clear, was not centrally directed but rather the product of various parties acting with various motivations—by latching onto and, in turn, reinforcing three broader shifts in the way that many white Americans spoke and wrote about racial differences and racial tensions.[42]

First, colonization advocates increasingly assessed racial prejudice in universal terms, not historically specific ones. In a basic sense, they asserted that prejudice was a natural and unchangeable part of the human condition, not a product of human actions. A late-1865 declaration by Frank Blair, made as part of his family's effort to get the reconstructed Democratic Party to rally around colonization and against Black suffrage, illustrates the point. God had "implanted" in all human "hearts," Frank proclaimed, a "natural antipathy" to all other races. The "Intention" of this aversive "instinct" was to "keep the races apart." Indeed, Frank added, the Civil War could be viewed as God's "punishment" for breaking these fundamental "laws"—a dramatic revision of the striking claim made by Reverend Robert Finley in 1816, and by many colonization advocates after, that God had conceived of American slavery and Black colonization as a divinely integrated means of bringing the blessings of civilization and Christianity to the African continent. Two decades later, in 1887, a former Confederate government official named Horace Fulkerson published a piece of colonization propaganda entitled *The Negro; As He Was; As He Is; As He Will Be*, in which he declared that "race antagonism" was one of the "unchangeable and eternal laws of human nature." A few years later, Senators John Morgan, Hampton, and Butler expressed the same universalizing sentiment regarding racial antipathy as they argued in favor of the Butler Bill and against the Lodge Bill. McKinley did the same in *An Appeal to Pharaoh:* "No natural laws are plainer or have vindicated their wisdom and binding force oftener than the law which from the beginning has compelled the separation of the races."[43]

Second, many colonization advocates also asserted, with increasing force and certainty, that Black Americans were intrinsically inferior to white Americans. This was not a new concept, of course. More than a century earlier in *Notes on the State of Virginia*, Jefferson, as noted in the introduction to this book, had indicated a strong inclination toward this view, qualified only by a minor expression of deference to the theory that racial differences were changeable, not fixed, and that they were the product of varying societal structures and climatic conditions. During the colonization movement's first four decades, some advocates, despite asserting a firm belief in the improvability of the Black race, acknowledged or implied that some differences between white and Black Americans might turn out to be fixed and biological. Such acknowledgments or implications became more common in colonization rhetoric from the mid-1860s onward, as the Blairs and others adopted the racial ideas disseminated by an emergent group of "ethnologists." For several years prior to this moment, the Blairs had embraced this group's assertion that hybrid populations (mixed races) were inherently degenerate. After the Civil War, they largely adopted the group's claim that the Black race was intrinsically inferior to the white race. An early instance of this shift in colonization rhetoric can be found in a speech given by Frank Blair in 1866: "If we refuse to grant them [Black Americans] social equality, it is because they are an inferior race ... and [it is for the same] reason, I say, that they should never be allowed to enjoy ... political equality." The shift became more pronounced during the 1880s and 1890s as the center of gravity for colonization promotion moved from the Upper South to the Lower South. Senator Morgan, in his 1890 *Arena* article, declared that "the inferiority of the negro race, as compared with the white race, is so essentially true, and so obvious, that, to assume it in argument, cannot be justly attributed to prejudice."[44]

Third, colonization advocates, throughout the postwar decades, repeatedly made the claim that Black expatriation was the key to effecting a final and sustainable reconciliation between the North and the South—in essence, recycling a tactic that advocates had used extensively between 1833 and 1853. In a speech that Frank Blair gave in late 1865, as part of the speaking tour that he and Montgomery conducted in their effort to reconstruct the Democratic Party, he declared, "Until this [racial separation] is done we shall not be free from strife in this country." Two decades later, in 1887, in *The Negro; As He Was; As He Is; As He Will Be,* Fulkerson proclaimed that the "separation of the races" was essential to the still incomplete effort, on the part of the American people, "to form a more perfect Union, establish Justice and secure domestic Tranquility"—a near-direct quotation from the Constitution. Grady, Morgan, Butler, Hampton, and McKinley, in various ways, all conveyed the same basic sentiment. In *An Appeal to Pharaoh,* McKinley invoked the same passage from the Constitution and went on to describe the history of sectional conflict in the United States using the same kind of blame-the-oppressed formula that Tennessee Representative Frederick Perry Stanton had used when promoting the Liberian steamer initiative during the early 1850s and that President Lincoln had used, to the great consternation of Black activists, in his much-publicized 1862 White House meeting with free Black Washingtonians: "Let the main proposition be set forth again, in the plainest terms: The Negro was the cause of the division of the United States into the two sections, the North and the South, and has been the cause of all the strife that has taken place" since.[45]

A set of remarks made by Morgan in 1889 and 1890 illuminates how these adjustments intertwined in colonization rhetoric in ways that contributed to the wider trend of diminishing the perceived significance of slavery's impact on the American past and the American present. In the 1890 article, mentioned above, Morgan made a bold assertion: the intense "aversion" that white Americans felt toward Black Americans was "not a result of slavery." In making this assertion, he amended, slightly but consciously, a statement he had made the prior year in an article in *Forum,* in which he had allowed for the possibility that "the aversion and incongruity of the races," which was "fixed and irreconcilable," might derive from "slavery in the United States" or "slavery in Africa." He wiped this possibility away in his 1890 article, a strong indication that the revised position better suited his political interests. Morgan went further as well. Not only did he disavow any causal relationship between anti-Black prejudice and slavery, but he also rejected the notion that the institution bore responsibility for the racial tensions that so powerfully afflicted the nation, especially its Southern portion: "It is the presence of seven or eight millions of negroes in this country and the friction caused by their political power and their social aspirations, and not the fact that they were recently in slavery, that agitates and distresses the people of both races."[46]

There was much irony, and almost certainly a measure of disingenuousness, in this striking assertion by Morgan. At the same time that he was using the history of the colonization movement as a political instrument, he was offering an account of the origins of racial prejudice, racial tension, and sectional conflict in the United States that would have perplexed many of the key historical figures, like Jefferson and Lincoln, that he and other post-1865 colonization advocates ritually invoked. The central animating fact of the pre-1865 colonization movement *was* the institution of slavery, specifically its tendency to endanger white Americans, to corrupt the nation's republican system of governance, and to undermine the stability of the Union. From the beginning, going back to the founding of the ACS and even further back to Jefferson's declarations in *Notes on the State of Virginia*, the movement's core ideology—that Black freedom was an enormous and intractable societal problem—had the fact of slavery as its cornerstone. Without the existence of this racialized institution, it is very hard to believe, perhaps even impossible to believe, that any movement to expatriate Black Americans would ever have formed.

But now, during the postslavery era, the Blairs, Fulkerson, Grady, Morgan, Butler, Hampton, McKinley, and other colonization advocates were characterizing racial antipathy as universal and primordial, an aversive force that predated any beliefs, practices, or institutions constructed by humans. They were asserting, without qualification, that the Black race was intrinsically subordinate to the white race. And they were, in turn, speaking about the problem of Black freedom, specifically escalating efforts to narrow its boundaries, as if it had little to no relation to the historical institution of slavery. In all of this, post-1865 colonization advocates diverged, without acknowledgment, from the history that they were so avidly invoking, on the last point most of all.

DISFRANCHISEMENT

In March 1891, the second session of the Fifty-First Congress ended, and the Lodge Bill, which members of the Senate, including James Z. George of Mississippi, had been filibustering for months, became a moot point. The Republican Party's first attempt, in many years, to augment the federal government's power to enforce the Fifteenth Amendment had failed. While it is hard to determine how much the Butler Bill speeches of Morgan, Butler, and Hampton, along with the larger moment of political performance that the bill's introduction had afforded, contributed to this failure, the failure was certainly a victory from their perspective. These Lower Southern senators wanted the federal government to leave the Southern states alone when it came to running their elections and especially when it came to determining who was eligible to vote. Over the next ten years, they largely got their wish. Congress, which was for the most part back in the hands of the Democratic Party, voted to repeal the outstanding Fifteenth Amendment enforcement measures still inscribed in federal lawbooks, a clear sign that Southern states would have considerable electoral latitude. The federal court system handed down several judgments that effectively bolstered the defensibility of electoral revisions made by Southern state constitutional conventions. While these federal actions unfolded, several Southern states followed Mississippi's lead and ratified constitutions that effectively disfranchised Black residents: Arkansas in 1891, South Carolina in 1895, Louisiana in 1898, North Carolina in 1900, Alabama in 1901, and Virginia in 1902.[47]

During this disfranchisement decade, various white Southerners continued to produce the kind of "Negro Problem" propaganda that McKinley, Grady, Morgan, Butler, Hampton, and George, during the late 1880s and early 1890s, had made highly visible in American politics. For the most part, this propaganda did not show up in the records of the state constitutional conventions that effected disfranchisement. All delegates enlisted in the disfranchisement cause understood that giving fiery speeches in favor of Black exclusion would not serve their goal of effecting disfranchisement in ways that steered clear of the Fifteenth Amendment's ban on race-based discrimination. "Negro Problem" rhetoric produced outside of the convention walls, however, had the potential to provide a kind of supportive and validating political atmosphere for the conventions' exclusionary work—something that Frederick Douglass had highlighted, in general terms, in speeches given in 1889 and 1890 and that he continued to point out, over the next few years, in his final appearances on the national speaking circuit.[48]

An 1894 book entitled *The Ills of the South*, for instance, written by a Mississippi school superintendent and released by one of the more venerable publishing houses in New York, made its case against Black suffrage and for Black expatriation by, among other moves, invoking the Jefferson quotation that the Blairs had, in the past, employed so frequently: "Nothing is more certainly written in the book of fate than that these people are to be free; nor is it less certain that the two races, equally free, cannot live in the same government." A North Carolina lawyer expressed similar sentiments in a book-length work published in 1898 entitled *A Solution of the Race Problem in the South*. And in 1900, John Temple Graves, a well-known Atlanta journalist, invoked the authority of several luminous, past colonization advocates to bolster the credibility and the appeal of his arguments. In a high-profile speech delivered at a three-day conference in Alabama, organized by the Southern Society for the Promotion of the Study of Race Conditions and Problems in the South, Graves, who at one point referred to the Fifteenth Amendment as "the American mistake of the century," stated that the position that he took on the matter of the nation's race "problem" was the very same as that espoused by Daniel Webster, Henry Clay, Thomas Jefferson, Abraham Lincoln, and Henry Grady: "Separation is the logical, the inevitable, the only way. No other proposed solution will stand the test of logic and experiment." The problem, he added, cannot be solved by "religion," "education," "time," or "politics." He then put particular stress on this last point. "No statute will permanently solve this problem," as the recent three-decade history of the Fifteenth Amendment had shown. "No anodyne of law, no counter-irritant of legislation will quiet it longer than the hour of its application."[49]

About five months before Graves gave his speech at the so-called "Race Problem" conference, Senator John Morgan of Alabama—now one of the most senior members of the chamber, having served continuously since 1877—spoke once again before the Senate on the subject of Black expatriation. Alabama had not yet followed in the footsteps of the various states that had disfranchised Black Americans over the past decade, but the likelihood of such a move in Morgan's home state was rising. The specific occasion for his speech was a resolution proposed by a Republican senator that denounced "any state" that effected, through whatever sly device, disfranchisement on the basis of racial "descent." As part of his strongly worded protest, Morgan asserted that the "negro voter" bore responsibility for much of the tension that had, for more than thirty years, persisted between the North and the South. Effectively, Morgan used the same kind of blame-the-oppressed rhetoric that Lincoln had used in his 1862 White House meeting with free Black Washingtonians and that colonization advocates, especially Tennessee Congressman Frederick Perry Stanton, had used, or at least implied, for the past eighty years. "Perfect accord between the former warring sections of the Union can never be attained," Morgan proclaimed, "so long as the negroes are forced upon the white people of the Southern states as full and equal participants in the ballot box." To these declarations, Morgan added the prospective threat of race war, thus invoking, at least implicitly, the century-old rhetoric of Jefferson. "If the basis of voting remains as it is," Morgan stated, "the finale will be the expulsion of the negro or his extermination."[50]

Morgan then closed this lengthy anti-Black-suffrage harangue by suggesting another possible solution to the nation's ever-vexing "race question." Perhaps "in the Philippine Archipelago," where the United States military was currently engaged in a war for territorial control, the Black American population might ultimately find a "happy home" where they might "grow into power beneath our flag."[51]

The following year, a state convention in Alabama amended the constitution such that it effectively disfranchised the state's Black residents. According to the 1900 census, Black Americans comprised nearly half of Alabama's total population.

The persistent promotion of Black expatriation during the several decades following the Civil War had a profound impact not just on the effort to oppose, undermine, discredit, and ultimately neutralize the Fifteenth Amendment but also on a much wider effort to restrict Black freedom: the construction of an exclusionary system of practices and laws colloquially known as Jim Crow. As was the case with the final moments of state-based disfranchisement during the 1890s and early 1900s, the impact was more indirect than direct. In many cases, though certainly not all of them, postwar efforts to impose exclusionary practices and laws operated within a tighter legal frame than prewar efforts, due to the existence of the Thirteenth, Fourteenth, and Fifteenth Amendments. In this particular context, the persistent promotion of Black expatriation fostered a validating and enabling atmosphere for the restriction of Black freedom. One of the main atmospheric contributions made by colonization advocates during the postwar decades, as this chapter has indicated throughout, was the idea that laws, especially federal laws, did not have the power to eliminate, or even significantly undermine, racial prejudice.[52]

Colonization advocates asserted this idea repeatedly from the mid-1860s onward. This idea was not new, of course. It had been easily inferable, for many decades, from the colonization movement's well-worn assertions regarding the ineradicability of anti-Black prejudice and, more broadly, the incongruity of Black freedom and white freedom. But it was an idea that became more common and explicit in colonization rhetoric during the postwar decades, as this chapter has shown. During the 1868 debates in Congress regarding the proposed fifteenth amendment, for instance, Senator James Doolittle had declared that the "attempt to make" Black Americans "equal" in the United States was "impossible to be carried into effect." Four years later, Senator Frank Blair had signed his name to a minority report, that, in forcefully protesting the prospect of additional Fifteenth Amendment enforcement measures, had tersely declared: "Man's puny statutes cannot repeal or nullify the immutable ordinances of the almighty."[53]

During the late 1880s, 1890s, and early 1900s, this idea appeared, in some form, in virtually every piece of "Negro Problem" propaganda issued by colonization advocates. Senator John Tyler Morgan, in the 1889 *Forum* article that he authored in advance of the Butler Bill moment in Congress, declared that "no human law" could overcome race "aversion," because no human law had "created this condition." Atlanta journalist John Temple Graves made the same point with similar force a decade later, when, in his address to the Alabama conference held in 1900, he insisted that "no statute," "no anodyne of law," and "no counter-irritant of legislation" would ever be effective in solving the nation's "race problems." And in the 1887 book *The Negro; As He Was; As He Is; As He Will Be,* Horace Fulkerson praised the Supreme Court's recent decision in the *Civil Rights Cases,* which effectively nullified major portions of the Civil Rights Act of 1875, as a "monument to the wisdom" of the federal judiciary and as a "living witness to the folly of the Government in undertaking to legislate a Nation's prejudices out of existence."[54]

Such claims, it is important to highlight, were not simply the province of those who continued, after 1865, to promote the issue of colonization. During the Butler Bill debate in the Senate, for instance, North Carolina Congressman Zebulon Vance, in a speech meant to give notice that he would *not* support the colonization appropriation, declared that it was impossible to resolve the "negro problem" through "legislation." In making this statement, Vance effectively aligned himself with the Butler Bill's larger, unspoken purpose: to object, preemptively, to the expected attempt by Republican congressmen to bolster the federal government's powers of electoral enforcement (Lodge Bill). In other remarks, Vance clarified that he also aligned with the bill's animating sentiment. The "presence" of a Black population in the United States, was "of course," Vance stated, a major societal problem. Indeed, "I should be happy to know that there was not one of them in the United States among us, to be the unwilling cause of everlasting contention between our people." The reason for his opposition to the bill, Vance explained, was that few Black Americans, in his view, would accept the offer of voluntary removal, thus leaving the core problem unchanged. A much more pragmatic approach, he advised, was for the Northern people to allow the Southern people to manage the problem as they saw fit. "Suppose you trust the southern people for awhile," he stated, and cease all of "your interference."[55]

Trust in the white South's capacity to deal with the issue of Black freedom was something that McKinley, Grady, Morgan, Butler, Hampton, Fulkerson, and, indeed, effectively all "Negro Problem" propagandists had demanded as they had persisted in promoting colonization and as they had used colonization movement ideology to normalize and justify Black exclusion. The *Civil Rights Cases* decision had been a significant step in this direction, as Fulkerson had indicated. The majority opinion, delivered by Associate Justice Joseph Bradley in 1883, had indicated that the federal government lacked the authority, under the auspices of the Thirteenth and Fourteenth Amendments, to assert several of the racial protections stipulated by the 1875 law. Interestingly, Bradley was a long-time friend of Frederick Frelinghuysen, the current secretary of state and, since 1869, a vice president of the American Colonization Society—a choice of affiliation almost certainly related to the fact that Frelinghuysen's father, Theodore, had been a leading figure of the colonization movement from the early 1820s until his death in the early 1860s. Another major step in this direction came in 1896, when the Supreme Court rendered its decision in *Plessy v. Ferguson*. In this instance, the court upheld a Louisiana state law that obligated "railway companies ... to provide equal, but separate, accommodations for the white and colored races," stipulated "fines or imprisonment" for "passengers" who refused to comply, and exempted "from liability" all railway companies that denied service to certain passengers on the grounds of noncompliance. The majority opinion in this case also cited the fundamental limits of the Thirteenth and Fourteenth Amendments, asserting that the Louisiana law was "not in conflict with the provisions [of] either." In aggregate, these decisions cleared out a broad legal space for the subsequent expansion of Jim Crow laws and practices throughout the South and, indeed, the North. As Associate Justice John Harlan put it in his dissenting opinion, the *Plessy* decision gave the states considerable latitude to continue "regulating the enjoyment of civil rights, upon the basis of race" and doing so in ways "cunningly devised" to work around the constitutional amendments that were the "legitimate results of the war."[56]

The published opinion in the *Plessy* case, written by Associate Justice Henry Billings Brown, a native of Massachusetts, contained a suggestive set of passages: "The [plaintiff's] argument . . . assumes that social prejudices may be overcome by legislation, and that equal rights cannot be secured to the negro except by an enforced commingling of the two races. We cannot accept this proposition." To this, Brown added, "Legislation is powerless to eradicate racial instincts . . . and the attempt to do so can only result in accentuating the difficulties of the present situation." The consonance between the opinion's language and the idea that colonization advocates had avidly broadcasted since the close of the Civil War was both clear and strong: The federal government could do little to block the prejudicial impulses of white Americans.[57]

CONCLUSION

> Colonization is no solution of the race problem. It is an evasion. It is not repenting of wrong but putting out of sight the people upon whom wrong has been inflicted. Its reiteration and agitation only serve to fan the flame of popular prejudice and encourage the hope that in some way or other, in time or in eternity, those who hate the negro will get rid of him.
> —FREDERICK DOUGLASS, *Lessons of the Hour*, 1894

> Between me and the other world there is ever an unasked question: unasked by some through feelings of delicacy; by others through the difficulty of rightly framing it. All, nevertheless, flutter around it. . . . How does it feel to be a *problem*?
> —W. E. B. DU BOIS, "Strivings of the Negro People," 1897

> Men will here learn that a race, as a family, may be true to itself without seeking to exterminate all others. That for the note of the feeblest there is room, nay a positive need, in the harmonies of God. . . . We would not deprecate the fact, then, that America has a Race Problem. It is guaranty of the perpetuity and progress of her institutions, and insures the breadth of her culture and the symmetry of her development.
> —ANNA JULIA COOPER, *A Voice from the South*, 1892

IN THE MOST BASIC SENSE, *Words Colliding* is a political history. It tells the story of a mainstream nineteenth-century political movement that, due to the influence of several framing conventions, has received less scholarly attention than the deep impressions that it left on the documentary record indicate it warrants. The book tracks, over a period of more than eighty years, from the late 1810s to the early 1900s, all of the major attempts made by white politicians to obtain support from the federal government for a project aimed at the large-scale expatriation of Black Americans. Some of the political moments that it covers have received noteworthy attention from historians, particularly the ACS's 1816–17 founding moment, the Slave Trade Act of 1819 and the subsequent founding of Liberia, the late-1820s debates in Congress regarding the ACS's two memorials, the Blair family's Republican Party campaign of the late 1850s, and the early-1860s promotion of colonization by Abraham Lincoln. The other key political moments in the book, however, have received very limited attention. This category includes Henry Clay's Land Bills of the 1830s, the ACS convention and the Kennedy Report of the early to mid-1840s, Frederick Perry Stanton's Liberian steamer proposal of the early 1850s, the Blairs' Democratic Party campaign of the late 1860s, and the Butler Bill of 1890. In most cases, only a handful of historians have noted these historical moments, and only one or two have analyzed them in any depth.

I constructed the chapters of this book with an aim of giving each moment significant analytical attention, both from the perspective of those promoting colonization and those opposing it, and of showing how each moment fit within the ongoing, intertwined debates regarding slavery and Black civil rights. I constructed the narrative thread that weaves through these chapters with a larger objective of showing points of continuity and contrast among these political moments. In essence, the final product, at least as I intend it, is a federally focused, long-arc political history of slavery and race in nineteenth-century America, one that integrates familiar moments with less familiar moments and that connects the pre-1865 political period, when enslavement was legal, with the post-1865 political period, when it was not, but when its influence was still strongly felt in myriad ways.

In a very important sense, this book is also an intellectual history. It tells the story of a racialized ideology that had taken root, over multiple centuries, in the English colonies and in the early United States, that crystallized during the era of revitalized nation-building that followed the War of 1812, and that served as the touchstone for an eight-decade political movement that profoundly influenced American attitudes toward slavery and racial equality. In its simplest form, this ideology identified Black freedom as one of the greatest and most intractable problems in American society, a problem that could only be resolved by removing Black Americans from the United States or, at a minimum, by excluding this population from key civil liberties enjoyed by white Americans. *Words Colliding* tells the story of this ideology in four main aspects.

First, it examines Thomas Jefferson's articulation in *Notes on the State of Virginia*—first published in 1787, the same year as the Constitutional Convention—of the colonization movement's core animating premises. Jefferson asserted that the long-standing use of enslaved labor, on a racialized basis, had made it impossible for white and Black Americans to coexist peacefully and prosperously on terms of equality. In essence, according to Jefferson, Black freedom and white freedom were incongruous. He also asserted that the institution of enslavement would not and should not survive indefinitely in the nation, because it fundamentally corrupted and endangered its white citizens and thus prevented the United States from realizing its full potential. In sum, Jefferson envisioned a future in which subsequent generations of politicians would effect, in integrated fashion, the abolition of slavery and the removal of the nation's Black population. On this latter endeavor, he indicated, the federal government would likely have a crucial role to play.

Second, the book analyzes, in close and careful detail, the founding rhetoric of the American Colonization Society, the organization that effectively launched the eight-decade effort to make Black expatriation a national priority. Taken as a whole, the documentary record of this founding moment was replete with complex, confusing, and even seemingly contradictory statements. In actual fact, however, there was a discernible coherence. In effect, this set of statements revealed two of the colonization movement's defining characteristics: the movement's primary objectives, which did indeed reflect a somewhat confusing but nonetheless quite deliberate ambivalence regarding slavery; and the chief promotional tactic that the organization's leaders planned to employ in pursuit of their campaign to obtain federal support. Virginia Congressman John Randolph provided the first revelation when he suggested that establishing a system of Black colonization would encourage manumissions and, at the same time, make slavery safer and more stable. Kentucky Congressman Henry Clay provided the second revelation when he asserted that the ACS's sole function was to facilitate the removal of *free* Black Americans, not to abolish slavery. This technically correct but intentionally misleading claim reflected the founders' recognition that seeking federal support for a project designed, in significant part, to encourage slavery's gradual eradication would require very careful politicking—states'-rights-based objections from the South, especially the Lower South, were almost certain to arise.

The historical significance of the founders' decision to adopt the political tactic that Clay exemplified cannot be overstated. In effect, the ACS's founding moment translated Jefferson's assertion regarding the incongruity of white freedom and Black freedom into the colonization movement's core Black-freedom-as-a-societal-problem ideology. As colonization advocates promoted this ideology over the next eighty years in national politics, mainly in support of efforts to persuade Congress to sponsor Black expatriation, they fostered an impression that Black freedom was at least as big a national problem as slavery, if not bigger. Colonization advocates conveyed this message quite clearly when they asserted, as Clay and many other Southern politicians often did, that while they strongly favored the prospect of slavery's ultimate abolition, they absolutely opposed the pursuit of abolition without a concomitant plan for removing the free Black population. In other words, no attempt should be made to address the problem of slavery until there was a national agreement to address the problem of Black freedom. Even in instances where colonization advocates did not make such an assertion, the implication was still present, easily inferable from the repeated and indeed ritualistic claim that the colonization movement dealt only with free Black Americans.

And while it was true that colonization advocates acknowledged, on many occasions over the years, that the term *free Black Americans,* as they conceived it, referred not just to individuals who were already free but also to those who might become free through manumission or abolition—thus signaling emancipatory intent—it was also true that, on many occasions, they did not make such an acknowledgment. Henry Clay's founding speech was but the first of many such instances. Furthermore, there were long periods of time when most colonization advocates, especially Southern ones, deliberately and systematically avoided acknowledgments of emancipatory intent. During these periods, the colonization movement's dominant promotional strategy was to characterize Black freedom as the nation's most divisive and volatile issue. Indeed, if we look holistically across the movement's eighty-year history, colonization advocates employed this strategy, on a dominant basis, more frequently than not. Roughly speaking, it was only from the mid-1820s through the mid-1830s and then again from the late 1850s through the mid-1860s that colonization advocates put clear and consistent emphasis on the movement's professed aim of facilitating slavery's eradication. Thus, even though the historical record of colonization advocacy strongly indicates that the movement originated in two motivations—to resolve the national problem of Black freedom *and* the national problem of slavery—the record indicates just as strongly that the first problem, for the majority of the movement's eight decades, was its leaders' primary concern.

Third, *Words Colliding* shows how changes in the political landscape prompted colonization advocates, in five distinct phases from 1817 through 1900, to modify their rhetoric and tactics. As they made these modifications, they asserted strong connections between colonization and a variety of potent national issues, including slave trade suppression, gradual abolition, "abolitionist" agitation, international trade, international power, "fugitive" slave enforcement, Unionism, Republican Party promotion, imperial expansion, civil war prevention, Civil War victory (for the Union), Southern reconstruction, postwar racial violence, and Black civil rights. Their main objective, in all instances, was to make the case that establishing a system of Black expatriation would aid in the pursuit of national objectives or support the task of ameliorating national challenges, or both. The overarching effect of the colonization movement's political efforts during this eighty-year period, the book argues, was to broaden and deepen the influence of its ideology in American society and culture, causing growing numbers of white Americans to view the exclusion of Black Americans—whether through geographic removal or through the denial of key civil liberties—as rational, necessary, morally defensible, and patriotic.

Fourth, *Words Colliding* explicates the main arguments used by Black activists to undermine the propagation and elaboration of colonization ideology. From the moment of the ACS's founding in the late 1810s through the disfranchisement efforts of the 1890s and early 1900s, Black activists engaged in ideological combat with colonization advocates. Black activists understood, from the beginning, that the fight against the colonization movement was about far more than undermining its efforts to obtain federal support and rejecting the movement's offers of funded, *voluntary* resettlement. The opposition movement was about countering and pushing back, to the greatest extent possible, the advances of an ideology that characterized Black freedom as an intractable and ever-worsening societal problem. Black activists repeatedly pointed out that the broader and deeper this ideology's influence became, the greater the impulse was for white politicians to pass laws that pushed Black Americans further and further toward the margins of civil society, in a very real sense "approximating" expatriation. In other words, the colonization movement, Black activists recognized, could repeatedly fail to accomplish its chief aims and yet still affect racial attitudes in the United States in ways that were profoundly detrimental to the lives of Black Americans.[1]

Frederick Douglass delivered one of the last significant public speeches of his life in early 1894 at the Metropolitan African Methodist Episcopal Church in Washington, DC, which lay just a few blocks north of the White House. One of the main subjects that he addressed was the horrific trend of anti-Black lynching. Over the last ten-plus years, white mobs, mainly but not exclusively in the South, had seized and killed at least one thousand Black Americans. Many of these killings had taken place in broad daylight as planned events, with large portions of the local white community in attendance. In other words, they were not clandestine affairs but rather violent public rituals orchestrated, in large part, Douglass asserted, with the "full sympathy" of the "upper classes of the South." These white mobs claimed to be reacting, Douglass explained, to a deeply concerning trend, the raping of white women by Black men, even though there was nothing in American history, Douglass pointedly observed, to suggest the plausibility of such a trend. Indeed, he added, there was a disturbing and painful irony reflected in these claims. The most significant and indisputable trend of interracial rape in American history, Douglass somberly observed, occurred under the auspices of "Slavery," which throughout its two-century tenure "was a system of legalized outrage upon the black women of the South."

The flurry of rape accusations in recent years should thus be seen, Douglass declared, not as a series of moves to obtain criminal justice but rather as part of a larger project—that included "well-known efforts . . . to degrade the negro by legislative enactments," to restrict Black suffrage, and to implement a "color line" in many "public places in the South"—to "blast and ruin the negro's character as a man and a citizen," thus "paving the way" to the full invalidation of Black citizenship.[2]

Over the course of his speech, which ran to thirty-six pages when subsequently published in pamphlet form, Douglass devoted a significant amount of time, as had been his habit in recent years, to a discussion of the "race problem"—or the "negro problem" as, he noted, it was often "mis-called." One of Douglass's chief objectives was to criticize, as he had before, two purported solutions that white Americans, especially white Southerners, had pushed, with a kind of relentless force, for decades: the expulsion of Black Americans from the electorate and the colonization of Black Americans outside the United States. The first approach, Douglass asserted, was, at its core, "a mean and cowardly proposition." It sent a disturbing and shameful message to Black Americans: "Your suffrage has been practically rendered a failure by violence, [and] we now propose to make it a failure by law." The second approach, Douglass declared, was as misguided and harmful as it had always been: "Colonization is no solution of the race problem. It is an evasion. It is not repenting of wrong but putting out of sight the people upon whom wrong has been inflicted." The ongoing "reiteration and agitation" of such "colonization nonsense," Douglass asserted, not only stoked "the flame of popular prejudice" but also fostered "doubt" and "despair" in the mind of the Black American by "forc[ing] upon him the idea that he is forever doomed to be a stranger and sojourner in the land of his birth." It was thus very troubling and frustrating, Douglass stated, to see that the "colonizing scheme," nearly eight decades after the founding of the ACS, continued "to have a strong hold on the public mind."[3]

After rejecting these two purported solutions to the "race problem," Douglass restated, as a kind of final act, the basic elements of the solution that Black activists had prescribed since the early 1870s. First, white Americans needed to stop "violating the amendments of the Constitution" and to begin abiding by the spirit of these enlightened laws. "If this were done, there would be no negro problem to vex the South, or to vex the nation."

Second, "the white people of the North and the South" needed to stop portraying their "prejudices" as fixed and instead make a serious and sustained effort to "conquer" them. If they did, they would soon come face-to-face with a striking fact. The core assumption that had animated so many racial decisions in American history—that it was necessary to oppress "the colored man" in order "to elevate the white man"—had never been true.[4]

Douglass died the year after he gave this speech in the nation's capital. He was close to eighty years old. For roughly five decades, he had been one of the most influential Black activists in the nation. In the years surrounding his death, two Black Americans of great present and future consequence entered the national scene: William Edward Burghardt Du Bois, who was born in Massachusetts in 1868, placing him in his late twenties when Douglass passed, and Anna Julia Cooper, who was born into enslavement in North Carolina in 1858, which placed her in her early thirties. Neither Du Bois nor Cooper said much about the colonization movement over the course of their very long lives. The cause had a diminishing number of high-profile public advocates during the closing years of the nineteenth century, as Douglass faded out and as Du Bois and Cooper faded in. Both individuals, however, had quite a bit to say about the racialized vision of exclusion and inequality that the colonization movement had done so much, over the past eighty years, to embed in American society.[5]

In 1897, Du Bois published an article in the venerable *Atlantic Monthly* that was titled "Strivings of the Negro People." This piece ultimately gained higher visibility six years later, when it was reprinted, almost verbatim, as the opening chapter of *Souls of Black Folk,* the most famous of all of his publications and arguably one of the most influential pieces of twentieth-century American literature and social commentary. At the time of the article's publication, Du Bois, who had just received his PhD in sociology from Harvard, was at the beginning of a long and distinguished university career. His dissertation, it is worth noting, was a two-century study of efforts in the former English colonies and the United States to suppress the "African Slave Trade." The topical focus ensured that he did, in fact, make several references to the American Colonization Society, specifically its role as the federal government's partner in returning "recaptives" to Africa. Although Du Bois did not offer much in the way of critical commentary on the colonization movement, the opening words of his *Atlantic* article called to mind the intertwined discourses of the "Negro Problem" and colonization: "Between me and the other world there is ever an unasked question: unasked by some through feelings of delicacy; by others through the difficulty of rightly framing it. All, nevertheless, flutter around it.... How does it feel to be a *problem?*" As Du Bois continued, the resonant undertones persisted: "It is a peculiar sensation, this double-consciousness.... One ever feels his two-ness,—an American, a Negro; two souls, two thoughts, two unreconciled strivings; two warring ideals in one dark body, whose dogged strength alone keeps it from being torn asunder."[6]

Later in the article, Du Bois asserted, as Douglass had, that the path of inclusion would yield greater benefits to the nation than the path of exclusion, but he made the point in a way that, at the same time, diverged significantly from that of Douglass. Rather than predicting, as Douglass and many other Black activists had throughout the nineteenth century, that the Black and white races would, over time, amalgamate into one, Du Bois suggested that racial distinctions should be, to a significant degree, retained and that there was great benefit to be derived from such retention. The Black American, Du Bois asserted, "does not wish to Africanize America, for America has too much to teach the world." Nor, he continued, did the Black American "wish to bleach his Negro blood in a flood of white Americanism, for he believes—foolishly, perhaps, but fervently—that Negro blood has yet a message for the world." The Black American, Du Bois further explained, "simply wishes to make it possible for a man to be both a Negro and an American without being cursed and spit upon by his fellows" and to have the opportunity to contribute to America's great republican experiment as a valued partner, instead of being treated like an "outcast and a stranger."[7]

Anna Julia Cooper offered a very similar message to the American public in her book *A Voice from the South,* published in 1892, five years before Du Bois's article and two years before Douglass's final speech. Cooper lived in Washington, DC, at the time of the book's publication, working as a teacher in the local school system. She had earned undergraduate and graduate degrees from Oberlin University during the 1880s. Later, during the 1920s, she would earn a PhD from the University of Paris and would become the president of Frelinghuysen University. Interestingly, this institution bore the name of Frederick Frelinghuysen, the former secretary of state and former United States senator who, for a time during the post–Civil War years, had supported the American Colonization Society and whose father, Theodore Frelinghuysen, had been a leading colonization advocate for nearly forty years. Cooper made clear, like Du Bois, that she did not believe that the American people would or should ultimately merge into one race. She made this point with considerable force, lumping those who favored amalgamation together with those who favored colonization, though presumably with less disdain for the former. "For the love of humanity," she declared toward the end of the book, "stop the mouth of those learned theorizers... who come out annually with their new and improved method of getting the answer and clearing the slate: amalgamation, deportation, colonization and all the other *ations* that were ever devised or dreamt of." Racial heterogeneity had been, from the beginning, she argued, one of the defining features of the United States. It was something to celebrate, not to bemoan. The various tensions and conflicts produced by this heterogeneity had been and continued to be greatly beneficial to the nation's progress: "Where a hundred free forces are lustily clamoring for recognition and each wrestling mightily for the mastery, individual tyrannies must inevitably be chiseled down, individual bigotries worn smooth and malleable, individual prejudices either obliterated or concealed." In the future, she continued, "men will here learn that a race, as a family, may be true to itself without seeking to exterminate all others."[8]

This might be the vision of an "optimist," she acknowledged, but it did not necessarily follow that the vision was impracticable. The United States, she asserted with firm conviction, was the "arena" where "political tyranny" and "caste illiberality" would ultimately be conquered, and racial diversity would play a crucial role in this realization. There was no logical reason, therefore, to "deprecate the fact... that America has a Race Problem," she asserted. "It is guaranty of the perpetuity and progress of her institutions, and insures the breadth of her culture and the symmetry of her development." Indeed, Cooper went on to declare, "the historian of American civilization will yet congratulate the country that she has had a Race Problem and that the descendants of the black race furnished one of its largest factors."[9]

In writing and publishing these important documents, Douglass, Du Bois, and Cooper were doing something that Black Americans had been doing for eight decades. They were asserting a vision of the nation's racial future that had, as its foundation, the principles of inclusion and equality, and they were doing so in ways that coopted the language that colonization advocates, and white Americans more broadly, had used throughout the nineteenth century to promote a contrary vision, one rooted in exclusion and inequality. From the beginning, Black activists had fought against the colonization movement fully aware that words, not just political victories, had great capacity for harm. As Frederick Douglass—one of the greatest rhetoricians in American history, not just as a composer of eloquent, precise, and compelling language but also as an analyst of others' compositions—observed in early 1894, as he denounced, once again, "Negro Problem" discourse in all of its aspects: "Words are things . . . a very bad thing in this case, since they give us a misnomer . . . [that] has a strong bias against the negro." This insidious linguistic "formula," he added, effectively "handicaps his cause with all the prejudice known to exist against him."[10]

For every bit of the colonization movement's eighty-year existence, prominent and influential white advocates, Black activists had consistently pointed out, had propagated and strengthened anti-Black prejudice throughout the United States. Whether the movement's early leaders had intended this effect or not was, from the perspective of Black Americans, largely immaterial. The rise of anti-Black prejudice, with its myriad oppressive consequences, was an empirical fact, and the colonization movement's significant role in fostering this rise was, as Black activists had repeatedly indicated, one rivaled only by the institution of slavery itself. At one point during his 1894 speech, Douglass made the following terse and conclusive observation on the matter of intention. "When [white Southerners] . . . prefixed 'negro' to the national problem, . . . [they] knew that the device would awaken and increase a deep-seated prejudice at once, and that it would repel fair and candid investigation."[11]

The contrary visions that Douglass, Du Bois, and Cooper asserted during the 1890s were not identical, as noted, but they did share a common attitude. They looked to the future with a sense of faith rather than fear—specifically, faith in the human capacity to adapt and progress, in contrast to fear grounded in rigid, backward-looking assumptions. The ideology of the colonization movement originated, most directly, in white anxiety and uncertainty regarding the institution of slavery. Jefferson had theorized that during the long period in which racialized slavery had spread throughout North America, the capacity of white and Black Americans to coexist on terms of equality had been irrevocably impaired. From that theory—which many white colonization advocates, especially those from the South, took to be a fact—the colonization movement had deduced the necessity of Black expatriation or, at a minimum, legal exclusion. If neither of these paths were taken, the consequences, they claimed, would be dire: a war of racial extermination or, at a minimum, a perpetual racial conflict. Douglass, Du Bois, and Cooper rejected this way of thinking, claiming that it had no substantive basis in human history and that it posited an unnecessarily constrained view of human potential. Why was it impossible to overcome racial prejudice in the future? Just because it had been a prominent feature of the American past did not predetermine its continuation. If it persisted in the United States, it did so because various groups of Americans, for reasons of self-interest, caused it to persist. Human agency was essential.[12]

Black activists had asserted these counterarguments for eight decades. They had done so with great conviction and, at the same time, without naiveté. They had acknowledged, without hesitation, that the eradication of racial prejudice would be difficult, especially in the near term. But they had also insisted that change was possible, especially if the people of the United States used the system of democracy to push change through the vehicle of the federal government. As Douglass repeatedly pointed out during his final decades on the national speaking circuit, the main reason that the United States had a "race problem" was that large numbers of white Americans refused to abide by the terms and spirit of the pivotal Thirteenth, Fourteenth, and Fifteenth Amendments. All that was needed to begin making these national reforms real and permanent was dedicated enforcement by the federal government. The deflective notion that the Black population was to blame for the "race problem," simply because of its ongoing existence, was preposterous, Douglass declared. Such an absurd ascription of blame only made sense if one operated within a very constrained and constructed frame of mind. The federal government had the legal instruments and the power necessary to undermine this frame of mind. More specifically, it had the capacity to prevent white Americans from implementing exclusionary laws and practices that used this way of thinking to justify such exclusion.

It would take the federal government another seventy years to assume the role of dedicated change agent. While the colonization movement, for the most part, was not a distinct force in American politics during this period, the movement's ideology, unsurprisingly, continued to have significant influence in American society. As long as large numbers of Americans sustained, elaborated, and defended the laws and practices of Jim Crow, they also perpetuated and reinforced, in various ways and to varying extents, the slavery-era notion that Black freedom was a problem and that Black exclusion was, in turn, necessary, inevitable, morally defensible, and even patriotic. Human agency, it bears repeating, was the driving force of persistence. Ideologies cannot survive otherwise.[13]

It is a striking fact that Du Bois and Cooper both lived long enough to see the federal government begin to take a firm stand against Jim Crow and, by extension, colonization ideology. In 1954, the Supreme Court effectively nullified the separate-but-equal doctrine as it pertained to public education, thus partially overturning *Plessy v. Ferguson*. During the late 1950s and early 1960s, Presidents Eisenhower and Kennedy put increasing pressure on Congress to take serious actions to guarantee and to enforce civic equality for all Americans. In the summer of 1964, less than twelve months after Du Bois died at the age of ninety-five and less than six months after Cooper passed at the age of 105, Congress followed through. The Civil Rights Act of 1964 effectively swept away the legal foundations that had enabled many state and local forms of Jim Crow discrimination and, along with the Civil Rights Act of 1965, dramatically increased the federal government's authority, and indeed its obligation, to prosecute violations of the new equal rights regime.

In combination, these laws directly repudiated the idea that Black freedom was a problem and that Black exclusion was thus in any sense necessary, inevitable, morally defensible, or patriotic. They also repudiated the associated idea, asserted by colonization advocates for eight decades and formally proclaimed in the 1896 *Plessy* decision, that racial prejudice was invulnerable to legal intervention.[14]

In a significant sense, these mid-1960s laws marked the end of a very long and contentious fight, one that stretched back to the administration of James Madison, the nation's fourth president, when Clay, Key, Mercer, Caldwell, Randolph, Washington, and many others had turned Jefferson's racialized vision into a political project. The great battle between colonization advocates and Black activists that raged over the next eighty years and that continued, at least in ideological terms, through the first two-thirds of the twentieth century had reached a conclusion. Colonization advocates, and their many ideological descendants, had lost the battle. Black activists, and their myriad supporters, had won. It was the latter's vision, not the former's, that the federal government adopted as national policy. And yet, in many ways, the great battle has continued.[15]

NOTES

ABBREVIATIONS

AC	*Annals of Congress*
AR	*African Repository*
CA	*Colored American*
CG	*Congressional Globe*
CR	*Congressional Record*
DM	*Douglass' Monthly*
FDP	*Frederick Douglass' Paper*
NE	*National Era*
NS	*North Star*
RD	*Register of Debates*
TAR	*The Annual Reports of the American Society for Colonizing the Free People of Colour of the United States*
TCR	*Christian Recorder*

INTRODUCTION

1. Jefferson, *Notes on the State of Virginia*, 272. For the full discussion, see 228–40, 270–73. In this note, I refer to the London edition published in 1787. The first edition published in the United States was issued in 1788 in Philadelphia.
2. Jefferson, *Notes on the State of Virginia*, 228–29.

3. Jefferson, *Notes on the State of Virginia,* 229.
4. Jefferson, "Memoir," 42.
5. Many historians have discussed the historical significance of Jefferson's remarks on Black expatriation (see, for instance, Fredrickson, *The Black Image in the White Mind;* Freehling, *The Road to Disunion, Vol. 1;* Guyatt, *Bind Us Apart;* Onuf, *The Mind of Thomas Jefferson;* and Staudenraus, *The African Colonization Movement*).
6. The most analogous interpretations of the colonization movement's history are Guyatt, *Bind Us Apart;* and Fredrickson, *The Black Image in the White Mind.* Both scholars recognize that the movement's exclusionary rhetoric made a deep and lasting impression on American society, one that persisted well beyond the abolition of slavery in 1865. To a significant degree, my book agrees with and builds upon these two very important works. Frederickson's book is the most comparable in chronological span, as it covers most of the nineteenth century, though it is not Fredrickson's aim to offer a thorough account, as I do in *Words Colliding,* of the ways in which colonization advocates broadened and deepened this societal impression over time by intertwining their exclusionary rhetoric with a changing array of high-profile political issues. Guyatt's book focuses mainly on the period before 1835 and thus, although quite astute, is largely suggestive, rather than demonstrative, of colonization ideology's long-term influence. Fredrickson's book is also the most comparable in the way it frames colonization ideology. The two core elements of colonization ideology, as I articulate them in *Words Colliding*—that Black freedom was a *problem* in American society and that the exclusion of Black Americans (either from the United States itself, or, at a minimum, from the rights enjoyed by white Americans within the United States) was necessary, inevitable, morally defensible, and even patriotic—essentially agree with his assertions, given in the book's concluding pages, that it was quite common during the nineteenth century for white Americans to view "racial prejudice or antipathy ... [as] a natural and inevitable" reaction to Black freedom and, furthermore, to maintain that a "biracial equalitarian (or 'integrated') society" was largely "impossible" to effect (321, specifically points 5 and 6). These assertions also agree, for the most part, with Guyatt's overarching claim that "racial separation ... [was] the principal means of imagining slavery's demise in the early republic" and that this way of thinking significantly informed the postemancipation system of Jim Crow segregation that dominated the United States for a hundred years following the Civil War (330). A notable difference between my book and Guyatt's, however, is that he uses the phrase "separate but equal," a reference to the *Plessy v. Ferguson* Supreme Court decision of 1896, to capture the essence of colonization ideology

(10–11), while, in contrast, I identify this essence as the notion that Black freedom was a societal *problem*. Guyatt's formulation has considerable merit and utility, to be clear, since, as he points out, *separate but equal* was indeed one of the colonization movement's core messages. There was, however, a major qualification to this message. For the most part, colonization advocates did not favor a policy of *separate but equal* while Black Americans continued to live in the United States. They favored it only in the case that Black Americans emigrated to a polity of their own, or to an existing polity where they could live as civic equals with the native population. Indeed, it is one of the core claims of *Words Colliding* that throughout the nineteenth century, both before and after the Civil War, colonization advocates insisted on the necessity of civic *inequality* and that they did so largely because they believed, or at least they professed to believe, that Black freedom was an intractable societal problem. On the subject of Black opposition to the colonization movement, the main monographic work is Power-Greene, *Against Wind and Tide*. For other important contributions, see Blight, *Frederick Douglass*; M. S. Jones, *Birthright Citizens*; Kantrowitz, *More Than Freedom*; Masur, *Until Justice Be Done*; Quarles, *Black Abolitionists*; Rael, *Black Identity and Black Protest*; Sinha, *The Slave's Cause*; and Winch, *A Gentleman of Color*.

7. Hening, *The Statutes at Large*, vol. 2, 267. I located this reference using the footnotes of Ira Berlin, *Slaves Without Masters*, 5. For colonial legal history on the matters of slavery and Black freedom, see ibid.; Berlin, *Many Thousands Gone*; and Jordan, *White Over Black*.
8. Hening, *The Statutes at Large*, vol. 2, 170; Berlin, *Slaves Without Masters*; Berlin, *Many Thousands Gone*; Jordan, *White Over Black*.
9. Berlin, *Slaves Without Masters*; Berlin, *Many Thousands Gone*; Jordan, *White Over Black*. The scholar who pointed out the distinctive strength of this attitude in the English colonies and in the United States was Orlando Patterson (*Slavery and Social Death*, 240–61).
10. For the 1691 Virginia law, see Hening, *The Statutes at Large*, vol. 3, 86–88. Berlin, *Slaves Without Masters*; Berlin, *Many Thousands Gone*; Jordan, *White Over Black*.
11. Berlin, *Slaves Without Masters*; Berlin, *Many Thousands Gone*; Jordan, *White Over Black*; Zilversmit, *The First Emancipation*.
12. Berlin, *Slaves Without Masters*; Berlin, *Many Thousands Gone*; Jordan, *White Over Black*; Zilversmit, *The First Emancipation*.
13. "From Thomas Jefferson to St. George Tucker, 28 August 1797," Founders Online, National Archives. On the history of the Prosser Conspiracy and the political aftermath, see Berlin, *Slaves Without Masters*; Berlin, *Many Thousands Gone*; Egerton, *Gabriel's Rebellion*; and Jordan, *White Over Black*.

14. "Colonization of People of Color of Virginia," in *American State Papers, Class X, Miscellaneous*, vol. 1 (Buffalo, 1988), 464-67 (quotation on 464); Berlin, *Slaves Without Masters*; Egerton, *Gabriel's Rebellion*; Jordan, *White Over Black*.
15. Fairfax, "Plan for Liberating the Negroes," 286. For the full text, see ibid., 285-87. On British colonization in Sierra Leone, see C. L. Brown, *Moral Capital*.
16. George Tucker, *Letter to a Member of the General Assembly*, 23.
17. George Tucker, *Letter to a Member of the General Assembly*, 14, 16.
18. St. George Tucker, *A Dissertation on Slavery*, 7, 89. The letter that Jefferson penned in 1797 characterizing the Haitian Revolution as the front end of a "revolutionary storm" had, in fact, been written to St. George, as a thank-you for sending Jefferson a copy of the pamphlet.
19. St. George Tucker, *A Dissertation on Slavery*, 94-95.
20. Egerton, *Charles Fenton Mercer*; Egerton, "'Its Origin Is Not a Little Curious.'" Egerton's accounts of the founding revise an earlier account offered in Staudenraus, *The African Colonization Movement*.
21. "Colony of Free Blacks," *Niles' Register* 10 (1816): 260; I. V. Brown, *Memoirs of the Rev. Robert Finley, D.D.*; Egerton, *Charles Fenton Mercer*; Egerton, "'Its Origin Is Not a Little Curious.'"
22. "Virginia House of Delegates," *National Intelligencer*, December 21, 1816; Egerton, *Charles Fenton Mercer*; Egerton, "'Its Origin Is Not a Little Curious.'" The language of the Virginia legislature's resolution differs somewhat in another contemporary source. See *A View of Exertions*, 4. There is a curious reference to the "North Pacific" in the resolution as reported in the *Intelligencer* that does not show up in any of the ACS's accounts of the resolution.
23. "Virginia House of Delegates," *National Intelligencer*, December 21, 1816.
24. *A View of Exertions*, 5-6, 10-11; "The Meeting on the Colonization of the Free Blacks," *National Intelligencer*, December 24, 1816.
25. The most readily accessible copy of Finley's pamphlet can be found in the *African Repository*, the official journal of the ACS (see Finley, "Thoughts on the Colonization of Free Blacks," 332-35 [quotations on 335]).
26. Finley, "Thoughts on the Colonization of Free Blacks," 335.
27. "A Counter Memorial," *National Intelligencer*, December 30, 1816.
28. Dain, *A Hideous Monster of the Mind*; Fredrickson, *The Black Image in the White Mind*; Horsman, *Race and Manifest Destiny*.
29. Jefferson, *Notes on the State of Virginia*, 229, 239; Dain, *A Hideous Monster of the Mind*, 26-39.
30. Finley, "Thoughts on the Colonization of Free Blacks," 334.
31. "A Counter Memorial," *National Intelligencer*, December 30, 1816.
32. Jefferson, *Notes on the State of Virginia*, 240.
33. Most colonization monographs have used the ACS or one of its auxiliary organizations as the primary unit of analysis, including Burin, *Slavery and the*

Peculiar Solution; Guyatt, *Bind Us Apart;* Staudenraus, *The African Colonization Movement;* and Tomek, *Colonization and Its Discontents.* For two exceptions, see Mills, *The World Colonization Made;* and Page, *Black Resettlement and the American Civil War.*

34. P. J. Staudenraus's *The African Colonization Movement, 1816-1865,* the first major scholarly monograph on the ACS and still one of the most cited, makes no mention of the Blair family's promotion of colonization. Eric Burin's influential and oft-cited *Slavery and the Peculiar Solution,* the second major scholarly monograph on the ACS, mentions Frank Blair Jr. briefly, though insightfully, on the last few pages of its excellent first chapter. Neither Staudenraus nor Burin addresses the post-1865 period in any substantive way. For two recently published works that do provide some coverage of the Blairs' efforts as colonization advocates, see Mills, *The World Colonization Made,* 167-95; and Page, *Black Resettlement and the American Civil War,* 99-188.

35. In arriving at this insight, I was aided immensely by several challenging conversations with James Campbell and James Oakes, both of whom pressed me to articulate why the colonization movement's repeated failures were historically significant. I was also influenced, conceptually speaking, by McCurry, *Confederate Reckoning.*

36. None of the monographs on the colonization movement provide any substantive coverage of both pre-1865 and post-1865 promotion of the issue, except for Page, *Black Resettlement and the American Civil War* (263-90). Two important nonmonographic works that provide both pre-1865 and post-1865 coverage are Campbell, *Middle Passages,* and, as noted earlier, Fredrickson, *The Black Image in the White Mind.* Other exemplary works of scholarship that influenced my decision to adopt a trans-1865 framing are Hahn, *A Nation Under Our Feet;* Hobbs, *A Chosen Exile;* Kantrowitz, *More Than Freedom;* and Masur, *Until Justice Be Done.*

37. For historians who have, to varying degrees, argued for an *antislavery* label, see Burin, *Slavery and the Peculiar Solution,* 2; Egerton, "Averting a Crisis," 147; Fredrickson, *The Black Image in the White Mind,* 8-12; Guyatt, *Bind Us Apart,* 267-72; and Tomek, *Colonization and Its Discontents,* xv-xx. For two historians who have characterized the ACS as essentially *proslavery,* see Ripley, *The Black Abolitionist Papers,* vol. 3, 7; and Tise, *Proslavery,* 50-54. For an article-length discussion of the interpretive constraints of binary frameworks, see Hammann, "Beyond *Antislavery* and *Proslavery.*"

38. Several historians have written about terminological problems in slavery scholarship. See, for instance, D. B. Davis, *The Problem of Slavery in the Age of Revolution,* 21-22; Freehling, *The Road to Disunion, Vol. 1,* 121-23; Kraditor, *Means and Ends in American Abolitionism,* 7-38; McDaniel, "The Bonds and Boundaries of Antislavery"; Polgar, *Standard-Bearers of Equality,* 19-21; and Tise,

Proslavery, xiii–xviii. For an extensive analysis of existing terminological problems, see Hammann, "Beyond *Antislavery* and *Proslavery*." On the potential for mutual misunderstanding among historians, see the excellent essays by Andrew Delbanco in *The Abolitionist Imagination* (3–55, 155–63).

39. Hammann, "Beyond *Antislavery* and *Proslavery*."
40. I have only been able to find one reference to the term *eventualism* in scholarship on enslavement in the United States, though I cannot say for sure that there are not others (see Fehrenbacher, *The Dred Scott Case*, 117–18). My thinking was influenced by Fehrenbacher's brief remarks; it was also influenced by Freehling's term "conditional termination" (see *The Road to Disunion, Vol. 1*, 121–43). Some historians have used the word *eventual* to describe the attitudes of Henry Clay and others toward slavery's future (see, for instance, Remini, *Henry Clay*, 670, 692; and Klotter, *Henry Clay*, 192). For a focused discussion and demonstration of this term's value, see Hammann, "Beyond *Antislavery* and *Proslavery*."
41. On the instability of this term and efforts to give it a standard definition, see, for instance, Delbanco, *The Abolitionist Imagination*, 3–55; Kraditor, *Means and Ends in American Abolitionism*, 7–38; Polgar, *Standard-Bearers of Equality*, 19–21; and Sinha, *The Slave's Cause*, 1–5.
42. For scholars who have stressed the distinction between *colonization* and *emigration*, see F. J. Miller, *The Search for a Black Nationality;* and Power-Greene, *Against Wind and Tide*.
43. Douglass, "The Nation's Problem," 728.

1. FOUNDING MOMENT

1. *A View of Exertions*, 14. For other accounts of the ACS's founding moment, see Burin, *Slavery and the Peculiar Solution;* Egerton, "'Its Origin Is Not a Little Curious'"; Guyatt, *Bind Us Apart;* Spooner, "'I Know This Scheme Is from God'"; and Staudenraus, *The African Colonization Movement*.
2. *A View of Exertions*, 5, 9–10. Several historians have noted the mixed-message nature of the ACS's founding rhetoric. See, for instance, Egerton, "Averting a Crisis"; Fredrickson, *The Black Image in the White Mind*, 8–12; Guyatt, *Bind Us Apart*, 267–72; and Spooner, "'I Know This Scheme Is from God.'"
3. For scholarship that has stressed the Upper Southern dimension of the ACS's founding moment, see Egerton, "'Its Origin Is Not a Little Curious'" and "Averting a Crisis"; Guyatt, *Bind Us Apart*, 267–72; and Spooner, "'I Know This Scheme Is from God.'"

4. For biographical information on Randolph, I have consulted Garland, *The Life of John Randolph of Roanoke;* and Johnson, *John Randolph of Roanoke.*
5. "The First Annual Report," in *TAR, Vols. 1-10*, 2.
6. Berlin, *Slaves Without Masters;* Berlin, *Many Thousands Gone;* Jordan, *White Over Black;* Patterson, *Slavery and Social Death.*
7. "The First Annual Report," in *TAR, Vols. 1-10*, 16, 19, 21.
8. "The First Annual Report," in *TAR, Vols. 1-10*, 17.
9. For scholarly works that note Randolph's countervailing claims, see Clegg, *The Price of Liberty*, 30-31; and Guyatt, *Bind Us Apart*, 268.
10. For biographical information on Clay, I have relied mainly on Heidler and Heidler, *Henry Clay;* Klotter, *Henry Clay;* Maness, "Henry Clay and the Problem of Slavery"; and Remini, *Henry Clay.*
11. Clay, "To the Electors of Fayette County," April, 16, 1798, in Clay, *Papers of Henry Clay,* ed. Hopkins and Hargreaves, vol. 1, 3-7 (quotations on 5-6).
12. For an example of Clay's increased candor regarding colonization's emancipatory potential, see "The Tenth Annual Report," in *TAR, Vols. 1-10*, 12-23.
13. For the full text of the founding constitution, see *A View of Exertions*, 11-12. For the petition, see ibid., 14-16. Two historians who have suggested that ACS founders employed politically motivated rhetorical deception during the founding sessions are Douglas Egerton and Nicholas Guyatt (Egerton, "'Its Origin Is Not a Little Curious,'" 113; and Guyatt, *Bind Us Apart*, 268).
14. One historian who has substantively discussed the political distinctions between promoting the colonization of *already free* Black Americans and *prospectively free* Black Americans is Lacy Ford (see *Deliver Us from Evil*, 299-328).
15. On the *national* dimensions of the ACS's message, see Staudenraus, *The African Colonization Movement*, 12-35.
16. *A View of Exertions*, 14.
17. "The First Annual Report," in *TAR, Vols. 1-10*, 10.
18. Carter and Sutch, *Historical Statistics of the United States.*
19. "The First Annual Report," in *TAR, Vols. 1-10*, 10.
20. For scholarly works that cover the early decades of Black opposition to the colonization movement, see M. S. Jones, *Birthright Citizens;* Miller, *The Search for a Black Nationality;* Power-Greene, *Against Wind and Tide;* Sinha, *The Slave's Cause;* and Winch, *A Gentleman of Color.*
21. For accounts of the two public protest meetings held in 1817, see Garrison, *Thoughts on African Colonization*, pt. 2, 9-13 (quotations on 13).
22. Garrison, *Thoughts on African Colonization*, pt. 2, 9. See also "The Colonization Scheme," in *Niles' Register* 17 (1820): 201-2; and Walker, *Walker's Appeal, in Four Articles*, 49-88.

23. Garrison, *Thoughts on African Colonization*, pt. 2, 10-11.
24. "Continued from No. 3," *Freedom's Journal,* April 13, 1827; "Colonization," *Rights of All,* July 17, 1829. Some of the dates for articles in the *Rights of All* are designated within issues. I have cited the dates on the front page of the issue in which the article appears.

2. ENDING SLAVERY

1. For a full record of this meeting, see "The Seventh Annual Report," in *TAR, Vols. 1-10,* 5-18.
2. "The Seventh Annual Report," in *TAR, Vols. 1-10,* 10-11.
3. "The Seventh Annual Report," in *TAR, Vols. 1-10,* 12.
4. "The Seventh Annual Report," in *TAR, Vols. 1-10,* 7-9, 13.
5. ACS leaders actually decided at the 1824 meeting that they would submit a new memorial to Congress in the next year, but ultimately they did not do so (see "The Seventh Annual Report," in *TAR, Vols. 1-10,* 111-15; "The Eighth Annual Report," in *Vols. 1-10,* 24; and Staudenraus, *The African Colonization Movement,* 169).
6. For the full text of the memorial, see *A View of Exertions,* 14-16 (quotations on 14). John Randolph was part of the eight-person committee that drafted the document. Other notable members were Robert Wright (United States representative from Maryland), Francis Scott Key, Elias Caldwell, and Richard Rush (United States attorney general, from Pennsylvania) (see *A View of Exertions,* 11). For the entry in the congressional record, see *AC,* 14th Cong., 2nd Sess., 481-83 (1816-17). For the ACS's early years of congressional politicking, see Burin, *Slavery and the Peculiar Solution;* Burin, "The Slave Trade Act of 1819"; Egerton, *Charles Fenton Mercer;* and Staudenraus, *The African Colonization Movement.*
7. For the report from the House committee, see *AC,* 14th Cong., 2nd Sess., 939-41 (1816-17) (quotations on 939).
8. *AC,* 14th Cong., 2nd Sess., 941 (1816-17). On the history of slave trade activism in Great Britain, see C. L. Brown, *Moral Capital.*
9. "The Second Annual Report," in *TAR, Vols. 1-10,* 12-16. Important secondary references for these points and for the events discussed in the remainder of this section include Burin, "The Slave Trade Act of 1819"; Clegg, *The Price of Liberty;* Egerton, *Charles Fenton Mercer;* and Staudenraus, *The African Colonization Movement.*
10. "The Third Annual Report," in *TAR, Vols. 1-10,* 46-49 (quotation on 48).

11. For the full memorial, see "The Fourth Annual Report," in *TAR, Vols. 1–10*, 23–30 (quotations on 26, 28).
12. On the founding of Liberia, see Clegg, *The Price of Liberty*; F. J. Miller, *The Search for a Black Nationality*; and Staudenraus, *The African Colonization Movement*.
13. For the early history of Liberia, see Clegg, *The Price of Liberty*; and F. J. Miller, *The Search for a Black Nationality*.
14. F. J. Miller, *The Search for a Black Nationality*.
15. F. J. Miller, *The Search for a Black Nationality*.
16. For auxiliary society data, see Adams, *The Neglected Period of Anti-Slavery in America*, 106. My Upper South-dominant interpretation builds on scholarly works such as Egerton, "'Its Origin Is Not a Little Curious'"; and Spooner, "'I Know This Scheme Is from God.'"
17. P. J. Staudenraus's account of the ACS's founding puts the Northern benevolence movement in the foreground, while acknowledging that several Upper Southerners were crucial contributors and early leaders (see Staudenraus, *The African Colonization Movement*, 12–35, 94–103, 117–35). For broader coverage of the benevolence movement, see Abzug, *Cosmos Crumbling*; Hammond, *The Politics of Benevolence*; Walters, *American Reformers*.
18. "The Seventh Annual Report," in *TAR, Vols. 1–10*, 9–12.
19. P. J. Staudenraus discusses the society's efforts to enhance its Northern appeal (see *The African Colonization Movement*, 69–135, 169–87).
20. The idea that ACS leaders, for promotional purposes, cultivated two founding narratives has received little notice from colonization scholars. For the most part, they have focused on debating whether the ACS's origins were predominantly Northern or Southern. An exemplar of the former view, as indicated above, is Staudenraus, *The African Colonization Movement*; exemplars of the latter view, also indicated above, are Egerton, "'Its Origin Is Not a Little Curious'"; and Spooner, "'I Know This Scheme Is from God.'"
21. "American Colonization Society," *AR* 1 (1826): 1–5 (quotations on 1 and 3).
22. "The Reports of the American Society for Colonizing the Free People of Colour in the United States.—1818, 19, 20, 21, 22, 23," *Christian Spectator* 5 (1823): 486; "Review on African Colonization," *Quarterly Christian Spectator* 2 (1830): 459–60.
23. "The Sixth Annual Report," in *TAR, Vols. 1–10*, 50. Beverly Tomek stresses the importance of the emancipatory-potential message in recruiting many white Pennsylvanians to the colonization cause (see Tomek, *Colonization and Its Discontents*, 43–62).
24. "The Rev. Leonard Bacon's Plea for Africa, and an Address in Behalf of the Colonization Society, by Peachy Grattan, Esq.," *AR* 1 (1826): 169–79 (quotations on 177); "Annual Meetings of Auxiliary Societies," 337–47 (quotations on 345).

25. In 1843, a House committee, under the leadership of Maryland Representative John Pendleton Kennedy, produced an enormous report on the subjects of colonization and Liberia in national politics. The appendix contained a fairly comprehensive catalogue of state legislative resolutions in favor of colonization up to that point (see House Committee on Commerce, Report of Mr. Kennedy, 926-35 [quotations on 927-28]).
26. *AR* 1 (1826): 161, 335. On the subject of rising opposition from the Lower South, see Freehling, *Prelude to Civil War;* Ford, *Deliver Us from Evil;* and Staudenraus, *The African Colonization Movement.*
27. For 1827, see *AR* 2 (1827): 325-26. For 1828, see *AR* 3 (1828): 321-23. It should be noted that the 1828 list, unlike the 1827 list, did not indicate which of the delegates were in attendance. Thus, it is possible that some of those named were not present. For context and analysis of the 1827 and 1828 annual meetings and the respective memorials, see Freehling, *Prelude to Civil War;* Ford, *Deliver Us from Evil;* and Staudenraus, *The African Colonization Movement.*
28. For Clay's speech, see "The Tenth Annual Report," in *TAR, Vols. 1-10,* 12-23 (quotations on 19, 23). Francis Scott Key gave a similarly forceful speech at the 1828 meeting (see "Annual Meeting of the American Colonization Society," *AR* 3 [1828]: 353-56).
29. "Memorial of the American Society for Colonizing the Free People of Color of the United States," 6 (1826-27).
30. Hayne gave two speeches in opposition to the memorial. For the first speech see *RD,* 19th Cong., 2nd Sess., 289-95 (1826-27); for the second speech, see 325-34 (quotations on 289, 329). Other senators voicing opposition were John Berrien (GA), William Rufus de Vane King (AL), and William Smith (SC) (ibid., 296). On Hayne's opposition and on other instances of opposition discussed in the remainder of this section, see Freehling, *Prelude to Civil War;* and Ford, *Deliver Us from Evil.*
31. "Colonization of the Free People of Color," 7 (1826-27); Turnbull, *The Crisis,* 126-38 (quotations on 131, 137).
32. "Resolutions of the Legislature of Georgia," 9 (1827-28); "Resolutions of a Special Committee of the Senate of South Carolina" (1827-28).
33. See [Tazewell Report] (1832-33) (quotations on 7, 13). The Senate Journal for the 20th Congress, 1st Session, indicates that the committee's report was printed in 1828, but I have not been able to locate it—hence my usage of a later printing.
34. Oates, *The Fires of Jubilee.*
35. *RD,* 22nd Cong., 1st Sess., 1537-38, 1662-63, 1674-76 (1831-32) (quotations on 1537). The two other Virginians were William Archer and Robert Craig. On the post-Nat-Turner inflection in colonization interest in the Upper South, see Ford, *Deliver Us from Evil;* and Goodyear Freehling, *Drift Toward Dissolution.*

36. Clay estimated this total five-year amount based on actual 1831 federal land revenues (see *RD,* 22nd Cong., 1st Sess., 1118-19 [1831-32]). To my knowledge, the paragraphs that follow offer the first in-depth analysis of the Clay Land Bill moment's significance to the larger history of the colonization movement. For other brief accounts, see Burin, *Slavery and the Peculiar Solution,* 22; and Staudenraus, *The African Colonization Movement,* 185-87. On the broader history of the public lands as a federal political issue, see Feller, *The Public Lands in Jacksonian Politics.*
37. *AR* 7 (1832): 370-72 (quotations on 370, 372). Both Madison and Marshall had been involved in the colonization movement for several years at this point (on Madison, see McCoy, *The Last of the Fathers;* and on Marshall, see Beveridge, *The Life of John Marshall*).
38. For Clay's entire speech, which took place in June 1832, see *RD,* 22nd Cong., 1st Sess., 1096-119 (1831-32) (quotations on 1116-17). Clay gave a second speech in January 1833 (see *RD,* 22nd Cong., 2nd Sess., 67-79 [1832-33]). Andrew Jackson, "Second Annual Message," December 6, 1830, online by Gerhard Peters and John T. Woolley, The American Presidency Project, http://www.presidency.ucsb.edu.
39. For the final vote in the Senate, see *RD,* 22nd Cong., 1st Sess., 1174 (1831-32).
40. For the final Senate vote on the bill in January 1833, see *RD,* 22nd Cong., 2nd Sess., 235 (1832-33). The objector in the House was Clement Clay. For his entire speech, see 1904-19 (quotations on 1911). For the final vote in the House, see 1920-21.
41. *RD,* 22nd Cong., 2nd Sess., 809 (1832-33).
42. *RD,* 23rd Cong. 1st Sess., 15, 17 (1833-34). For Clay's full speech, see 14-18. For Clay's claim regarding a congressional override, see 1603.
43. For Jackson's message to Congress explaining his pocket veto, see "Message from the President of the United States" (1833-34). For the Senate votes on removing "colonization" from the bill text, see *RD,* 22nd Cong., 1st Sess., 1166 (1831-32); 22nd Cong., 2nd Sess., 230-31 (1832-33). During a speech in the spring of 1834 in favor of a new Land Bill (with colonization, internal improvements, and education added back in), Clay indicated that he strongly believed that the president had planned to veto the 1833 bill mainly because of the "provision . . . specifying colonization" (see 1603). For the text of Clay's new bill (and for the revision discussed below), see S. 6, 23rd Cong., 1st Sess. (1833-34). This bill eventually died in the Senate and thus did not make it as far as the earlier bill. Before that happened, the Committee on Public Lands revised the text by removing "colonization of free persons of color" as an allowable expense category. Since the committee allowed the other designated categories to remain, this revision went further than the one made by the House in early 1833. In effect, it prohibited the states from using their

allocated funds for colonization. Clay made yet another attempt in late 1835 and early 1836. This time, the Committee on Public Lands struck colonization, as well as all other expense categories, thus repeating the 1833 House revision. Once again, the bill failed to pass. For the text of the original and the revised versions, see S. 40, 24th Cong., 1st Sess. (1835-36).

44. On the multiyear conflict between South Carolina and the federal government, see Cooper, *The South and the Politics of Slavery*; Ford, *Deliver Us from Evil*; and Freehling, *The Road to Disunion, Vol. 1*.

3. STRENGTHENING THE UNION

1. Scholarly accounts of the founding of the American Anti-Slavery Society are numerous. For those that emphasize its continuity with earlier Black activist efforts, see Pease and Pease, *They Who Would Be Free*; Power-Greene, *Against Wind and Tide*; Quarles, *Black Abolitionists*; Sinha, *The Slave's Cause*; and Winch, *A Gentleman of Color*.
2. Mayer, *All on Fire*; Power-Greene, *Against Wind and Tide*; Winch, *A Gentleman of Color*; Wyatt-Brown, *Lewis Tappan*.
3. *Proceedings of the Anti-Slavery Convention* (1833): 12-16 (quotation on 15).
4. The South Carolinian representatives were James Henry Hammond and Henry Laurens Pinckney (see *RD*, 24th Cong., 1st Sess., 2450 [1835-36]; *CG*, Appendix, 24th Cong., 1st Sess., 768 [1835-36]). On the history of the Gag Rule era, see W. J. Cooper, *The South and the Politics of Slavery*; Freehling, *The Road to Disunion, Vol. 1*; and W. L. Miller, *Arguing About Slavery*.
5. For the text of the bill that Clay proposed and that the Committee on Public Lands rejected, without amendment, see S. 31, 24th Cong., 2nd Sess. (1836-37). For the brief debate in the Senate, see *CG*, 24th Cong., 2nd Sess., 30, 67 (quotation on 67). Clay tried to revive the Land Bill (with colonization in it) at least one more time. This failed as well. On the way to this outcome, the Committee on Public Lands again struck colonization and the other two expense categories from the bill text. For the original and revised versions, see S. 2, 27th Cong., 1st Sess. (1841).
6. One of the anecdotes Clay offered as justification for incorporation was the fact that former President James Madison had felt compelled to donate funds, from his will, indirectly to the ACS by bequeathing them directly to one of the ACS's officers, Reverend Ralph Gurley.
7. For the debate on the ACS incorporation memorial, see *CG*, 24th Cong., 2nd Sess., 129-31 (1836-37) (quotations on 129-30). These proceedings were also

summarized, fairly thoroughly, in "Application for a Charter," *AR* 13 (1837): 41–47.

8. For the final vote against referring the memorial to committee, see *CG*, 24th Cong., 2nd Sess., 138 (1836–37).

9. On the strengthening of Southern political solidarity during the mid- to late 1830s, see W. J. Cooper, *The South and the Politics of Slavery;* and Freehling, *The Road to Disunion, Vol. 1.* On the principle of *nonintervention,* see M. A. Morrison, *Slavery and the American West,* 9, 22, and passim.

10. Most monographs on the colonization movement have characterized the 1830s and 1840s as a time of political challenges and adjustments and have noted the cautious rhetoric adopted by many advocates, especially those from the South, with respect to slavery (see, for instance, Burin, *Slavery and the Peculiar Solution,* 22–27; and Staudenraus, *The African Colonization Movement,* 224–50). The most important historiographical intervention made in this chapter is the story told around the first adjustment: in essence, that colonization advocates took a basic message of Unionist appeal, which had been part of the movement's rhetoric for years, and raised it to an entirely new level of intensity and centrality. An excellent chapter in Richard Blackett's *The Captive's Quest for Freedom* highlights the use of Unionist rhetoric by colonization advocates during the early 1850s (88–134).

11. "To Our Patrons," *Freedom's Journal,* March 16, 1827. On the founding and significant influence of *Freedom's Journal,* see James, *The Struggles of John Brown Russwurm;* F. J. Miller, *The Search for a Black Nationality;* and Power-Greene, *Against Wind and Tide.*

12. Interestingly, prior to the newspaper's founding, Cornish had become involved with the American Bible Society (ABS). This made him an affiliate of an organization that counted Bushrod Washington and Francis Scott Key, two of the ACS's founders, as long-standing vice presidents. While there is no record of Cornish commenting on this institutional convergence, it was a fact that he certainly would not have relished. For biographical information on Cornish, I have relied on Swift, *Black Prophets of Justice.* For Russwurm, I have relied on James, *The Struggles of John Brown Russwurm.*

13. *Freedom's Journal,* August 31, 1827.

14. James, *The Struggles of John Brown Russwurm.*

15. "Liberia," *Freedom's Journal,* February 14, 1829; "Liberia," *Freedom's Journal,* February 21, 1829; "Colonization," *Freedom's Journal,* March 14, 1829; James, *The Struggles of John Brown Russwurm.*

16. "Barbarism in America," *Rights of All,* August 7, 1829.

17. "Barbarism in America," *Rights of All,* August 7, 1829; *Resolutions of the People of Color at a Meeting Held on the 25th of January, 1831,* 7. On the history of the incidents in Cincinnati, see Taylor, *Frontiers of Freedom.*

18. Hamilton, *Address to the Fourth Annual Convention of the Free People of Color of the United States* (1834), 5–6. See also *Minutes and Proceedings of the Second Annual Convention, for the Improvement of the Free People of Colour* (1832): 18–19, 32–33; *Minutes and Proceedings of the Third Annual Convention, for the Improvement of the Free People of Colour* (1833): 26–28, 34–36. For the escalation in state-level racial oppression during this period and the intertwined history of Black civil rights activism, see Bell, *A Survey of the Negro Convention Movement*; Berlin, *Slaves Without Masters*; Berwanger, *The Frontier Against Slavery*; M. S. Jones, *Birthright Citizens*; Litwack, *North of Slavery*; Masur, *Until Justice Be Done*; Rael, *Black Identity and Black Protest*; and Winch, *A Gentleman of Color*.
19. Ruggles, *The "Extinguisher" Extinguished!*, 39–40.
20. "Twenty-First Annual Meeting of the American Colonization Society," *AR* 14 (1838): 17–29.
21. "Twenty-First Annual Meeting of the American Colonization Society," *AR* 14 (1838): 17–29. On the various challenges the ACS encountered during the several years following the founding of the AASS, see Burin, *Slavery and the Peculiar Solution*; Staudenraus *The African Colonization Movement*; and Tomek, *Colonization and Its Discontents*.
22. "Twenty-First Annual Meeting of the American Colonization Society," *AR* 14 (1838): 18. During the speech, Clay made a qualifying remark in which he noted that most ACS members felt that slavery, in the abstract, was a "deplorable evil" (18).
23. "Remarks of the Hon. James Garland, of Virginia," *AR* 14 (1838): 43–47 (quotations on 43–45).
24. "To the People of the United States," *AR* 14 (1838): 130–35 (quotations on 134).
25. Clay, *Speech of the Hon. Henry Clay, in the Senate of the United States, on the Subject of Abolition Petitions, February 7, 1839*, 12–14.
26. *RD*, 22nd Cong., 2nd Sess., 75 (1832–33); J. C. Calhoun, "Speech on the Reception of Abolition Petitions, February, 1837," 225; Clay, *Speech of the Hon. Henry Clay, in the Senate of the United States, on the Subject of Abolition Petitions, February 7, 1839*, 16. On the ongoing rejection of perpetualism by many Upper Southern politicians, see Ford, *Deliver Us from Evil*; Freehling, *The Road to Disunion, Vol. 1*; and Hammann, "Beyond *Antislavery* and *Proslavery*."
27. "Clay to Jacob Gibson," July 25, 1842, in Clay, *Papers of Henry Clay*, ed. Hopkins and Hargreaves, vol. 9, 745–47 (quotations on 746).
28. Clay, *Speech of the Hon. Henry Clay, in the Senate of the United States, on the Subject of Abolition Petitions, February 7, 1839*, 16; Hammann, "Beyond *Antislavery* and *Proslavery*."
29. Ford, *Deliver Us from Evil*; Freehling, *The Road to Disunion, Vol. 1*; Hammann, "Beyond Antislavery and Proslavery." It is worth noting that the year before

Clay's speech, Alexis de Tocqueville issued the first American edition of *Democracy in America*. This enormously influential work contained a section that mentioned the colonization movement and that asserted a view of slavery's future that resonated with past and present colonization rhetoric. Although Tocqueville stated that he had little faith in the practicability of colonization, he essentially agreed with colonization advocates on the incongruity of Black freedom and white freedom. "I do not imagine," he wrote, "that the white and black races will ever live in any country upon an equal footing"—to which he added, "I believe the difficulty to be still greater in the United States than elsewhere." He also expressed great uncertainty, as Clay and others were doing through their eventualist remarks, as to how and when slavery would ultimately come to an end in America (Tocqueville, *Democracy in America*, 336–61 [quotations on 353]). For a discussion of Tocqueville and the colonization movement, see Fredrickson, *The Black Image in the White Mind*, 21–25.

30. "Proposals and Plan of a Newspaper for the People of Color," "Title of This Journal," *CA*, March 4, 1837. On the history of the *Colored American*, see Pease and Pease, *They Who Would Be Free*; and Quarles, *Black Abolitionists*.
31. "From *The Emancipator*: Great Anti-Colonization Meeting in New York," *CA*, January 19, 1839. For biographical information on Wright, I have relied mainly on Swift, *Black Prophets of Justice*.
32. "American Colonization Society," *CA*, July 29, 1837.
33. "*The Colonization Herald*," *CA*, January 27, 1838; "Colonization Convention," *CA*, June 2, 1838; "Communications—The Late Colonization Meeting," *CA*, July 7, 1838.
34. "What Have Colonizationists Done?" *CA*, July 13, 1839.
35. Cornish and Wright, *The Colonization Scheme Considered*, 7; "Great Anti-Colonization Meeting," *CA*, January 12, 1839; "Wrongs of the Colored People," January 30, 1841 (emphasis added).
36. Berlin, *Slaves Without Masters*; Berwanger, *The Frontier Against Slavery*; Litwack, *North of Slavery*.
37. "Philadelphia Correspondence," *CA*, January 27, 1838. See also "Misrepresentation Exposed," March 29, 1838. For the full text of the memorial, see "The Climax Capped," March 15, 1838. I have used the *Colored American* as the original source because I have not been able to locate the document in the state convention's official record or in the journals of the Pennsylvania House of Representatives or of the Senate. For more on this political moment in Pennsylvania, see Wood, "A Sacrifice on the Altar of Slavery."
38. "Our Next President," *CA*, March 29, 1838; "For *The Colored American*," *CA*, September 22, 1838.
39. "Henry Clay's Speech," *CA*, February 16, 1839.

40. "Wrongs of the Colored People," *CA*, January 30, 1841; Cornish and Wright, *The Colonization Scheme Considered*, 26.
41. On the early 1840s political environment in Washington, see Freehling, *The Road to Disunion, Vol. 1*; Holt, *The Rise and Fall of the American Whig Party*; H. Jones, *To the Webster-Ashburton Treaty*; and Karp, *This Vast Southern Empire*.
42. For the convention's various participants and speeches, see *Proceedings of a Convention of the Friends of African Colonization* (1842). For background on the planning of the convention, see "African Colonization. Important Meeting in Washington," *AR* 17 (1842): 121-25. Surprisingly, the ACS's 1842 convention and the congressional committee reports and debates that followed over the next two years have received little to no attention from historians.
43. *Proceedings of a Convention of the Friends of African Colonization* (1842): 34-49 (quotations on 46).
44. *Proceedings of a Convention of the Friends of African Colonization* (1842): passim.
45. "Mr. Key's Address," *AR* 4 (1829): 298-305 (quotations on 302-3).
46. *Proceedings of a Convention of the Friends of African Colonization* (1842): 7-21 (quotations on 12, 16).
47. *Proceedings of a Convention of the Friends of African Colonization* (1842): 1-4 (quotations on 4).
48. *Proceedings of a Convention of the Friends of African Colonization* (1842): 50-64 (quotations on 57).
49. *Proceedings of a Convention of the Friends of African Colonization* (1842): 57-58. On the tendency of Clay and the emergent Whig Party to support colonization while simultaneously opposing native dispossession, see Portnoy, *Their Right to Speak*.
50. For the ACS's 1842 memorial, see "Report of Mr. Kennedy," 7-16 (1842-43) (quotations on 14, 16).
51. "Report of Mr. Kennedy," 6 (1842-43). Appended to the seven-page summary of committee findings were hundreds of documents that, in aggregate, amounted to an archival history of colonization advocacy. Brief mentions of the Kennedy Report can be found in Mills, *The World Colonization Made*, 135-36; and Staudenraus, *The African Colonization Movement*, 307.
52. "African Slave Trade" (1843-44).
53. "African Slave Trade" 5 (1843-44).
54. "Constitution of the Republic of Liberia," *AR* 24 (1848): 1-3 (quotations on 1-2). For historical scholarship on Liberian independence, see Clegg, *The Price of Liberty*; Mills, *The World Colonization Made*; and Tyler-McGraw, *An African Republic*.
55. *AR* 25 (1849): 55. See also ibid., 52-60. On the colonization movement's efforts to promote the recognition of Liberia, see Mills, *The World Colonization Made*, 129-62; and Page, *Black Resettlement and the American Civil War*, 31-38.

56. "Late from Liberia," *AR* 25 (1849): 225-27 (quotations on 226). See also, for instance, "An Oration—by J. S. Payne," *AR* 24 (1848): 18-28.
57. "New York Colonization Society," *AR* 24 (1848): 237-40 (quotations on 239).
58. *CG*, 30th Cong., 2nd Sess., 189-90, 204-10 (1848-49) (quotations on 189).
59. *CG*, 30th Cong., 2nd Sess., 190, 206 (1848-49). See also *CG*, 31st Cong., 1st Sess., 1803-5 (1849-50).
60. *CG*, 30th Cong., 2nd Sess., 206-7 (1848-49). On this moment in Kentucky politics, see Tallant, *Evil Necessity*.
61. "Clay to Richard Pindell," February 17, 1849, in Clay, *Papers of Henry Clay*, ed. Hopkins and Hargreaves, vol. 10, 574-81 (quotations on 576-77). On the contrast between Clay's late-1790s attitude toward gradual abolition and his late-1840s attitude, see Hammann, "Beyond *Antislavery* and *Proslavery*."
62. On the history of the late-1840s congressional debate over slavery, see W. J. Cooper, *The South and the Politics of Slavery*; Foner, *Free Soil, Free Labor, Free Men*; Freehling, *The Road to Disunion, Vol. 1*; and M. A. Morrison, *Slavery and the American West*.
63. *CG*, 30th Cong., 2nd Sess., 209-10 (1848-49).
64. Sen. Ex. Doc. No. 75, 31st Cong., 1st Sess., 31 (1849-50); *Senate Journal*, 31st Cong., 1st Sess., 629 (1849-50).
65. "Addresses Delivered at the Annual Meeting," *AR* 25 (1849): 52-60 (quotations on 53-54).
66. *CG*, Appendix, 31st Cong., 1st Sess., 115-27 (1849-50) (quotation on 127).
67. [Stanton Report] (1849-50); H.R. 367, 31st Cong., 1st Sess. Historians have written relatively little about the colonization movement's high-profile and widely endorsed efforts during the early 1850s to obtain federal funding for Liberian steamship lines. Good but limited coverage can be found in Blackett, *The Captive's Quest for Freedom*, 92-94; Burin, *Slavery and the Peculiar Solution*, 28-29; and Karp, *This Vast Southern Empire*, 202-4. See also Blight, *Frederick Douglass*, 238-39.
68. [Stanton Report], esp. 3-4 (1849-50). See also the endorsement speech given by Andrew Ewing, a Democrat from Tennessee who served in the House at the same time as Stanton (*CG*, 31st Cong., 1st Sess., 1887-90) and the promotional pamphlet *Remarks on the Colonization of the Western Coast of Africa*.
69. Millard Fillmore, "First Annual Message," December 2, 1850, online by Gerhard Peters and John T. Woolley, The American Presidency Project, http://www.presidency.ucsb.edu. For secondary works on the Compromise of 1850 and the idea that it was a final settlement of slavery-related sectional conflict, see M. A. Morrison, *Slavery and the American West*; and Potter and Fehrenbacher, *The Impending Crisis*.

70. "Minutes of the Annual Meeting of the American Colonization Society," *AR* 27 (1851): 85-91.
71. Clay, "Speech of the Hon. H. Clay, Delivered at the Annual Meeting of the Am. Col. Society, January 21, 1851," 105-14 (quotations on 106, 109). The transcript of the speech indicated moments of notable applause. For a more detailed analysis of Clay's speech, see Hammann, "Beyond *Antislavery* and *Proslavery*."
72. Clay, "To the Electors of Fayette County," 6.
73. Clay, "Speech of the Hon. H. Clay, Delivered at the Annual Meeting of the Am. Col. Society, January 21, 1851," 109.
74. Stanton had his address read into the congressional record in February 1851 at the end of a speech that he gave in the House on behalf of the proposed Liberian steamer appropriation (see *CG*, Appendix, 31st Cong., 2nd Sess. [1850-51], 203-4 [quotations on 203]). For some reason, the *African Repository* did not reprint his speech.
75. *CG*, Appendix, 31st Cong., 2nd Sess., 203 (1850-51). For other relevant remarks given by Stanton between 1850 and 1851, see *CG*, 31st Cong., 1st Sess., 1861-64, 1914-20 (1849-50); *CG*, Appendix, 31st Cong., 2nd Sess., 200-203; *CG*, 31st Cong., 2nd Sess., 754-55.
76. *CG*, Appendix, 31st Cong., 2nd Sess., 203 (1850-51).
77. S. Doc. Misc. No. 19, 31st Cong., 2nd Sess., 1 (1850-51); *CG*, 31st Cong., 2nd Sess., 246 (1850-51). Records of other petitions are scattered throughout the *Congressional Globe,* the *House Journal,* and the *Senate Journal* (see, for instance, *CG*, 31st Cong., 2nd Sess., 246, 491, 503, 623).
78. The *Sun* (Baltimore), February 28, 1851; *AR* 27 (1851): 280-81 (quotation on 280). Reprints of articles from various newspapers can be found on 52-53, 204-6, 209-11, 347-48, and in *Colonization of the Western Coast of Africa*.
79. For a full account of the 1852 annual meeting, see *AR* 28 (1852): 70-91. For Stanton's speech, see 71-81 (quotations on 77).
80. For Webster's full 1852 speech, see *AR* 28 (1852): 86-89 (quotations on 86, 89). For the relevant portions of Webster's earlier speech, see *CG*, Appendix, 31st Cong., 1st Sess., 275-76 (1849-50).
81. "Extract—The New Colonization Scheme," *NS*, December 5, 1850. For good coverage and analysis of Black opposition to colonization promotion during the 1840s and early 1850s, see Power-Greene, *Against Wind and Tide*, 95-128. For Black opposition to the Liberian steamer proposal, see Blackett, *The Captive's Quest for Freedom*, 95-97.
82. "Convention of Colored Citizens," *NS*, April 10, 1851.
83. On the national- and state-level trends of Black oppression during this period, see Berlin, *Slaves Without Masters;* Berwanger, *The Frontier Against Slavery;* Blackett, *The Captive's Quest for Freedom;* Blight, *Frederick Douglass;* and Litwack, *North of Slavery*.

84. On the long history of Black civil rights activism, see Blight, *Frederick Douglass;* M. S. Jones, *Birthright Citizens;* Masur, *Until Justice Be Done;* Pease and Pease, *They Who Would Be Free;* Rael, *Black Identity and Black Protest;* Sinha, *The Slave's Cause;* and Winch, *A Gentleman of Color.*
85. For biographical information on Douglass, I have relied mainly on Blight, *Frederick Douglass.*
86. "Great Anti-Colonization Meeting in New York," *NS,* May 11, 1849. For biographical information on Ray, see Work, "The Life of Charles B. Ray."
87. "A New Party Question," *FDP,* March 18, 1853.
88. "Hon. Horace Greeley and the People of Color," *FDP,* January 29, 1852. For Article XIII and its context, see Mitchell, *Report of the Agent of the Indiana Colonization Society;* and Berwanger, *The Frontier Against Slavery.*
89. "Hon. Horace Greeley and the People of Color," *FDP,* January 29, 1852; *Journal of the Senate of the State of New-York; at Their Seventy-Fifth Session* (Albany, 1852), 21-25. See also "Extract from the Message of Governor Hunt," *AR* 28 (1852): 34-37.
90. "Henry Clay," *NS,* March 23, 1849. For the document that Douglass critiqued, see "Clay to Richard Pindell," 574-81. David Blight has also highlighted Douglass's particular concerns about Clay (Blight, *Frederick Douglass,* 190-91).
91. What made this cycle particularly self-reinforcing was the fact that many colonization advocates, as Black activists noted, were the very same politicians who voted for and, in some cases, spearheaded exclusionary legislation. Henry Clay, Daniel Webster, and Frederick Perry Stanton, for instance, had endorsed the Fugitive Slave Law in speeches before Congress and had voted in favor of the law's ultimate passage.
92. "Great Anti-Colonization Meeting in New York," *NS,* May 11, 1849; "A New Party Question," *FDP,* March 18, 1853. On the post-1850 increase in Black emigration, see "Table of Emigrants Settled in Liberia by the American Colonization Society," in *TAR, Vols. 44-53,* 56-64. On the debate among Black Americans regarding emigration, see Levine, *Martin Delany, Frederick Douglass, and the Politics of Representative Identity;* F. J. Miller, *The Search for a Black Nationality;* and Power-Greene, *Against Wind and Tide.*
93. *Proceedings of the Colored National Convention, Held in Rochester* (1853): 8 (emphasis added).
94. "Thirty-First Annual Report of the American Colonization Society," *African Register* 24 (1848): 65-79 (quotations on 69); "The American Colonization Society," *NS,* March 24, 1848. There was also a notable increase, between 1848 and 1850, in the number of Black Americans emigrating to Liberia (see "Table of Emigrants Settled in Liberia by the American Colonization Society," in *TAR, Vols. 44-53,* 56-64).

95. "The American Colonization Society," *NS*, March 24, 1848; "The Relations of Our Government to Liberia," *FDP*, March 25, 1853. On the number of Black American emigrants, see "Table of Emigrants Settled in Liberia by the American Colonization Society," 56–64. On Black Americans' complicated reaction to Liberia's independence, see Clegg, *The Price of Liberty*; Levine, *Martin Delany, Frederick Douglass, and the Politics of Representative Identity*; F. J. Miller, *The Search for a Black Nationality*; Mills, *The World Colonization Made*; Power-Greene, *Against Wind and Tide*; and Tyler-McGraw, *An African Republic*.
96. "Communications. The West—The West," *NS*, January 26, 1849; "Colonization and Emigration," *NS*, March 2, 1849. For Garnet's earlier criticism, see "Springfield, Mass. March 1848," *NS*, April 7, 1848. For biographical information on Garnet, see Pasternak, *Rise Now and Fly to Arms*.
97. "Cortlandville, Feb. 1849," *NS*, February 9, 1849.
98. *NS*, January 14, 1848.
99. "Anniversaries," *FDP*, May 27, 1853. For other indications, see "For *Frederick Douglass' Paper*: From our Toronto Correspondent," *FDP*, June 23, 1854; and *CG*, 33rd Cong., 1st Sess., 1590–1604 (1853–54); "Steam to Liberia," and "The United States and Liberia," *AR* 31 (1855): 11–16.
100. *CG*, 31st Cong., 1st Sess., 1866–1868 (1849–50) (quotations on 1867–68); *CG*, 31st Cong., 2nd Sess., 756–58 (1850–51) (quotations on 758).
101. "Letter from J.C. Holly," *FDP*, April 29, 1852.
102. For evidence of the expansion of the ACS's officer rolls, see *AR* 30 (1854): 45. For Everett's speech, see *AR* 29 (1853): 50–61. For Fillmore's letter, see 72–73 (quotations on 73).

4. PREVENTING DISUNION

1. For biographical information on Francis Preston Blair Sr., Frank Blair, and Montgomery Blair, see Parrish, *Frank Blair*; E. B. Smith, *Francis Preston Blair*; and W. E. Smith, *The Francis Preston Blair Family in Politics*.
2. Francis P. Blair, Jr., *Speech of Hon. Frank P. Blair, Jr., of Missouri, on the Acquisition of Territory in Central and South America*, 4. The speech also appears in *CG*, 35th Cong., 1st Sess., 293–98 (1857–58). The only colonization monographs to analyze the Blair's 1858–60 promotional efforts in depth are Mills, *The World Colonization Made*, 163–82; and Page, *Black Resettlement and the American Civil War*, 99–118. Both are recent publications. The subject, however, is not new to historians, despite its relative lack of coverage in colonization-focused scholarship. For older works that provide excellent analyses, see Foner, *Free Soil, Free*

Labor, Free Men, 267–80; Sewell, *Ballots for Freedom*, 316–36; and W. E. Smith, *The Francis Preston Blair Family in Politics*, vol. 1, 443–52 and passim. For a more recent work, see Escott, *Lincoln's Dilemma*, 14–37, 71–82.

3. For the history of Transylvania University, see http://www.transy.edu/about/our-history.
4. E. B. Smith, *Francis Preston Blair*; W. E. Smith, *The Francis Preston Blair Family in Politics*.
5. E. B. Smith, *Francis Preston Blair*; W. E. Smith, *The Francis Preston Blair Family in Politics*.
6. See, for instance, Blair Sr., *Letter of Francis P. Blair, Esq., to the Republican Association of Washington, D.C.*; and Blair Sr., *Letter from Francis P. Blair. to My Neighbors*. The latter document was also printed in the Republican Party newspaper the *National Era* (see October 2, 1856). See also W. E. Smith, *The Francis Preston Blair Family in Politics*.
7. *Official Proceedings of the Republican Convention Convened in the City of Pittsburgh, Pennsylvania* (1856): 5; Blair Sr., *Letter from Francis P. Blair. to My Neighbors*, 2.
8. Blair Sr., *Letter from Francis P. Blair. to My Neighbors*, 1. I used the following website for my election data: https://www.presidency.ucsb.edu/statistics/elections/1856.
9. Howard, *Report of the Decision of the Supreme Court of the United States, and the Opinions of the Judges Thereof, in the Case of Dred Scott versus John F. A. Sanford*. On the slavery controversy in Kansas during the Buchanan administration, see Freehling, *The Road to Disunion, Vol. 1*; Freehling, *The Road to Disunion, Vol. 2*; and M. A. Morrison, *Slavery and the American West*. On the Dred Scott case, see Fehrenbacher, *The Dred Scott Case*; and W. E. Smith, *The Francis Preston Blair Family in Politics*.
10. Howard, *Report of the Decision of the Supreme Court of the United States, and the Opinions of the Judges Thereof, in the Case of Dred Scott versus John F. A. Sanford*, 13, 17; Fehrenbacher, *The Dred Scott Case*; W. E. Smith, *The Francis Preston Blair Family in Politics*.
11. Blair Jr., *The Destiny of the Races of This Continent*, 19.
12. Blair Jr., *The Destiny of the Races of This Continent*, 24. This strategizing moment has been astutely discussed in Foner, *Free Soil, Free Labor, Free Men*, 267–80; and W. E. Smith, *The Francis Preston Blair Family in Politics*, vol. 1, 443–52.
13. Freehling, *The Road to Disunion, Vol. 1*; M. A. Morrison, *Slavery and the American West*.
14. *CG*, Appendix, 31st Cong., 1st Sess., 972 (1849–50). On Upper Southern attitudes toward slavery and on the diffusion theory, see Freehling, *The Road to Disunion, Vol. 1*.

15. Blair Jr., *Speech of Hon. Frank P. Blair, Jr., of Missouri, on the Acquisition of Territory in Central and South America*, 4.
16. Blair Jr., *Speech of Hon. Frank P. Blair, Jr., of Missouri, on the Acquisition of Territory in Central and South America*, 7. A substantive discussion of the Blairs' contrasting approach can be found in Mills, *The World Colonization Made*, 164–82. See also Page, *Black Resettlement and the American Civil War*, 109.
17. Blair Jr., *The Destiny of the Races of This Continent*, 35. For an extensive discussion of imperialism as a promotional theme, see Mills, *The World Colonization Made*, 164–82. See also Foner, *Free Soil, Free Labor, Free Men*, 272–74.
18. Blair Jr., *The Destiny of the Races of This Continent*, 21, 26.
19. Blair Jr., *Colonization and Commerce*, 2. Over the past several decades, ACS spokespeople had also argued, in various ways, against racial amalgamation, but for the most part they had not invoked the emergent theory of racial hybrids as biologically inferior. For the various theories of racial origins and differences that held sway in the United States during the nineteenth century, see Dain, *A Hideous Monster of the Mind;* Fredrickson, *The Black Image in the White Mind;* and Horsman, *Race and Manifest Destiny*.
20. *AR* 28 (1852): 100. Dayton, for instance, delivered a speech at the ACS's 1848 annual meeting and was a member of the Board of Managers of the New Jersey Colonization Society (see "Thirty-First Annual Report of the American Colonization Society," *AR* 24 [1848]: 33–34 [his speech was mentioned but not printed]). Corwin was a vice president of the American Colonization Society and had been involved in colonization promotion for nearly two decades (see Matijasic, "Conservative Reform in the West: The African Colonization Movement in Ohio, 1826–1839."). On colonization interest among Northern anti-extension politicians, see Berwanger, *The Frontier Against Slavery*.
21. Blair Jr., *Speech of Hon. F. P. Blair, Jr., of Missouri: At the Cooper Institute*, 6, 10.
22. For the appendix, see Blair Jr., *The Destiny of the Races of This Continent*, 29–38.
23. Blair Jr., *The Destiny of the Races of This Continent*, 32. For other endorsements, see the pamphlet's appendix and the very meticulous footnotes given in Foner, *Free Soil, Free Labor, Free Men*, 267–80; and Sewell, *Ballots for Freedom*, 316–36.
24. "Political. The Campaign in Missouri. Speech of Hon. F. P. Stanton at St. Louis," *New York Times*, July 27, 1860.
25. *CG*, 36th Cong., 1st Sess., 1629–35 (1859–60) (quotations on 1632). Other Republican notables in Congress were Senator James Harlan of Iowa, Representative Cadwallader Washburn of Wisconsin, and Senator James Ashley of Ohio (see *CG*, 36th Cong., 1st Sess., Appendix, 57, 265, 373–77 [1859–60]). Again, for the endorsements in this paragraph and the next, the scholarship of Eric Foner and Richard Sewell has been invaluable (see *Free Soil, Free Labor, Free Men*, 267–80; and *Ballots for Freedom*, 316–36).

26. For Wade, see *CG*, Appendix, 36th Cong., 1st Sess., 150–57 (1859–60) (quotation on 155). For Trumbull, see *CG*, 36th Cong., 1st Sess., 53–61 (quotations on 60–61).
27. *CG*, 36th Cong., 1st Sess., 59 (1859–60); *CG*, Appendix, 36th Cong., 1st Sess., 155.
28. "Jefferson's Birthday in Washington," *NE*, April 21, 1859. See also "Tropical Colonization," *NE*, February 24, 1859; "'The Harper's Ferry Affair as Party Capital'—The Danger of Using It," *NE*, November 3, 1859. For an example of an earlier denunciation of the ACS, see "Oppressive Legislation—Colonization," *NE*, May 27, 1852. The editors' main criticism of ACS proponents was that their consent rhetoric was a sham. Echoing criticisms repeatedly made by Black activists, the editors accused the society of engaging in coercion by "instigating oppressive legislation" and then citing such legislation as the "strongest argument" in favor of expatriation. During the late 1850s, in contrast, the editors did not acknowledge that forceful declarations in favor of racial separation—like those made by the Blairs, Trumbull, Wade, Doolittle, and by the editors themselves—could also be construed as coercive. Support from the *National Era* is documented in Foner, *Free Soil, Free Labor, Free Men*, 267–80.
29. "Colonization. Sailing of the Liberian Packet," *NS*, September 14, 1849; "The Twelfth Volume of Frederick Douglass' Paper," *DM*, January 1859. Like several historians, I have assumed that Douglass wrote all uncredited articles.
30. "F. P. Blair's Lecture in Boston," *DM*, March 1859.
31. "The Colored Citizens of New York and the African Civilization Society," *The Liberator*, May 4, 1860; "Twenty-Seventh Anniversary of the American Anti-Slavery Society," *The Liberator*, May, 18, 1860. Edward Bates was a Missouri politician whose name was considered for the presidential nomination at the 1860 Republican National Convention. Horace Greeley was the editor of the *National Tribune*. For other statements of opposition against the Republican Party and its support for expatriation, see "F. P. Blair's Lecture in Boston," *DM*, March 1859; "Dr. Pennington and The African Civilization Society," *Weekly Anglo-African*, April 21, 1860; "Twenty-Seventh Anniversary of the American Anti-Slavery Society," *National Anti-Slavery Standard*, May 26, 1860; and "Sunday Evening. Remarks by H. Ford Douglass," *Anti-Slavery Bugle*, October 6, 1860.
32. For annual meeting accounts and published lists of ACS officers in the years 1855 to 1860, see *AR* 31 (1855): 41–42; *AR* 32 (1856): 40–48; *AR* 33 (1857): 33–34; *AR* 34 (1858): 33–48; *AR* 35 (1859): 89–90; *AR* 36 (1860): 52–53; and "Fortieth Annual Report," in *TAR*, Vols. 34–43, 49–50. For additional analysis of what the ACS was doing during the mid- to late 1850s, see Page, *Black Resettlement and the American Civil War*, 38–53.

33. *AR* 34 (1858): 33-39 (quotations on 35).
34. *AR* 34 (1858): 39.
35. See *AR* 35 (1859): 225-38 (quotations are on 228, 235). For the other cities where Latrobe gave this speech, see the *Repository*'s footnote on 225.
36. See *AR* 36 (1860): 151-54 (quotations on 151).
37. For the 1859 appropriation, see "Chap. LXXV—An Act making Appropriations for the Consular and Diplomatic Expenses of the Government for the Year ending the thirtieth of June, eighteen hundred and sixty,'" in Sanger, *The Statutes at Large*, vol. 11, 402-4. For the 1860 appropriation, see "Chap. CXXXVI—An Act to amend an Act entitled 'An Act in addition to the Acts Prohibiting the Slave Trade,'" in Sanger, *The Statutes at Large*, vol. 12, 40-41.
38. *CG*, 35th Cong., 2nd Sess., 1057 (1858-59). For key moments in the debate regarding these bills and examples of resistance from Lower Southern Democrats, see *CG*, 35th Cong., 2nd Sess., 1053-57; and *CG*, 36th Cong., 1st Sess., 2303-9 (1859-60).
39. Foner, *Free Soil, Free Labor, Free Men*, 270. See also Luthin, "Organizing the Republican Party in the 'Border-Slave' Regions."
40. M. Blair, *Address of Montgomery Blair, before the Maryland State Republican Convention at Baltimore, April 26, 1860*, 3.
41. Bates, *Diary of Edward Bates, 1859-1866*, ed. Beale, 111-14 (quotations on 113). For information on the Blairs' recruitment of Crittenden and Bates and their efforts to promote Bates's nomination at the Republican convention, see Luthin, "Organizing the Republican Party in the 'Border-Slave' Regions"; and W. E. Smith, *The Francis Preston Blair Family in Politics*.
42. Lincoln, "Eulogy on Henry Clay," in Lincoln, *Collected Works of Abraham Lincoln*, ed. Basler, vol. 2, 121-32 (quotation on 132); "Speech at Springfield, Illinois," ibid., 398-410 (quotations on 409); W. E. Smith, *The Francis Preston Blair Family in Politics*. For biographical analysis of Lincoln, I have relied mainly on Foner, *The Fiery Trial*; and Oakes, *Freedom National*.
43. Lincoln, "Address at Cooper Institute," in Lincoln, *Collected Works of Abraham Lincoln*, ed. Basler, vol. 3, 541.
44. On Everett, see Mason, *Apostle of Union*. On Bell, see Parks, *John Bell of Tennessee*.
45. "The Chicago Nominations," *DM*, June 1860; "The Late Election," *DM*, December 1860. See also "The Republican Party," *DM*, August 1860.
46. "Speech of Frederick Douglass. Delivered at Geneva, N.Y., August 1, 1860, on the Occasion of the Twenty-Sixth Anniversary of Emancipation in the British West Indies," *DM*, September 1860.

5. ENDING THE CIVIL WAR

1. Lincoln, "Second Annual Message," December 1, 1862, Online by Gerhard Peters and John T. Woolley, The American Presidency Project. http://www.presidency.ucsb.edu. Throughout this chapter, for analyses of Lincoln's evolving policy toward slavery during the Civil War, I have relied most on Escott, *Lincoln's Dilemma;* Foner, *The Fiery Trial;* Harris, *Lincoln and the Border States;* and Oakes, *Freedom National.*
2. Lincoln, "Second Annual Message," December 1, 1862.
3. Lincoln, "Second Annual Message," December 1, 1862. One other qualification Lincoln offered was a rejection of the claim that expatriation was necessary to prevent a postemancipation decline in the "wages of white labor."
4. Lincoln, "Second Annual Message," December 1, 1862.
5. For other important accounts of the Blairs' relationship with Lincoln and, more broadly, of the Blairs' efforts to promote colonization during the Civil War, see Escott, *Lincoln's Dilemma;* Parrish, *Frank Blair;* and W. E. Smith, *The Francis Preston Blair Family in Politics.*
6. Escott, *Lincoln's Dilemma.*
7. Lincoln, "'A House Divided': Speech at Springfield Illinois," in Lincoln, *Collected Works of Abraham Lincoln,* ed. Basler, vol. 2, 461; "Address at Cooper Institute," ibid., vol. 3, 539. For important secondary references, see Escott, *Lincoln's Dilemma;* Foner, *The Fiery Trial;* Oakes, *Freedom National;* Parrish, *Frank Blair;* and W. E. Smith, *The Francis Preston Blair Family in Politics.*
8. Francis P. Blair, Sr. to Lincoln, November 16, 1861, Abraham Lincoln Papers. See also Lincoln to Caleb B. Smith, October 23, 1861. This was not the first time Blair had written to Lincoln about colonization. He had broached the subject in a letter, in May 1860, congratulating Lincoln on his presidential nomination (see Francis P. Blair, Sr. to Lincoln, May 26, 1860, Abraham Lincoln Papers).
9. For the history of the Chiriqui colonization effort, see Page, *Black Resettlement and the American Civil War;* Page, "Lincoln and Chiriqui Colonization Revisited"; and Scheips, "Lincoln and the Chiriqui Colonization Project."
10. Foner, *The Fiery Trial;* Harris, *Lincoln and the Border States;* Oakes, *Freedom National.*
11. Lincoln, "First Annual Message." December 3, 1861, Online by Gerhard Peters and John T. Woolley, The American Presidency Project, http://www.presidency.ucsb.edu.
12. The analysis in this section is very much informed by Foner, *The Fiery Trial;* Harris, *Lincoln and the Border States;* and Oakes, *Freedom National.*
13. For the vote on Doolittle's amendment, see *CG,* 37th Cong., 2nd Sess., 1522-23 (1861-62). For Doolittle's speech in support of the colonization amendment,

see "Emancipation. Speech of Hon. J. R. Doolittle, of Wisconsin, in the Senate, March 19, 1862," Appendix, 83-86 (quotations on 85). For the final Senate vote on the bill, which included the colonization appropriation, see 1526. For the final House vote, see 1648-49.

14. Lincoln to Congress, April 16, 1862, Abraham Lincoln Papers.

15. For the $500,000 appropriation, see "Chap. CLXXXII—An Act making supplemental Appropriations for sundry Civil Expenses of the Government for the Year ending June thirtieth, eighteen hundred and sixty-three, and for the Year ending June thirtieth, eighteen hundred and sixty-two, and for other Purposes," in Sanger, *The Statutes at Large*, vol. 12, 582-83.

16. "Report of Select Committee on Emancipation," 35-36 (1861-62).

17. "Report of Select Committee on Emancipation," 1 (1861-62) (emphasis added). See also *CG*, 37th Cong., 2nd Sess., 1563.

18. "Report of Select Committee on Emancipation," 33 (1861-62). The six Southern representatives were Frank Blair (MO), George Fisher (DE), Kellian Whaley (VA), Samuel Casey (KY), Andrew Jackson Clements (TN), and Cornelius Leary (MD). Clements's name is misspelled as "Clemens." The two Northern representatives were William Lehman (PA) and Albert White (IN).

19. For the bill's text, see "Report of Select Committee on Emancipation," 32-33 (1861-62) (quotation on 32). The $180 million compensation cap had been determined by assuming the prospective emancipation of 600,000 enslaved individuals in the Border States (considerably less than the 1 million-plus indicated in the 1860 Census) and multiplying that figure by $300. The report did not provide detailed rationale for the population difference, but contemporary debate in Congress suggested that committee members assumed that war had already diminished the size of each state's enslaved population.

20. "Report of Select Committee on Emancipation," 13-14 (1861-62). For the full discussion of colonization, see 13-31. For further evidence that the bill envisioned compulsory colonization for the emancipated, see the remarks of Senator John Henderson of Missouri: *CG*, 37th Cong., 3rd Sess., 613 (1862-63). The proposed bill, he stated, "did not leave it voluntary with the slave, but required deportation and gave $20,000,000 therefor."

21. Lincoln, "Address to Border State Representatives," July 12, 1862, Abraham Lincoln Papers. It should be noted that Lincoln had, around this time, submitted his own version of a Border State emancipatory aid bill to Congress. On this political moment, see Escott, *Lincoln's Dilemma*; Foner, *The Fiery Trial*; Harris, *Lincoln and the Border States*; and Oakes, *Freedom National*.

22. For the majority position, see Border State Congressmen to Lincoln, July 14, 1862, Abraham Lincoln Papers. For the minority position, see Border State Congressmen to Abraham Lincoln, July 15, 1862, Abraham Lincoln Papers.
23. See, for instance, remarks made by Senators Willard Saulsbury of Delaware and Lazarus Powell of Kentucky (*CG*, 37th Cong., 2nd Sess., 1332-33, 1523 [1861-62]). On the resistance of Border State congressmen, see Escott, *Lincoln's Dilemma;* Foner, *The Fiery Trial;* Harris, *Lincoln and the Border States;* and Oakes, *Freedom National.*
24. *CG,* 37th Cong., 2nd Sess., 1371 (1861-62) (emphasis added).
25. Border State Congressmen to Lincoln, July 14, 1862.
26. *CG,* 37th Cong., 2nd Sess., 1266 (1861-62).
27. *CG,* 37th Cong., 2nd Sess., 1333-34, 1350-53, 1358-59 1522-23 (1861-62) (quotations on 1353, 1522). The second senator was James Harlan of Iowa.
28. *CG,* 37th Cong., 2nd Sess., 1904 (1861-62). For other such remarks by Davis, see 1338, 1371. For similar remarks by other Border State congressmen, see John Carlile (VA, soon to be WV), 1157-58; and Waitman Willey (VA, soon to be WV), 1604-7.
29. For the Second Confiscation Act, see "Chap. CXCV—An Act to suppress Insurrection, to punish Treason and Rebellion, to seize and confiscate the Property of Rebels, and for other Purposes," in Sanger, *The Statutes at Large,* vol. 12, 589-92. The voluntary colonization provision is on 592. The language of the colonization provision in the $500,000 appropriation, it should be noted, was a bit vague (see "Chap. CLXXXII—An Act making supplemental Appropriations for sundry Civil Expenses of the Government," 582). The restriction, however, was implied since Congress connected the appropriation directly to the DC Abolition Act and to the Second Confiscation Act, both of which were explicit and clear on the subject.
30. On the practice and frequency of embedding expatriation conditions in offers of manumission see Burin, *Slavery and the Peculiar Solution;* and Staudenraus, *The African Colonization Movement.*
31. Lincoln, "Address to Border State Representatives," July 12, 1862.
32. Lincoln, "Address on Colonization to a Deputation of Negroes, August 14, 1862," in Lincoln, *Collected Works of Abraham Lincoln,* ed. Basler, vol. 5, 370-75 (quotations on 371-72).
33. Lincoln, "Address on Colonization to a Deputation of Negroes, August 14, 1862," 372-73.
34. "The First Annual Report," 10.
35. "The Colonization of People of African Descent," *New York Daily Tribune,* August 15, 1862.

36. For scholarly analyses of this meeting, see Blight, *Frederick Douglass,* 371–72; Masur, "The African American Delegation to Abraham Lincoln: A Reappraisal"; and Oakes, *Freedom National,* 308–10.
37. "The President and His Speeches," *DM,* September 1862; "[Letter to Editor]," *TCR,* September 27, 1862. On the strong negative reaction of Douglass and other Black Americans, see Blight, *Frederick Douglass,* 372–77.
38. "To the Colored People of the United States," *TCR,* September 20, 1862.
39. "Washington Correspondence," *TCR,* August 30, 1862 (emphasis added). For additional evidence of this trend, see "Washington Correspondence," August 30, 1862 [different article]; and "For *The Christian Recorder,*" November 8, 1862.
40. "Letter to the President," *DM,* October 1862; "Indiana Conference," *TCR,* September 6, 1862.
41. "Mrs. Frances E. Watkins on the War and the President's Colonization Scheme," *TCR,* September 27, "Washington Correspondence," October 4, 1862.
42. "The Spirit of Colonization," "The President and His Speeches," *DM,* September 1862.
43. *Proceedings of the National Emigration Convention of Colored People, Held at Cleveland, Ohio* (1854): 33. On the number of Liberian emigrants between 1851 and 1861, see "Table of Emigrants Settled in Liberia by the American Colonization Society," in *TAR, Vols. 44–53,* 56–64. On the rising interest in Black emigration during this time, see Campbell, *Middle Passages;* F. J. Miller, *The Search for a Black Nationality;* and Power-Greene, *Against Wind and Tide.*
44. In one article in the *North Star,* Delany characterized Liberia "as a source of subsequent enterprise, which no colored American should permit himself to lose sight of." In the same article, however, he offered no endorsement of emigration and had only vitriol for the "scheme" of the ACS, which he described as "degrading, expatriating, insolent, [and] slaveholding." But there was, in his view, something to what the Liberian people had done that, at a minimum, warranted the further attention of Black Americans (see "Liberia," *NS,* March 2, 1849). For biographical information on Delany, see Levine, *Martin Delany.*
45. "The African Civilization Society," *TCR,* December 7, 1861. On Delany, Garnet, and the African Civilization Society, see Levine, *Martin Delany;* F. J. Miller, *The Search for a Black Nationality;* and Pasternak, *Rise Now and Fly to Arms.* For the African Civilization Society's constitution, see https://www.blackpast.org/african-american-history/constitution-african-civilization-society-1796/.

46. "African Civilization Society," *DM*, February 1859; "The Colored Citizens of New York and the African Civilization Society," *The Liberator*, May 4, 1860. On the debate over Black emigration, see F. J. Miller, *The Search for a Black Nationality*; and Power-Greene, *Against Wind and Tide*.
47. "Colored Men Petitioning to Be Colonized," *DM*, May 1862. See also "Brooklyn Correspondence," *TCR*, May 30, 1863.
48. "The President's Message," *DM*, January 1863; "Letter from H. Ford Douglas," *DM*, February 1863; "Frederick Douglass at the Cooper Institute," *DM*, March 1863.
49. "The Meeting of the Colored Loyalist," "The Present and Future of the Colored Race in America," "Valedictory," *DM*, June 1863. It should be noted that the Union army had informally employed Black soldiers, on a smaller scale, prior to 1863. On the recruitment and service of Black soldiers during the Civil War, see Cornish, *The Sable Arm*; and McPherson, *The Negro's Civil War*.
50. John B. Henderson to Lincoln, July 21, 1862, in Edward McPherson, *The Political History of the United States of America, during the Great Rebellion*, 218–20. I have not been able to locate an original copy of this document. For accounts of Henderson's actions during this time, see Harris, *Lincoln and the Border States*; and Mattingly, "Senator John Brooks Henderson."
51. *Proceedings of the Missouri State Convention* (1862): 72–84, 98–104 (quotation on 99).
52. For biographical background on Henderson, I have relied mainly on Mattingly, "Senator John Brooks Henderson."
53. *Speech Delivered by Hon. J. B. Henderson, at Hannibal, MO., on the 20th of August, 1862*, 24–25, 27, 36. See also John B. Henderson to Lincoln, September 3, 1862, Abraham Lincoln Papers.
54. S. 434, 37th Cong., 3rd Sess. (1862–63).
55. *CG*, 37th Cong., 3rd Sess., 780 (1862–63). Historians have devoted relatively little time and attention to analyzing the debates surrounding Henderson's bill in the Senate or the alternate bill in the House. The most detailed coverage can be found in Harris, *Lincoln and the Border States*; and Mattingly, "Senator John Brooks Henderson."
56. *CG*, 37th Cong., 3rd Sess., 351–57, 611–25 (1862–63) (quotations on 355, 613) (emphasis added).
57. The congressman was Orville Browning (see *CG*, 37th Cong., 2nd Sess., 1520–22 [1861–62]).
58. *CG*, 37th Cong., 3rd Sess., 795 (1862–63).
59. *CG*, 37th Cong., 3rd Sess., 802 (1862–63). For the final vote, see 903. For oppositional speeches by Senators Anthony Kennedy (MD), Lazarus Powell (KY), and Willard Saulsbury (DE), see 624–25, 792–93, 800–805, 897–900.

60. *CG*, Appendix, 37th Cong., 3rd Sess., 143-48 (1862-63) (quotations on 144, 147). For the other speeches, see ibid., 137-38, 148-51.
61. The Henderson quotations are from a letter quoted in Mattingly, "Senator John Brooks Henderson," 98. For Sumner, see *CG*, 37th Cong., 3rd Sess., 903 (1862-63). For indications of Sumner's aversion to appropriating federal funds for voluntary colonization, see his votes against the DC Abolition Act colonization amendments (*CG*, 37th Cong., 2nd Sess., 1333, 1522-23 [1861-62]).
62. *CG*, 38th Cong., 1st Sess., 145 (1863-64). Henderson was one of several senators who proposed immediate abolition constitutional amendments during this congressional session.
63. The history of this political shift is complicated. For analyses of what happened in Missouri and Maryland, where the shift was most significant, see Fields, *Slavery and Freedom on the Middle Ground;* Harris, *Lincoln and the Border States;* and Wagandt, *The Mighty Revolution.*
64. See McPherson, *The Negro's Civil War;* Oakes, *Freedom National;* Wagandt, *The Mighty Revolution.*
65. *Address of the Unconditional Union State Central Committee to the People of Maryland, September 16th, 1863,* 9; *Immediate Emancipation in Maryland. Proceedings of the Union State Central Committee, at a Meeting Held in Temperance Temple, Baltimore, Wednesday, December 16, 1863,* 15-18 (quotations on 18). For background on Kennedy, see Tuckerman, *The Life of John Pendleton Kennedy.*
66. For Henderson's speech, see *Proceedings of the Missouri State Convention* (1863): 198-212 (quotations on 204, 206). For the text of the resolution and Henderson's vote in favor of tabling, see *Journal of the Missouri State Convention* (1863): 47-48. It should be noted that Henderson did not, at the 1863 state convention, recommend the kind of immediate abolition that he would propose, on a national basis, six months later. Instead, he proposed a plan of gradual abolition that would take place between 1870 and 1878.
67. For the Senate vote, see *CG*, 38th Cong., 1st Sess., 1490 (1863-64). For analysis of the Thirteenth Amendment debates, see Foner, *The Second Founding;* and Oakes, *Freedom National.*
68. *CG*, 38th Cong., 1st Sess., 1459-65 (1863-64) (quotations on 1459-61).
69. *CG*, 38th Cong., 1st Sess., 1461 (1863-64).
70. *CG*, Appendix, 38th Cong., 1st Sess., 3262 (1863-64). For the repeal law, see "Chap. CCX—An Act making Appropriations for sundry Civil Expenses of the Government for the Year ending the Thirtieth of June, eighteen hundred and sixty-five, and for other Purposes" in Sanger, *The Statutes at Large,* vol. 13, 344-53 (the repeal is on 352). See also the "Report of the Secretary of the Interior," *CG*, Appendix, 38th Cong., 1st Sess., 25-26.
71. *CG*, 38th Cong., 1st Sess., 1465 (1863-64).

72. For perspectives on Lincoln's decision to remain publicly silent on colonization after December 1862, see Foner, *The Fiery Trial*, 258–61; and Page, *Black Resettlement and the American Civil War*, 246–56. Some discussion of the Blairs' persistent interest in colonization can be found in Escott, *Lincoln's Dilemma*; and W. E. Smith, *The Francis Preston Blair Family in Politics*.
73. "The Government Attempts at Negro Colonization. Letter from the Secretary of the Interior to the Senate," *New York Times*, April 5, 1864. On the Chiriqui and Île-à-Vache incidents, see Page, *Black Resettlement and the American Civil War*; Page, "Lincoln and Chiriqui Colonization Revisited." On the political complexities of the 1864 presidential election, from Lincoln's perspective, see Escott, *Lincoln's Dilemma*; Foner, *The Fiery Trial*; and Oakes, *Freedom National*.
74. Blair, "Speech at the Union Mass Convention, Concord, N.H., June 17, 1863," in *Comments on the Policy Inaugurated by the President, in a Letter and Two Speeches*, 13–20 (quotations on 17–20). See also "Speech at the Meeting Held at Cleveland, May 20, 1863," 8–12.
75. Henry Wilson to Lincoln, August 21, 1863, October 25, 1863, Abraham Lincoln Papers
76. *CG*, Appendix, 38th Cong., 1st Sess., 46–51 (1863–64) (quotations on 48). See also Blair Jr., *Speech of Francis P. Blair, Jr., of Missouri, Delivered in the House of Representatives, February 5, 1864*; and *Speech of F. P. Blair, of Missouri, Delivered in the House of Representatives, April 23, 1864*. On the growing tension between the Blairs and many Republican Party leaders, see Escott, *Lincoln's Dilemma*; Parrish, *Frank Blair*; and W. E. Smith, *The Francis Preston Blair Family in Politics*.
77. Lincoln to Montgomery Blair, September 23, 1864, Montgomery Blair to Lincoln, September 23, 1864, Abraham Lincoln Papers. See also Francis P. Blair, Jr. to Francis P. Blair, Sr., September 30, 1864.
78. M. Blair, *Speech of the Hon. Montgomery Blair, at the Cooper Institute, N.Y. to Ratify the Union Nominations, September 27, 1864*.
79. "Hon. Montgomery Blair on Emancipation," *New York Times*, March 8, 1862. This letter was reprinted in 1863 as part of a pamphlet issued by the Blairs (see M. Blair, *Comments on the Policy Inaugurated by the President, in a Letter and Two Speeches*, 3–7). For Montgomery's attempt to get colonization included in the resolution, see Montgomery Blair to Lincoln, March 5, 1862, Abraham Lincoln Papers.
80. Blair Jr., *Speech of Hon. F. P. Blair, Jr. of Missouri, on the Policy of the President for the Restoration of the Union and Establishment of Peace; Delivered in the House of Representatives, April 11, 1862*, 7.
81. *Proceedings of the National Convention of Colored Men, Held in the City of Syracuse, N.Y.* (1864): 9, 42. David Blight also notes the convention's declaration against colonization (see Blight, *Frederick Douglass*, 440).

82. Foner, *The Fiery Trial;* Oakes, *Freedom National.*
83. "Army Correspondence," *TCR,* March 25, 1865.
84. *CG,* 38th Cong., 1st Sess., 672-75, 3262 (1863-64) (quotations on 673, 675, 3262). The first senator was Reverdy Johnson. The second was James Henry Lane.
85. *CG,* 38th Cong., 1st Sess., 1465 (1863-64). On the ongoing concerns of Black Americans, see Blight, *Frederick Douglass;* Du Bois, *Black Reconstruction in America;* and Masur, *Until Justice Be Done.*
86. *Proceedings of the National Convention of Colored Men* (1864): 56.

6. OPPOSING BLACK SUFFRAGE

1. *Proceedings of the First Annual Meeting of the National Equal Rights League, Held in Cleveland, Ohio* (1865). On Black civil rights activism from the mid-1860s through the late 1870s, see Blight, *Frederick Douglass;* Du Bois, *Black Reconstruction in America;* Foner, *Reconstruction;* and Hahn, *A Nation Under Our Feet.*
2. *Proceedings of the First Annual Meeting of the National Equal Rights League, Held in Cleveland, Ohio* (1865): 37, 39. On the history of the Forten family, see Winch, *A Gentleman of Color.*
3. *Proceedings of the First Annual Meeting of the National Equal Rights League, Held in Cleveland, Ohio* (1865): 52. On the post-Civil War history of the Blairs, see Parrish, *Frank Blair;* and W. E. Smith, *The Francis Preston Blair Family in Politics.* While both historians mention the Blairs' ongoing interest in colonization, neither gives the subject significant attention.
4. "Ratification Meeting at the Cooper Institute," *New York Times,* October 19, 1865.
5. While, to my knowledge, no historian has argued that white politicians used colonization ideology, from the mid-1860s through the early 1900s, as a main political instrument in the fight against Black suffrage, Thomas Upchurch has argued (as I do) that during the 1889-91 congressional session, Southern politicians revived the issue of federal support for colonization by proposing the Butler Bill, which I discuss later in this chapter, not because they had an expectation of actually securing a colonization appropriation but rather because the proposal afforded them an opportunity to give lengthy speeches inflected with colonization rhetoric through which they hoped to create a headwind for a federal elections enforcement bill (Lodge Bill) expected to come up during the session (see Upchurch, *Legislating Racism,* 23-45). See also Upchurch, "Senator John Tyler Morgan and the Genesis of Jim Crow Ideology, 1889-1898."

6. To date, there is no thorough historical study of the post-1865 colonization movement. Good but scattered coverage, most of which focuses on the ACS and on Black Americans interested in emigrating to Liberia with ACS support, can be found in Campbell, *Middle Passages;* Hahn, *A Nation Under Our Feet;* Painter, *Exodusters;* and Redkey, *Black Exodus.* See also Frederickson, *The Black Image in the White Mind;* and Page, *Black Resettlement and the American Civil War.*
7. Fields and Fields, *Racecraft,* 111–48 (quotation on 146). See also Fields, "Ideology and Race in American History."
8. "Ratification Meeting at the Cooper Institute," *New York Times,* October 19, 1865.
9. Blair, *Proscription in Maryland,* 9–10; "A Grand Conservative Mass-Meeting at the Courthouse at Jefferson City," *Missouri Republican,* June 18, 1866. For other relevant speeches Frank made during this time, see "Speech at Mass Convention in St. Louis," October 27, 1865, "General Blair at the Home of Henderson," May 17, 1866. On the Blair's political tactics, see Parrish, *Frank Blair;* and W. E. Smith, *The Francis Preston Blair Family in Politics.*
10. Blair Jr., *Speech of Gen. F. P. Blair, Democratic Candidate for Vice President,* 11–12. See also "A Splendid Flag-Raising. Speech of Gen. F. P. Blair," *Missouri Republican,* October 19, 1868. The *Missouri Republican* of St. Louis, in its coverage of the Democratic Party canvass, made the phrase a recurrent headline as it reported on Frank's speaking tour: "Democratic Ticket—In favor of a white man's Government: opposed to Negro Suffrage and Negro Equality" (see, for instance, *Missouri Republican,* September 3, 21, November 2, 1868).
11. *CG,* 40th Cong., 3rd Sess., 1010–12 (1868–69) (quotations on 1011). For a similar speech by Doolittle during the prior session, see *CG,* 40th Cong., 2nd Sess., 2868–70 (1867–68). On the debate over the prospective Fifteenth Amendment, see Foner, *The Second Founding.*
12. On the political history of the 1870s and 1880s, see Du Bois, *Black Reconstruction in America;* Foner, *Reconstruction;* Perman, *The Road to Redemption;* and White, *The Republic for Which It Stands.*
13. On electoral violence—and other forms of electoral manipulation—in the South during the postwar decades, see Du Bois, *Black Reconstruction in America;* Litwack, *Trouble in Mind;* Perman, *Struggle for Mastery;* and Williamson, *The Crucible of Race.*
14. "Report of the Joint Select Committee to Inquire into the Condition of Affairs in the Late Insurrectionary States," 289–588 (1871–72) (quotations on 516). See also Parrish, *Frank Blair.*
15. "Report of African Emigration—N.J. Conference," *TCR,* May 30, 1878. On the rising trend of racial oppression, see Du Bois, *Black Reconstruction in America;* Litwack, *Trouble in Mind;* and Williamson, *The Crucible of Race.*

16. On the migration and emigration of Black Southerners during this time, see Campbell, *Middle Passages;* Hahn, *A Nation Under Our Feet;* and Painter, *Exodusters.*
17. Alexander T. McGill, "Patriotism, Philanthropy, and Religion," *AR* 53 (1877): 72-78 (quotation on 72); John H. B. Latrobe, "Liberia: Its Origin, Rise, Progress and Results," *AR* 56 (1880): 90-99 (quotations on 97).
18. "Ought the Negro to Be Disfranchised? Ought He to Have Been Enfranchised?" Montgomery was one of eight distinct contributors to this article. For his full essay, see 262-67 (quotations are on 263, 266). For the congressional report, see "Report and Testimony of the Select Committee of the United States Senate to Investigate the Causes of the Removal of the Negroes from the Southern States to the Northern States" (1879-80).
19. Fredrickson, *The Black Image in the White Mind,* 262-68. The arguments that I make in this section have benefited not only from Fredrickson's analysis of the propaganda campaign but also by his identification of several of the campaign's key documents. See also Upchurch, *Legislating Racism,* 23-45. Beyond the documents and speeches of McKinley, Grady, and Morgan, three other significant sources contributing to this Lower Southern-led discourse were Fulkerson, *The Negro; As He Was; As He Is; As He Will Be;* Simpson, *A Treatise on Negro Colonization;* and Scomp, "Can the Race Problem Be Solved?" Fulkerson held multiple positions in the Confederate government during the Civil War. Afterward, he was a merchant and an individual of some regional prominence in the Presbyterian Church. Scomp was a faculty member at Emory University. I do not have biographical information on Simpson.
20. McKinley, *An Appeal to Pharaoh,* 38, 126, 200-205.
21. Grady, "The Race Problem in the South," 197, 199, 209, 212. See also Grady, "In Plain Black and White: A Reply to Mr. Cable."
22. Grady, "The Race Problem in the South," 217.
23. Morgan, "Shall Negro Majorities Rule?" 589; Morgan, "The Race Question in the United States," 387, 398.
24. For the bill's full text, see *CR,* 51st Cong., 1st Sess., 802.
25. Upchurch, *Legislating Racism,* 23-45. The argument that I make here, as mentioned in an earlier footnote, bears similarity to the one that Upchurch makes. The main difference is my contention that the Butler Bill moment in Congress was part of a multidecade, Southern effort, stretching back to the mid-1860s, to use colonization ideology as a political instrument in the fight against Black suffrage. See also Redkey, *Black Exodus,* 47-72; and Upchurch, "Senator John Tyler Morgan and the Genesis of Jim Crow Ideology, 1889-1898."

26. For the full speeches of each senator, see *CR,* 51st Cong., 1st Sess., 419-31, 622-31, 971-74 (1889-90) (quotations on 420, 623, 972). See also Hampton, "The Race Problem," 132-38.
27. *CR,* 51st Cong., 1st Sess., 428, 972-73 (1889-90).
28. For the Lodge Bill debate and its broader historical context, see Perman, *Struggle for Mastery;* and Upchurch, *Legislating Racism.*
29. For George's speech, see *CR,* Appendix, 51st Cong., 2nd Sess., 46-83 (1890-91) (quotations on 52, 67-68). For the claim that some Mississippians were quite explicit about the convention's disfranchisement aim, see, for instance, *Daily Clarion Ledger,* December 22, 1890; and Perman, *Struggle for Mastery,* 28.
30. *Proceedings of the National Convention of the Colored Men of America, Held in Washington, D.C.* (1869): VI-VII (Appendix). See also *Proceedings of the Colored National Labor Convention, Held in Washington, D.C.* (1869, published in 1870), 31; "Colonization," *TCR,* August 21, 1869.
31. "Annual Convention of the National Labor Union," *New National Era,* January 12, 1871, "African Colonization," December 19, 1872. See also "The American Colonization Society," April 3, 1873.
32. Campbell, *Middle Passages;* Hahn, *A Nation Under Our Feet;* Painter, *Exodusters.*
33. Frederick Douglass, "The Negro Exodus from the Gulf States," 47. The *Christian Recorder* published numerous anti-emigration articles during this time (see, for instance: "The Colored Man of the United States," *TCR,* March 7, 1878; "Emigration: What Thought of It," *TCR,* April 11, 1878; "A Lively Discussion," *TCR,* May 23, 1878; "Report of African Emigration—N.J. Conference," *TCR,* May 30, 1878).
34. For another account of this newspaper debate, see Redkey, *Black Exodus,* 30-42.
35. "For *The Christian Recorder:* Advisory Committee on African Colonization," *TCR,* December 7, 1882.
36. "Bishop Turner's Reply," *TCR,* January 25, 1883; "The African Question," *TCR,* February 22, 1883. According to a January 4 article, Turner appears to have sent one additional letter that was not reprinted or that is not in the *Christian Recorder* archive.
37. "For *The Christian Recorder:* Advisory Committee on African Colonization," *TCR,* December 7, 1882; "Bishop Turner's Reply," *TCR,* January 25, 1883; "The African Question Again," *TCR,* June 21, 1883.
38. "Bishop Turner on the Advisory Committee," *TCR,* January 4, 1883. Frederick Douglass offered a similar criticism of *race patriotism* in a speech that he gave in Washington, DC, in the spring of 1889. Douglass lamented that "race pride" had become such a common feature of Black discourse. By promoting this

absurd idea, he stressed, Black Americans were inviting white Americans to grasp their own sense of "race pride," the root cause of Black oppression, more tightly. "The ice under us in this country is very thin," Douglass observed. "At no time in the history of the conflict between slavery and freedom has the character of the Negro... been made the subject of a fiercer and more serious discussion." In such discomfiting circumstances, Black Americans would do well, he admonished, not to hand rhetorical weapons to their white "critics." The ongoing "battle with popular prejudice, requires on our part the utmost circumspection in word and in deed" (Douglass, "The Nation's Problem," 726, 731-32).

39. Douglass, "The Nation's Problem," 728; Douglass, *The Race Problem*, 8. On Douglass's efforts to discredit and rebut "Negro Problem" rhetoric, see Blight, *Frederick Douglass*, 687-89, 736-44, and passim.
40. Douglass, "The Nation's Problem," 726; "Henry Clay," *NS,* March 23, 1849.
41. Douglass, "The Nation's Problem," 737; Douglass, *The Race Problem*, 8.
42. For scholarship on the minimization and distortion of the subject of slavery in American memory, see Blight, *Race and Reunion;* and Horton and Horton, *Slavery and Public History*.
43. "Speech at Mass Convention in St. Louis," *Daily Missouri Republican,* October 27, 1865; Fulkerson, *The Negro; As He Was; As He Is; As He Will Be,* 108; *CR,* 51st Cong., 1st Sess., 420, 628, 972 (1889-90); McKinley, *An Appeal to Pharaoh,* 200.
44. "A Grand Conservative Mass-Meeting," *Daily Missouri Republican,* June 16, 1866; Morgan, "The Race Question in the United States," 390. On the complex history of the racialized attitudes of white Americans, see Dain, *A Hideous Monster of the Mind;* Fredrickson, *The Black Image in the White Mind;* and Horsman, *Race and Manifest Destiny*.
45. "Speech at Mass Convention in St. Louis," *Daily Missouri Republican,* October 27, 1865; Fulkerson, *The Negro; As He Was; As He Is; As He Will Be,* 104; McKinley, *An Appeal to Pharaoh,* 18.
46. Morgan, "The Race Question in the United States," 387, 390. For the prior year's article, see Morgan, "Shall Negro Majorities Rule?" 593.
47. Perman, *Struggle for Mastery*.
48. Douglass, "The Nation's Problem"; Douglass, *The Race Problem;* Douglass, *Lessons of the Hour*. Three references for the persistence of "Negro Problem" rhetoric are Fredrickson, *The Black Image in the White Mind;* Upchurch, *Legislating Racism;* and Upchurch, "Senator John Tyler Morgan and the Genesis of Jim Crow Ideology, 1889-1898."
49. Otken, *The Ills of the South,* 251; Simmons, *A Solution of the Race Problem in the South;* Graves, "[Speech]," 54-56. For other contemporary publications that

highlight Black suffrage as a societal problem and that offer favorable views of Black expatriation, see Holley, *The Race Problem and Other Critiques;* and W. P. Calhoun, *The Caucasian and the Negro in the United States.* For a later instance, see Pickett, *The Negro Problem,* which was published in 1909, when the trend of state-based disfranchisement was largely complete but when efforts to sustain or to strengthen disfranchisement mechanisms were still very much ongoing.

50. Morgan, *Negro Suffrage in the South,* 2, 11-12, 15.
51. Morgan, *Negro Suffrage in the South,* 16. Black expatriation to the Philippines was something that Morgan discussed on other occasions during the 1890s and early 1900s (see Baylen and Moore, "Senator John Tyler Morgan and Negro Colonization in the Philippines, 1901 to 1902"; and Scribner, "'A Splendid Investment': Black Colonization and America's Pacific Empire, 1898-1904").
52. For scholarship that asserts a connection between colonization ideology and Jim Crow laws and practices, see Fredrickson, *The Black Image in the White Mind,* 262-68, 320-32; and Upchurch, "Senator John Tyler Morgan and the Genesis of Jim Crow Ideology, 1889-1898."
53. *CG,* 40th Cong., 2nd Sess., 2869 (1867-68); "Report of the Joint Select Committee to Inquire into the Condition of Affairs in the Late Insurrectionary States," 516 (1871-72).
54. Fulkerson, *The Negro; As He Was; As He Is; As He Will Be;* 115; Morgan, "Shall Negro Majorities Rule?" 593; Graves, "[Speech]," 55.
55. *CG,* 51st Cong., 1st Sess., 969-70 (1889-90).
56. "Civil Rights Cases," 537-38; "Plessy v. Ferguson," 560-61.
57. "Plessy v. Ferguson," 551.

CONCLUSION

1. The idea of civic exclusion as an "approximation" of colonization is one that George Fredrickson explores in *The Black Image in the White Mind* (262-68, 320-25). On 268, he states: "An image of the fruits of racial separation could easily lead to efforts to strengthen the barriers of segregation, in an effort to approximate total separation without actual deportation."
2. Douglass, *Lessons of the Hour,* 6, 15-16. As Douglass made these remarks, he was well aware that colonization advocates, for many decades, had been quick to point to racial violence as strong evidence that white freedom and Black freedom were irrevocably incongruous and that race war would be the certain

result of emancipation without expatriation. The 1872 minority report that Senator Frank Blair had signed and submitted to Congress had, in essence, characterized Southern electoral violence as unfortunate but also logical and unsurprising. White Southerners were reacting fiercely to what they saw as an attempt to use the lever of Black political equality to subordinate their interests. Sixteen years later, the Southern author of *A Treatise on Negro Colonization* cited, in similar fashion, the fact that the two races were "killing each other in many parts of the country" as powerful evidence that white and Black Americans simply could not coexist on "terms of equality." Around the same time, Horace Fulkerson's book-length work of colonization propaganda included a section devoted to highlighting newspaper excerpts from around the country that demonstrated the pervasive and horrific extent of contemporary racial violence. "We are now in the shadow of... coming events," Fulkerson warned. "And what is the result of continued and increasing friction [between the races]? Fire! Nothing less" (see "Report of the Joint Select Committee to Inquire into the Condition of Affairs in the Late Insurrectionary States," 516 (1871-72); Simpson, *A Treatise on Negro Colonization,* 7; and Fulkerson, *The Negro; As He Was; As He Is; As He Will Be,* 88-101 [quotation on 88]). On Douglass's *Lessons of the Hour* speech, see Blight, *Frederick Douglass,* 736-47. On the rising trend of lynching and other forms of racial violence, see Litwack, *Trouble in Mind;* and Williamson, *The Crucible of Race.*
3. Douglass, *Lessons of the Hour,* 3, 22-23, 25-27.
4. Douglass, *Lessons of the Hour,* 33.
5. For biographical information on Cooper, see Belle, "Anna Julia Cooper." For Du Bois, see Lewis, *W. E. B. Du Bois.*
6. Du Bois, "Strivings of the Negro People," 194-98 (quotation on 194, emphasis added).
7. Du Bois, "Strivings of the Negro People," 194-95.
8. A. J. Cooper, *A Voice from the South,* 164, 168, 171-72 (emphasis added).
9. A. J. Cooper, *A Voice from the South,* 165, 168, 173-74.
10. Douglass, *Lessons of the Hour,* 29-30. For a similar statement on the capacity of "words" to do harm, see Douglass, *The Race Problem,* 3-4. (Due to a printing error in the original pamphlet, page 4 is mislabeled as page 5, and vice versa.)
11. Douglass, *Lessons of the Hour,* 30.
12. The point about human agency is one that, as noted earlier, Barbara Fields has compellingly made in her influential scholarship on *race* (see Fields and Fields, *Racecraft,* 111-48; and Fields, "Ideology and Race in American History").
13. From the mid-1890s to the mid-1960s, there were scattered efforts to keep the cause of Black expatriation alive. Two of the most high-profile white colonization advocates were Earnest Sevier Cox, a Tennessee-born minister

and author, and Theodore Bilbo, a Mississippi governor and congressman. Both promoted colonization during the 1930s and 1940s (Sevier in the 1920s, as well) and both frequently quoted Lincoln, among other historical colonization advocates, as they did so. For colonization propaganda by Bilbo and Cox, see Bilbo, *Take Your Choice;* Cox, *White America;* and Cox, *Let My People Go.* For scholarship on Bilbo and Cox, see Fitzgerald, "'We Have Found Moses'"; Fleegler, "Theodore G. Bilbo"; Fredrickson, *The Black Image in the White Mind;* Jackson and Winston, "The Last Repatriationist"; and D. Smith and *Dictionary of Virginia Biography,* "Earnest Sevier Cox." Black-led emigration efforts manifested during this period as well, mainly under the leadership of Marcus Garvey and Mitt Maude Lena Gordon, who headed the Universal Negro Improvement Association and the Peace Movement of Ethiopia, respectively. As had been the case throughout the nineteenth century, only a small minority of Black Americans expressed interest in either effort. On the histories of the Peace Movement of Ethiopia and the UNIA, see Blain, *Set the World on Fire;* and T. Martin, *Race First.* On the larger claim that colonization ideology continued to shape racial attitudes in the United States after 1900, see Fredrickson, *The Black Image in the White Mind,* 320–32; and Guyatt, *Bind Us Apart,* 9–13. On the assertion that ideologies cannot survive without human agency, see, as already indicated, Fields and Fields, *Racecraft,* 146.

14. On the long civil rights movement, see Dudziak, *Cold War Civil Rights.* Gilmore, *Defying Dixie;* and Marable, *Race, Reform, and Rebellion.*

15. One specific instance of the battle's continuation can be found in the publications of the American Renaissance, a Virginia-based organization that, over the last three decades, has repeatedly promoted colonization ideology and that has done so, in significant part, by invoking the names and rhetoric of famous eighteenth- and nineteenth-century colonization advocates (see, for example, Bradley, "What Should White Americans Do?" [2024]; Hood, "James Madison and the American Colonization Society" [2021]; and Taylor, "What the Founders Really Thought About Race" [2012]).

BIBLIOGRAPHY

SELECTED ARCHIVES AND MANUSCRIPT COLLECTIONS

American Colonization Society Records, Library of Congress
Blair Family Papers, Library of Congress
Blair Family Papers, Princeton University
Francis Scott Key Papers, Maryland Center for History and Culture
Historical Society of Pennsylvania
Mary Custis Lee Papers, Virginia Museum of History and Culture
Mary Randolph Custis Lee Papers, Virginia Museum of History and Culture
Library Company of Philadelphia
Abraham Lincoln Papers, Library of Congress
Maryland State Colonization Society Records, Maryland Center for History and Culture
Charles Fenton Mercer Papers, Virginia Museum of History and Culture
Missouri State Historical Society
Princeton Library Special Collections
Princeton Theological Seminary Special Collections
Joseph Rogers Underwood Papers, Western Kentucky University
University of Virginia Special Collections
Virginia Colonization Society, Virginia Museum of History and Culture
Yale Divinity School Special Collections
Yale Library Special Collections

GOVERNMENT PUBLICATIONS

Annals of Congress
Congressional Globe
Congressional Record
House Journal

Register of Debates
Senate Journal

"African Slave Trade." Senate Committee on Foreign Affairs. H.R. Doc. No. 469, 28th Cong., 1st Sess., 1843-44.

"Civil Rights Cases." In *United States Reports, Volume 109, Cases Adjudged in the Supreme Court of the United States at October Term, 1883,* 3-62. New York: Banks & Brothers, 1884.

"Colonization of the Free People of Color." House Select Committee. H.R. Rep. No. 101, 19th Cong., 2nd Sess., 1826-27.

Hening, William Waller, ed. *The Statutes at Large: Being a Collection of All the Laws of Virginia, from the First Session of the Legislature, in the Year 1619.* Vol. 2. Richmond: Samuel Pleasants, 1810.

Hening, William Waller, ed. *The Statutes at Large: Being a Collection of All the Laws of Virginia, from the First Session of the Legislature, in the Year 1619.* Vol. 3. Philadelphia: Thomas Desilver, 1823.

Howard, Benjamin C., ed. *Report of the Decision of the Supreme Court of the United States, and the Opinions of the Judges Thereof, in the Case of Dred Scott versus John F. A. Sanford. December Term, 1856.* Washington, DC: Cornelius Wendell, 1857.

Journal of the Missouri State Convention, Held in Jefferson City, June, 1862. St. Louis: George Knapp, 1862.

Journal of the Missouri State Convention, Held in Jefferson City, June, 1863. St. Louis: George Knapp, 1863.

"Memorial of the American Society for Colonizing the Free People of Color of the United States." H.R. Doc. No. 64, 19th Cong., 2nd Sess., 1826-27.

"Message from the President of the United States, Returning, With his objections, the bill entitled 'An act to appropriate, for a limited time, the proceeds of the sales of the public lands of the United States, and for granting land to certain States.'" S. Doc. No. 3, 23rd Cong., 1st Sess., 1833-34.

"Plessy v. Ferguson." In *United States Reports,* vol. 163: *Cases Adjudged in the Supreme Court of the United States at October Term, 1895,* 537-64. New York: Banks & Brothers, 1896.

Proceedings of the Missouri State Convention, Held in Jefferson City, June, 1862. St. Louis: George Knapp, 1862.

Proceedings of the Missouri State Convention, Held in Jefferson City, June, 1863. St. Louis: George Knapp, 1863.

Report of Mr. Kennedy, of Maryland, from the Committee on Commerce of the House of Representatives of the United States, on the Memorial of the Friends of African Colonization, Assembled in Convention in the City of Washington, May, 1842. H.R. Rep. No. 283, 27th Cong., 3rd Sess., 1842-43.

"Report and Testimony of the Select Committee of the United States Senate to Investigate the Causes of the Removal of the Negroes from the Southern States to the Northern States." S. Rep. No. 693, 3 parts, 46th Cong., 2nd Sess., 1879-80.

"Report of the Joint Select Committee to Inquire into the Condition of Affairs in the Late Insurrectionary States." S. Rep. No. 41, 42nd Cong., 2nd. Sess., 1871-72.

"Report of Select Committee on Emancipation." H.R. Rep. No. 148, 37th Cong., 2nd Sess., 1861-62.

"Report of a Special Committee of the Senate of South Carolina, on the Resolutions Submitted by Mr. Ramsay, on the Subject of State Rights." S. Doc. No. 29, 20th Cong., 1st Sess., 1827-28.

"Resolutions of the Legislature of Georgia, in Relation to the American Colonization Society." S. Doc. No. 31, 20th Cong., 1st Sess., 1827-28.

Sanger, George P., ed. *The Statutes at Large, Treaties, and Proclamations, of the United States of America, from December 3, 1855, to March 3, 1859.* Vol. 11. Boston: Little, Brown, 1859.

Sanger, George P., ed. *The Statutes at Large, Treaties, and Proclamations, of the United States of America, from December 5, 1859, to March 3, 1863.* Vol. 12. Boston: Little, Brown, 1863.

Sanger, George P., ed. *The Statutes at Large, Treaties, and Proclamations of the United States of America, from December 1863, to December 1865.* Vol. 13. Boston: Little, Brown, 1866.

[Stanton Report]. House Committee on Naval Affairs. H.R. Rep. No. 438, 31st Cong., 1st Sess., 1849-50.

[Tazewell Report]. Senate Committee on Foreign Relations. H. R. Rep. No. 277, 22nd Cong., 1st. Sess., 1832-33.

NEWSPAPERS AND PERIODICALS

African Repository
Arena Magazine
Christian Recorder
Christian Spectator
Colored American
Douglass' Monthly
Frank Leslie's Popular Monthly
Forum Magazine
Freedom's Journal
Frederick Douglass' Paper

The Liberator
Maryland Colonization Journal
Missouri Republican
National Era
National Intelligencer
New National Era
New York Times
Niles' Register
North American Review
North Star
The Sun (Baltimore)

PUBLISHED PRIMARY SOURCES

Address of the Unconditional Union State Central Committee to the People of Maryland, September 16th, 1863. Baltimore: Sherwood, 1863.

The Annual Reports of the American Society for Colonizing the Free People of Colour of the United States: Volumes 1-10, 1818-27. New York: Negro Universities Press, 1969.

The Annual Reports of the American Society for Colonizing the Free People of Colour of the United States: Volumes 11-20, 1828-36. New York: Negro Universities Press, 1969.

The Annual Reports of the American Society for Colonizing the Free People of Colour of the United States: Volumes 21-33, 1838-50. New York: Negro Universities Press, 1969.

The Annual Reports of the American Society for Colonizing the Free People of Colour of the United States: Volumes 34-43, 1851-60. New York: Negro Universities Press, 1969.

The Annual Reports of the American Society for Colonizing the Free People of Colour of the United States: Volumes 44-53, 1861-70. New York: Negro Universities Press, 1969.

The Annual Reports of the American Society for Colonizing the Free People of Colour of the United States: Volumes 54-63, 1871-80. New York: Negro Universities Press, 1969.

The Annual Reports of the American Society for Colonizing the Free People of Colour of the United States: Volumes 64-93, 1881-1910. New York: Negro Universities Press, 1969.

Bates, Edward. *The Diary of Edward Bates, 1859-1866.* Edited by Howard K. Beale. Washington DC: US Government Printing Office, 1933.

Bilbo, Theodore G. *Take Your Choice; Separation or Mongrelization.* Poplarville, MS: Dream House, 1947.

Blair, Francis Preston, Jr. *Colonization and Commerce: An Address Before the Young Men's Mercantile Library Association of Cincinnati, Ohio, November 29, 1859.* N.p., n.d. Harvard College Library Charles Elliott Perkins Memorial Collection, 1915.

Blair, Francis Preston, Jr. *The Destiny of the Races of This Continent. An Address Delivered Before the Mercantile Library Association of Boston, Massachusetts. On the 26th of January, 1859.* Washington, DC: Buell & Blanchard, 1859.

Blair, Francis Preston, Jr. *Speech of F. P. Blair, of Missouri, Delivered in the House of Representatives, April 23, 1864.* Washington, DC: L. Towers, 1864.

Blair, Francis Preston, Jr. *Speech of Francis P. Blair, Jr., of Missouri, Delivered in the House of Representatives, February 5, 1864.* Washington, DC: Constitutional Union Office, 1864.

Blair, Francis Preston, Jr. *Speech of Gen. F. P. Blair, Democratic Candidate for Vice President. Delivered September 24th, 1868, at Indianapolis. Before the Largest Political Meeting Ever Held in Indiana.* Blair Family Papers. Manuscript Division, Library of Congress, Washington DC.

Blair, Francis Preston, Jr. *Speech of Hon. F. P. Blair, Jr., of Missouri: At the Cooper Institute, New York City, Wednesday, January 25, 1860.* Washington, DC: Buell & Blanchard, 1860.

Blair, Francis Preston, Jr. *Speech of Hon. F. P. Blair, Jr. of Missouri, on the Policy of the President for the Restoration of the Union and Establishment of Peace; Delivered in the House of Representatives, April 11, 1862.* Washington, DC: Congressional Globe Office, 1862.

Blair, Francis Preston, Jr. *Speech of Hon. Frank P. Blair, Jr., of Missouri, on the Acquisition of Territory in Central and South America, to Be Colonized with Free Blacks, and Held as a Dependency by the United States. Delivered in the House of Representatives, on the 14th Day of January, 1858. with an Appendix.* Washington, DC: Buell & Blanchard, 1858.

Blair, Francis Preston, Sr. *Letter from Francis P. Blair. to My Neighbors.* New York: New York Evening Post, 1856.

Blair, Francis Preston, Sr. *Letter of Francis P. Blair, Esq., to the Republican Association of Washington, D.C.* Washington, DC: Buell & Blanchard, 1855.

Blair, Francis Preston, Sr. "Paper Submitted to the Convention, in Behalf of His Southern Constituents, by Francis P. Blair, President of the Convention." In *Official Proceedings of the Republican Convention Convened in the City of Pittsburgh, Pennsylvania, on the 22d of February, 1856,* 5–8. Washington, DC: Buell & Blanchard, 1856.

Blair, Francis Preston, Sr. *A Voice from the Grave of Jackson!—Letter from Francis P. Blair, Esq., to a Public Meeting in New York, Held April 29, 1856.* N.p., 1856.

Blair, Montgomery. *Address of Montgomery Blair, before the Maryland State Republican Convention at Baltimore, April 26, 1860.* Washington, DC: Buell & Blanchard, 1860.

Blair, Montgomery. *Comments on the Policy Inaugurated by the President, in a Letter and Two Speeches.* New York: Hall, Clayton & Medole, 1863.

Blair, Montgomery. *Letter of Hon. Montgomery Blair, Postmaster General, to the Meeting Held at the Cooper Institute, New York, March 6, 1862.* Washington, DC: Congressional Globe, 1862.

Blair, Montgomery. *Proscription in Maryland. Speeches of the Hon. Montgomery Blair, as President of the Anti-Registry Convention, to the Convention and to the Legislature of Maryland, Delivered 24th and 25th of January, 1866.* Washington, DC: Joseph L. Pearson, 1868.

Blair, Montgomery. *Speech of the Hon. Montgomery Blair, at the Cooper Institute, N.Y. to Ratify the Union Nominations, September 27, 1864.* New York: Daniel W. Lee, 1864.

Blair, Montgomery. *Speech of the Hon. Montgomery Blair, on the Causes of the Rebellion and in Support of the President's Plan of Pacification, Delivered Before the Legislature of Maryland, at Annapolis, on the 22d of January, 1864.* Baltimore: Sherwood, 1864.

Blair, Montgomery. *Speech of the Hon. Montgomery Blair, (Postmaster General,) on the Revolutionary Schemes of the Ultra Abolitionists, and in Defence of the Policy of the President. Delivered at the Unconditional Union Meeting, Held at Rockville, Montgomery Co., Maryland, on Saturday, October 3, 1863.* New York: D. W. Lee, 1863.

Bradley, Peter. "What Should White Americans Do?" *American Renaissance*, June 26, 2024. https://www.amren.com/features/2024/06/what-should-white-americans-do/.

Brown, Isaac V. *Memoirs of the Rev. Robert Finley, D.D.* New Brunswick, NJ: Terhune & Letson, 1819.

Calhoun, John C. "Speech on the Reception of Abolition Petitions, February, 1837." In *Speeches of John C. Calhoun. Delivered in the Congress of the United States from 1811 to the Present Time*, 222–26. New York: Harper & Brothers, 1843.

Calhoun, William Patrick. *The Caucasian and the Negro in the United States: They Must Separate. If Not, Then Extermination. A Proposed Solution: Colonization.* Columbia, SC: R. L. Bryan, 1902.

Clay, Henry. "An Address Delivered to the Colonization Society of Kentucky, at Frankfort, December 17, 1829, by the Hon. Henry Clay, at the Request of the Board of Managers." *African Repository* 6 (1831): 1–26.

Clay, Henry. "Mr. Clay's Remarks." *African Repository* 12 (1836): 297–301.

Clay, Henry. *The Papers of Henry Clay.* Edited by James F. Hopkins and Mary W. M. Hargreaves. 10 vols. Lexington: University of Kentucky Press, 1959.

Clay, Henry. *Speech of the Hon. Henry Clay, in the Senate of the United States, on the Subject of Abolition Petitions, February 7, 1839.* Boston: James Monroe, 1839.

Clay, Henry. "Speech of the Hon. H. Clay, Delivered at the Annual Meeting of the Am. Col. Society, January 21, 1851." *African Repository* 27 (1851): 105–14.

Clay, Henry. "Speech of Mr. Clay, at the Mass Meeting in Lexington, KY, on Saturday November 13, 1847." *Niles' National Register* 73 (1848): 197–200.

Colonization of the Western Coast of Africa, by Means of a Line of Mail Steam Ships. New York: W. L. Burroughs, 1851.

Constitution of the American Society of Free Persons of Colour, for Improving Their Condition in the United States; for Purchasing Lands; and for the Establishment of a Settlement in Upper Canada, Also, The Proceedings of the Convention with Their Address to Free Persons of Colour in the United States. Philadelphia: J. W. Allen, 1831.

Cooper, Anna Julia. *A Voice from the South.* Xenia, OH: Aldine, 1892.

Cornish, Samuel E., and Theodore S. Wright. *The Colonization Scheme Considered, In Its Rejection by the Colored People—In Its Tendency to Uphold Caste—In Its Unfitness for Christianizing and Civilizing the Aborigines of Africa, and for Putting a Stop to the African Slave Trade: In a Letter to the Hon. Theodore Frelinghuysen and the Hon. Benjamin F. Butler.* Newark, NJ: Aaron Guest, 1840.

Cox, Earnest Sevier. *Let My People Go.* Richmond: White America Society, 1925.

Cox, Earnest Sevier. *White America.* Richmond: White America Society, 1923.

Douglass, Frederick. *Frederick Douglass: Selected Speeches and Writings.* Edited by Philip Sheldon Foner and Yuval Taylor. Chicago: Lawrence Hill Books, 1999.

Douglass, Frederick. *Lessons of the Hour: Metropolitan A.M.E. Church.* Baltimore, MD: Thomas & Evans, 1894.

Douglass, Frederick. "The Nation's Problem, Speech Delivered Before the Bethel Literary and Historical Society, Washington D.C., April 16, 1889." In *Frederick Douglass: Selected Speeches and Writings,* edited by Philip Sheldon Foner and Yuval Taylor, 725-40. Chicago: Lawrence Hill Books, 1999.

Douglass, Frederick. "The Negro Exodus from the Gulf States." *Frank Leslie's Popular Monthly* 9 (1880).

Douglass, Frederick. *The Race Problem. Great Speech of Frederick Douglass, Delivered Before the Bethel Literary and Historical Association, in the Metropolitan A.M.E. Church, Washington D.C., October 21, 1890.* Library of Congress.

Du Bois, William Edward Burghardt. *Black Reconstruction in America: 1860-1880.* With an introduction by David Levering Lewis. New York: Free Press, 1998.

Du Bois, William Edward Burghardt. *The Souls of Black Folk: Essays and Sketches.* Chicago: A. C. McClurg, 1903.

Du Bois, William Edward Burghardt. "Strivings of the Negro People." *Atlantic Monthly* 80 (1897): 194-98.

Du Bois, William Edward Burghardt. *The Suppression of the African Slave-Trade to the United States of America, 1638-1870.* New York: Longmans, Green, 1904.

Fairfax, Ferdinando. "Plan for Liberating the Negroes within the United States." *American Museum* 8 (1790): 285-87.

Finley, Robert. "Thoughts on the Colonization of Free Blacks." *African Repository* 9 (1834): 332-35.

Fulkerson, H. S. *The Negro; As He Was; As He Is; As He Will Be.* Vicksburg, MS: Commercial Herald, 1887.

Garrison, William Lloyd. *Thoughts on African Colonization.* Boston: Garrison and Knapp, 1832.

Grady, Henry W. "In Plain Black and White: A Reply to Mr. Cable." *The Century* 29 (1885): 909-17.

Grady, Henry W. "The Race Problem in the South: A Speech Delivered at the Annual Banquet of the Boston Merchants' Association, December, 1889." In *The Complete Orations and Speeches of Henry W. Grady*, edited by Edwin DuBois Shurter, 190-220. New York: Hinds, Noble & Eldredge, 1910.

Graves, John Temple. "The Problem of the Races." In *The Possibilities of the Negro in Symposium: A Solution of the Negro Problem Psychologically Considered. The Negro Not "A Beast,"* 5-34. Atlanta: Franklin Printing and Publishing, 1904.

Graves, John Temple. "[Speech]." In *Race Problems of the South: Report of the Proceedings of the First Annual Conference Held Under the Auspices of the Southern Society for the Promotion of the Study of Race Conditions and Problems in the South at Montgomery Alabama*, 48-57. Richmond: B. F. Johnson, 1900.

Hamilton, William. *Address to the Fourth Annual Convention of the Free People of Color of the United States. Delivered at the Opening of Their Session in the City of New-York, June 2, 1834.* New York: S. W. Benedict, 1834.

Hampton, Wade. "The Race Problem." *The Arena* 2 (1890): 132-38.

Henderson, John. *Speech Delivered by Hon. J. B. Henderson, at Hannibal, MO., on the 20th of August, 1862, Before a Mass Meeting of the Citizens of Marion and Ralls Counties.* N.p., n.d.

Hoffman, Frederick. *Race Traits and Tendencies of the American Negro.* New York: Macmillan Company for the American Economic Association, 1896.

Holley, H.W. *The Race Problem and Other Critiques.* Buffalo: Charles Wells Moulton, 1891.

Hood, Gregory. "James Madison and the American Colonization Society." *American Renaissance*, August 9, 2021. https://www.amren.com/news/2021/08/james-madison-and-the-american-colonization-society/.

Immediate Emancipation in Maryland. Proceedings of the Union State Central Committee, at a Meeting Held in Temperance Temple, Baltimore, Wednesday, December 16, 1863. Baltimore: Bull & Tuttle, 1863.

Jefferson, Thomas. "Memoir." In *Memoir, Correspondence, and Private Papers of Thomas Jefferson*, edited by Thomas Jefferson Randolph, vol. 1, 1-94: London: Henry Colburn and Richard Bentley, 1829.

Jefferson, Thomas. *Notes on the State of Virginia.* London: John Stockdale, 1787.

Lease, Mary Elizabeth. *The Problem of Civilization Solved.* Chicago: Laird and Lee, 1895.

Lincoln, Abraham. *Abraham Lincoln, Slavery, and the Civil War: Selected Writing and Speeches.* Edited by Michael P. Johnson. 2nd ed. Boston: Bedford/St. Martin's, 2010.

Lincoln, Abraham. *Collected Works of Abraham Lincoln.* Edited by Roy Basler. 9 vols. New Brunswick, NJ: Rutgers University Press, 1953.

McKinley, Carlyle. *An Appeal to Pharaoh: The Negro Problem and Its Radical Solution.* New York: Fords, Howard & Hulbert, 1889.

McPherson, Edward. *The Political History of the United States of America, during the Great Rebellion.* 2nd ed. Washington, DC: Philp & Solomons, 1865.

Minutes and Proceedings of the First Annual Convention of the People of Color, Held by Adjournments in the City of Philadelphia, from the Sixth to the Eleventh of June, Inclusive, 1831. Philadelphia: Committee of Arrangements, 1831.

Minutes and Proceedings of the Second Annual Convention, for the Improvement of the Free People of Colour in These United States, Held by Adjournments in the City of Philadelphia, from the 4th to the 13th of June Inclusive, 1832. Philadelphia: Martin & Boden, 1832.

Minutes and Proceedings of the Third Annual Convention, for the Improvement of the Free People of Colour in These United States, Held by Adjournments in the City of Philadelphia, from the 3d to the 13th of June Inclusive, 1833. New York, 1833.

Minutes of the Fifth Annual Convention for the Improvement of the Free People of Colour in the United States; Held by Adjournments, in the Wesley Church, Philadelphia; from the First to the Fifth of June, Inclusive; 1835. Philadelphia: William P. Gibbons, 1835.

Minutes of the Fourth Annual Convention for the Improvement of the Free People of Colour, in the United States; Held by Adjournments in the Asbury Church, New York, from the 2nd to the 12th of June, Inclusive, 1834. New York: S. W. Benedict & Co., 1834.

Minutes of the National Convention of Colored Citizens: Held at Buffalo, on the 15th, 16th, 17th, 18th and 19th of August, 1843. New York: Piercy & Reed, 1843.

Mitchell, James. *Report of the Agent of the Indiana Colonization Society, Showing the Operations of Said Agency During the Year 1852, in Answer to a Resolution of the Senate.* Indianapolis: J. P. Chapman, 1853.

Morgan, John T. "Shall Negro Majorities Rule?" *The Forum* 6 (1889): 586–99.

Morgan, John T. "The Race Question in the United States." *The Arena* 2 (1890): 385–98.

Morgan, John T. *Negro Suffrage in the South. Mr. Pritchard's Resolution. Speech of the Hon. John T. Morgan, of Alabama, in the Senate of the United States, January 8, 1900.* Washington, DC, 1900.

Official Proceedings of the Republican Convention Convened in the City of Pittsburgh, Pennsylvania, on the 22d of February, 1856. Washington, DC: Buell & Blanchard, 1856.

Otken, Charles H. *The Ills of the South; or, Related Causes Hostile to the General Prosperity of the Southern People.* New York: G. P. Putnam's Sons, 1894.

"Ought the Negro to Be Disfranchised? Ought He to Have Been Enfranchised?" *North American Review* 128 (1879): 225–83.

Pickett, William P. *The Negro Problem: Abraham Lincoln's Solution.* New York: G. P. Putnam's Sons, 1909.

Proceedings of a Convention of the Friends of African Colonization. Washington, DC: Alexander and Barnard, 1842.

Proceedings of the Anti-Slavery Convention, Assembled at Philadelphia, December 4, 5, and 6, 1833. New York: Dorr & Butterfield, 1833.

Proceedings of the Colored National Convention, Held in Rochester, July 6th, 7th and 8th, 1853. Rochester, 1853.

Proceedings of the Colored National Labor Convention, Held in Washington, D.C., on December 6th, 7th, 8th, 9th, and 10th, 1869. Washington, DC: The New Era, 1870.

Proceedings of the Convention of the Colored People of VA., Held in the City of Alexandria, Aug. 2, 3, 4, 5, 1865. Alexandria: Cowing & Gillis, 1865.

Proceedings of the First Annual Meeting of the National Equal Rights League, Held in Cleveland, Ohio, October 19, 20, and 21, 1865. Philadelphia: E. C. Markley & Son, 1865.

Proceedings of the National Convention of the Colored Men of America, Held in Washington, D.C., on January 13, 14, 15, and 16, 1869. Washington, DC, 1869.

Proceedings of the National Convention of Colored Men, Held in the City of Syracuse, N.Y., October 4, 5, 6, and 7, 1864; with the Bill of Wrongs and Rights, and the Address to the American People. Boston: J. S. Rock and Geo. L. Ruffin, 1864.

Proceedings of the National Emigration Convention of Colored People, Held at Cleveland, Ohio, Thursday, Friday and Saturday, the 24th, 25th and 26th of August 1854. Pittsburgh: A. A. Anderson, 1854.

Proceedings of the State Convention of Colored People, Held at Albany, New-York, on the 22d, 23d and 24th of July, 1851. Albany: Charles Van Benthuysen, 1851.

Proceedings of the State Equal Rights' Convention, of the Colored People of Pennsylvania, Held in the City of Harrisburg February 8th, 9th, and 10th, 1865: Together with a Few of the Arguments Presented Suggesting the Necessity for Holding the Convention, and an Address of the Colored State Convention to the People of Pennsylvania. N.p., 1865.

Remarks on the Colonization of the Western Coast of Africa, by the Free Negroes of the United States, and the Consequent Civilization of Africa and Suppression of the Slave Trade. New York: W. L. Burroughs, 1850.

Resolutions of the People of Color at a Meeting Held on the 25th of January, 1831. With an Address to the Citizens of New-York, in Answer to Those of the New-York Colonization Society. New York, 1831.

Ruggles, David. *The "Extinguisher" Extinguished! Or David M. Reese, M.D. "Used Up."* New York: D. Ruggles, 1834.

Scomp, Henry A. "Can the Race Problem Be Solved?" *The Forum* 8 (1890): 365–76.

Shufeldt, R. W. *The Negro: A Menace to Civilization.* Boston: Richard G. Badger, 1907.

Simmons, Enoch Spencer. *A Solution of the Race Problem in the South.* Raleigh, NC: Edwards & Broughton, 1898.

Simpson, Samuel. *A Treatise on Negro Colonization. A Plan for Colonizing All the Negroes in the United States on Foreign Territory.* N.p., 1888.

Sparks, Jared. *Historical Outline of the American Colonization Society, and Remarks on the Advantages and Practicability of Colonizing in Africa the Free People of Color from the United States.* Boston: O. Everett, 1824.

Taylor, Jared. "What the Founders Really Thought About Race." *American Renaissance,* February 17, 2012. https://www.amren.com/news/2022/02/what-the-founders-really-thought-about-race-jared-taylor/.

Tocqueville, Alexis de. *Democracy in America.* Translated by Henry Reeve. Second American Edition. New York: George Adlard, 1838.

Tucker, George. *Letter to a Member of the General Assembly of Virginia, on the Subject of the Late Conspiracy of the Slaves; with a Proposal for Their Colonization.* Baltimore: Bonsal & Niles, 1801.

Tucker, St. George. *A Dissertation on Slavery with a Proposal for the Gradual Abolition of It, in the State of Virginia.* Philadelphia: Matthew Carey, 1796.

Turnbull, Robert. *The Crisis: Or, Essays on the Usurpations of the Federal Government.* Charleston: A. E. Miller, 1827.

A View of Exertions Lately Made for the Purpose of Colonizing the Free People of Colour, in the United States, in Africa, or Elsewhere. Washington, DC: Jonathan Elliot, 1817.

Walker, David. *Walker's Appeal, in Four Articles; Together with a Preamble, to the Coloured Citizens of the World, but in Particular, and Very Expressly, to Those of the United States of America.* 3rd ed. Boston: D. Walker, 1830.

SECONDARY SOURCES

Abbott, Richard H. *The Republican Party and the South, 1855–1877: The First Southern Strategy.* Chapel Hill: University of North Carolina Press, 1986.

Abzug, Robert H. *Cosmos Crumbling: American Reform and the Religious Imagination.* Oxford: Oxford University Press, 1994.

Adams, Alice Dana. *The Neglected Period of Anti-Slavery in America, 1808–1831.* Boston: Ginn, 1908.

Aidt-Guy, Anita Louise. "Persistent Maryland: Antislavery Activity Between 1850 and 1864." PhD diss., Georgetown University, 1994.

Ambrose, Andy. "John Temple Graves and the Southern Race Problem." Atlanta History Center, 2023. https://www.atlantahistorycenter.com/blog/john-temple-graves-and-the-southern-race-problem/.

Ayers, Edward L. *Southern Crossing: A History of the American South, 1877–1906.* Oxford: Oxford University Press, 1998.

Baylen, Joseph O., and John Hammond Moore. "Senator John Tyler Morgan and Negro Colonization in the Philippines, 1901 to 1902." *Phylon* (1960–) 29, no. 1 (1968): 65–75.

Bell, Howard Holman. *A Survey of the Negro Convention Movement.* New York: Arno, 1969.

Bellamy, Donnie. "Slavery, Emancipation, and Racism in Missouri, 1850–1865." PhD diss., University of Missouri, 1971.

Belle, Kathryn Sophia. "Anna Julia Cooper." In *The Stanford Encyclopedia of Philosophy*, edited by Edward N. Zalta and Uri Nodelman, Winter 2023. https://plato.stanford.edu/archives/win2023/entries/anna-julia-cooper/.

Bennett, Charles Raymond. "All Things to All People: The American Colonization Society in Kentucky, 1829–1860." PhD diss., University of Kentucky, 1980.

Berlin, Ira. *Many Thousands Gone: The First Two Centuries of Slavery in North America.* Cambridge, MA: Belknap Press of Harvard University, 1998.

Berlin, Ira. *Slaves Without Masters: The Free Negro in the Antebellum South.* With a new preface. New York: New Press, 2007.

Berwanger, Eugene H. *The Frontier Against Slavery: Western Anti-Negro Prejudice and the Slavery Extension Controversy.* Urbana: University of Illinois Press, 1967.

Berwanger, Eugene H. *The West and Reconstruction.* Urbana: University of Illinois Press, 1981.

Beveridge, Albert Jeremiah. *The Life of John Marshall.* Vols. 3–4. Boston: Houghton Mifflin, 1919.

Billington, Ray Allen. "James Forten: Forgotten Abolitionist." *Negro History Bulletin* 13, no. 2 (1949): 31–45.

Blackett, R. J. M. *The Captive's Quest for Freedom: Fugitive Slaves, the 1850 Fugitive Slave Law, and the Politics of Slavery.* Cambridge: Cambridge University Press, 2018.

Blain, Keisha N. *Set the World on Fire: Black Nationalist Women and the Global Struggle for Freedom.* Philadelphia: University of Pennsylvania Press, 2018.

Blight, David W. *Frederick Douglass: Prophet of Freedom.* New York: Simon & Schuster, 2018.

Blight, David W. *Race and Reunion: The Civil War in American Memory.* Cambridge, MA: Harvard University Press, 2001.

Brackett, Jeffrey Richardson. *The Negro in Maryland: A Study of the Institution of Slavery.* Baltimore: Johns Hopkins University, 1889.

Bradford, Antuian Rivarius. "The Mississippi State Colonization Society and the Key Leaders in the Mississippi Colonization Scheme." Master's thesis, Morgan State University, 2010.

Brown, Christopher Leslie. *Moral Capital: Foundations of British Abolitionism.* Chapel Hill: Omohundro Institute and University of North Carolina Press, 2006.

Bureau of the Census. *A Century of Population Growth, 1790-1900*. Washington, DC: Government Printing Office, 1909.

Burin, Eric. "Rethinking Northern White Support for the African Colonization Movement: The Pennsylvania Colonization Society as an Agent of Emancipation." *Pennsylvania Magazine of History and Biography* 127, no. 2 (2003): 197-229.

Burin, Eric. "The Slave Trade Act of 1819: A New Look at Colonization and the Politics of Slavery." *American Nineteenth Century History* 13, no. 1 (2012): 1-14.

Burin, Eric. *Slavery and the Peculiar Solution: A History of the American Colonization Society*. With a new preface. Gainesville: University Press of Florida, 2008.

Campbell, James T. *Middle Passages: African American Journeys to Africa, 1787-2005*. New York: Penguin Books, 2007.

Canney, Donald L. *Africa Squadron: The U.S. Navy and the Slave Trade, 1842-1861*. Washington, DC: Potomac Books, 2006.

Carter, Susan B., and Richard Sutch, eds. *Historical Statistics of the United States*. Millennial Edition. New York: Cambridge University Press, 2006.

Clegg, Claude Andrew. *The Price of Liberty: African Americans and the Making of Liberia*. Chapel Hill: University of North Carolina Press, 2004.

Coates, Ta-Nehisi. *Between the World and Me*. New York: Random House, 2015.

Cogliano, Francis D. *Thomas Jefferson: Reputation and Legacy*. Edinburgh: Edinburgh University Press, 2006.

Coleman, Charles H. *The Election of 1868: The Democratic Effort to Regain Control*. New York: Columbia University Press, 1933.

Cooper, William J., Jr. *The South and the Politics of Slavery, 1828-1856*. Baton Rouge: Louisiana State University Press, 1978.

Cornish, Dudley Taylor. *The Sable Arm: Negro Troops in the Union Army, 1861-1865*. With a new foreword. Lawrence: University Press of Kansas, 1987.

Crofts, Daniel W. *Reluctant Confederates: Upper South Unionists in the Secession Crisis*. Chapel Hill: University of North Carolina Press, 1989.

Dain, Bruce. *A Hideous Monster of the Mind: American Race Theory in the Early Republic*. Cambridge, MA: Harvard University Press, 2002.

Davis, David Brion. "The Emergence of Immediatism in British and American Antislavery Thought." *Mississippi Valley Historical Review* 49, no. 2 (1962): 209-30.

Davis, David Brion. *The Problem of Slavery in the Age of Emancipation*. New York: Vintage Books, 2015.

Davis, David Brion. *The Problem of Slavery in the Age of Revolution, 1770-1823*. With a new preface. Oxford: Oxford University Press, 1999.

Davis, David Brion. *The Problem of Slavery in Western Culture*. Oxford: Oxford University Press, 1988.

Davis, Hugh. *Leonard Bacon: New England Reformer and Antislavery Moderate*. Baton Rouge: Louisiana State University Press, 1998.

Davis, Hugh. *"We Will Be Satisfied with Nothing Less": The African American Struggle for Equal Rights in the North During Reconstruction.* Ithaca, NY: Cornell University Press, 2011.

Delbanco, Andrew. *The Abolitionist Imagination.* Cambridge, MA: Harvard University Press, 2012.

Dillon, Merton Lynn. *The Abolitionists: The Growth of a Dissenting Minority.* DeKalb: Northern Illinois University Press, 1974.

Du Bois, William Edward Burghardt. *Black Reconstruction in America: 1860–1880.* With an introduction by David Levering Lewis. New York: Free Press, 1998.

Du Bois, William Edward Burghardt. *The Souls of Black Folk: Essays and Sketches.* Chicago: A. C. McClurg, 1903.

Du Bois, William Edward Burghardt. "Souls of White Folk." In *Darkwater: Voices from Within the Veil,* 29–52. New York: Harcourt, Brace and Howe, 1920.

Dudziak, Mary L. *Cold War Civil Rights: Race and the Image of American Democracy.* With a new preface. Princeton, NJ: Princeton University Press, 2011.

Dumond, Dwight Lowell. *Antislavery: The Crusade for Freedom in America.* Ann Arbor: University of Michigan Press, 1961.

Dyer, Brainerd. "The Persistence of the Idea of Negro Colonization." *Pacific Historical Review* 12, no. 1 (1943): 53–65.

Edwards, Laura F. *A Legal History of the Civil War and Reconstruction: A Nation of Rights.* Cambridge: Cambridge University Press, 2015.

Egerton, Douglas R. "Averting a Crisis: The Proslavery Critique of the American Colonization Society." In *Rebels, Reformers, & Revolutionaries: Collected Essays and Second Thoughts,* 147–59. New York: Routledge, 2002.

Egerton, Douglas R. *Charles Fenton Mercer and the Trial of National Conservatism.* Jackson: University Press of Mississippi, 1989.

Egerton, Douglas R. *Gabriel's Rebellion: The Virginia Slave Conspiracies of 1800 and 1802.* Chapel Hill: University of North Carolina Press, 1993.

Egerton, Douglas R. "'Its Origin Is Not a Little Curious': A New Look at the American Colonization Society." In *Rebels, Reformers, & Revolutionaries: Collected Essays and Second Thoughts,* 107–20. New York: Routledge, 2002.

Ely, Melvin Patrick. *Israel on the Appomattox: A Southern Experiment in Black Freedom from the 1790s Through the Civil War.* New York: Vintage Books, 2005.

Escott, Paul D. *Lincoln's Dilemma: Blair, Sumner, and the Republican Struggle over Racism and Equality in the Civil War Era.* Charlottesville: University of Virginia Press, 2017.

Etcheson, Nicole. *Bleeding Kansas: Contested Liberty in the Civil War Era.* Lawrence: University Press of Kansas, 2004.

Etcheson, Nicole. *The Emerging Midwest: Upland Southerners and the Political Culture of the Old Northwest, 1787–1861.* Bloomington: Indiana University Press, 1996.

Fehrenbacher, Donald. *The Dred Scott Case: Its Significance in American Law and Politics.* Oxford: Oxford University Press, 2001.

Feller, Daniel. *The Public Lands in Jacksonian Politics.* Madison: University of Wisconsin Press, 1984.

Fields, Barbara J. "Ideology and Race in American History." In *Region, Race, and Reconstruction: Essays in Honor of C. Vann Woodward,* edited by James M. McPherson and J. Morgan Kousser, 143–77. Oxford: Oxford University Press, 1982.

Fields, Barbara J. *Slavery and Freedom on the Middle Ground: Maryland during the Nineteenth Century.* New Haven, CT: Yale University Press, 1985.

Fields, Karen E., and Barbara Jeanne Fields. *Racecraft: The Soul of Inequality in American Life.* London: Verso Books, 2012.

Filler, Louis. *The Crusade Against Slavery.* New York: Harper & Row, 1960.

Fischer, David Hackett, and James C. Kelly. *Bound Away: Virginia and the Westward Movement.* Charlottesville: University of Virginia Press, 2000.

Fitzgerald, Michael W. "'We Have Found a Moses': Theodore Bilbo, Black Nationalism, and the Greater Liberia Bill of 1939." *Journal of Southern History* 63, no. 2 (1997): 293–320.

Fladeland, Betty. *James Gillespie Birney: Slaveholder to Abolitionist.* New York: Greenwood, 1969.

Fleegler, Robert L. "Theodore G. Bilbo and the Decline of Public Racism, 1938–1947." *Journal of Mississippi History* 68, no. 1 (2006): 1–27.

Foner, Eric. *The Fiery Trial: Abraham Lincoln and American Slavery.* New York: W. W. Norton, 2011.

Foner, Eric. *Free Soil, Free Labor, Free Men: The Ideology of the Republican Party Before the Civil War.* With a new introduction. Oxford: Oxford University Press, 1995.

Foner, Eric. *Freedom's Lawmakers: A Directory of Black Officeholders During Reconstruction.* Oxford: Oxford University Press, 1993.

Foner, Eric. "Lincoln and Colonization." In *Our Lincoln: New Perspectives on Lincoln and His World,* edited by Eric Foner, 135–66. New York: W. W. Norton, 2008.

Foner, Eric. *Reconstruction: America's Unfinished Revolution, 1863–1877.* New York: Harper & Row, 1988.

Foner, Eric. *The Second Founding: How the Civil War and Reconstruction Remade the Constitution.* New York: W. W. Norton, 2019.

Ford, Lacy K. *Deliver Us from Evil: The Slavery Question in the Old South.* Oxford: Oxford University Press, 2009.

Ford, Lacy. "Reconfiguring the Old South: 'Solving' the Problem of Slavery, 1787–1838." *Journal of American History* 95, no. 1 (2008): 95–122.

Foster, Frances Smith. "A Narrative of the Interesting Origins and (Somewhat) Surprising Developments of African-American Print Culture." *American Literary History* 17, no. 4 (December 1, 2005): 714–40.

Fredrickson, George M. *The Black Image in the White Mind: The Debate on Afro-American Character and Destiny, 1817-1914*. With a new preface. Middletown, CT: Wesleyan University Press, 1987.

Freehling, William W. *Prelude to Civil War: The Nullification Controversy in South Carolina, 1816-1836*. New York: Harper & Row, 1966.

Freehling, William W. *The Road to Disunion, Vol. 1: Secessionists at Bay, 1776-1854*. Oxford: Oxford University Press, 1990.

Freehling, William W. *The Road to Disunion, Vol. 2: Secessionists Triumphant, 1854-1861*. Oxford: Oxford University Press, 2007.

Friedman, Lawrence. *Gregarious Saints: Self and Community in American Abolitionism, 1830-1870*. Cambridge: Cambridge University Press, 1982.

Friedman, Lawrence. "Purifying the White Man's Country: The American Colonization Society Reconsidered, 1816-1840." *SOCIETAS—A Review of Social History* 6, no. 1 (Winter 1976): 1-24.

Fry, Joseph A. "John Tyler Morgan's Southern Expansionism." *Diplomatic History* 9, no. 4 (1985): 329-46.

Fuente, Alejandro de la, and Ariela J. Gross. *Becoming Free, Becoming Black: Race, Freedom, and Law in Cuba, Virginia, and Louisiana*. Cambridge: Cambridge University Press, 2020.

Gardner, Eric. *Black Print Unbound: The Christian Recorder, African American Literature, and Periodical Culture*. Oxford: Oxford University Press, 2015.

Garland, Hugh A. *The Life of John Randolph of Roanoke*. New York: D. Appleton, 1860.

Gates, Henry Louis, Jr. *Stony the Road: Reconstruction, White Supremacy, and the Rise of Jim Crow*. New York: Penguin, 2020.

Gillette, William. *The Right to Vote: Politics and the Passage of the Fifteenth Amendment*. Baltimore: Johns Hopkins University Press, 1969.

Gilmore, Glenda Elizabeth. *Defying Dixie: The Radical Roots of Civil Rights, 1919-1950*. New York: W. W. Norton, 2009.

Goldman, Robert Michael. *Reconstruction and Black Suffrage: Losing the Vote in Reese and Cruikshank*. Lawrence: University Press of Kansas, 2001.

Goodyear Freehling, Alison. *Drift Toward Dissolution: The Virginia Slavery Debate of 1831-1832*. Baton Rouge: Louisiana State University Press, 1982.

Grant, Colin. *Negro with a Hat: The Rise and Fall of Marcus Garvey*. Oxford: Oxford University Press, 2008.

Greenidge, Kerri K. *Black Radical: The Life and Times of William Monroe Trotter*. New York: Liveright, 2020.

Griffin, Appleton Prentiss Clark, ed. *Select List of References on the Negro Question*. 2nd ed. Washington, DC: Library of Congress, 1906.

Gross, Ariela J. *Double Character: Slavery and Mastery in the Antebellum Southern Courtroom*. Athens: University of Georgia Press, 2006.

Guasco, Suzanne Cooper. *Confronting Slavery: Edward Coles and the Rise of Antislavery Politics in Nineteenth-Century America.* DeKalb: Northern Illinois University Press, 2013.

Guyatt, Nicholas. "America's Conservatory: Race, Reconstruction, and the Santo Domingo Debate." *Journal of American History* 97, no. 4 (2011): 974–1000.

Guyatt, Nicholas. *Bind Us Apart: How Enlightened Americans Invented Racial Segregation.* New York: Basic Books, 2016.

Guyatt, Nicholas. "'The Future Empire of Our Freedmen': Republican Colonization Schemes in Texas and Mexico, 1861–1865." In *Civil War Wests: Testing the Limits of the United States,* edited by Adam Arenson, 95–117. Berkeley: University of California Press, 2015.

Guyatt, Nicholas. "'An Impossible Idea?': The Curious Career of Internal Colonization." *Journal of the Civil War Era* 4, no. 2 (2014): 234–63.

Guyatt, Nicholas. "'The Outskirts of Our Happiness': Race and the Lure of Colonization in the Early Republic." *Journal of American History* 95, no. 4 (2009): 986–1011.

Guyatt, Nicholas. *Providence and the Invention of the United States, 1607–1876.* Cambridge: Cambridge University Press, 2007.

Hahn, Steven. *A Nation Under Our Feet: Black Political Struggles in the Rural South, from Slavery to the Great Migration.* Cambridge, MA: Belknap Press of Harvard University Press, 2003.

Hall, Richard L. *On Afric's Shore: A History of Maryland in Liberia, 1834–1857.* Baltimore: Maryland Center for History and Culture, 2004.

Halpin, Dennis Patrick. *A Brotherhood of Liberty: Black Reconstruction and Its Legacies in Baltimore, 1865–1920.* Philadelphia: University of Pennsylvania Press, 2019.

Hammann, Andrew F. "Beyond *Antislavery* and *Proslavery:* A New Term, *Eventualism,* and a Refined Interpretive Approach." *American Nineteenth Century History* 23, no. 3 (2022): 229–53.

Hammann, Andrew F. "Emancipation and Exclusion: The Politics of Slavery and Colonization, 1787–1865." PhD diss., Stanford University, 2017.

Hammond, John L. *The Politics of Benevolence: Revival Religion and American Voting Behavior.* Norwood, NJ: Ablex, 1979.

Harris, William C. *Lincoln and the Border States: Preserving the Union.* Lawrence: University Press of Kansas, 2011.

Hartman, Saidiya V. *Lose Your Mother: A Journey Along the Atlantic Slave Route.* New York: Farrar, Straus and Giroux, 2007.

Hartman, Saidiya V. *Scenes of Subjection: Terror, Slavery, and Self-Making in Nineteenth-Century America.* Oxford: Oxford University Press, 1997.

Hawkins, Merrill. "Charles H. Otken." In *Mississippi Encyclopedia.* Center for Study of Southern Culture, 2020. http://mississippiencyclopedia.org/entries/otken-charles-h/.

Heidler, David Stephen, and Jeanne T. Heidler. *Henry Clay: The Essential American.* New York: Random House, 2011.

Henry, Raquel L. "The Colonization Movement in Indiana, 1820–1864: A Struggle to Remove the African American." PhD diss., Indiana University, 2008.

Hetrick, Matthew J. "African American Colonization and Identity: 1780–1925." PhD diss., University of Delaware, 2013.

Hill, Robert A., ed. *The Marcus Garvey and Universal Negro Improvement Association Papers.* Berkeley: University of California Press, 1983.

Hobbs, Allyson. *A Chosen Exile: A History of Racial Passing in American Life.* Cambridge, MA: Harvard University Press, 2016.

Holt, Michael F. *The Rise and Fall of the American Whig Party: Jacksonian Politics and the Onset of the Civil War.* Oxford: Oxford University Press, 2003.

Horsman, Reginald. *Race and Manifest Destiny: The Origins of American Racial Anglo-Saxonism.* Cambridge, MA: Harvard University Press, 1981.

Horton, James Oliver, and Lois E. Horton, eds. *Slavery and Public History: The Tough Stuff of American Memory.* Chapel Hill: University of North Carolina Press, 2008.

Howe, Daniel Walker. *What Hath God Wrought: The Transformation of America, 1815–1848.* Oxford: Oxford University Press, 2007.

Jackson, John P., and Andrew S. Winston. "The Last Repatriationist: The Career of Earnest Sevier Cox." In *Race and Science: Scientific Challenges to Racism in Modern America,* edited by Paul Farber and Hamilton Cravens, 58–80. Corvallis: Oregon State University Press, 2009.

James, Winston. *The Struggles of John Brown Russwurm: The Life and Writings of a Pan-Africanist Pioneer, 1799–1851.* New York: New York University Press, 2010.

Johnson, David. *John Randolph of Roanoke.* Baton Rouge: Louisiana State University Press, 2012.

Jones, Howard. *To the Webster-Ashburton Treaty: A Study in Anglo-American Relations, 1783–1843.* Chapel Hill: University of North Carolina Press, 1977.

Jones, Martha S. *Birthright Citizens: A History of Race and Rights in Antebellum America.* Cambridge: Cambridge University Press, 2018.

Jordan, Winthrop D. *White Over Black: American Attitudes Toward the Negro, 1550–1812.* Chapel Hill: University of North Carolina Press, 1968.

Kantrowitz, Stephen. *Ben Tillman and the Reconstruction of White Supremacy.* Chapel Hill: University of North Carolina Press, 2015.

Kantrowitz, Stephen. *More Than Freedom: Fighting for Black Citizenship in a White Republic, 1829–1889.* New York: Penguin Books, 2012.

Karp, Matthew. *This Vast Southern Empire: Slaveholders at the Helm of American Foreign Policy.* Cambridge, MA: Harvard University Press, 2016.

Kendi, Ibram X. *Stamped from the Beginning: The Definitive History of Racist Ideas in America.* New York: Bold Type Books, 2017.

Keyssar, Alexander. *The Right to Vote: The Contested History of Democracy in the United States.* Rev. ed. New York: Basic Books, 2009.

Kierner, Cynthia A. *Martha Jefferson Randolph, Daughter of Monticello: Her Life and Times.* Chapel Hill: University of North Carolina Press, 2012.

Klotter, James C. *Henry Clay: The Man Who Would Be President.* Oxford: Oxford University Press, 2018.

Knupfer, Peter B. *The Union as It Is: Constitutional Unionism and Sectional Compromise, 1787–1861.* Chapel Hill: University of North Carolina Press, 1991.

Kraditor, Aileen S. *Means and Ends in American Abolitionism: Garrison and His Critics on Strategy and Tactics, 1834–1850.* Chicago: Ivan R. Dee, 1989.

Lee, Deborah Ann. "'Life Is a Solemn Trust': Ann R. Page and the Antislavery Movement in the Upper South." PhD diss., George Mason University, 2003.

Levine, Robert S. *Martin Delany, Frederick Douglass, and the Politics of Representative Identity.* Chapel Hill: University of North Carolina Press, 1997.

Lewis, David Levering. *W. E. B. Du Bois: A Biography.* New York: Henry Holt, 2009.

Litwack, Leon F. *North of Slavery: The Negro in the Free States.* Chicago: University of Chicago Press, 1965.

Litwack, Leon F. *Trouble in Mind: Black Southerners in the Age of Jim Crow.* New York: Vintage Books, 1999.

Logan, Rayford W. *The Betrayal of the Negro: From Rutherford B. Hayes to Woodrow Wilson.* Boston: Da Capo, 1997.

Luthin, Reinhard H. "Organizing the Republican Party in the 'Border-Slave' Regions: Edward Bates's Presidential Candidacy in 1860." *Missouri Historical Review* 38, no. 2 (January 1944): 138–61.

Mabry, William Alexander. "Disfranchisement of the Negro in Mississippi." *Journal of Southern History* 4, no. 3 (1938): 318–33.

Magliocca, Gerard N. *Washington's Heir: The Life of Bushrod Washington.* Oxford: Oxford University Press, 2022.

Magness, Phillip W., and Sebastian N. Page. *Colonization After Emancipation: Lincoln and the Movement for Black Resettlement.* Columbia: University of Missouri Press, 2011.

Maness, Lonnie Edward. "Henry Clay and the Problem of Slavery." PhD diss., Memphis State University, 1980.

Marable, Manning. *Race, Reform, and Rebellion: The Second Reconstruction and Beyond in Black America, 1945–2006.* 3rd ed. Jackson: University Press of Mississippi, 2007.

Martin, Asa Earl. *The Anti-Slavery Movement in Kentucky, Prior to 1850.* Louisville: Standard Printing Company of Louisville, 1918.

Martin, Tony. *Race First: The Ideological and Organizational Struggles of Marcus Garvey and the Universal Negro Improvement Association.* Dover, MA: Majority, 1986.

Mason, Matthew. *Apostle of Union: A Political Biography of Edward Everett.* Chapel Hill: University of North Carolina Press, 2016.

Masur, Kate. "The African American Delegation to Abraham Lincoln: A Reappraisal." *Civil War History* 56, no. 2 (2010).

Masur, Kate. *Until Justice Be Done: America's First Civil Rights Movement, from the Revolution to Reconstruction.* New York: W. W. Norton, 2021.

Matijasic, Thomas David. "Conservative Reform in the West: The African Colonization Movement in Ohio, 1826–1839." PhD diss., Miami University, 1982.

Mattingly, Arthur Herman. "Senator John Brooks Henderson, United States Senator from Missouri." PhD diss., Kansas State University, 1971.

May, Gregory. *A Madman's Will: John Randolph, 400 Slaves, and the Mirage of Freedom.* New York: Liveright, 2023.

Mayer, Henry. *All on Fire: William Lloyd Garrison and the Abolition of Slavery.* New York: W. W. Norton, 2008.

McAward, Jennifer Mason. "Defining the Badges and Incidents of Slavery." *University of Pennsylvania Journal of Constitutional Law* 14, no. 3 (2012): 561–630.

McCoy, Drew R. *The Last of the Fathers: James Madison and the Republican Legacy.* Cambridge: Cambridge University Press, 1991.

McCurry, Stephanie. *Confederate Reckoning: Power and Politics in the Civil War South.* Cambridge, MA: Harvard University Press, 2010.

McDaniel, W. Caleb. "The Bonds and Boundaries of Antislavery." *Journal of the Civil War Era* 4, no. 1 (2014): 84–105.

McMillen, Neil R. "Reconstruction and Its Aftermath: Mississippi History, 1865–1890." *Journal of American History* 77, no. 1 (1990): 239–46.

McPherson, James M. *The Negro's Civil War: How American Blacks Felt and Acted During the War for the Union.* New York: Vintage Books, 2008.

McPherson, James M. *The Struggle for Equality: Abolitionists and the Negro in the Civil War and Reconstruction.* Princeton, NJ: Princeton University Press, 1964.

Mehlinger, Louis R. "The Attitude of the Free Negro Toward Colonization." *Journal of Negro History*, 1 (1916): 276–301.

Miller, Floyd John. *The Search for a Black Nationality: Black Emigration and Colonization, 1787–1863.* Urbana: University of Illinois Press, 1975.

Miller, William Lee. *Arguing About Slavery: John Quincy Adams and the Great Battle in the United States Congress.* New York: Vintage Books, 1998.

Mills, Brandon. *The World Colonization Made: The Racial Geography of Early American Empire.* Philadelphia: University of Pennsylvania Press, 2020.

Morrison, Michael A. *Slavery and the American West: The Eclipse of Manifest Destiny.* Chapel Hill: University of North Carolina Press, 1997.

Morrison, Toni. *The Origin of Others.* Cambridge, MA: Harvard University Press, 2017.
Moses, Wilson Jeremiah. *The Golden Age of Black Nationalism, 1850-1925.* Oxford: Oxford University Press, 1988.
Newman, Richard S. *The Transformation of American Abolitionism: Fighting Slavery in the Early Republic.* Chapel Hill: University of North Carolina Press, 2002.
Oakes, James. *Freedom National: The Destruction of Slavery in the United States, 1861-1865.* New York: W. W. Norton, 2012.
Oates, Stephen B. *The Fires of Jubilee: Nat Turner's Fierce Rebellion.* New York: Harper Collins, 1990.
Oliver, Albert. "The Protest and Attitudes of Blacks Towards the American Colonization Society and the Concepts of Emigration and Colonization in Africa, 1817-1865." PhD diss., St. John's University, 1978.
Omi, Michael, and Howard Winant. *Racial Formation in the United States: From the 1960s to the 1990s.* 2nd ed. New York: Routledge, 1994.
Onuf, Peter S. *Jefferson's Empire: The Language of American Nationhood.* Charlottesville: University of Virginia Press, 2000.
Onuf, Peter S. *The Mind of Thomas Jefferson.* Charlottesville: University of Virginia Press, 2007.
Page, Sebastian N. *Black Resettlement and the American Civil War.* Cambridge: Cambridge University Press, 2021.
Page, Sebastian N. "Lincoln and Chiriqui Colonization Revisited." *American Nineteenth Century History* 12, no. 3 (2011): 289-325.
Painter, Nell Irvin. *Exodusters: Black Migration to Kansas After Reconstruction.* Lawrence: University Press of Kansas, 1986.
Paludan, Phillip Shaw. "Lincoln and Colonization: Policy or Propaganda?" *Journal of the Abraham Lincoln Association* 25, no. 1 (2004): 23-37.
Parkinson, Robert G. *The Common Cause: Creating Race and Nation in the American Revolution.* Chapel Hill: University of North Carolina Press, 2016.
Parks, Joseph H. *John Bell of Tennessee.* Baton Rouge: Louisiana State University Press, 1950.
Parrish, William Earl. *Frank Blair: Lincoln's Conservative.* Columbia: University of Missouri Press, 1998.
Pasternak, Martin B. *Rise Now and Fly to Arms: The Life of Henry Highland Garnet.* New York: Garland, 1995.
Patterson, Caleb Perry. *The Negro in Tennessee, 1790-1865: A Study in Southern Politics.* Austin: University of Texas, 1922.
Patterson, Orlando. *Rituals of Blood: Consequences of Slavery in Two American Centuries.* New York: Basic Books, 1998.
Patterson, Orlando. *Slavery and Social Death: A Comparative Study.* With a new preface. Cambridge, MA: Harvard University Press, 2018.

Pease, Jane H., and William Henry Pease. *They Who Would Be Free: Blacks' Search for Freedom, 1830–1861.* Urbana: University of Illinois Press, 1990.

Perman, Michael. *The Road to Redemption: Southern Politics, 1869–1879.* Chapel Hill: University of North Carolina Press, 1984.

Perman, Michael. *Struggle for Mastery: Disfranchisement in the South, 1888–1908.* Chapel Hill: University of North Carolina Press, 2001.

Peterson, Merrill D. *The Jefferson Image in the American Mind.* Charlottesville: University of Virginia Press, 1998.

Polgar, Paul J. *Standard-Bearers of Equality: America's First Abolition Movement.* Chapel Hill: University of North Carolina Press, 2019.

Portnoy, Alisse. *Their Right to Speak: Women's Activism in the Indian and Slave Debates.* Cambridge, MA: Harvard University Press, 2005.

Potter, David Morris, and Don Edward Fehrenbacher. *The Impending Crisis, 1848–1861.* New York: Harper & Row, 1976.

Power-Greene, Ousmane K. *Against Wind and Tide: The African American Struggle against the Colonization Movement.* New York: New York University Press, 2014.

Quarles, Benjamin. *Black Abolitionists.* Oxford: Oxford University Press, 1969.

Quarles, Benjamin. *Lincoln and the Negro.* Oxford: Oxford University Press, 1962.

Rael, Patrick. *Black Identity and Black Protest in the Antebellum North.* Chapel Hill: University of North Carolina Press, 2002.

Redkey, Edwin S. *Black Exodus: Black Nationalist and Back-to-Africa Movements, 1890–1910.* New Haven, CT: Yale University Press, 1969.

Remini, Robert Vincent. *Henry Clay: Statesman for the Union.* New York: W. W. Norton, 1993.

Richardson, Heather Cox. *West from Appomattox: The Reconstruction of America After the Civil War.* New Haven, CT: Yale University Press, 2007.

Ripley, C. Peter. *The Black Abolitionist Papers.* 5 vols. Vol. 3. Chapel Hill: University of North Carolina Press, 1985.

Riser, R. Volney. "Disfranchisement, the U.S. Constitution, and the Federal Courts: Alabama's 1901 Constitutional Convention Debates the Grandfather Clause." *American Journal of Legal History* 48, no. 3 (2006): 237–79.

Robinson, Michael D. *A Union Indivisible: Secession and the Politics of Slavery in the Border South.* Chapel Hill: University of North Carolina Press, 2021.

Russell, John Henderson. "The Free Negro in Virginia, 1619–1895." PhD diss., Johns Hopkins University, 1913.

Scheips, Paul J. "Lincoln and the Chiriqui Colonization Project." *Journal of Negro History* 37, no. 4 (1952): 418–53.

Schmidt, Benno C. "Principle and Prejudice: The Supreme Court and Race in the Progressive Era. Part 3: Black Disfranchisement from the KKK to the Grandfather Clause." *Columbia Law Review* 82, no. 5 (1982): 835–905.

Scribner, Jolie Colette. "'A Splendid Investment': Black Colonization and America's Pacific Empire, 1898-1904." Master's thesis, University of Montana, 2021.

Seeley, Samantha. "Beyond the American Colonization Society." *History Compass* 14, no. 3 (2016): 93-104.

Seeley, Samantha. *Race, Removal, and the Right to Remain: Migration and the Making of the United States.* Chapel Hill: University of North Carolina Press, 2021.

Semmes, John Edward. *John H. B. Latrobe and His Times, 1803-1891.* Baltimore: The Norman Remington Co., 1917.

Sewell, Richard H. *Ballots for Freedom: Antislavery Politics in the United States, 1837-1860.* New York: W. W. Norton, 1980.

Sherwood, Henry Noble. "The Formation of the American Colonization Society." *Journal of Negro History* 2 (1917): 209-28.

Simmons, William J. *Men of Mark: Eminent, Progressive and Rising.* Cleveland: Geo. M. Rewell, 1887.

Sinha, Manisha. *The Slave's Cause: A History of Abolition.* New Haven, CT: Yale University Press, 2016.

Sklar, Kathryn Kish. *Catharine Beecher: A Study in American Domesticity.* New York: W. W. Norton, 1976.

Smith, Douglas, and *Dictionary of Virginia Biography*. "Earnest Sevier Cox (1880-1966)." Encyclopedia Virginia, 2020. https://encyclopediavirginia.org/entries/cox-earnest-sevier-1880-1966/.

Smith, Elbert B. *Francis Preston Blair: A Biography.* New York: Free Press, 1980.

Smith, William Ernest. *The Francis Preston Blair Family in Politics,* vol. 1-2. New York: Macmillan, 1933.

Smith-Rosenberg, Carroll. *This Violent Empire: The Birth of an American National Identity.* Chapel Hill: Omohundro Institute and University of North Carolina Press, 2012.

Smock, Raymond W. *Booker T. Washington: Black Leadership in the Age of Jim Crow.* Chicago: Ivan R. Dee, 2010.

Snay, Mitchell. *Horace Greeley and the Politics of Reform in Nineteenth-Century America.* Lanham, MD: Rowman & Littlefield, 2011.

Spooner, Matthew. "'I Know This Scheme Is from God:' Toward a Reconsideration of the Origins of the American Colonization Society." *Slavery & Abolition* 35, no. 4 (2014): 559-75.

Stabler, John Burgess. "A History of the Constitutional Union Party: A Tragic Failure." PhD diss., Columbia University, 1954.

Staudenraus, P. J. *The African Colonization Movement, 1816-1865.* New York: Columbia University Press, 1961.

Stauffer, John. *The Black Hearts of Men: Radical Abolitionists and the Transformation of Race.* Cambridge, MA: Harvard University Press, 2002.

Stein, Judith. *The World of Marcus Garvey: Race and Class in Modern Society*. Baton Rouge: Louisiana State University Press, 1986.

Stewart, James Brewer. *Abolitionist Politics and the Coming of the Civil War*. Amherst: University of Massachusetts Press, 2008.

Stewart, James Brewer. *Holy Warriors: The Abolitionists and American Slavery*. New York: Hill and Wang, 1976.

Swift, David Everett. *Black Prophets of Justice: Activist Clergy Before the Civil War*. Baton Rouge: Louisiana State University Press, 1989.

Tallant, Harold D. *Evil Necessity: Slavery and Political Culture in Antebellum Kentucky*. Lexington: University Press of Kentucky, 2003.

Taylor, Alan. *The Internal Enemy: Slavery and War in Virginia, 1772–1832*. New York: W. W. Norton, 2013.

Taylor, Nikki Marie. *Frontiers of Freedom: Cincinnati's Black Community, 1802–1868*. Athens: Ohio University Press, 2005.

Thornbrough, Emma Lou. "The National Afro-American League, 1887–1908." *Journal of Southern History* 27, no. 4 (1961): 494–512.

Thornbrough, Emma Lou. *The Negro in Indiana Before 1900: A Study of a Minority*. Bloomington: Indiana University Press, 1993.

Tindall, George B. "The Campaign for the Disfranchisement of Negroes in South Carolina." *Journal of Southern History* 15, no. 2 (1949): 212–34.

Tise, Larry E. *Proslavery: A History of the Defense of Slavery in America, 1701–1840*. Athens: University of Georgia Press, 1987.

Tomek, Beverly C. *Colonization and Its Discontents: Emancipation, Emigration, and Antislavery in Antebellum Pennsylvania*. New York: New York University Press, 2011.

Tomek, Beverly C., and Matthew J Hetrick, eds. *New Directions in the Study of African American Recolonization*. Gainesville: University Press of Florida, 2018.

Tuckerman, Henry T. *The Life of John Pendleton Kennedy*. New York: G. P. Putnam & Sons, 1871.

Tyler-McGraw, Marie. *An African Republic: Black & White Virginians in the Making of Liberia*. Chapel Hill: University of North Carolina Press, 2007.

Upchurch, Thomas A. *Legislating Racism: The Billion Dollar Congress and the Birth of Jim Crow*. Lexington: University Press of Kentucky, 2004.

Upchurch, Thomas A. "Senator John Tyler Morgan and the Genesis of Jim Crow Ideology, 1889–1898." *Alabama Review* 57, no. 2 (2004): 110–31.

Van Sickle, Eugene S. "A Transnational Vision: John H. B. Latrobe and Maryland's African Colonization Movement." PhD diss., West Virginia University, 2005.

Vance, Joseph Carroll. "Thomas Jefferson Randolph." PhD diss., University of Virginia, 1957.

Vanderford, Chad. *The Legacy of St. George Tucker: College Professors in Virginia Confront Slavery and Rights of States, 1771-1897.* Knoxville: University of Tennessee Press, 2015.

Vorenberg, Michael. "Abraham Lincoln and the Politics of Black Colonization." *Journal of the Abraham Lincoln Association* 14, no. 2 (1993): 22-45.

Vorenberg, Michael. *Final Freedom: The Civil War, the Abolition of Slavery, and the Thirteenth Amendment.* Cambridge: Cambridge University Press, 2001.

Wagandt, Charles Lewis. *The Mighty Revolution: Negro Emancipation in Maryland, 1862-1864.* Baltimore: Maryland Historical Society, 2004.

Walters, Ronald G. *American Reformers, 1815-1860.* Rev. ed. New York: Hill and Wang, 1997.

Walters, Ronald G. *The Antislavery Appeal: American Abolitionism After 1830.* New York: W. W. Norton, 1984.

Wesley, Charles H. "Lincoln's Plan for Colonizing the Emancipated Negroes." *Journal of Negro History* 4 (1919): 7-21.

White, Richard. *The Republic for Which It Stands: The United States During Reconstruction and the Gilded Age, 1865-1896.* Oxford: Oxford University Press, 2017.

Whitman, T. Stephen. *The Price of Freedom: Slavery and Manumission in Baltimore and Early National Maryland.* Lexington: University Press of Kentucky, 1997.

Wilentz, Sean. *No Property in Man: Slavery and Antislavery at the Nation's Founding, with a New Preface.* 2nd ed. Cambridge, MA: Harvard University Press, 2019.

Wilkerson, Isabel. *Caste: The Origins of Our Discontents.* New York: Random House, 2020.

Williamson, Joel. *The Crucible of Race: Black-White Relations in the American South Since Emancipation.* Oxford: Oxford University Press, 1984.

Winch, Julie. *A Gentleman of Color: The Life of James Forten.* Oxford: Oxford University Press, 2003.

Wolf, Eva Sheppard. *Race and Liberty in the New Nation: Emancipation in Virginia from the Revolution to Nat Turner's Rebellion.* Baton Rouge: Louisiana State University Press, 2006.

Wood, Nicholas. "'A Sacrifice on the Altar of Slavery': Doughface Politics and Black Disenfranchisement in Pennsylvania, 1837-1838." *Journal of the Early Republic* 31, no. 1 (2011): 75-106.

Woodson, Carter Godwin. "Colonization As a Remedy for Migration." In *A Century of Negro Migration*, 61-80. Washington, DC: Association for the Study of Negro Life and History, 1918.

Woodson, Carter Godwin. *The History of the Negro Church.* Washington, DC: Associated Publishers, 1921.

Work, M. N. "The Life of Charles B. Ray." *Journal of Negro History* 4, no. 4 (October 1919): 361-71.

Wyatt-Brown, Bertram. "The Civil Rights Act of 1875." *Western Political Quarterly* 18, no. 4 (1965): 763–75.

Wyatt-Brown, Bertram. *Lewis Tappan and the Evangelical War Against Slavery.* Baton Rouge: Louisiana State University Press, 1997.

Zilversmit, Arthur. *The First Emancipation: The Abolition of Slavery in the North.* Chicago: University of Chicago Press, 1967.

INDEX

AASS. *See* American Anti-Slavery Society
abolitionist, use of term, 24, 26-27
ACS. *See* American Colonization Society
Africa: colonization as way to bring Christianity to, 15-16, 55, 146, 221, 224; as geographic focus of colonization, 9, 15-16, 52-55, 145, 146, 147, 208, 212, 221; US trade with, 96, 108. *See also* Liberia; Sierra Leone
African Civilization Society, 176-77
African Methodist Episcopal (AME) Church, 75, 173, 218-20
African Repository (ACS publication), 45-46, 59-60, 62-63, 69-70, 85, 97, 102, 126, 138, 208
Alabama, 206, 228-30
American and Foreign Anti-Slavery Society (AFASS), 124, 140, 176
American Anti-Slavery Society (AASS), 21, 75-77, 85, 89-90, 116, 140, 144, 176
American Bible Society, 39, 58, 61, 76
American Board of Commissioners for Foreign Missions, 58, 61
American Colonization Society (ACS): Blairs' colonization project and, 128, 136, 145-49, 209; decline in prestige and membership, 85, 87, 136, 145, 147; eventualism rhetoric of, 80, 97, 125, 128, 146; federal support and, 12, 22, 29, 33, 38-39, 47-52, 64-66, 85, 148, 189, 237; founding of, 14-15, 28-29, 33-34, 59-60, 76, 113, 236, 237-39, 252n20; free Black Americans as primary focus, 34, 37-41, 147, 238; Gag Rule's effect on, 85; goals of, 29, 36-37, 40, 47, 52, 79, 257n20; incorporation memorial and, 78-79, 260n6; Land Bills and, 69-74; Liberia as geographic focus for colonization, 15-16, 80, 99-100, 136, 145-47, 177, 203; Lower South and, 29, 51, 63-68, 74, 96; memorials to Congress, 39, 44, 49-52, 54, 64-67, 74, 99-100, 236, 256n5; Northern states' support sought by, 21, 29, 41, 48-51, 58-63, 85; peak of political import in early to mid-1850s, 126; perpetualism and, 61, 86; political parties and, 67-68, 79, 152; post–Civil War, 200, 209; slavery and emancipation, as subjects requiring special handling, 37-41, 50, 61-63, 65, 74, 80, 97, 138, 146-47, 149, 238; slave trade politics and, 51-58, 148; states' rights and, 29, 39, 47, 63-65, 67; Unionism and, 30, 80, 86-89, 92, 97-98, 100, 104-7, 111, 120, 125, 239, 261n10; voluntary consent of free Black Americans and, 41-43, 172, 271n28

American Party (Know Nothing), 130, 132, 180
American Society for Colonizing the Free People of Colour of the United States (earlier name of ACS). *See* American Colonization Society
American Temperance Society, 39
anti-extension principle, 112, 131-32, 134-36, 138-39, 142, 151, 153
antislavery, use of term, 24-25, 26
Arkansas, 228

Bacon, Leonard, 58, 61
Banks, Nathaniel, 143
Bates, Edward, 150-51
Bell, John, 152-53
benevolent society movement, 58-59, 61, 76
Bilbo, Theodore, 286n13
Birney, James, 85
Black Americans' opposition to colonization movement, 32, 43-46, 74, 93-94, 174-78, 239-40, 245; AASS and, 75-76; ACS and, 43-46, 48, 84; Black newspapers as vehicles of, 81-82, 89-94, 116; Blairs' colonization campaign, 30, 129, 140, 143-45, 154, 197, 217; countermemorial to *National Intelligencer* (1816), 17, 19-20; discord among Black activists, 177-78; expansion of, 80-84; National Equal Rights League and, 200; Philadelphia protest (1817), 44-45, 75; protesting Liberian steamer project, 114; right to live in United States same as white Americans, 32, 44-45, 197, 199-200; second-generation leadership of, 116; strengthened in 1833-53 period, 30, 89-94; Syracuse convention of Black leaders (1864), 195-98, 279n81; Tanner and, 220; use of term "colonization," 27
Black-led emigration, 83, 175-78, 208, 218-20
Black suffrage, 199-230; Black activists for, 31, 217-23; Blairs and, 202-4; colonization movement and, 202-3, 212, 215, 223, 230, 280n5; election-related violence, 206-8, 214, 218; Enforcement Act (1870), 206-7; Jefferson and, 209, 217; literacy tests and poll taxes as restrictive measures, 214, 216; in Lower South, 206; Morgan on, 229-30; Republican Party and, 201-2, 206. *See also* disfranchisement of Black Americans; Fifteenth Amendment
Blair, Francis Preston, Sr.: as colonization movement leader, 30, 127-28; combining emancipation with expatriation, 134; death of (1876), 207; disagreement with Kansas-Nebraska Act, 131-32; Lincoln and, 157, 273n8; Republican Party and, 130-31; as slaveholder, 134, 195. *See also* Blair family's colonization campaign
Blair, Francis (Frank) Preston, Jr., 4, 129, 253n34; death of (1875), 207; as Democrat, 207; on disfranchisement, 209, 224; Douglass's criticism of, 143; important speeches (1858-60), 127-28, 133-34, 136, 139-40, 143, 151, 166, 193; on incongruity of white freedom and Black freedom, 204-5; on inferiority of Black race, 225; Jefferson's views espoused by, 135-36, 204-5; on Joint Select Committee to Inquire into the Condition of Affairs in the Late Insurrectionary States, 207,

231; Lincoln and, 157–58; as Missouri's congressional representative, 30, 128, 141, 154, 157, 165; on Select Committee on Emancipation (for Border States), 157, 165, 195, 274n18; as senator, 207; as slaveholder, 134, 195; as vice-presidential running mate to Seymour (1868), 214

Blair, Montgomery, 4, 30, 129; Black suffrage and, 204; Border State Resolution and, 194; Cooper Institute speech (1865), 200–201; death of (1883), 210; *Dred Scott* and, 132; as Lincoln cabinet member, 157–58, 191; "Ought the Negro to Be Disfranchised? Ought He to Have Been Enfranchised?" (essay), 209–10; resignation from Lincoln's cabinet, 193, 204; as slaveholder, 134, 195; speeches in favor of colonization (1863), 191–92

Blair family's colonization campaign, 22, 30–31, 127–53, 190–210, 253n34; ACS and, 128, 136, 145–49, 209; background of, 127, 129–30; Black-freedom-as-a-problem ideology and, 129, 195, 201, 227; Black response to, 30, 129, 140, 143–45, 154, 197, 217; Black suffrage and, 202–4, 210, 224; Democratic Party's resurgence and, 200–204, 207–8, 213, 224–25, 236; eventualism and, 128, 138, 139; fusing North and Upper South to support, 22, 30, 127, 188; gradualism and, 138, 160; immediate abolition and, 193; on incongruity of white freedom and Black freedom, 128–29, 201–2, 204–5, 209, 225; Jefferson's influence on, 128, 135–36, 142, 201, 204–5, 228; Lincoln and, 31, 157–62, 191, 193–95, 197, 204; on mixed races' inferiority, 225; post–Civil War, 200–204; Republican Party politics and, 30, 128–30, 134–35, 139–42, 149–51, 158–59, 180, 193–94; as slaveholders, 195

Border State Resolution (1862), 164–68, 179, 180, 187, 194; Border States' negotiations, 161, 168–73; Select Committee on Emancipation and, 157, 164–66, 179, 182, 195, 274n18

Border States: failure of colonization and, 189, 193–95; failure to take federal offers for emancipatory actions, 179–85, 274n21; Missouri Emancipation Bill and, 183; remaining part of Union and essential to Union victory, 155, 159, 163–66; thirteenth constitutional amendment and, 188; Unconditional Unionism and, 186–88. *See also specific states*

Bradley, Joseph, 232
Breckinridge, John C., 152–53
Brown, B. Gratz, 158
Brown, Henry Billings, 233
Buchanan, James, 132, 148
Butler, Benjamin, 92, 94, 190
Butler, Matthew: and proposed Butler Bill, 217, 225, 227–28, 236, 280n5; race aversion's ineradicability and, 224, 231–32; seeking federal funding for colonization, 213–16

Caldwell, Elias, 13, 14–15, 33, 58–60, 248, 256n6
Calhoun, John, 26, 78, 88, 118, 222
Canada, Black emigration to, 82–83, 175
Caribbean as colonization destination, 136–37, 208
Carroll, Charles, 36, 84–85

Cary, Lott, 57-58
Central America. *See* South America/Central America as colonization destination
Chambers, Ezekiel, 65, 72
Chiriqui Improvement Company, 160, 191
Christianity: benevolent society movement and, 61; colonization as way to bring to Africa, 15-16, 55, 146, 221, 224
Christian Recorder (Black newspaper), 21, 173-74, 208, 219-20
Cincinnati, Black population's relocation to Canada, 83
Civil Rights Act (1875), 231
Civil Rights Act (1964), 248
Civil Rights Act (1965), 248
Civil Rights Cases (1883), 231-32
Civil War, US, 30-31, 155-98; abolishing slavery as key to ending, 155-56; Black leaders' optimism and, 178; Black soldiers in, 178-79, 186, 199-200, 277n49; colonization movement losing traction in and failing after, 22, 157, 202-3; congressional composition's change opening up new possibilities during, 159-60, 185; federal colonization appropriations, 162-63; self-emancipation during, 159-60; Union army as emancipatory force in, 160-61, 163, 186
Clay, Clement, 259n40
Clay, Henry: on abolition and manumission conditioned on colonization, 42-43, 104-5, 172, 238; on ACS's incorporation memorial, 78-79, 260n6; Black criticism of, 44-45; Black-freedom-as-a-problem ideology and, 23-24, 50, 109, 112, 118; as colonization movement leader, 4, 14-15, 22-24, 29, 33-34, 38, 50, 57, 60, 64-69, 79, 81, 84-89, 108-9, 112, 114, 141-42, 149, 170-71, 202, 248; death of (1852), 113, 149; on dissolution of Union, 107-8; Douglass's criticism of, 143-44, 222; eventualism and, 26, 88-89, 97, 104, 109-11, 254n40; Fugitive Slave Law and, 267n91; gradual abolition and, 104, 118, 128, 184; on incongruity of white freedom and Black freedom, 23, 45-46, 229; Indian Removal Act and, 99; Liberian steamer proposal and, 114; Lincoln eulogy for, 151; misleading rhetoric on slavery and colonization, 38, 40, 51, 63, 238; perpetualism and, 88; Randolph and, 54-55; return to Senate (1850), 107; Senate speech on Unionism (1839), 87-89, 97, 104, 110, 120; as slaveholder, 35, 85; on slavery as "deplorable evil," 262n22; states' rights and, 73; as US presidential candidate (1844), 92-94; on white antipathy toward free Black Americans as ineradicable, 45. *See also* Land Bills
Clayton, John, 106
Colfax, Schuyler, 205
Colombia as colonization destination, 160, 191
colonization and colonization movement: analogy to resettlement of Native Americans, 98-99, 103, 215; anti-Black prejudice traced to, 4-5, 32, 45-46, 48, 83, 94, 175, 226, 245; benevolent society movement and, 59-60; Black suffrage debate and, 202-3, 212, 215, 223, 230, 280n5; Border States and, 165, 169-73; Civil

War as turning point for, 22, 157, 189, 194, 202-3; Cox and Bilbo promoting during 1920s-40s, 286n13; eventualism and, 29-30, 91-92, 146; exclusion and exclusionary laws influenced by, 22, 30-31, 92, 115, 117, 119, 144, 177, 217-18, 225, 228-29, 239, 240, 267n91; federal colonization appropriations, 162-63; Fifteenth Amendment and, 211-13, 230; Jefferson and, 3-4, 6, 8-9, 12, 14, 125, 128, 134, 141-42, 157, 162, 202, 237; Lincoln and, 4, 31, 151, 155-56, 161, 163, 171-74, 178, 190-95, 197, 213, 215-16, 236, 286-87n13; peaks of political import, 30, 126, 156-57, 161-62; post-Civil War advocates, 22, 31, 203, 210-17, 224-32, 281n6; potential to prevent civil war, 30, 239; as safety measure for white Americans, 23-24, 36-37, 50, 91, 109, 113-14, 237-38; splintering of, 133-39; state-level, 68-69, 85-86, 118; Tocqueville's opinion of, 263n29; Tuckers on, 11-12, 15, 16; Unionism and patriotism rhetoric of, 80, 86, 92, 120, 152, 211, 215; use of term "colonization," 24, 27-28; word choices and terminological problems, 24-28, 210, 253nn37-38. *See also* American Colonization Society; Blair family's colonization campaign; "Negro Problem"

Colored American (Black newspaper), 21, 89-94, 115-17

Compromise of 1850, 107-14, 130, 134-35, 149, 152, 162

Connecticut, 62-63

Constitution, US: Article I, Section 8, 65; Lincoln's three proposed constitutional amendments (1862), 155, 163, 192; white Americans failing to live by, 225, 241, 246. *See also specific amendments*

Constitutional Union Party, 152-53, 180

Cooper, Anna Julia, 235, 242; background of, 243-44; on racial future of America, 244-48

Cornish, Samuel, 30, 75-76, 81-83, 89-90, 92, 116, 176

Corwin, Thomas, 139, 270n20

Cox, Earnest Sevier, 286n13

Crittenden, John J., 126

Custis, George Washington Parke, 49-50, 59

danger of Black population to white Americans: enslaved population's uprisings, 6, 8, 26, 41, 46; free Black population as catalyst of, 16, 36-37; Jefferson on, 3, 227; race war, 138, 170, 230, 285n2

Davis, Garrett, 167-71, 183, 194

Davis, Jefferson, 105-6

Day, Jeremiah, 58

Dayton, William, 105, 139, 270n20

DC Abolition Act (1862), 162-63, 170, 275n29; Border States' opposition to, 167; slaveholder compensation under, 165; voluntary colonization appropriation and, 162, 165, 169, 195

Delany, Martin, 116, 176-77, 219, 276n44

Delaware, 112, 132, 153, 159, 163-65

Democratic Party: 1860 presidential election, 152; 1868 presidential and congressional elections, 205; Blairs' departure to Republican Party, 30, 128, 130; Blairs' return to, 200-204, 207-8, 225, 236; disunion demands

Democratic Party (*continued*)
and threats of, 139; Fifteenth Amendment and, 205, 228; formation of, 55, 71, 73, 204; Key as member of, 95; Lodge Bill and, 216; opposed to ACS's incorporation memorial, 79; reconstruction and resurgence in the South, 200-204, 207-8, 213, 224-25, 236. *See also* Jacksonian Democrats

Democratic-Republican Party, conflict within, 55

Dennison, William, 147-48

diffusion theory, 135

disfranchisement of Black Americans, 211, 216, 223, 228-30, 241

disunion, prevention of (1854-60), 30, 127-45; ACS exerting caution in sensitive political era, 149; Democratic Party's demands and threats of disunion, 139; Lincoln's 1860 election as portent of disunion, 153; Republicans seeing colonization proposal as way to unite both sides, 142. *See also* Blair family's colonization campaign

Doolittle, James, 141-42, 154, 162-63, 169-70, 205-6, 209, 231

Douglas, Stephen, 126, 151-53, 158

Douglass, Frederick, 30, 116-23, 240-42; background of, 116; on Black suffrage and disfranchisement, 218, 241; on Clay's rhetoric, 118-19; on Liberian steamer proposal, 124; on Liberia's independence, 121-22; Lincoln and, 153, 158, 173; on lynchings of Black Americans, 240-41; on "Negro Problem" propaganda, 221-23, 228, 241, 245-46; opposed to colonization, 28, 30, 143-45, 178-79, 196, 219, 222-23, 235, 241; on racial violence incited by colonization advocates, 175, 218; on Republican Party, 153-54; Gerrit Smith and, 86, 140; at Syracuse convention of Black leaders (1864), 195-96; Underground Railroad and, 84. *See also Douglass' Monthly; Frederick Douglass' Paper; North Star*

Douglass' Monthly (newspaper), 1, 143-44, 153, 174, 179

Downing, George, 116, 144-45, 153, 177

Dred Scott v. Sandford (1857), 132-33, 136

Du Bois, W. E. B., 235; background of, 242-43; on racial future of America, 244-48

Ellsworth, Henry Leavitt, 98

Emerson, Ralph Waldo, 134, 143

emigration, use of term, 27-28

Enforcement Act (1870), 206-7

eventualism: ACS adopting rhetoric of, 80, 97, 125, 128, 146; Blair family rejecting, 128, 138, 139; Clay and, 26, 88-89, 97, 104, 109-11, 254n40; colonization movement and, 29-30, 91-92, 146; diffusion theory and, 135; Southern states and, 29-30, 89, 135, 146; Tocqueville on, 263n29; use of term, 25-26, 254n40

Everett, Edward, 126, 152

exclusion and exclusionary laws: colonization movement's causal relationship with, 22, 30-31, 92, 115, 117, 119, 144, 177, 217-18, 225, 228-29, 239-40, 247, 267n91; *Dred Scott* and, 133; Du Bois and Cooper on, 242; of English colonies, 5; federal government's ability to prevent, 246-47; Jim Crow, 200, 230, 233, 247-48, 250n6; language of Lower Southern

propagandists and, 210-11; newly emancipated Black population forced to leave home state, 7, 12, 115, 119, 171; use of term "exclusion," 27-28. *See also* Black suffrage; disfranchisement of Black Americans; Jim Crow
expatriation, use of term, 27-28

Fairfax, Ferdinando, 9
fear of enslaved uprisings, 6, 8, 26, 41, 46
Fifteenth Amendment (1870), 203-17; Black activists and, 31, 217-23; colonization movement and, 31, 202-3, 212, 215, 223, 230; Democratic Party and, 205, 228; disfranchisement constructed to steer clear of, 228; effect of, 230; enforcement of, 206-7, 214, 246-47; fighting against, 203-6, 231; Lower South's discrediting of, 210-13, 229; neutralizing of, 213-17; passage of, 206; Republican Party and, 205-6, 208, 214, 227-28; undermining of, 206-10; white Americans refusing to abide by, 241, 246
Fillmore, Millard, 109, 113-14, 126, 132, 148, 150
Finley, Robert, 13-16, 19, 58-61, 146, 224
First Confiscation Act (1861), 160-61, 163
Forten, James, 29, 44, 48, 75-76, 115-16, 145
Forten, William, 116, 199-200, 217-18
Fourteenth Amendment (1868), 230; *Civil Rights Cases* (1883), 232; *Plessy v. Ferguson* (1896), 232-33; white Americans refusing to abide by, 241, 246
Frederick Douglass' Paper (Black newspaper), 21, 116-19, 123, 125, 143

free Black Americans: ACS focused on, 34, 37-41, 147, 238; as alleged cause of unrest among the enslaved, 34, 36; newly emancipated forced to leave home state, 7, 115, 171; sectionalism blamed on, 30, 111, 120, 225-27; Southern states' desire to decrease number of, 47. *See also* Black Americans' opposition to colonization movement
Freedmen's Bureau, 197
Freedom's Journal (Black newspaper), 76, 80-82, 90, 116
Frelinghuysen, Frederick, 232, 243-44
Frelinghuysen, Theodore, 58, 92, 94, 232, 244
Fremont, John C., 132, 134
Fugitive Slave Act (1850), 30, 107-8, 111-12, 115, 117, 136, 175, 239; effect on emigration, 119-20
Fulkerson, Horace, 224-25, 227, 231-32, 286n2

Gabriel Prosser Conspiracy (Virginia, 1800), 8, 12
Gag Rule (US House of Representatives, 1836-44), 77, 85, 95
Garland, James, 86-87
Garnet, Henry Highland, 116, 121-23, 176-77, 179, 218-19
Garrison, William Lloyd, 27, 76, 90, 185
Garvey, Marcus, 287n13
George, James Z., 216-17, 227-28
Gordon, Mitt Maude Lena, 287n13
Grady, Henry, 210-13, 225, 227-29, 232
Grant, Ulysses S., 205
Graves, John Temple, 229, 231
Greeley, Horace, 117-18, 154, 172, 271n31
Gurley, Ralph, 59, 67-68, 87, 97-98, 106

Haiti, 19, 121, 137, 156–57
Haitian Revolution (1791–1804), 8, 10
Hampton, Wade, 213–17, 224–25, 227–28, 232
Harlan, John, *Plessy* dissent by, 233
Harper, Frances Ellen Watkins, 116, 175
Harper, Robert Goodloe, 36–37, 49–51, 59
Hayne, Robert, 65, 67, 215
Henderson, John, 179–90, 198
Holly, James Theodore, 136–37
Homestead Act (1862), 150

Illinois, 115, 117, 119, 121
immediatism, use of term, 25
Indiana, 62–63, 112, 115, 117–19
Indian Removal Act (1830), 98–99
Ingersoll, Joseph R., 101–2
Iowa, 115

Jackson, Andrew: Blair and, 129; Democratic Party and, 55, 204; Key and, 95; Land Bill pocket veto by, 70, 72–73, 124; as president, 69; on separation of races, 141
Jacksonian Democrats, 67–68, 73
Jefferson, Thomas: Black suffrage and, 209, 217; Blair family's beliefs and, 128, 135–36, 142, 201, 204–5, 228; combining emancipation with expatriation, 6, 125, 128–29, 134, 141–42, 157, 160, 162, 170, 202, 215, 237, 248; comments and predictions on slavery, 1–4, 9, 15, 18–20, 34–35, 57, 64, 68, 134–37, 160, 162, 170, 224, 227, 237; on danger presented by enslaved population and race war, 3, 8, 46, 170; on incongruity of white freedom and Black freedom, 3–4, 7, 11, 19–20, 142, 150, 159, 198, 204–5, 217, 228–29, 237–38, 246; Lincoln's references to, 151–52, 159; Louisiana Purchase and, 161; Northwest Ordinance and, 131, 135–36; on potential colonization sites for Black expatriation, 8, 12, 14; on public land revenue's use to fund colonization, 69; as slaveholder, 35; St. George Tucker disagreeing with, 11; on theory of race, 18–20, 224
Jenifer, Daniel, 68–69
Jim Crow, 200, 230, 233, 247–48, 250n6

Kansas, 130, 132, 152, 208
Kansas-Nebraska Act (1854), 128, 130–32, 134–35, 139, 152, 180
Kennedy, John Pendleton, 99, 187, 213
Kennedy Report (1843), 95–100, 106, 236
Kentucky, 6, 38, 87, 104–6, 118–19, 153, 170; remaining part of Union, 159, 163–65
Key, Francis Scott: ACS and, 87, 95–98, 258n28; as American Bible Society member, 261n12; as colonization movement leader, 4, 13–14, 60, 95, 149, 248, 256n6; gradualism and, 128; on Liberia-US relations, 95–96, 99; linking colonization and emancipation, 97, 202; as slaveholder, 35, 97
King, Rufus, 69, 215
Know Nothing (American Party), 130, 132, 180
Ku Klux Klan, 206

Land Bills (proposed by Clay, 1831–33), 68–74, 236, 259n36; Clay's speech on, including prediction of end of slavery, 87–88; Jackson's pocket veto of, 72–74, 124; new versions (1834–37), 71–72, 78, 124, 259–60n43, 260n5; Senate passage, 69–71, 79

Latrobe, John, 147

Liberia: ACS's colonization focus on, 15–16, 80, 99–100, 136, 145–47, 177, 203; Black Americans opposed to emigration to, 82, 170, 276n44; challenges to life in, 57; Delany and Garnet's emigration project and, 176–77; founding of, 56–58, 236; Gurley's report on, 106; independence of, 57–58, 101–2, 120–21, 125; Key on, 95–96; manumissions conditioned on consent to emigration to, 165, 171; Monrovia as capital of, 56; return of enslaved Africans seized by US Navy to, 53–54, 56, 78, 103, 145, 148; Russwurm emigrating to, 82; steamship project and, 108–15, 123–24, 138, 140, 149, 226, 236, 265n67; Tanner on emigration to, 220; as US ally in Africa, 108; US fact-finding mission sent to, 106; US recognition of independence of, 157; voluntary emigration to, 56–57, 82, 120, 175–76, 218, 267n94

Liberty Party, 85

Lincoln, Abraham: assassination of (1865), 204; background of, 158–59; Black Washingtonians' meeting with, 171–73, 197, 226, 229; Blair family and, 31, 157–62, 191, 193–95, 197, 204; Border State resistance and, 166–69; Border State Resolution and negotiations with Border States, 169–73; Clay eulogy by, 151; colonization and, 4, 31, 151, 155–56, 161, 163, 171–74, 178, 190–95, 197, 213, 215–16, 236, 286–87n13; Cooper Union for the Advancement of Science and Art speech (1860), 151, 200; Emancipation Proclamation (1863), 178, 186, 191, 196; end of slavery, three constitutional proposals linked to (1862), 155–57, 163; first annual message to Congress, 161; on incongruity of white freedom and Black freedom, 171–72, 202, 205, 217, 229; Jefferson's influence on, 151–52, 159; Preliminary Emancipation Proclamation (1862), 163; presidential election of 1860, 151–53; second annual message to Congress, 155, 217; on self-emancipated Black Americans, 161

Lodge Bill, 216, 224, 227, 232

Louisiana, 206, 219, 228, 232–33

Louisiana Purchase, 130, 161

lynchings of Black Americans, 240–41

Madison, James, 69–70, 84, 141, 248, 260n6

Marshall, John, 33, 35, 69–70

Maryland: ACS's article of incorporation from, 78; Border State Resolution and, 186–87; colonization appropriation by legislature, 85; colonization movement in, 6, 13, 68–69, 85, 92; Land Bills and, 71; Liberian steamer project and, 112; manumission restrictions in, 7; presidential election of 1860 and, 153; remaining part of Union, 159, 163–65; Republican Party and, 132, 149–50; size of enslaved population in, 42; size of free Black population in, 7, 42–43

Maryland Colonization Society, 98, 147

Massachusetts, 62-63
McKinley, Carlyle, 210-15, 224-28, 232
McLane, Robert, 107
Mercer, Charles Fenton: ACS and, 49-54, 59, 64-65, 67-68, 87, 95, 97; chairing House committee reviewing ACS's 1827 memorial, 67, 81; as colonization movement leader, 13-14, 22, 33, 50, 60, 149, 248; gradualism and, 128; Nat Turner Revolt and, 68; as slaveholder, 35, 49
Metcalfe, Thomas, 103-6
Mississippi, 206, 216-17, 219, 228
Missouri: presidential election of 1860 and, 153; proposed Emancipation Bill (1862-63), 179-87, 192; remaining part of Union, 159, 163-65; Republican convention in, 149
Missouri Compromise (1820), repeal of, 130-32, 134
Mitchell, James, 171-72, 190
mixing of races: American people merging into one race, 20, 221, 243-44; as cause of degeneration, 137-38, 225, 270n19
Monroe, James, 4, 8, 12, 54-56, 141, 148
Morehead, James T., 95, 97
Morgan, John Tyler, 4, 31, 210-17, 224-32
Morton, Samuel, 18, 138

National Emigration Convention (Cleveland 1854), 176
National Equal Rights League, 199-200, 217
National Republican Party, 55, 67, 71, 79, 127
Native Americans' resettlement as analogy to expatriation of Black Americans, 98-99, 103, 215

Nat Turner Revolt (1831), 8, 68, 83, 92
"Negro Problem" (or "race problem"), 210-12; Black counterarguments to, 217-23; colonization and, 210-17, 222; Cooper on, 244; Douglass on, 221-23, 241, 245-46; Du Bois on, 243; federal government's ability to enforce laws and, 206-7, 214, 246-47; Morgan on, 226, 230; Southern propaganda on, 214, 228, 231, 245
New Jersey, 7, 62-63, 112
New York, 62-63, 112, 118, 121, 205
New York Committee of Vigilance, 84, 117
nonaction (nonintervention) principle (1830s-60s), 79, 88, 110, 183, 189, 232
North Carolina, 124-25, 153, 228
North Star (Black newspaper), 114, 116, 121-23, 143
Northwest Ordinance (1787), 131, 135-36
Northwest Territory, 141
Nott, Josiah, 18, 138

Ohio, 62-63, 112, 148

Page, John, 8-9, 12
Pennsylvania, 2-3, 7, 62-63, 88, 93, 112
Pennsylvania Anti-Slavery Society (PASS), 114
Pennsylvania Colonization Society (PCS), 220-21
perpetualism: ACS and, 61, 86; advocates of, 88, 153; rejection of, 88, 137, 141, 156; use of term, 25-26
Philippines, Black expatriation to, 230, 285n51

Plessy v. Ferguson (1896), 232-33, 247, 250-51n6
Pomeroy, Samuel, 160
proslavery, use of term, 24-26
Prosser, Gabriel, 8
Purvis, Harriet Forten, 116
Purvis, Robert, 116, 144-45, 151, 153
Purvis, Sarah Forten, 116

race, definition in late eighteenth and nineteenth century, 17-21
"race patriotism," 221
racial hybridity, 138, 225, 270n19
Randolph, John: ACS memorials presented to Congress by, 51, 54-55, 256n6; background of, 35; Black Americans' criticism of, 44; on colonization movement making slavery more secure, 91, 237-38; as early colonization movement leader, 13, 29, 33-34, 40, 46-47, 55, 59-60, 237, 248; as slaveholder, 35
Ray, Charles Bennet, 116-17, 119
recaptured enslaved Africans. *See under* US Navy
Reconstruction Act (1867), 205-6
Reese, David M., 84
religious purpose of colonization. *See* Christianity
Republican Party: abolition without colonization and, 188-89, 191-94, 197; anti-extension as cornerstone of, 134-35, 139, 142, 153; Black suffrage and, 201-2; Blair family joining (late 1850s) and colonization campaign, 30, 128-30, 134-35, 139-42, 144, 149-51, 158-59, 174, 180, 193-94; Blair family leaving (1865), 203-4; Border State resistance and, 167-68; Butler Bill and, 231-32; Cooper Institute rally (NY 1860), 139, 151; DC Abolition Act and, 169; Douglass on, 153-54; emancipatory moves and, 162-63; federal oversight in the South and, 208; Fifteenth Amendment and, 205-6, 208, 214, 227-28; formation of, 130-31; Missouri Emancipation Bill and, 180, 183, 185; presidential election of 1860, 150-51, 153; presidential election of 1868, 205; readmitted Southern States and Black voters, 206; Stanton joining, 140
Revolutionary War, 9, 159
Rhett Report (1844), 100-101, 113, 124
Rives, William C., 95
Roberts, Joseph Jenkins, 102
Rollins, James, 184
Ruggles, David, 84, 116
Rush, Richard, 64
Russwurm, John, 81-82

Saint-Domingue (now Haiti), slave rebellion in, 8, 10
Second Confiscation Act (1862), 163, 167, 170, 275n29
separate-but-equal doctrine, 232, 247, 251n6
Seymour, Horatio, 204-5, 214
Sierra Leone, 9, 52-53, 55, 69
Slaughter, Phillip, 146-47
slaveholder compensation for emancipated individuals, 155, 163, 165, 168, 181, 183-86, 274n19
slavery and enslaved persons: Border States' shift of stance on, 185-90; diminishing memory of slavery, 223-27; expansion in US west and

326 INDEX

slavery and enslaved persons (*continued*)
  anti-extension principle, 104, 106-8, 112, 128, 130-32, 134-36, 138-39, 151; growth of enslaved population (1790-1850), 16, 42, 80, 110; sectional tensions heightened by mid-1840s, 104
slave trade, 51-58, 96, 239; end of international trade for US, 53; Liberia and, 56, 96, 108
Slave Trade Act (1819), 56, 96, 148, 236
Smith, Caleb Blood, 160
Smith, Gerrit, 85-86, 140
Smith, Samuel Stanhope, 17-18
South America/Central America as colonization destination, 136-37, 141, 171, 190
South Carolina, 66-68, 73, 188, 206, 219, 228
Southern opposition to colonization movement, 29, 51, 63-68, 72-74, 105-6, 124
Stanton, Frederick Perry: in ACS and colonization movement, 108-9, 111-14, 140-41, 229; Douglass on, 120; Fugitive Slave Law and, 267n91; Liberian steamer proposal and, 108-9, 113-14, 123, 138, 140, 172, 226, 236; Unionism and patriotism in rhetoric of, 120
state-level colonization movement, 68-69, 85-86, 118
states' rights: ACS and, 29, 39, 47, 63-65, 67; Northern and Southern politicians agreeing about, 105; Randolph and, 55
suffrage. *See* Black suffrage
Sumner, Charles, 184-85, 204
Syracuse convention of Black leaders (1864), 195-99, 279n81

Taney, Roger, 11, 132-33
Tanner, Benjamin, 219-21
Tappan, Arthur, 76
Tariff of 1828 (Tariff of Abominations), 67-68
Tariff of 1832, 73
Tariff of 1833 (Compromise Tariff), 73
Tazewell Report (1828), 67, 100, 124
Teague, Colin, 57-58
Tennessee, 153, 159, 164-65
terminology challenges, 24-28, 253nn37-38, 254n40
Texas, 198
Thirteenth Amendment (1865), 2, 4; congressional proposal of, 157, 185-90, 196-98, 201; effect of, 157, 230; ratification of, 157, 197, 199
Tocqueville, Alexis de, 263n29
Trumbull, Lyman, 141-42, 154
Tucker, George, 9-10, 15-16, 34
Tucker, St. George, 10-12, 15, 34
Turnbull, Robert, 66-68
Turner, Henry McNeal, 174-75, 197, 219-21
Turner, Nat. *See* Nat Turner Revolt

Unconditional Unionism, 186-88
Underground Railroad, 84
Underwood, Joseph R., 95, 99, 103-6, 135
Unionism: colonization movement using rhetoric of, 30, 80, 86-89, 92, 97-98, 104-7, 111, 120, 125, 152, 239, 261n10; prevention of disunion, 127-45; Rhett Report and, 100; Unconditional Unionism, 186-88
US Navy: British interference with, 95-96; Liberia steamship proposal and, 108; seizure of enslaved Africans

and return to Africa, 53-54, 56, 78, 103, 145, 148; 170. *See also* Black Americans' opposition to colonization movement

Vance, Zebulon, 231-32
Venable, Abraham, 124-25
Vermont, 62-63, 112
Virginia: 1860 presidential election and, 153; colonial period, 5-6; colonization and, 9-11, 13-14, 68-69, 71, 85, 92, 252n22; colonization appropriation by legislature, 85; disfranchisement of Black Americans in, 228; exclusionary laws and manumission restrictions, 7; free Black population in, 7, 42; Liberian steamer project and, 112; size of enslaved population in, 16, 42; uprisings by enslaved population, 8, 12, 16, 68
voluntariness of Black Americans' expatriation, 12, 110, 240; ACS and, 41-43, 172, 271n28; Blairs' proposal and, 140; Border States Resolution and, 165, 169-73; vs. coerced consent, 42-43, 119-20, 156, 161, 170-72, 174; in DC Abolition Act (1862), 162, 169; incentives for, 182; in Second Confiscation Act (1862), 162,

Wade, Benjamin, 141-42, 154
Walker, David, 84
Walker, Robert J., 107
War of 1812, 14, 16, 37, 55, 159
Washington, Bushrod, 33, 35-37, 49-50, 54, 60, 85, 141, 188, 248
Webster, Daniel: in ACS and colonization movement, 113-14, 215; in African trade talks with Britain, 96; Fugitive Slave Law and, 267n91; Gurley's report and, 106; on incongruity of white freedom and Black freedom, 202, 217, 229; Unionism and patriotism in rhetoric of, 120
Western territories, 150, 162, 167, 198. *See also* anti-extension principle
Whig Party, 55, 71, 79, 93-95, 99-100; collapse of, 130-31, 145, 149
Whittlesey, Elisha, 95
Wilmot Proviso (1848), 105, 108, 134
Wilson, Henry, 148, 170, 189, 192-93, 197-98, 203-4
Wright, Theodore, 90, 92, 94, 116, 176
Wythe, George, 10, 38

Recent books in the series
A NATION DIVIDED: STUDIES IN THE CIVIL WAR ERA

After the Fire: Richmond in Defeat
NELSON D. LANKFORD

From Dakota to Dixie: George Buswell's Civil War
EDITED BY JONATHAN W. WHITE AND REAGAN CONNELLY

Reconstruction beyond 150: Reassessing the New Birth of Freedom
ORVILLE VERNON BURTON AND J. BRENT MORRIS, EDITORS

Dueling Cultures, Damnable Legacies: Southern Violence and White Supremacy in the Civil War Era
JAMES HILL WELBORN III

The Civil War Political Tradition: Ten Portraits of Those Who Formed It
PAUL D. ESCOTT

The Weaker Sex in War: Gender and Nationalism in Civil War Virginia
KRISTEN BRILL

Young America: The Transformation of Nationalism before the Civil War
MARK POWER SMITH

Black Suffrage: Lincoln's Last Goal
PAUL D. ESCOTT

The Cacophony of Politics: Northern Democrats and the American Civil War
J. MATTHEW GALLMAN

My Work among the Freedmen: The Civil War and Reconstruction Letters of Harriet M. Buss
EDITED BY JONATHAN W. WHITE AND LYDIA J. DAVIS

Colossal Ambitions: Confederate Planning for a Post–Civil War World
ADRIAN BRETTLE

Newest Born of Nations: European Nationalist Movements and the Making of the Confederacy
ANN L. TUCKER

The Worst Passions of Human Nature: White Supremacy in the Civil War North
PAUL D. ESCOTT

Preserving the White Man's Republic: Jacksonian Democracy, Race, and the Transformation of American Conservatism
JOSHUA A. LYNN

American Abolitionism: Its Direct Political Impact from Colonial Times into Reconstruction
STANLEY HARROLD

A Strife of Tongues: The Compromise of 1850 and the Ideological Foundations of the American Civil War
STEPHEN E. MAIZLISH

The First Republican Army: The Army of Virginia and the Radicalization of the Civil War
JOHN H. MATSUI

War upon Our Border: Two Ohio Valley Communities Navigate the Civil War
STEPHEN I. ROCKENBACH

Gold and Freedom: The Political Economy of Reconstruction
NICOLAS BARREYRE, TRANSLATED BY ARTHUR GOLDHAMMER

www.ingramcontent.com/pod-product-compliance
Lightning Source LLC
Chambersburg PA
CBHW030605230426
43661CB00053B/1852